BRITISH WRITERS AND PARIS 1830–1875

British Writers and Paris
1830–1875

ELISABETH JAY

OXFORD
UNIVERSITY PRESS

OXFORD
UNIVERSITY PRESS

Great Clarendon Street, Oxford, OX2 6DP,
United Kingdom

Oxford University Press is a department of the University of Oxford.
It furthers the University's objective of excellence in research, scholarship,
and education by publishing worldwide. Oxford is a registered trade mark of
Oxford University Press in the UK and in certain other countries

First Edition published in 2016

Published in the United States of America by Oxford University Press
198 Madison Avenue, New York, NY 10016, United States of America

British Library Cataloguing in Publication Data

Data available

Library of Congress Control Number: 2015943754

ISBN 978–0–19–965524–3

For Kathleen Davies

Acknowledgements

Over the years this book has taken I have benefited from casual conversations, interested questions, and the timely and sage advice of those who read early draft chapters. In this last category I would like to thank Kathleen Davies, Charmian Hearne, Judy Lee, Gail Marshall, Andrew McNeillie, Jane Potter, and the two anonymous readers for Oxford University Press. Other scholars have replied generously and promptly to my questions: Sabine Chaouche, Diana Cooper-Richet, Gowan Dawson, Janet Howarth, Brian Maidment, Jeremy MacClancy, Katy Mullin, Glyn Redpath, and Catherine Seville spring instantly to mind, although there are many others whose conference papers, publications, and chance remarks have sparked questions about my own research. A multidisciplinary conference at the University of Oslo in 2008 on nineteenth-century London and Paris, to which Christina Horvath invited me, was particularly stimulating.

Thanks are also due to my former colleagues in the English department at Oxford Brookes who believed in this project sufficiently to allow me a research semester, despite knowing that such a slow-burner would not yield instant REF dividends. This enabled me to take advantage of a visiting research fellowship at the Armstrong-Browning Library in Waco, Texas, where I enjoyed access to the correspondence of Robert and Elizabeth Barrett Browning and of a number of other Paris-loving Victorian writers. I also have cause to be immensely grateful for the resources of the British Library, the Bibliothèque Nationale de France, and the Bodleian: special mention must be made of Grant Hibberd, historian at the Foreign and Commonwealth Office, of the staff at the Librairie Galignani, and of the unstinting help always given by Sue Usher of Oxford University's English Faculty Library. Erna Cooper's invitation to accompany her to a gathering in the British Embassy in Paris, and her generosity in allowing me to use her Parisian eyrie, turned a brief research trip into an unexpected pleasure.

Contents

PART III. THE FICTIONAL FORMATTING OF PARIS

List of illustrations

Map

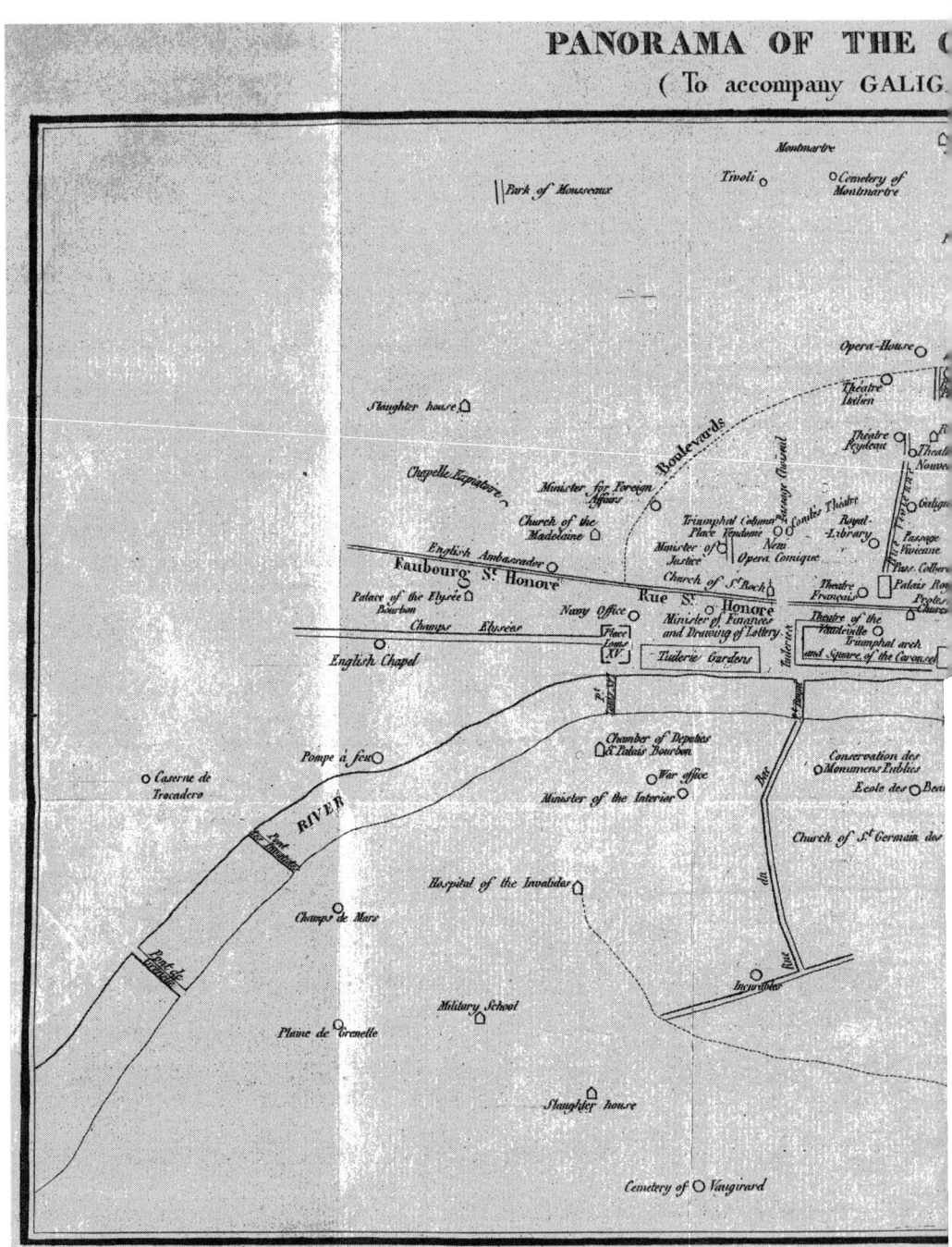

Map: 'Panorama of the Curiosities of Paris', in Galignani's *New Paris Guide, or Stranger's Companion...*, May 1827 (by courtesy of the Bodleian Libraries, The University of Oxford, Per.20481 f.6 (1827), fold-out map between pp. lx and lxi).

Slaughter house

Hospital St Louis

of St Lazare

of the Varieties of Custom house Theatre of Gymnase

Rue St

Theatre of the Porte St Martin

New Spelnigt Comique

Gate or Triumphal arch of St Denis

Gate or Triumphal arch of St Martin

Franconi

Gaiete Theatre

Exchange

the Temple

Cafe Turc

Slaughter house

Cemetery of Pere la Chaise

Conservatory of Art and Manufactures

Library

Rue St Martin

Post Office

Church of St Eustache

Archives of France

Mont de Piete

Corn Market

Church of St Germain of the re

Town Hall

Place Royale

Prison of the Force

Church of St Gervais

Rue

Fountain of the Elephant or Bastille

St

Antoine

County of Justice Police Passeports

Palace Prefecture for Police

Celestins ex a Convent Now Barracks

Hospital of Quinze-Vingts

Plate Glass Manufactory

Mint of the Institute

Church of Notre Dame

ISLAND OF St LOUIS

Hotel Dieu

Arsenal

Wine Market

RIVER

School of Medicine

Palais des Thermes

Rue St

College of France

Garden of Plants

Church of St Sulpice

Sorbonne

College of Louis le Gd

Church of St Etienne du Mont

Foundling Hospital

Odeon Theatre

St Genevieve or Pantheon

Hospital of Salpetriere

Palace of the Luxembourg & Chamber of Peers

Prison of Ste Pelagie

Deaf and Dumb Institution

Rue St Jacques

Hospital or Church of Val-de-Grace

Gobelins Tapistry Manufactory

Slaughter house

Observatory

Introduction

> We should think...of identity as a 'production' which is never complete, always in process, and always constituted within, not outside representation.[1]

The significant role Paris played as part of the creative environment of many mid-nineteenth-century British writers is a largely forgotten story. This book offers a historically grounded account of the many ways in which this neighbouring capital touched the career and work of both major and minor writers. It is concerned both with the materiality of writers' engagements with Paris and with the ways in which these experiences became absorbed and expressed within the Victorian imaginary. Just as Dickens's London was a real place, exerting identifiable influences on his life and writing, and yet in another sense never existed outside his imagination, so this book holds in tension Paris at a specific historical moment and Paris as a literary confection.

More than a century ago, Hilaire Belloc laid the blame for the move from history as experience to history as abstraction, and its disastrous consequences for the perception of France's real cultural influence on Great Britain, at the feet of Thomas Carlyle's enormously influential *French Revolution* (1837).[2] Anglo-French and Roman Catholic, Belloc might be considered as *parti pris*; nevertheless his arguments have some merit. Driven by the conviction that 'in every object there is inexhaustible meaning; the eye sees in it what the eye brings means of seeing', Carlyle's history was as conducive to ascribing a symbolic identity to the French nation as the view he was combatting.[3] France as an object lesson in the results of poor government replaced a view of the French as bearers of a noxious contagious disease best resisted by means of an actual and metaphorical *cordon sanitaire*. Belloc's other claim, that Carlyle's perspective on France encouraged a disproportionate estimate of the Teutonic influence on Victorian Britain, was doubtless fuelled by resentments dating back to the Franco-Prussian war; but this privileging of Germany, its Romantic literature and its Higher Critics, as the leading European cultural influence on Victorian Britain continued for much of the twentieth century.

---

[1] S. Hall, 'Cultural Identity and the Diaspora', in *Identity, Community, Culture, Difference*, ed. J. Rutherford (London: Lawrence & Wishart, 1990), 222.

[2] T. Carlyle, *The French Revolution*, intro. H. Belloc (2 vols, London: J. M. Dent & Sons, 1906), pp. v–xvi.

[3] Quoted in *The French Revolution*, in *The Works of Thomas Carlyle*, ed. H. D. Traill (30 vols, London: Chapman & Hall, 1896–1901), ii, 5.

Recent scholarship concerned with Victorian literature's engagement with Europe has often taken its lead from Linda Colley's influential study, *Britons: Forging the Nation 1707–1837* (1992), in which she argued that the concept of Britishness took form in relation to the 'other' of the French. The focus of work in this vein has therefore been self-reflexive, attending to the politics of Victorian identity formation, and noting the ways in which travel variously estranged, unsettled, or transformed a writer's conception of self and home, rather than concentrating upon the objective aspect of his or her engagement with foreign life. Social historians, meanwhile, have enthusiastically co-opted literature as a primary source, but have rarely interested themselves in literary aesthetics or questioned the extent to which contact with a foreign culture showed itself in the literary and artistic forms, structures, and genres employed at home.

Conceiving of cultural impact more broadly than as an influence on an élite band of writers, this study cuts a broad swathe across genres (including fiction, poetry, the essay, drama, journalism, travel writing, the diary, biography, and autobiography). The breadth of this database enables the consideration of broad questions, such as what made Paris such a honeypot for writers at this time—perhaps less easy to understand than the attraction it held for artists and musicians, who were professionally less dependent on a working knowledge of French for absorbing what Paris had to offer them. Examining a wide spectrum of writing over the course of almost half a century also reveals ways in which the accounts by writers were so often indebted (whether they realized it or not) to preconceptions formed variously from encounters with French exiles, artistic representations of the city, newspaper articles, or the accounts given by previous British visitors.

A letter from Charles Dickens, written on the day of arrival on his first trip to France in 1837, neatly encapsulates the way in which, although neither he nor the recipient had previously set foot on French soil, he assumes they are both in a position to recognize 'Frenchness' when they see it:

> We went this afternoon in a barouche to some gardens where the people dance, and where they were footing it most heartily—especially the women who in their short petticoats and light caps look uncommonly agreeable. A gentleman in a blue surtout and silken Berlins accompanied us from the Hotel and acted as Curator he even waltzed elegantly too. We rang for slippers after we came back, and it turned out that this gentleman was the "Boots". Isn't this French?[4]

The always potentially dangerous *peuple*, or masses, disporting themselves; their scantily but decoratively attired women—possibly offering further promise of making themselves 'agreeable'; and the disregard for class barriers—all form part of a spectacle pleasingly confirming the national characteristics Dickens's sightseeing expedition had sought out.

The satisfying impression of continuity provided by national stereotypes was of course tempered in the period covered by this book by a disquieting sense of Paris

---

[4] *The Pilgrim Edition of the Letters of Charles Dickens*, ed. G. Storey et al. (12 vols, Oxford: Clarendon Press, 1965–2002), i, 281.

as a city undergoing almost constant change. The turbulent years between 1830 and the aftermath of the Franco-Prussian war afforded plenty to contemplate to those across the Channel, and even writing ostensibly strongly focused on one shore or the other can be seen to be informed by the impulse to make national comparisons. It has, for instance, been argued that Walter Bagehot's classic work *The English Constitution* (1867) was as much stimulated by contemplating the contrast between the overweening Emperor Napoleon III and Great Britain's monarchy, or (in the 1872 edition) the experimental arrangements of the Third Republic's parliamentary system against that of Great Britain, as by considering the changes wrought by the Second Reform Bill of 1867.[5] Extending this book's span to include the immediate aftermath of the Franco-Prussian war and the birth-pangs of the Third Republic, when France's sense of its supreme position in European affairs and the capital's self-assurance both momentarily faltered, helps in understanding why the history of mid-nineteenth-century Paris continued to haunt the British imagination.

The first part of this book, 'Finding one's bearings in Paris', undertakes a chronologically organized exploration of the historical, topographical, and social dimensions of the city encountered by British writers in the mid-nineteenth century. Rather than encouraging a myth of progress, this approach is based upon a dynamic model, both of Paris and of writers' interaction with it. A writer's growing fame could change the nature of his or her Parisian experiences: for instance, in the early 1830s Thackeray's social circle was mainly confined to the camaraderie of indigent would-be artists and journalists, but by the 1850s, in the wake of *Vanity Fair*'s success, the salons of the upper echelons of Franco-British society had opened to embrace him.

Abrupt regime changes were accompanied by ambitious government programmes for redesigning the city's physical and social contours. Chapters 4 and 5 attend both to Paris as physical experience and to the self-conscious assessment of the sensations it provoked. The spectacular nature and speed of these developments prompted British writers who made frequent cross-Channel forays to repeated topographical 'readings' of Paris, and sometimes to bouts of reflection on earlier selves from which they now seemed irretrievably estranged by the wholesale destruction of the buildings, streets, and enclaves where they had formerly wandered.

If acquiring lodgings on the left or right bank of the Seine, in a hotel or rented apartment, alone or with family or friends, necessarily influenced the way in which a visitor experienced Paris, so did the nature of the social encounters the city opened or withheld. Since the days of the wandering medieval scholar it had been the custom to write letters of introduction for friends and protégés to European colleagues, while wealthy travellers had servants or hired guides who saw to their practical needs.[6] By the mid-nineteenth century, however, an increasing number of

[5] *Bagehot: The English Constitution*, ed. P. Smith (Cambridge: Cambridge University Press, 2001), 45, 218–21.

[6] R. C. Dales, *The Intellectual Life of Western Europe in the Middle Ages* (Leiden: E. J. Brill, 1992), 222, 290–91; H. Brown and G. Dow (eds), *European Connections: Readers, Writer, Salonnières* (Oxford: Peter Lang, 2011), 2.

middle-class British travellers were thrown upon their own resources to access informal networks for negotiating social interaction in a foreign city. Chapters 6 and 7 pursue the nature and extent of British sociability in Paris. Chapter 6 considers the ways in which gender predetermined the Paris it was possible to experience, the extent to which British writers could ever become intimate with native Parisians, and the part played by the British Embassy. Chapter 7 is devoted to the role of the Parisian *salon*, an institution which the British identified as quintessentially French and to which they prized entry, while also regarding its sophisticated management of social intercourse as evidence of French worldliness and superficiality.

Establishing a network of contacts, usually amongst their own compatriots, was a vital prerequisite for the Anglophone journalists whose careers form the subject of the middle part of this book. The journalistic revolution of the 1830s and 1840s exposed a new generation to the technological inventions and new commercial practices taking place in the printing industries of France, England, and Germany. Although it is no part of my thesis to deny the wider European context of the London–Paris axis, Chapter 8 pays particular attention to the press conditions which made Paris the launchpad for so many British journalists. Chapter 9 offers a taxonomy of the British men and women who found their way from very diverse backgrounds into journalism in Paris. Chapter 10 discusses the rapidly evolving working conditions and the qualities requisite for success in a period when journalism became increasingly professionalized. Chapter 11 explores the numerous ways in which the highly competitive market of Parisian Anglophone journalism—which placed a premium on the ability to recognize, adapt, or if necessary plagiarize new print fashions—influenced Thackeray's work as both writer and illustrator.

The third and final part of this book engages directly with the literary nature of the writings produced as a consequence of British writers' contact with Paris. Excluding only drama from its purview, since the cross-Channel trade in translation and acting styles would demand a full-length separate study, this part is devoted to fictional accounts of Paris. The brief, introductory Chapter 12 examines the use of French within Anglophone texts during a period when fiction became cheaply available to a far wider audience. Chapter 13 starts by considering the paradoxical narrowness of the literary palette from which British writers confected their pictures of Paris at a time usually heralded as one of British fiction's most inventive phases, before distinguishing the subgenres most frequently employed by novelists. Finally, Chapter 14 addresses the underlying structures, stock characters, and recurrent themes through which British prejudices about Paris emerged, revealing how often these tropes were themselves dependent upon previous literary sources. The book's concluding paragraphs suggest what this study contributes to the voluminous literature of Victorian studies.

Having indicated the book's purpose and outlined its contents, it is time to say something of its methodology. Seeking quantitative evidence for my claim that nineteenth-century Paris, as a real city, existing in time and space, impinged on mainstream British culture, I turned to the search engine of the *Oxford Dictionary of National Biography*. Using 1830–1875 as the dates between which writers involved in 'Literature, journalism and publishing' were active, with Paris a significant place in their life-story, the search yielded 127 entries, whereas substituting 'Germany' for Paris, but keeping the other search terms, yielded only 77 entries.

These bald statistics mask complicating factors. In the case of briefer entries, a short period in Paris may not have been deemed sufficiently important for mention, or may have been incorporated under a larger entity such as travel in France, or even Europe. A few of the writers discussed in this book were considered too insignificant for inclusion; others occur in more than one category, and still others fail to feature in the category 'Literature, journalism and publishing'. A search in cognate areas brought up 130 names under the term 'art', 25 under 'theatre and live entertainment', and 42 for 'music'. Even then this omitted some names without which any literary guide to the period would seem incomplete, such as John Stuart Mill, for whom a teenage year spent in France proved formative. It was a French text to which he turned to lift his spirits during his nervous breakdown of 1826–27: Jean-François Marmontel and his four-volume *Mémoires d'un père* (1804) are not names that resonate in current histories of nineteenth-century English literature, but Ruskin too acknowledged both author and book as seminal.[7] The reforming agenda behind Mill's political writing of the 1830s was heavily influenced by his personal acquaintance with the Saint-Simonians, and by his experience of the1830 uprising. From 1833 Paris would also offer a regular rendezvous for his meetings with Harriet Taylor, the woman who won his lifelong devotion.[8]

The notion of a 'national biography' to which I resorted for these statistics also deserves comment, since the United Kingdom of Great Britain and Ireland had only been formally constituted as recently as 1801. Whereas the English, sometimes seemingly unselfconsciously, arrogated 'Britishness' for themselves, the Irish, Scots, and Welsh were frequently more alive to national difference. This study will follow nineteenth-century practice in using 'English' and 'British' interchangeably, but differentiating other constituents of the kingdom when appropriate, particularly in producing a taxonomy of Anglophone journalists.

Residual, largely sentimental notions of connection lingered between the Scots and the French, dating from the 'auld alliance' which in 1295 had promised mutual aid in the event of England attacking either territory. Enlightenment philosophy brought about a renewed eighteenth-century rapprochement between Edinburgh and Paris: this lingered in the tendency of Scotland's nineteenth-century intelligentsia and professional classes to pursue further training in Paris rather than immediately adopting the more familiar migratory route south of the border.[9]

Despite the atheistic excesses of the French Revolution, nineteenth-century Irish Catholics were disposed to believe that their co-religionists in France would

---

[7] *The Works of John Ruskin*, ed. E. T. Cook and A. Wedderburn (39 vols, London: George Allen; New York: Longmans, Green, 1903–12), xviii, 48.

[8] F. A. Hayek, *John Stuart Mill and Harriet Taylor: Their Correspondence and Subsequent Marriage* (London: Routledge & Kegan Paul, 1951).

[9] T. Nairn, *The Break-Up of Britain: Crisis and Neo-nationalism* (Altona, Vic.: Common Ground, 2003), 112; S. Reynolds, *Paris–Edinburgh: Cultural Connections in the* Belle Époque (Aldershot: Ashgate, 2007), 5–11.

offer a more sympathetic milieu than Protestant England. Paris indeed served as a convenient perch for many who felt themselves culturally alienated by upbringing, politics, religion, or long-time service abroad, from the 'centre' represented by Great Britain's capital city. Nevertheless, Parisian scorn for the provincial probably served to offset much of the romanticization of the affinities between Great Britain's Celtic fringes and the French regions, practised on either side of the Channel by pseudo-ethnographers such as Matthew Arnold or Ernest Renan.

This book's use of a multiplicity of literary discourses differentiates it from much existing scholarship on Anglo-French literature and culture which has typically fallen into case-history approaches to genres such as travel writers and their work;[10] books chronicling individual canonical writers' engagement with France;[11] or survey works, ranging from the panoptic social history with a long historical sweep[12] to books showing a more marked interest in literary matters.[13] Walter Benjamin's claim for Paris as 'the capital of the nineteenth century' has notably received attention from literary scholars focusing on fiction. Priscilla Parkhurst Ferguson reads Paris as the recurrent stage of revolution which defined the narrative terms of those four canonical French novelists, Flaubert, Hugo, Vallès and Zola, while those scholars of comparative literature Franco Moretti and Robert Alter attend to native novelists' treatment of their own capital cities, Paris and London, in arguing that the swiftly growing nineteenth-century European city was crucial in effecting an imaginative shift of consciousness and a consequent change in literary taste.[14]

The decision to cast the literary net more widely was founded on the belief that this would more aptly capture the ambience of mid-nineteenth-century print cul-

[10] L. Withey, *Grand Tours and Cook's Tours: A History of Leisure Travel 1750–1915* (London: Aurum, 1998) and R. Mullen and J. Munson *'The Smell of the Continent': The British Discover Europe* (Basingstoke: Macmillan, 2009) offer historical narratives. G. Robb, *The Discovery of France* (London: Picador, 2007) and M. Morgan, *National Identities and Travel in Victorian Britain* (Basingstoke: Palgrave, 2001) employ copious travel literature in building, for their different purposes, on the identity formation thesis provided by L. Colley in *Britons: Forging the Nation 1707–1837* (New Haven, Conn.: Yale University Press, 1992). J. Buzard, *The Beaten Track: European Tourism, Literature, and the Ways to 'Culture' 1800–1900* (Oxford: Clarendon Press, 1993) devotes greater attention to the literary qualities of his primary sources.

[11] e.g. R. Gridley, *The Brownings and France: A Chronicle with Commentary* (London: Athlone Press, 1982); J. Rignall (ed.), *George Eliot and Europe* (Aldershot: Scolar, 1996); J. Rignall, *George Eliot, European Novelist* (Aldershot: Ashgate, 2011); *Dickens on France*, ed. J. Edmondson (Oxford: Signal Books, 2006).

[12] Two recent examples are R. Tombs and I. Tombs, *That Sweet Enemy: The British and the French from the Sun King to the Present* (London: Pimlico, 2007) and P. Thorold, *The British in France: Visitors and Residents since the Revolution* (London: Continuum, 2008).

[13] The somewhat idiosyncratic C. Campos, *The View of France from Arnold to Bloomsbury* (Oxford: Oxford University Press, 1965) focuses on canonical authors, as does C. Crossley and I. Small (eds), *Studies in Anglo-French Cultural Relations* (Basingstoke: Macmillan, 1988). C. A. Simmons, *Eyes Across the Channel: French Revolutions, Party History, and British Writing 1830–82* (Amsterdam: Harwood Academic, 2000) selects material to comment on France's role as political touchstone for Tory and Whig writers. D. Rainsford, *Literature, Identity and the English Channel: Narrow Seas Expanded* (Basingstoke: Palgrave, 2002) attempts to cover two centuries of literature from both sides of the Channel.

[14] P. P. Ferguson, *Paris as Revolution: Writing the Nineteenth-Century City* (Berkeley: University of California Press, 1994); F. Moretti, *Atlas of the European Novel 1800–1900* (London: Verso, 1998); R. Alter, *Imagined Cities* (New Haven, Conn.: Yale University Press, 2005).

ture. During this period of exceptionally rapid expansion and democratization, before Modernism sought to reinscribe the division between the 'highbrow' text designed for a limited readership and the 'lowbrow' production aimed at a mass market, the lines were by no means as finely drawn. The migration of illustration to a staple of the mid-century press from both ends of a market where it had existed in the form of lurid woodcuts for the cheap press or expensive engravings witnessed a period when image and text, writer and illustrator, briefly held out the promise in Great Britain of the more equal status that seemed to pertain in France. The precise ranking of various literary genres was no more stable. The versatility demanded of writers who had cut their teeth on highly competitive piece-rate work in Paris produced a generation of writers ready to try their hand at a range of genres, including drama, travel writing, art criticism, historical sketches, memoirs and life-writing. By considering these occasional pieces as interventions in a contemporary debate, this study provides a context in which to evaluate writings previously seen as difficult to place in the oeuvres of major writers.

The readiness of so many of these writers, both male and female, to slip back and forth between the genres of journalism and novel writing in their accounts of Paris suggests both the abundant possibilities of their subject matter and the consequent difficulty of establishing a steady gaze or fixed position on this swiftly evolving city. Indeed, the competing perspectives and complex movements, often observable in the same piece of journalism or travel writing, between such positions as holding France up as a mirror capable of revealing England's worst traits to herself, using its ethos as a simple contrast to Great Britain's religious or moral worth, or simply noting different cultural practices, lent themselves readily enough to the polyphonic world of fiction. Nevertheless, in fiction and non-fiction alike, deep-seated ambivalence and irresolvable plurality of view remains a characteristic note.

This book's attention to the journalism and fiction of the mid-nineteenth century corroborates Benedict Anderson's claim for the significance of the emergence in the previous century of the novel and the newspaper as joint providers of the 'technical means for "re-presenting" the *kind* of imagined community that is the nation'.[15] The desire to strike a fresh note and gain individual recognition, while labouring under the anonymity of the ubiquitous title 'our Paris Correspondent', fostered—most notably in the generation of writers of the 1830s and 1840s—an impulse to fashion personae through which they could alternately empathize with or rebuke their readers' supposed views of Paris and the French.

Above all, the ensuing study repeatedly reveals an ever-present tension between these writers' interest in the urban life of Paris—different in so many ways from their own capital—and the tendency to respond to, or lapse into, the easy cliché and literary stereotype, when they sought to encapsulate their impressions of Paris for their readers at home.

[15] B. R. O'G. Anderson, *Imagined Communities: Reflections on the Origin and Spread of Nationalism,* 2nd edn. (London: Verso, 2006), 25.

PART I

FINDING ONE'S BEARINGS IN MID-NINETEENTH-CENTURY PARIS

The seven chapters in this first section of this book are devoted to picturing Paris as it appeared to nineteenth-century British writers. The initial three chapters are historical in scope: the first provides a skeleton history of regime change, the second, British eyewitness accounts of these events as they were played out on the streets of Paris, and the third is concerned with texts where turbulence in Paris is evaluated in terms of its likely impact on British shores. Chapters 4 and 5 focus on the topography of the Paris with which the British were most familiar, and the ways in which this urban experience, in many ways so different from their own, struck them at a sensory level. Chapters 6 and 7 consider the variety and quality of Parisian social experience open to British writers of either sex.

1

Regime change on the streets of Paris

This chapter provides the minimum information necessary to make sense of the references to political systems, events and allegiances which occur in the rest of the book. It cannot hope to serve as a substitute for the more sophisticated accounts by professional historians of the period.[1] It is further limited by treating Paris as an entity largely separable from France as a whole: this is an important caveat, in that, just as political life and discussion in nineteenth-century London were influenced by the industrial life of Manchester, so the silk weavers of Lyon played their part in the deliberations and tactics employed by the government in Paris.

1.1 BOURBON MONARCHY, 1814–1830

The period covered by this book opens with the summary ousting of Charles X from his throne in 1830. The Bourbon monarchy, restored in 1814 under Louis XVIII (1814–24), had lasted until 1830, with the brief exception of 'the Hundred Days' (March to July 1815) during which Napoleon I returned from exile in Elba, launched a further campaign, and was finally defeated by a coalition of European armies at the battle of Waterloo. Charles X (1824–30) succeeded Louis XVIII: both were brothers and heirs of the executed Louis XVI.

Louis XVIII tempered his restoration of the old order by the symbolic act of moving his court from Versailles to Napoleon's I's official residence at the Tuileries in Paris, and agreeing to a constitutional monarchy supported by a bicameral government. His successor, Charles X, was more reactionary. He nailed his colours to the mast by introducing legislation that favoured the dispossessed nobility and re-established the influence of the Roman Catholic clergy. In the face of increasing liberal opposition to his policies, Charles declared that he would rule by decree. In March

---

[1] Two volumes of the *Nouvelle Histoire de Paris* are devoted to the mid-19th c.: P. Vigier, *Paris pendant la Monarchie de Juillet* (Paris: Association pour la publication d'une histoire de Paris, 1991) and L. Girard, *La Deuxième République et le Second Empire* (Paris: Association pour la publication d'une histoire de Paris,1981). C. Jones, *Paris: Biography of a City* (London: Penguin, 2006) offers chapters on this period together with an extremely useful annotated bibliographical guide, covering general accounts of the 19th-c. city, and more specialized guides to e.g. its different arrondissements, social groups, occupations, music, art, theatre, and architecture, both civic and domestic. A. Hussey, *Paris: the Secret History* (London: Penguin, 2007) offers a readable synopsis, claiming to emphasize the viewpoint of the marginalized, disruptive classes of Paris. A cultural history, concentrating on the public topoi of the city, is to be found in C. Prendergast, *Paris and the Nineteenth Century* (Oxford: Blackwell, 1992). The artefacts in the relevant rooms of Paris's Musée Carnavalet provide another excellent method for introducing newcomers to the history and culture of Paris in this period.

1830 he dissolved the Chamber of Deputies for resisting his reforms and, at the end of April, particularly offended Paris by dismissing the city's voluntary corps, the National Guard. His July ordinances, published on 26 July 1830, censored a hostile press, reduced the membership and power of the Chamber of Deputies, and imposed restrictions which affected the ability of the commercial classes to become deputies. Workers, deprived of their living by employers who had closed their business concerns in protest, barricaded the narrow Parisian streets against the troops sent in to quell them.

1.2 THE JULY MONARCHY OF LOUIS-PHILIPPE, 1830–1848

At the conclusion of three days of rioting between 27 and 29 July 1830 (known as *les Trois Glorieuses*), Louis-Philippe, duc d'Orléans, head of the cadet branch of the Bourbons, and conveniently at hand in the Palais-Royal, accepted the throne by popular acclaim, rather than supporting the candidature of Charles's young grandson, as the abdicating monarch had wished. Nicknamed the 'Citizen King', Louis-Philippe bore the official title 'King of the French', rather than 'King of France', indicating that he ruled at his subjects' pleasure rather than by hereditary right as previous monarchs had done. The mutual suspicion that had long existed between the two branches of the Bourbons now sharply divided the aristocracy of the *ancien régime* into supporters of the older branch, known as Legitimists, and supporters of Louis-Philippe and his heirs, referred to as Orléanists.

The July Monarchy, as it became known, lasted eighteen years. Despite his efforts at appeasing the forces that had toppled Charles X, Louis-Philippe's tenure of the last French kingship was to be troubled. He commissioned a column honouring those who had fallen in the July revolution to be erected in the Place de la Bastille, symbolic site of the inaugural events of the 1789 Revolution where the throne of his predecessor, Charles X, had been dragged and burnt. He back-pedalled on Charles X's public displays of the close bond between the Roman Catholic Church and the throne, which had caused such offence to liberal thinkers. Endeavouring to distance his regime from that of Charles X, and to suggest continuity with the nation's heroic past, he caused Napoleon's remains to be brought back from St Helena in December 1840 and ceremoniously interred in Les Invalides. The new king's public image, frock-coated and sporting an umbrella rather than a sword, was designed to demonstrate his solidarity with a bourgeois spirit that saw more profit in peace than revolution.

Nevertheless, this king, who had spent so much of his life in exile and continued to surround himself with foreigners, was not popular. The commercial prosperity on display in the new *grands magasins* and covered arcades, and the growth of rich suburban enclaves, demanded hordes of immigrant workers. This growth in Paris's urban population, which doubled between 1800 and mid-century, was not matched by corresponding government expenditure on the poor during times of illness or unemployment. Nor did the Church, previously a principal conduit for charitable endeavour, see a corresponding increase in the number of its parish clergy. The way in which the cholera epidemic of 1832 differentially affected the poor and the rich during a time of economic recession spoke to the growing gap between the dangerously overcrowded conditions in which the lowest classes lived and the new developments augmenting the housing available to the comfortably-off. These overt inequities fuelled the fire of radical ideologies and revolutionary fervour. By the mid-1840s, when Karl Marx first encountered Friedrich Engels in a café in the Palais-Royal, the city had become a hub for European revolutionaries.

The economic divide which opened up between the eastern districts of the city where the working classes congregated, and the more affluent northern and north-western parts fomented paranoia about the extent of the thievery, violence, and insurrectionary tendencies believed to be lurking in the shadows. These fears were in turn fanned by a slew of publications, both fictional and non-fictional, about urban crime.[2] Judging by their letters home, British tourists seemed to have relished incidents which allowed them to confirm that the streets of Paris were more dangerous than those of London. Visiting as an undergraduate in 1829, Thackeray claimed that a swordstick trumped the umbrella as the essential item for venturing out onto the Champs-Élysées at night.[3]

The tightly packed five-storey houses which hemmed the narrow streets in the older parts of the city were home to legendary victims as well as aggressors.[4] In 1834 government troops sent to quell an uprising in the Beaubourg neighbourhood (the 4th arrondissement), where barricades had been erected, allegedly reacted to sniper fire coming from the Rue Transnonain. Bursting into number 12, they killed twelve defenceless inhabitants. The official explanation that these deaths had occurred only as a consequence of the troops being forced to defend themselves received short shrift in the radical press. The artist Honoré Daumier, who lived only three blocks away, perpetuated the memory of the event in a lithograph showing men, women, and a baby, dressed in their nightclothes and lying dead in a bedroom where they had clearly been sleeping moments before (Fig. 1).

Charles X's downfall had been precipitated by his determination to silence a critical press. Louis-Philippe's reign had seemed to promise a more liberal approach, but in September 1835 the freedom of the press was once again, as Thackeray

[2] T. McDonough, 'City of Strangers', in *The Invisible Flâneuse? Gender, Public Space, and Visual Culture in Nineteenth-Century Paris*, ed. A. D'Souza and T. McDonough (Manchester: Manchester University Press, 2006), 148–63.

[3] *The Letters and Private Papers of William Makepeace Thackeray*, ed. G. N. Ray (4 vols, Cambridge, Mass: Harvard University Press, 1945–6), i, 89, 102–3, 357. See also *The Pilgrim Edition of the Letters of Charles Dickens*, ed. G Storey et al. (12 vols, Oxford: Clarendon Press, 1965–2002), iv, 676.

[4] The thesis driving R. D. E. Burton, *Blood in the City: Violence and Revelation in Paris, 1789–1945* (Ithaca, NY: Cornell University Press, 2001) is that a martyrology, welcomed by the more extreme Roman Catholics and the radical left alike, fuelled the political unrest and street violence of the July monarchy, even effecting a short-lived rapprochement between the crucifix and the liberty tree in the events leading up to 1848.

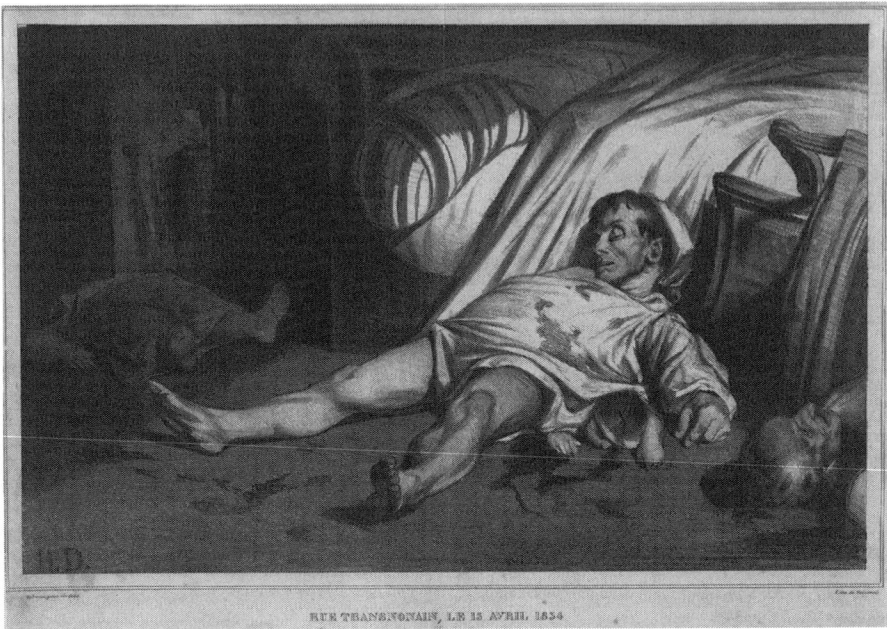

Fig. 1. 'Rue Transnonain, le 15 Avril 1834', lithograph by Honoré Daumier (by courtesy of Yale University Art Gallery, Everett V. Meeks, B.A. 1901, Fund).

neatly expressed it, 'calmly strangled by the Monarch who had gained his crown for his supposed championship of it'.[5] The outlawing of press discussion of the king, his family, and the legitimacy of the monarchy was part of a wider response to one of the potentially more serious attempts at toppling the regime. The Corsican Fieschi's attempt on the life of Louis-Philippe as the king and his sons were reviewing the National Guard was only one of seven plots against the monarch uncovered in 1835. Popular uprisings periodically recurred within the city; meanwhile, Louis-Napoleon launched two attempts, in 1836 and 1840, to regain the throne for the Bonapartistes.

Read in the context of these repeated attacks upon Louis-Philippe's authority, Thackeray's serial *The History of the Next French Revolution, from a forthcoming history of Europe*, published in *Punch* in the spring of 1844, reads more as informed political satire than as comic fantasy.[6] When, in February 1848, his opponents succeeded in overthrowing Louis-Philippe, the event formed the prelude to a series of political upheavals in Europe and beyond, predicated (economically speaking) on the failure of governments to address the decline of living conditions amongst the labouring

---

[5] 'Caricatures and Lithography', in *The Paris Sketch Book*, vol. ii of *The Oxford Thackeray*, ed. G. Saintsbury (London: Oxford University Press, 1910), 178. First published as 'Parisian Caricatures' in the *London and Westminster Review* 32 (Apr. 1839), 282–305.

[6] *The History of the Next French Revolution, from a forthcoming history of Europe* (*Punch*, 24 Feb.–20 Apr. 1844); repr. in *Oxford Thackeray*, vii, 315–53.

poor. The immediate provocation for the Parisian revolt was Louis-Philippe's ban on a series of fund-raising banquets, largely supported by the middle classes and designed to circumvent the outlawing of political gatherings and demonstrations. Unenfranchised as they were, the Parisian working classes resorted to their accustomed symbol of protest, the barricades. Confronted with the prospect of his troops turning against him, Louis-Philippe abdicated and fled to England, under a pseudonym in keeping with his bourgeois persona, Mr William Smith. The way in which the English harboured France's successive waves of political exiles, who while there often used British shores for the purpose of plotting their return to power, no doubt fostered the distrust of perfidious Albion among the masses of the Parisian poor who were unlikely ever to be able to avail themselves of Great Britain's shelter.

1.3 THE SECOND REPUBLIC, 1848–1851

The pressure of popular protest rendered impracticable the temporizing procedures of putting Louis-Philippe's 9-year-old grandson on the throne. Meanwhile, bourgeois liberal supporters of the newly declared Second Republic became alarmed by the radical nature of the proposed reforming measures, which included universal male suffrage along with immediate steps to alleviate the conditions of the working classes. On 21 June 1848 the provisional government rescinded its aid for the unemployed, and in the June Days Uprising (24–6 June) the eastern districts of working-class Paris fought the bourgeois faubourgs of the west. The street-by-street engagement was bitter, and resulted in a death toll of over 4,000 civilians and some 1,000 soldiers.

The ensuing crackdown by the triumphant liberal republicans over the forces of democratic socialism was merciless. Of the 11,000 imprisoned, some 4,000 were deported to Algeria. General Cavaignac, who had led the troops, was appointed interim head of state until an election could be held in December for a president who was to enjoy considerable executive power but was limited to a single four-year period of office. The long-term exile Louis-Napoleon Bonaparte, nephew and surviving heir to Napoleon I, was in part the default candidate, preferred to his rivals because, unlike any of them, he was not intimately associated with any one of the warring factions in recent events. He was carried to power not so much by the political élite of Paris as by the vote of the rural peasantry, who associated his name with the favours they had enjoyed when Napoleon I had restored order, confidence, and a degree of prosperity to the nation after the reign of terror.

In the first years of his presidency Louis-Napoleon attempted to please all parties. However, as the end of his four-year tenure came in sight, it became clear both that his right-wing supporters had always seen him as a stop-gap bridge to the restoration of monarchy, and that the National Assembly would brook no alteration to the law limiting his presidency to a single term. Aware of the popular support that Louis-Napoleon was whipping up by touring the provinces and by encouraging the press in its criticism of government reforms, in July 1851 the

National Assembly rescinded the legislation that had introduced universal male suffrage. In a carefully planned manoeuvre, on 2 December 1851 Louis-Napoleon deployed his troops in the centre of Paris, swiftly arrested his leading opponents, dissolved the National Assembly, and restored universal male suffrage. Ardent republicans such as Victor Hugo, who was to continue his anti-Napoleonic crusade during the twenty years of his ensuing exile, led an insurrection in Paris, but this was swiftly crushed by the evening of 4 December, and in the regions the army remained loyal to Louis-Napoleon. In Paris some 200 lay dead, thousands were arrested, and many political opponents were deported to the French colonies.

1.4 THE SECOND EMPIRE, 1852–1870

At the start of the next year Louis-Napoleon proceeded to deal with the other major constitutional threat to his rule: on 22 January 1852 he confiscated the property of the House of Orléans. A year to the day after his effective seizure of power, on 2 December 1852, the Second Empire came into being, with Napoleon III confirmed as its Emperor by a national referendum.

The Second Empire swiftly became a byword for opulent display, and later for overblown decadence. The redesign of Paris, carried out by Napoleon III in conjunction with Baron Haussmann, lay at the heart of a modernizing enterprise driven by social, economic, and political motives. The wholesale destruction of *le vieux Paris*, where the easily barricaded medieval alleyways of the slums had afforded a site of resistance for the radicalized working classes, went hand in hand with its inhabitants' relocation to the outskirts of the city, where growing numbers of factories offered some chance of employment. In 1868, when the British journalist Henry Vizetelly wanted to run a series of feature articles on life in the poor quarters of Paris, he was told by the Paris police that since Hausmannization there 'was no special low quarter, such as existed in London. The new boulevards...had pierced it through.' Their eighty miles of new streets had swept away the ancient rookeries, so that now there were no regular thieves' haunts or vagabonds' places of resort.'[7]

If the motives behind Haussmann's redesign were 'security, circulation and salubrity',[8] the scale of the work required to rip up existing streets and realign them in accordance with a coherent grand plan, and the accompanying power to requisition property and shift people, formed a monument to the power and efficiency of the imperial machine. Whereas in London the potential threat to property prices combined with fierce competition between numerous railway companies to prevent the kind of logical distribution of termini that worked to make cross-city travel easy for passengers, French government policy enabled Haussmann to create radial road links for Paris's vastly extended major stations.[9] As Queen Victoria

---

[7] H. Vizetelly, *Glances Back through Seventy Years: Autobiographical and Other Recollections* (2 vols, London: Kegan Paul, Trench, Trübner,1893), ii, 209.

[8] Quoted in Jones, *Paris*, 348.

[9] J. White, *London in the Nineteenth Century* (London: Jonathan Cape, 2007), pp. 41–7; J. Harter, *World Railways of the Nineteenth-Century: A Pictorial History in Victorian Engravings* (Baltimore, Md.: Johns Hopkins University Press, 2005), 139–40.

ruefully reflected when she visited Napoleon in 1855, he clearly enjoyed greater personal power than she did.

The particular occasion that prompted Victoria to this conclusion was Napoleon's careful staging of a magnificent farewell to her at Boulogne, where he reviewed the massed French troops on the precise spot where Napoleon I had planned to invade England. Throughout her stay she had been busily observing the sheer numbers of troops at his disposal. When she and her retinue entered Paris on the evening of 18 August 1855, she noted:

> There were troops along the whole line from the *Gare* [de Strasbourg]to the Palace...There were 40,000 troops, besides the 20,000 national Guards—60,000 in all; besides the 40,0000 I saw at Boulogne: artillery, cavalry, *Cent-Gardes* (who are splendid), and last, but not least, to my great delight, at the bridge of Boulogne, near the village and Palace of St. Cloud, the Zouaves—splendid troops in splendid dress...[10]

The Paris Exposition of 1867 was similarly used as an occasion to dazzle foreign potentates with a grand military display.

1.5 THE FRANCO-PRUSSIAN WAR AND THE SIEGE OF PARIS, 1870–1871

Troops who managed elegant drill formations on the parade ground, however, did not, it transpired, necessarily perform equally well on the battlefield. By 1870, when Napoleon III rashly declared war on Prussia, many Parisians had already begun to feel that they were paying too dearly for the privilege of acting as the Second Empire's showcase. On 4 September 1870, the day when news arrived of the Emperor's humiliating defeat and capture at the battle of Sedan on 2 September, there was a popular demonstration in the city in favour of France reverting to a republic. Following a well-established tradition of deposed French rulers, Napoleon took refuge in England in March 1871.

Meanwhile, the Prussian armies had advanced on Paris, which was protected by those regular French troops who had escaped Sedan, together with some 350,000 of the National Guard, and the stout city walls which had been strengthened as recently as 1840. Rather than attack Paris, the Prussians camped outside and concentrated on subduing French forces gathered in Metz and elsewhere. The siege of Paris was to last from 19 September 1870 to 28 January 1871, when the combined effects of starvation, lack of fuel during an exceptionally harsh winter, and enemy bombardment forced Paris to surrender. On 17 February, Prussian troops celebrated their victory in a symbolic parade through the heart of Paris.

The political hiatus in Paris caused by the withdrawal to Versailles of the unpopular provisional French government further fomented the divisions already visible

[10] *Queen Victoria: Leaves from a Journal: A Record of the Visit of the Emperor and Empress of the French to the Queen, and of the Visit of the Queen and H.R.H the Prince Consort to the Emperor of the French*, 1855, intro. R. Mortimer (London: André Deutsch, 1961), 149, 76–7.

within the city during the siege. The working classes, who felt that the poor had born the brunt of the siege's privations, were distrustful of the personal commercial interests which they believed had prompted their new government to concede Alsace and Lorraine to the Prussians rather than countenance further financial loss themselves. A government out to appease the German Emperor, might, they also feared, repudiate republicanism and elect to restore monarchy.

For its part, the provisional government, keen to maintain peace within the city, cancelled the allowance to the National Guard, which had compensated many working-class men for the loss of their normal employment during the siege, and attempted to decommission some of their armaments. When, on 18 March, soldiers were dispatched by the government to the working-class stronghold of Montmartre to repossess cannons from the National Guard, rioting ensued, and some of the government troops threw in their lot with the rioters. Adolphe Thiers, head of the provisional government, ordered those troops who remained loyal, and the police and civil servants, to evacuate Paris, effectively leaving the city in the hands of a National Guard accustomed to electing their own officers.

1.6 THE COMMUNE

By 28 March 1871 an elected committee of ninety-two, composed of radicalized workers, professionals, and intellectuals, announced the rule of the Commune—their symbol the red flag of socialism rather than the tricolour of moderate republicanism. Although they embarked upon a legislative programme, and attempted to coordinate the organizational efforts of the different areas of Paris, this revolution was inherently local in its administration and disparate in its political aims, which ranged from social democracy to the anarchic. The Commune's internationalist strain was promoted by the city's contingent of foreign political exiles, and achieved its symbolic moment in the demolition of the Vendôme column, monument to Napoleon I's imperialist conquests. Neither the government nor the Commune demonstrated much enthusiasm for open engagement. Instead, government troops mounted a second siege outside the city walls. On 21 May a triumphal concert in the garden of the Tuileries was interrupted by rumours that the western walls of the city had been breached. During *la Semaine Sanglante* ('the Bloody Week') that followed, vicious street-by-street combat ensued as government troops, with instructions to take no hostages, fought their way across Paris, finally penetrating the working-class strongholds in the east. During their enforced retreat, buildings of which the Second Empire had been so proud, and many others besides, were destroyed in a plume of fire: these acts of destruction were subsequently attributed to a scorched earth policy conducted by the Communards.

The reprisals were immediate and draconian, and included anyone known to have supported the Commune. Estimates of the Communards who died in this week vary wildly between 10,000 and 50,000—although the latter figure may include those subsequently executed—whereas most records agree in registering government losses at about 1,000. On the last day of *la Semaine Sanglante*, 147 rebels were hunted down to Père Lachaise cemetery in the working-class suburbs of Belleville, and shot against its walls: their corpses were soon joined by 1,000 more summarily executed in other parts of the city. Of those spared immediate execution, 35,000 or more were rounded up and marched out of the city to Versailles, for imprisonment and trial: almost 5,000 received life transportation to New Caledonia. As in previous regime changes, those who could fled to Great Britain, Europe, and the United States.

1.7 THE AFTERMATH OF THE COMMUNE AND THE BIRTH OF THE THIRD REPUBLIC

Determined to expunge the possibility of further rebellion, the government introduced a curfew and stamped out the prolific leftist newsprint that had sprung up in Paris during the Siege and the Commune. The early years of the Third Republic were bedevilled by political division. Those who favoured the return of monarchical rule were again split between supporters of the House of Bourbon and the Orléanists. Meanwhile the various republican factions were by no means all supportive of the policies espoused by Thiers as provisional President. When the Third Republic finally came into being as a legal entity in 1875, Thiers, whose reign had been cut short by his opponents in 1873, claimed that it would serve only as the form of government least divisive for France. It was to endure until 1940.

While the government cautiously remained at Versailles until 1879, it marked its grip on the city, as previous regimes had done, by erecting symbolic monuments. In 1873 the basilica of Sacré Cœur was commissioned in expiation of the sins of the Commune and positioned on the commanding peak of Montmartre, surveying the quarter where the insurrection had begun. The following year saw the rebuilding of the Vendôme column. These were both merely the preface to a building programme which, ironically, further rolled out Haussmann's designs for glorifying the Second Empire. In 1878 a third Paris Exposition was mounted, designed, through its monumental scale, to announce to the world France's recovery from the Franco-Prussian war.

In the time that it had taken France to convert from monarchy to republicanism, to Empire, to incipient anarchy and back to republicanism again, the English throne had passed from George IV (active as regent since 1811, and king from 1820 to1830) to William IV (1830–37), and then to Queen Victoria, who in the event would rule uninterruptedly until 1901. In retrospect, and by comparison with France, gradualism might well appear to have been the watchword of the Hanoverians. Indeed, the fact that as the century advanced the British showed themselves capable of surviving virtually unscathed by any comparable degree of public protest was frequently used to suggest how different the two nations were, in terms both of their constitutional arrangements and of their national character.

And yet to those who lived through them, these mid-century years in Great Britain did not seem to promise the slow inevitability of peaceful change. For one thing, during this period and especially at the beginning, at their back the British, whether conservative or radical, always heard the tumbrils of the French Revolution sounding the death knell of the *ancien régime*. It proved difficult to allay the suspicion that discontented portions of the English lower classes might be susceptible to being incited into mob action by agitators taking their lead from French radical socialism. The present tense, to which Thomas Carlyle's dramatic history of *The French Revolution* (1837) frequently reverted, served simultaneously to revive the terrors unleashed in 1789 and to underline the fact that the British too now lived in a 'a world not fixable; not fathomable!'.[11] The next two chapters, dealing with British writers' reactions to the events outlined in this chapter, dispel the notion of a uniform 'British' response to the regime changes taking place in the neighbouring capital.

[11] *The Works of Thomas Carlyle*, ed. H. D. Traill (30 vols, London: Chapman & Hall, 1896–1901), ii, 6.

2

British eyewitness accounts of regime change

This chapter deals with accounts produced by those British writers who for a variety of reasons happened to enjoy a ringside seat at the various *émeutes*, or outbreaks of seditious violence, occurring in the French capital between 1830 and 1871. The primary purpose of these reports was to convey the immediacy of the felt experience of life under crisis conditions. Reports of the earlier uprisings characteristically take multiple forms, from the journal entry and letter to the episode in a memoir or the focused retrospective volume. By 1870 the newspaper report dominated the field.

Read as a collection spanning half a century, these accounts prompt the following observations. British residents, living a life largely secluded from contact with those who took to the barricades, were usually taken by surprise by the uprisings. Once over the initial shock, however, their letters and journals often convey a barely concealed excitement at being on hand to experience such dramatic events. The sheer volume of published eyewitness narratives that succeeded each turbulent regime change suggest a degree of British interest in what was happening just over the water that is missing from British literary histories of this period.

Perhaps most significantly for the purposes of this book, taken together with the professional reporting of the siege and Commune, these accounts supplied the telling images and details that would provide fodder for later fictional accounts, thus suggesting that Benedict Anderson's claim that newsprint demonstrates how 'fiction seeps quietly and continuously into reality' could with equal justification be reversed.[1] Sometimes an incidental anecdote could make as striking an impression of the fear these political upheavals inspired in British residents as any of the longer, more detailed accounts. Joseph Archer Crowe, for instance, recalled, as a 5-year-old, seeing a certain Mrs Pennell, one of his parents' neighbours, so fearful during the 1830 revolution, that she hung her 'silver teapot, ewers, spoons and forks, in a mass under her petticoats, and at every step she emitted sounds like those of a musical triangle'.[2] It is more than possible that, living in Batignolles, a village on the outskirts of Paris, and thus cheaper than any central location, Mrs Pennell was carrying around with her all the valuables that such an economic refugee had left in the world.

---

[1] B. R. O'G. Anderson, *Imagined Communities: Reflections on the Origin and Spread of Nationalism*, 2nd edn (London: Verso, 2006), 36.

[2] J. Crowe, *Reminiscences of Thirty-Five years of My Life* (London: John Murray, 1895), 4.

2.1 1830

The accounts provided by eyewitnesses were inflected by class loyalties, political sympathies, and gender. The sense of becoming an intrepid explorer, when scouting for up-to-date information, is particularly strong in female accounts, where the sudden release from the ritual of everyday routines seems to have created an exultant sense of agency out of dangerous forays into the war-torn city. The accounts of *les Trois Glorieuses* of 1830 written by Mary Clarke and Lady Blessington, though produced from diametrically opposite points of view, both bear this out.

Mary Clarke lived with her disabled mother in the student quarter on the left bank of the Seine, where she socialized with the politicians, writers, and intellectuals who resented Charles X's oppressive regime. Hearing of the growing insurrection, she determined to cross the river and find out for herself. Writing up her adventures only a week or so later, she had already composed them into a dramatic account, nicely spiced with humour, to reassure the extended circle of family and friends around whom she might reasonably assume this communiqué would pass. 'On the Tuesday, at four o'clock, I went out and took an omnibus. The whole of the Rue St-Honoré was packed with common people, angry but not armed—nearly all the shops were shut—and I heard some firing at five.' Having no weapons but 'old pikes, halberds and sticks', the crowds were described as using whatever lay to hand to construct barricades from paving stones and omnibuses. 'On Wednesday, the air was full of the sound of the tocsin, and cannons, and gunshots. In the end I was so excited, so longing to go and fight, that off I sped to Joséphine's house, which was in the thick of the worst fighting, to see what was happening.' She attempted to make her way back across the river that night, but, 'seeing that there was a whole army beyond the Palais Royal, and noticing a corpse lying on the ground (covered, but with its bloody leg sticking out)', stayed with her friend overnight. 'On Thursday, I got home at six in the morning... When I came in, Mama said: "Tell me the news, for Heaven's sake—I have been quaking in my shoes!" I said: "But I told you that I would take great care." "Oh," said she: "it was not you I was worried about: it was the common people."'[3]

Lady Blessington, by contrast, enjoyed a vantage point on the wealthy, fashionable right bank. Her journal account of these events, however, was to remain unpublished until 1841, whether because her views might have been unpopular in the reformist agitations leading up to the great Reform Bill of 1832, or because of the personal scandal in which she found herself enveloped in 1831, or because only later did her financially precarious position make it necessary for her to use this material, is unclear.[4] Born plain Margaret Gardiner (1789–1849), to minor Irish Catholic gentry, she had changed her name on marriage to Marguerite and simultaneously adopted the manners of a *grande dame*. Fed a constant flow of information by leading French aristocrats and politicians known to her lover, Count d'Orsay,

---

[3] M. Lesser, *Clarkey: A Portrait in Letters of Mary Clarke Mohl (1793–1883)* (Oxford: Oxford University Press, 1984), 85–7.

[4] In 1831 the scandal of Lord Blessington's daughter having been married off to his wife's lover, Count d'Orsay, became public knowledge when the Count's wife left him.

on 27 July she merely noted the gathering crowds, the disappearance of carriages from the boulevards, and the servants and courtiers deserting the Tuileries, and reminded herself how quickly the civil authorities in London would have seen off such a 'commotion'. On 28 July she recorded:

> We have now entrenched ourselves in the front drawing-rooms, with the external shutters, which are stuffed to exclude noise, closed, but which we open occasionally, in order to see what is going on. Sitting in darkness, with the sound of firing, and the shouts of the people, continually in our ears, I can hardly bring myself to think that all that is now passing is not a dream.

Deeply irritated by the pleasure her servants derived from any rumour of the evidence of 'the power of the people', she fulminated:

> Misguided men! can they hope that servitude will be lightened by their being employed by some *parvenus*, elevated from the dregs of the people by a revolution which sets floating to the top the worst ingredients of the reeking caldron [*sic*] from which it is formed, instead of owning the more gentle and infinitely less degrading sway of those born to, and accustomed to rule?

On day three, she determined to visit an elderly royalist friend, and so, 'surprised at my own courage', she ventured out alone for the first time. The journey to a neighbouring street involved climbing a barricade, and, nearing the top, she encountered a citizen determined to help her. Drunkenly gallant, he declared himself 'one of the *bons enfans* of the revolution…We *les braves, des braves*, wage no war against women; *au contraire*, we love the pretty creatures. Here, take my hand, and I will assist you over the barricades.' With which, he reached forward, lost his balance and toppled out of sight. Although she felt that the labouring classes were 'totally incapacitated by ignorance from being able to comprehend even the causes alleged for this popular outbreak', in the aftermath of the uprising, she admitted that, despite her premonitions of death, destruction and degradation, there had been little looting and the populace had been surprisingly good-mannered. Nevertheless, her disapproval of the new king's constitutional position, at the beck and call of his subjects, prompted her to return to Great Britain that November.[5]

The same evidence of the potential political power of the populace aroused 'the utmost enthusiasm' in the young John Stuart Mill, who hoped that 'the higher classes might be made to see that they had more to fear from the poor when uneducated, than when educated'. He hastened to Paris that August, where he sent home running commentaries on the way that the mob, who had behaved so bravely in ridding themselves of a bad government, were now being let down by the educated and wealthy, who had joined in only belatedly and seemed in no hurry to provide much-needed leadership. Yet for all his 'intercourse with several of the active chiefs of the extreme popular party' and with the elderly General Lafayette, who threw his support behind the new regime, his accounts lack the passionate involvement combined with the journalist's eye for detail manifest in David

[5] Countess of Blessington, *The Idler in France* (2 vols, London: Henry Colburn, 1841), ii, 153, 166–7, 180, 201, 217, 235–40.

Turnbull's *The French Revolution of 1830; the events which produced it, and the scenes by which it was accompanied* (1830).[6]

Turnbull (1793?–1851), a roving European correspondent for the *Times* and a noted abolitionist in the slavery cause, was a wholehearted admirer of the 'innate love of freedom' of the French populace, gave unstinted praise to the prudent way in which even the very poorest of the rebels had conducted themselves, and was delighted by the way in which the action had sprung from the 'sansculottes' of the press. His preface spoke also of the way in which English residents had contributed: an English printer showed his solidarity with the French papers that Charles X had censored by closing his own business, and British medical students provided succour for the wounded on the barricades.[7]

2.2 1848

The revolution of 1848 was a longer-drawn-out and, it seemed to many British observers, almost ramshackle affair. The account sent by Mary Clarke, or Madame Mohl as she had recently become, to the Nightingale family in England conveys this sense of its impromptu origins:

> You can't imagine how quick the whole thing came about. On Tuesday I went out to see the people go to the banquet in the Champs Elysées—very peaceful they seemed.... Wednesday we heard of the change of ministry—the regency in the evening—on Thursday the Republic—all this with an accompaniment of pop-guns on all sides. M Mohl served three nights last week in the Garde Nationale—to make a show, for they had not a ball or cartridge or ounce of powder in the whole arrondissement.[8]

Anne Thackeray Ritchie[9] recalled that her grandparents' daily walks in the English quarter continued, the only difference being that they 'used to wear little tricolour rosettes to show their sympathies with the Republic'.[10]

To the Chartists, Irish republicans, and British sympathizers who flocked to Paris to celebrate the liberation of the French working classes from their oppressors, the slow pace at which the bourgeois provisional government worked for the next three months, and the failure of the radical left to carry the day, were profoundly disappointing. Arthur Hugh Clough arrived on 1 May and spent the

---

[6] *Autobiography and Literary Essays*, in *Collected Works of John Stuart Mill*, ed. J. M. Robson and J. Stillinger (33 vols, Toronto: University of Toronto Press, 1963–91), i, 178–9; and *The Earlier Letters of John Stuart Mill, 1812–1848*, ed. F. E. Minneka, intro. F. A. Hayek (2 vols, London: Routledge & Kegan Paul, 1996), i, 54–67.

[7] D. Turnbull, *The French Revolution of 1830* (London: Henry Colburn & Richard Bentley, 1830), 43–4, v–xv.

[8] Lesser, *Clarkey*, 122.

[9] W. M. Thackeray's elder daughter published variously under the names of Miss Thackeray, Anne Ritchie, Anne Thackeray Ritchie, and Lady Ritchie, but for the sake of continuity she will be known throughout this book as Anne Thackeray Ritchie.

[10] A. T. Ritchie, *Chapters from Some Memoirs* (London: Macmillan, 1894), 40.

ensuing five weeks sampling meetings at a variety of socialist clubs, frequently in the company of Geraldine Jewsbury, who had also hastened across the Channel to be in at the birth of the new Republic.[11] He reported his discouragement to his friend, Arthur Penrhyn Stanley:

> Ichabod Ichabod, the glory is departed. Liberty, Equality, and Fraternity, driven back by shopkeeping bayonet, hides her red cap in dingiest St. Antoine. Well-to-do-ism shakes her Egyptian scourge to the tune of Ye are idle, ye are idle; the tale of bricks will be doubled, and Moses and Aaron of Socialism can at the best only pray for plagues,— which perhaps will come—paving stones for vivats, and emeutes in all their quarters.
> Meantime the glory and the freshness of the dream is departed. The very garde mobile has dropped its dear blouse and red trimmings for a bourgeoisie-praetorian uniform with distinctive green hired-soldier epaulettes. The voice of the clubs is silenced…

Clough was not alone in reaching for a sub-Carlylean rhetoric. John Palgrave Simpson (1807–87), his travels abroad suddenly interrupted by his father's financial failure, adopted not only an imitation of the master's style but Carlyle's narrative device of keeping topographically distant events simultaneously within his purview. The grim series of tableaux depicting the blood and terror of this 'fearful drama', which he sold to the *Times*, *Blackwood's Magazine*, and *Bentley's Miscellany*, were strangely at odds with the byline of 'The Flâneur in Paris', which he employed in the last of these papers.[12]

The Marquess of Normanby, British Ambassador to Paris throughout 1848, allowed five years to elapse after his tour of duty before publishing *A Year of Revolution* (1857). Like Simpson, he was inclined to blame the bad faith of clever men in government for the uprising; but his narrative, woven from an edited account of his dispatches, was fettered on the one hand by the diplomatic code of discretion and, on the other, by the knowledge that the man who had emerged as President of the Republic in December 1848 was now very firmly established as Emperor.[13]

By contrast, the daily journal entries, starting from 14 May 1848, of the political economist Nassau Senior (1790–1864) were a model of frankness, which is probably why they remained unpublished until after his death. Almost as well-acquainted with the leading French statesmen of the day as Normanby,[14] he recorded conversations with diplomats and with the leading protagonists, alongside chance encounters in railway carriages or on street corners, and his journals paint a picture of a city awash with ever-changing rumours of incidents that have occurred only just out of sight. Opposing Carlyle's view of this revolution as a just protest against a 'sham king', Senior argued that, whereas in 1830 the King had

[11] *The Correspondence of Arthur Hugh Clough,* ed. F. L. Mulhauser (2 vols, Oxford: Clarendon Press, 1957), I, 203–15; S. K. Howe, *Geraldine Jewsbury, Her Life and Errors* (London: Allen & Unwin, 1935), 98–9.

[12] J. P. Simpson, *Pictures from Revolutionary Paris: sketched during the first phase of the Revolution of 1848* (2 vols, Edinburgh: William Blackwood & Sons, 1849), 34.

[13] C. H. Phipps, *A Year of Revolution from a Journal kept in Paris in 1848 by the Marquess of Normanby* (London: Longman, Green, Longmans, & Roberts, 1857), xiii.

[14] M. C. M. Simpson, *Many Memories of Many People* (London: Edward Arnold, 1898), 52.

been the aggressor, in 1848 the people had taken this role. Unsurprisingly, his analysis also concluded that the French relied too heavily on the notion of efficacious state intervention.[15]

2.3 DECEMBER 1851

Although their opinion of Louis-Napoleon's assumption of the role of Emperor differed, British eyewitness accounts seem to have agreed on a core of shared observations: the instant news blackout achieved by Napoleon's peremptory press censorship; the ubiquity of the troops; the sense of the fighting as highly localized; and the surprising speed at which urban life (on the surface at least) seemed to return to normal. On 1 December Elizabeth Barrett Browning reassured her anxious sister, who had read rumours of impending trouble in the British press, 'Where is the danger, as long as one stays in the house? In these Champs Élysées, they could only hear the sound of the cannons at a distance in the last revolution.'[16] From this privileged position she and Robert watched Louis-Napoleon ride by on horseback, leading his troops in celebrating the anniversary of Austerlitz. 'The dramatic effect', she wrote home, could not be exaggerated: 'these things are like an electric shock, & thrilling to you much the same.'[17] On the night of 4 December, when Napoleon's troops turned their fire on the people, she 'shrank from going quietly to sleep while human beings were dying in heaps perhaps, within earshot', but refused to regard the opposition to Louis-Napoleon as amounting to more than 'a little popular scum, cleared off at once by the troops'.[18] Within a couple of days she and Robert were able to inspect the sites of destruction on the boulevards from their carriage. As Madame Mohl told a British correspondent, less than a week later, Paris was as safe as London, 'providing you keep your thoughts entirely to yourself'.[19]

Those already ensconced in the safer parts of the city may have found their life remarkably little disturbed by Napoleon's seizure of power, but British journalists had trouble in penetrating a city where public transport had come to an abrupt halt. The young George Augustus Sala was one of a number of tyro reporters who rushed across in the hope of making a name for himself, only to be revolted by 'the horrible ferocity and brutality of this ruthless soldiery'. He unashamedly reported that during the opening day of the troops' sweeping clear of the boulevards with rounds of cannon fire, he and seven English companions took refuge in the cellar of their hotel in the Rue St Honoré; this made him all the more prepared to suspect

[15] *Journals kept in France and Italy from 1848 to 1852, with a Sketch of the Revolution of 1848 by the late Nassau William Senior*, ed. M. C. M. Simpson (2 vols, 1871; repr. New York: Da Capo Press, 1973), 102–3, 35–6, v–ix.

[16] *Elizabeth Barrett Browning: Letters to her Sister, 1846–1859*, ed. L. Huxley (London: John Murray, 1929), 148–9.

[17] *Elizabeth Barrett Browning's Letters to Mrs. David Ogilvy, 1849–1861*, ed. P. N. Heydon and P. Kelley (New York: Browning Institute, 1973), 59.

[18] *Letters of the Brownings to George Barrett*, ed. P. Landis and R. E. Freeman (Urbana: University of Illinois Press, 1958), 156–9; *Elizabeth Barrett Browning: Letters to her Sister*, ed. Huxley, 149.

[19] Letter of 10 Dec. 1848, quoted in Lesser, *Clarkey*, 133.

and mock the heroic boasts of English residents encountered on the boulevards a few days later.

Sala and other British journalists such as Henry Sutherland Edwards were also struck by the extraordinary sight of soldiers bivouacking in the heart of the city along the Seine, eating their breakfast of sausages and red wine, but ready at a moment's notice to muster, and fire indiscriminately into crowds of unarmed civilians. In his memoirs Edwards pointed out that the barricades, composed of five- to six-foot walls of stones, each weighing up to a couple of pounds, might have withstood musketry, but not the combined artillery force at the troops' disposal. Amidst reports of reprisals and executions, Sala personalized his account by mentioning an excursion to buy a bottle of soda water at an English chemist's he knew in the Rue de la Paix, only to find that the chemist lay dead upstairs, having fallen victim to a random military fusillade. Sala, thanking heaven he was an Englishman, concluded his report by asking his readers to contemplate this 'extraordinary people' who, with 'the blood not yet dry on the Boulevards; with corpses lying about the streets…with a brutal military in almost every printing office, tavern, café…with the city in a siege, without a legislature, without laws, without a government' were to be found the night after such catastrophic slaughter, 'dancing and flirting at the Salle Valentino, or the Prado, lounging in the *foyers* of the Italian Opera, gossiping over their *eau sucrée*, or squabbling over their dominoes outside and inside the cafes'.[20]

2.4 1870

When, almost two decades later, hostilities commenced between France and Prussia, many of the city's English residents were taking their annual vacation abroad. The Mohls, for instance, were in England and, little foreseeing how long the siege would last, simply prolonged their stay: he returned the following March and she only after the Commune. In effect, the continuous reporting of the long period covering the declaration of war on 19 July 1870 and the siege of Paris, lasting from 19 September 1870 to 28 January 1871, was mainly in the hands of a cadre of professional journalists, who were by this time more often salaried employees of British newspapers than freelance reporters.[21] The swift republication of their articles in volume form, and a steady stream of journalistic memoirs, speak to a British readership fascinated by accounts of the devastation of a city which increasing numbers had begun to regard as a favoured holiday destination. Nevertheless, as one of a number of journalists who continued to recycle his memory of events long after the siege, Henry Vizetelly observed that the Parisians had street-fighting down to such a well-rehearsed formula that it behoved reporters to develop an individualistic approach.[22] George Augustus Sala's self-aggrandizing memoirs, Vizetelly's social history, and Henry Labouchère's acerbic impressions of

---

[20] [G. A. Sala,] 'Liberty, Equality, Fraternity, and Musketry', *Household Words*, 27 Dec. 1851, 92, 313–18; H. S. Edwards, *Personal Recollections* (London: Cassell, 1900), 19–23.

[21] Further discussed in section 10.4.

[22] H. Vizetelly (ed.), *Paris in Peril* (2 vols, London: Tinsley Brothers, 1882), i, 18.

this period demonstrate something of the way in which the intense competition between newspapers fostered this concept of the foreign correspondent with a 'personal angle'.

As a long-time habitué of Paris, Sala was well placed in late July 1870 to take the capital's temperature on behalf of the *Daily Telegraph*. He noted the populace's admiring glances at the richly caparisoned troops and the way the city's churches were suddenly filled with women eager to light votive tapers. After a quick trip to the imperial headquarters at Metz, he returned at the end of the first week in August to find a changed scene. The capital was in a state of panic: British residents were thronging the Embassy wishing to leave their plate and jewellery in its vaults, and the authorities were preparing for a siege by stockpiling grain and importing hordes of cattle and sheep to graze in the Bois de Boulogne. By the time his memoirs appeared, Sala rather than the residents of Paris had taken centre stage: unable to report the sufferings of the siege from his next posting in Rome, his own narrow escape from being executed as a spy when the Republic fell on 4 September closed his narrative.[23]

Although Henry Vizetelly had been living in Paris for five years before the war began, he left Paris to report from the front in November 1870, which may help to explain the very detailed but impersonal narrative he co-authored with his eldest son. *Paris in Peril* (1882) is an illustrated political and social history of the siege, recording the care taken in the early stages to protect national treasures, or to barricade the wild animals in the Jardin des Plantes to prevent their escape. He notes the way that fashionable Parisians changed the route of their normal daily parade of carriages along the Champs-Élysées to tour the ramparts on fine autumn afternoons. As hunger gripped, the city's eating habits are catalogued and details supplied of the way in which transport and communication problems were surmounted. He records the heated discussions that took place about the difficult choices to be made. Should horses, so vital for transport, continue to be fed when they consumed the daily rations of ten people? Was gas best expended on keeping the city at least dimly lit, or should it be reserved for filling the balloons so necessary for communication with the rest of France?

Henry Labouchère's *Diary of the Besieged Resident in Paris, reprinted from the Daily News* (1871) paused only to add a preface, and one or two articles which had not made it back to England, before appearing between hardback covers. His reports had started on 18 September, the day before the siege started. Imagining that affairs would resolve themselves within the month, he eventually found himself trapped for the next five months, living in a hotel room, and so this episodic collection offers a fine impression of the siege as experienced in real time. From the first, Labouchère used his column inches to try to influence British government policy, in the early days imploring them to prevent Bismarck's alleged intentions of burning Paris to the ground, and, when the siege broke, urging the British to step up their relief aid. Nor was he afraid to name and shame the British Embassy staff for what he perceived as their cowardice in retreating to safer parts of France.

---

[23] *The Life and Adventures of George Augustus Sala written by himself*, 2nd edn (2 vols, London: Cassell, 1895), ii, 201–27.

This campaigning journalism coexisted with a running commentary on the social mores of besieged Paris. Although, like fellow journalists, Labouchère was unimpressed by the way in which English residents, who had been warned to leave while there was still time, now mobbed the Embassy in the hope of a safe passage home, his amused contempt was mainly trained on the French, who are treated as anthropological specimens hailing from a tribe whose every custom is remote and wonderful to the British gaze. The following sentence is typical: 'It is almost impossible for an Englishman to realise the intense delight which a Frenchman has in donning a uniform, strutting about with a martial swagger, and listening to a distant cannonade.'[24] The braggadocio of the well-rewarded National Guard, the humbug of the specious oratory preached at street corners and in the French newspapers, the profiteering as goods became more scarce, are regularly contrasted with the real suffering endured by women and children in an ice-bound city where fuel and food were in scant supply. Labouchère's fellow journalists acknowledged his mastery of the medium, and the wide British readership his articles achieved were said to have secured the fortunes of the *Daily News*. His humorous, occasionally satirical mode of treating the French as a species wholly distinct from the English played its part in shifting British attitudes from Carlyle's 'look and learn' approach to French politics to an altogether more detached appraisal of an inherently alien state of affairs.

2.5 THE COMMUNE

Labouchère returned to England on 10 February 1871, but in the ensuing month the fragile peace in a capital overseen by a provisional government, still based in Versailles, broke down. When Thiers evacuated the administrative cadre from Paris, Anne Thackeray Ritchie became so concerned for the fate of a cousin that she rushed to Paris to rescue her, arriving there on the very day that government troops started to clash with the siege-hardened citizenry of Montmartre. Her diary record of this mercy-dash reveals her curious sense of the absurdity of individuals' behaviour even in the presence of imminent death: these memories would later be fed almost verbatim into her fictional picture of this period:

March 18th…The fortresses and outlying fortifications all round Paris terribly grim…everyone in black—empty streets. Drove to Versailles next day. German notices on the walls. To St. Cloud, burnt, utterly destroyed—sunshine—people singing. Frenchman to me—"Ecoutez-les. Ils chantent avec leur pays en ruines."

March 19. Awakened by the cannon of Belleville. News of a Revolution—murder of the generals. *People acting* in the streets as they described it all to one another. Woman comes up, "Vous êtes Anglaise. Fuyez, fuyez!"

March 21. Drove up Rue Pigalle, saw a barricade. Dined with D'Eychtals in the evening. Met M. Bercier and heard of arrests.

---

[24] [H. Labouchère,] *Diary of the Besieged Resident in Paris, reprinted from the Daily News with Several New Letters and Preface* (London: Hurst & Blackett, 1871), 24.

> *March* 22. To Madame Mohl's in the sunshine, met hurrying crowds of figures who looked as if they had come straight out of the French Revolution. Massacre in Place Vendôme. Charlotte and I were out together, we rushed across fire of the guns to escape. We took refuge in the Church of St Roch; Rue St. Roch crowded with people turning out to fight, others running way, while others stood joking in their balconies.[25]

Meanwhile, the regular Paris correspondent for the *Daily News*, George Morland Crawford, who had been evacuated with his family to Tours for the duration of the siege, had resumed his duties in the capital and occupied a regular slot throughout the Commune and its aftermath in the 'Latest Telegraphs' section of the paper. The paper was held for his midnight report, often his fourth telegraph of the day. His columns offered translations of the statements put out by opposing sides; accounts of the stance taken by various French newspapers; lists of the Commune's edicts and actions; and a personal assessment of the state of play on the boulevards usually frequented by English tourists. Together these offered a picture of barely controlled anarchy. On 30 March, for instance, it was reported that the Central Committee of the Commune had burnt not only the police papers pertaining to themselves but also those relating to common thieves and criminals. On 25 April the Commune was reported to have ordered the restoration to the Paris Gas Company of 70,000 francs seized from its cash-box by a renegade battalion of the National Guard four days previously.

During the destruction that took place in the *Semaine Sanglante*, later reports would often contradict those sent earlier in the day: on 27 May, for example, it was first reported that Sainte-Chapelle had been destroyed in the conflagration that swept the Palais de Justice, but this was later rescinded. The same day's communiqué announced that, despite the fires raging everywhere, the greatest danger now lay in being denounced as in any way connected with the Commune. Although the phrase 'terror has come again' was repeatedly used, and from the start the *Daily News* sided with the 'forces of order', when it was clear that the provisional government's troops had been ordered to make no accommodation with the Commune and the corpses of the slain lay rotting on the streets, the paper's correspondent was driven to write, 'Conquered they will and must be, but at a price which must raise a fearful question whether the Government, facing the choice of two evils, did not act unwisely in assuming the terrible responsibilities with which it has charged itself.'[26] On 30 May the reports described the terrible vengeance that had been wreaked, while the view of Paris from Versailles spoke of a city engulfed in flame and suffering 'apocalytpic woes'. The following day's missives reported the first hint of normality restored as shops started to reopen, but also spoke of the need for instant cremation as bodies piled up in the mounting heat.

---

[25] *Anne Thackeray Ritchie: Journals and Letters. Biographical Commentary and Notes by Lilian Shankman*, ed. A. B. Bloom and J. Maynard (Columbus: Ohio State University Press, 1994), 145–6. Cf. *Mrs Dymond*, in *The Works of Miss Thackeray* (10 vols, London: Smith, Elder, 1890), x, 489.

[26] *Daily News*, 22 May 1871.

2.6 AFTER THE COMMUNE

In the years since the 1830 uprising, the British had come to regard the occasional political ferment in Paris almost in the light of a peculiar French peccadillo. In 1830, 1848, and 1851 there had been no repetition of terror on the scale unleashed by the French Revolution. The deportations to the French colonies were of little concern to the average Englishman; successive French governments had proved able to quell these civil disturbances, and the comparative brevity of the actual fighting had tended to cause only brief dips in the numbers of British who visited Paris.[27] When William Rossetti visited in late August 1871, he 'went about chiefly to look at ruins—Tuileries, Finances (the worst), Cour d'Escomptes [*sic*], Luxembourg and Arc de Triomphe slight; especially the former'. By comparison with the tales of the ravages wrought by the siege, and the corresponding talk of French reprisals he had heard on every side during his travels from Italy to Paris, he was surprised to find the city remarkably intact.[28]

Yet the notion of a cultivated people reduced to eating elephants, camels, dogs, and rats, followed by the concept of an anarchic city whose citizens would rather see it destroyed than submit to national government, and this same government then exacting brutal reprisals within the immediate vicinity of Paris, rather than in some far-flung territory, all contributed to increase the British sense of estrangement from its nearest European neighbour. Certainly, Francophile British journalists felt that the events of 1870–71 marked a deep rupture between past and present not only for Paris itself but for the relationship the British maintained with Paris. Readers of the *Daily News* were informed on 30 May 1871 that post-Commune Paris loathed the English because they were suspected of being part of the foreign insurgency manning the barricades. Crawford himself thought it implausible that Englishmen had played any substantial role, other, once again, than as medical students tending the wounded. It had however been suggested to him that so many of the Communards had spent their Second Empire exile in either Great Britain or the United States that English had become their lingua franca.

Blanchard Jerrold, who had published *Paris for the English* as recently as 1867, felt it behoved him in July 1871 to open a comic work, *The Cockaynes in Paris, or 'Gone Abroad with sketches by Gustave Doré and other illustrations of the English Abroad from a French point of view*, with a preface deploring recent events and making it clear that the English would no longer find a welcome in this greatly changed capital. Jerrold was an unashamed apologist for the Second Empire and went on to produce a four-volume biography of the deposed Emperor. His friend Sala was equally nostalgic. Despite the title of his *Paris Herself Again in 1878–9* (1879), a reprint of illustrated articles for the *Daily Telegraph* apparently designed

[27] The statistics can be found in P. Gerbod, 'Voyageurs et Résidents Britanniques en France en XIXe Siecle', *Acta Geographica* 76 (1988).

[28] *The Diary of W. M. Rossetti 1870–1873*, ed. O. Bornand (Oxford: Clarendon Press, 1977), 112–13.

to celebrate the city's renewed gaiety and wealth, the subtext was a threnody over a city now departed, which in hindsight seemed innocent in comparison with the tawdry glitter of the Third Republic.

One other facet of the eyewitness reporting of these revolutionary moments requires comment. Photography was in its infancy, and even by the time of the Commune had not quite progressed to the stage where it was possible to take instantaneous rather than static or posed images. This meant that the immediate reporting of the violence in which the Commune ended still leant more heavily on the word than on photojournalism. Photographs comparing the cityscape familiar to visitors at the close of the Second Empire could be juxtaposed with those of a post-Commune city depicting holes where once familiar buildings had stood, but for a sense of what it felt like to be in a city at the mercy of warring factions, the visual image had not as yet superseded the power of the word.

In his *Autobiography* J. S. Mill noted how atypical he was of his generation in that a teenage stint in Paris had given him a strong and continuing interest in Continental Liberalism: this, he felt, had freed him from 'the error always prevalent in England...of judging universal questions by a merely English standard'.[29] What distinguishes the commentaries and representations in the following chapter from the eyewitness reports featured here is the strength of their focus on the impact that events in Paris might hold for Great Britain. In particular, they reveal the threatening role that the working classes occupied in the English middle-class imagination during this period.

[29] *Autobiography*, in *Collected Works of John Stuart Mill*, ed. Robson and Stillinger, i, 63.

3

Regime change as viewed from English shores

Although some of the writers dealt with in this chapter also happened to have first-hand experience of political turbulence on the streets of Paris, the texts discussed here show a more pronounced focus upon the significance of these events for the British.

3.1 1830

In 1830 some of an older generation were still alive who had shared the hopes of the early Romantics at the dawn of the French Revolution before witnessing the Terror, the rise and fall of Napoleon, and the restoration of the Bourbons. Wordsworth's admirers would have to wait until 1850 for *The Prelude* to offer his thoughts about the Revolution, some of which he had witnessed at close quarters.[1] His direct experience of the Terror had opened his eyes to see:

> That Liberty, and Life, and Death would soon
> To the remotest corners of the land
> Lie in the arbitrement of those who ruled
> The capital City...

From this insight sprang his continuing commitment to the cause of Great Britain's rural poor, and his distrust of the urban masses. Meanwhile his letters and publications left little doubt of his continuing interest in French politics, his wholehearted opposition to Napoleon I, and his growing repudiation of radical paths to reform.[2]

Some Romantics, however, kept faith with the revolutionary fervour of their youth. Wordsworth's contemporary, the novelist and poet Amelia Opie (1769–1853), had reputedly been left 'in such a state of uncontrollable enthusiasm' by Napoleon's assumption of the position of First Consul in 1799 that 'all the visions of human perfectibility which the friends of her childhood had associated with the French Revolution rushing on her brain' led her, 'while sitting in the boulevards', to sing 'in her clear, brilliant soprano, Fall, tyrants, fall!'[3] The problem, as so many

---

[1] W. Wordsworth, *The Prelude*, bk X, ll. 108–11. The episodes in *The Prelude* which discuss this period of Wordsworth's life were first formulated in 1805 and last revised in 1839.

[2] For a fuller account see A. G. Hill, 'Wordsworth, Louis-Philippe, and "England in 1840"', *Modern Language Review* (July 2002), 529–38. See also S. Bainbridge, *Napoleon and English Romanticism* (Cambridge: Cambridge University Press, 1995).

[3] G. T. Mayer, *Women of Letters* (2 vols, London: Richard Bentley, 1894), ii, 82 and 101–2.

commentators found during the nineteenth century, was in distinguishing libera-
tors from tyrants. Opie, however, remained determined to see the beneficial aspect
of revolutions. In 1830 her 'fascinated interest in revolutions' led her to set off on
her own for Paris and subsequently report the July Monarchy and its overturning
of the Bourbons as one of the 'triumphs of constitutional freedom', partly, one
suspects, because it was endorsed by General Lafayette, 'the hero of my childhood,
the idol of my youth'.[4]

Charles X's repressive measures, and the assertion of the Parisian populace's will
in this so-called triumph of constitutional freedom, were felt to be highly pertinent
to the contemporary politics of contemporary England. It had been the fear that
Charles X's excesses would encourage the Tories to similar measures in England
that had prompted Elizabeth Barrett Browning to write, 'No English ear ought to
like hearing the chain clanking over our sea'.[5] The popular riots and disturbances
of 1831 in London, the Midlands, and the southwest, protesting against the House
of Lords' repeated refusal to pass the Reform Bill, all took place in an atmosphere
still febrile with reports of *les Trois Glorieuses*.

The electoral qualifications eventually encoded in the Great Reform Act (1832)
contrived to drive a wedge between Great Britain's working and middle classes.
It was therefore the class aspect of the French events of 1830 that the radical
G. W. M. Reynolds chose to address in his 1839 novel, *Alfred de Rosann; or, the
Adventures of a French Gentleman*. The novel is predicated upon the paradox that
while the respectable bourgeois are often at the mercy of thieves and fraudsters so,
when the moment comes, these elements, working together in pursuit of liberty,
can defeat the forces of tyranny and oppression. So strong, Reynolds claimed, is
the instinct for freedom that it displaces all other motives. In a passage footnoted,
'me ipso teste', Reynolds tells how Mr Atkins, Rothschild's agent, managed to
transport cash from London to the Bank of France in Paris unmolested, and the
Palace of the Tuileries remained unharmed, while criminals willingly sacrificed their
lives on the barricades. The novel emphasizes that such unifying action can never
be accidental, but is the result of deep-laid plans by secret forces working behind
the scenes long in advance of the uprising.

Nevertheless, Reynolds exhibited a certain nervousness about the internecine
slaughter occasioned by revolution. The following celebratory passage retreats into
a tableau of the aggrieved rather than engaging with the reality of street fighting:

> Many a widow avenged her slaughtered husband's massacre—many a veteran, with
> hoary locks and wrinkled brow, laid aside the staff that for years had supported his
> tottering limbs, and brandished the glittering sword. The tri-coloured banner waved
> in all directions—cries of "Freedom!" echoed on every side; and the rash monarch
> repented his audacity when too late. [6]

---

[4] A. Opie, 'A Morning at Paris in 1829', in *The Aurora Borealis, a Literary Annual*, ed. The Society
of Friends (Newcastle upon Tyne, 1833), 239.

[5] Quoted in R. Gridley, *The Brownings and France: A Chronicle with Commentary* (London: Athlone
Press, 1982), 9.

[6] G. W. M. Reynolds, *Alfred de Rosann: or, the Adventures of a French Gentleman* (London: J. W.
Southgate, 1839), 223–4.

3.2 THE JULY MONARCHY, AND THE RETURN
OF NAPOLEON'S REMAINS

The volatility of the French political scene had a way of wrong-footing prejudices the other side of the Channel. If Charles X, a monarch with at least a hereditary entitlement to rule, had provoked his people into rebellion, what were the British to make of the concept of a king elected by his people? To the Irish novelist Charles Lever, neither was acceptable. In *The Martins of Cro' Martin* (1856), he devoted chapters to the 1830 uprising which were clearly designed to align feckless absentee Irish landlords with the expatriate aristocracy of Europe, to be found carelessly enjoying life under Charles X's regime. However, Louis-Philippe's reign proved no more acceptable to his liberal sympathies, and the close of the novel finds characters with radical leanings despatched to America as the only place likely to satisfy these. Lever's ambivalence about the revolutionary spirit as it manifested itself in France was incarnated in the repeated portraits of Napoleon he drew in his military novels.[7]

British writers with less cause for split loyalties than Lever still found it hard to decide what to make of King Louis-Philippe's recuperation of that former revolutionary, and Great Britain's old enemy, 'Boney'. It had been one thing for Wordsworth to denounce him in 1809 as an unprincipled 'Adventurer' deserving to meet a 'violent and ignominious death', but, after Napoleon's second imprisonment on St Helena, some British radicals were of the opinion that his far-flung exile was symptomatic only of their own government's desire to wreak a shameful vengeance. Napoleon's death in 1821 might reasonably have been considered to have ended the matter; but the growing French clamour for the reinterment of the Emperor's remains in Paris threw British opinion into further confusion. Reynolds solved the dilemma facing those of a radical disposition to his own satisfaction by condemning Napoleon the tyrant while praising Napoleon as warrior and statesman.[8] Carlyle, delivering his last lecture on 22 May 1840, in a series published as *On Heroes, Hero-Worship, and the Heroic in History* (1841), chose Napoleon to illustrate his lecture 'The Hero as King', in the belief that, though tyrannical and deeply flawed, his achievements, particularly in restoring order, entitled him to this status.[9]

The return of the Emperor's body to Paris in December 1840, in an elaborate ceremony orchestrated by Louis-Philippe, prompted Thackeray, who had witnessed the event, to lengthy reflection on the proposition that 'It is no easy task in this world to distinguish between what is great in it, and what is mean'.[10] His three-chapter work *The Second Funeral of Napoleon* (1841) does not seek to resolve so much as

---

[7] See esp. *Charles O'Malley, the Irish Dragoon* (1841); and *Tom Burke of 'Ours'* (1844), repr. in *The Novels of Charles Lever*, edited by his daughter (36 vols, London: Downey, 1897–99).

[8] Reynolds, *Alfred de Rosann*, 79–81.

[9] See also D. Sorensen, '"Je suis la Révolution française": Carlyle, Napoleon, and the Napoleonic Mythus', *Carlyle Studies Annual* 22 (Spring 2006), 283–302.

[10] *The Second Funeral of Napoleon*, in *The Oxford Thackeray*, ed. G. Saintsbury (17 vols, London: Oxford University Press, 1910), iii, 397.

to open up a series of puzzling contrasts. The diplomatic courtesies between the English garrison and the French party collecting Napoleon's remains from St Helena sat strangely, Thackeray considered, with the ingrained enmity simultaneously playing itself out on the field of international politics. Moreover, the French determination to do lasting honour to their fallen Emperor had been oddly expressed, Thackeray noted, in tawdry decorative statuary, swiftly erected over the site of monuments hitherto devoted to republican heroes such as Lafayette.

Elizabeth Barrett Browning's poem 'Napoleon's Return' offered even franker expression of her inability to arrive at a clear judgement on this 'despot', who nevertheless had 'The genius to be loved' by his people. She concluded its twenty-eight stanzas,

> But whether
> The crowned Napoleon or the buried clay
> Be worthier, I discern not: angels may.[11]

3.3 1848

When Louis-Philippe was deposed in February 1848, many British writers were to be found welcoming France's return to republicanism. J. S. Mill was of the opinion that 'there never was a time when so great a drama was being played out in one generation'. He told a correspondent that he foresaw a domino effect so that 'all the rest of Europe, except England and Russia, will be republicanised in ten years, and England itself probably before we die'.[12] In a widely read piece of 4 March, Carlyle represented the barricades raised by the 'wild men in blouses' against the 'Sham King' and his corrupt practices as part and parcel of a revolution, begun by 'the Bastillers of '89', but as yet unaccomplished.[13] George Eliot approved of Carlyle's piece, and on 8 March, in 'sansculottish' spirits, wrote: 'Certainly our deposed monarchs should be pensioned off: we should have a hospital for them, or a sort of Zoological Garden, where these worn-out humbugs may be preserved.' She drew the line, however, at the British working classes with their 'selfish radicalism and unsatisfied, brute sensuality (in the agricultural and mining districts especially)' being allowed to take the lead.[14]

The aspersion Eliot cast on Great Britain's radicalized workers was doubtless prompted by the violent demonstrations that had taken place in Trafalgar Square on 6 March, when the government had already declared a Chartist demonstration illegal. G. W. M Reynolds took the chair at this event and asked the demonstrators to vote in favour of the revolution in Paris, which they duly did. Amidst riotous

---

[11] First published under this title in The *Athenæum*, 4 July 1840, it subsequently appeared in E. B. Browning, *Poems of 1844* as 'Crowned and Buried'.

[12] *The Earlier Letters of John Stuart Mill, 1812–1848*, ed. F. E. Minneka, intro. F. A. Hayek (2 vols, London: Routledge & Kegan Paul, 1996), ii, 732.

[13] 'Louis-Philippe', first published in *The Examiner*, 4 Mar. 1848; repr. in *Rescued Essays of Thomas Carlyle*, ed. P. Newberry (London: Leadenhall Press, 1892), 4.

[14] *The George Eliot Letters*, ed. G. S. Haight (9 vols, New Haven, Conn.: Yale University Press, 1954–6, 1978), i, 253–4.

support he then led the crowd down the Strand to his house in Wellington Street, where he addressed them from the balcony.

Matthew Arnold, who was 'in the great mob in Trafalgar Square', had already been impressed by the way in which Carlyle's commentary on recent events in Paris had 'put aside the din and whirl and brutality which envelop a movement of the masses, to fix his thought on its ideal invisible character'. Convinced that 'the hour of the hereditary peerage & eldest sonship and immense properties' was over, Arnold was equally certain that there was no danger of the British monarchy being toppled: 'It will be *rioting* here, only.'[15]

On 13 March Reynolds again played a prominent role in a demonstration on Kennington Common in support of the French Revolution. Thackeray, who had known Reynolds in Paris, reported the proceedings at length in the *Morning Chronicle,* in such a way as to suggest that 'the great Kennington-common demonstration' had been something of a damp squib.[16] Arnold, who was impressed by the calibre of Chartist speakers at their National Convention on 4 April, where Reynolds had also spoken, nevertheless thought it unlikely that they would ever form a government.[17] Characteristically, Arnold found it easiest to forge his own opinions in argument with a silent interlocutor. His two sonnets entitled 'To a Republican Friend, 1848' applaud the idealistic hopes of his more radical friend, Arthur Hugh Clough, while remaining sceptical of socialism's capacity to triumph over circumstance and a fallen human nature.[18]

The Oxford liberal circles to which Arnold and Clough had so recently belonged seem to have been given a particular fillip by the birth of the new republic. James Anthony Froude, who later claimed that '[a] fight for liberty is always inspiriting to the young and hopeful', recalled that, whilst friends such as Clough had gone to Paris, 'to see with his own eyes what was going on', his own contribution to the revolution had been to persuade a brass band to play the Marseillaise under the Vice Chancellor's window.[19] Benjamin Jowett led an Easter party of Balliol pupils to Paris in April 1848: it included Francis Palgrave, then accounted 'the wildest and most écervelé ['rash, hare-brained'] republican going'.[20] By 1887, it seems worth noting, Palgrave proved happy to compose an ode for Queen Victoria's jubilee.

The corpses on the boulevards in the June Days Uprising provided graphic illustration for many British observers of the difference between the republican aspirations nursed by youthful members of England's privileged middle classes and the realities of democratic socialism. The conservatively inclined Frances Trollope used

---

[15] *The Letters of Matthew Arnold*, ed. C. Y. Lang (6 vols, Charlottesville: University Press of Virginia, 1996–2001), i, 91.

[16] *William Makepeace Thackeray's Contributions to the* Morning Chronicle, ed. G. N. Ray (Urbana: University of Illinois Press, 1955), 192–8.

[17] *Letters of Matthew Arnold*, ed. Lang, i, 101.

[18] Published in *The Strayed Reveller and Other Poems*, 1849. For dating, see *The Poems of Matthew Arnold*, ed. K. Allott (London: Longmans, 1965), 101–3.

[19] Quoted in W. H. Dunn, *James Anthony Froude: A Biography* (2 vols, Oxford: Clarendon Press, 1961), i, 98.

[20] *The Correspondence of Arthur Hugh Clough*, ed. F. L. Mulhauser (2 vols, Oxford: Clarendon Press, 1957), i, 216.

her novel of this period, *The Old World and the New* (1849), to hammer home this message. Her intrepid English observer disguises herself to venture out to the barricades, but claims that the fighting spirit there is counterbalanced among the general populace of Paris by an equally strong undercurrent of bourgeois disapproval and a desire for order to be restored. Remarking upon the French predilection for trying out every style of government in swift succession, she claims that 'the shoe-blacks and chimney-sweepers are...tired of sans culottism and the red republic', before concluding with considerable prescience, 'The time is ripe for a president. But if I were a married woman, and wore diamonds, I would not put them on till there was an emperor to look smilingly upon them.'[21]

Only the most convinced of republican sympathisers felt the sacrifices had advanced the cause. Anxious to gainsay Matthew Arnold's 'sadly cynical' view of recent events, on his return to England Clough wrote to Tom Arnold, Matthew's younger brother, that 'France's prospects are dubious and dismal enough' but that 'the cruelties are unquestionably exaggerated....On the whole one accepts the whole thing with gratitude. It will, I think, on the whole accelerate change in England.'[22] By December 1848, Chartism might have seemed a spent political force, but Dickens, who deplored its tactics, nevertheless went into Carlylean mode in an excoriating attack upon a judge who had claimed, in the course of a Chartist trial, that the poor in France had been better off before than after the French Revolution. Observing that educated Chartist lecturers could make great political capital out of such false assertions, the underlying message of Dickens's article was the folly, in danger of being repeated on this side of the Channel, of ignoring the 'struggle on the part of the people for social recognition and existence'.[23]

The way in which England's liberal intelligentsia had given at least a cautious welcome to the 1848 coup suggests that the British government was right to view the subsequent chain of European revolutions that year, and the unrest at home, with some trepidation.

3.4 LOUIS-NAPOLEON BECOMES EMPEROR

The rise of Louis-Napoleon, his assumption of the imperial title, and his initial systematic suppression of opposition to the Second Empire further divided middle-class British opinion. The Browning household was riven with disagreement. Elizabeth Barrett Browning held that strong leadership was preferable to the vacillations of the Provisional Government of the Republic, and that, furthermore, the national referendum of 1852 had legitimated Napoleon's position as the people's choice. Robert Browning, by contrast, had a visceral distrust of a ruler who employed violence, arrests, and deportation, ostensibly to secure sound government for his people. Having another base in Florence widened the couple's interest in the com-

---

[21] F. Trollope, *The Old World and the New* (3 vols, London: Henry Colburn, 1849), iii, 281–2.

[22] *Correspondence of Clough*, ed. Mulhauser, i, 207 and 215.

[23] C. Dickens, 'Judicial Special Pleading', *The Examiner*, 23 Dec. 1848; repr. in *Dickens' Journalism*, ed. M. Slater (4 vols, London: J. M. Dent, 1994–2000), ii, 140.

plicated game Napoleon III went on to play in Italy, where his support for the Papal States appealed to right-wing Catholics, and his support for Italian nationalism appealed to liberals. Such contradictions made it hard for those with the republican sympathies of William Rossetti and his circle to know whether to regard Napoleon III as hero or villain.[24]

Napoleon's desire to cut a figure on the European political stage aroused suspicion of his intentions towards Great Britain. In early 1852, Coventry Patmore wrote to the *Times* advocating the formation of English rifle clubs as a pre-emptive measure of self-defence against the feared militaristic ambitions of this new tyrant.[25] Tennyson and his wife each contributed £5 to Patmore's fighting fund, and the poet dashed off some doggerel on the subject. The following stanza offers an adequate flavour:

> Ready, be ready! They mean no good,
> Ready, be ready! The times are wild!
> Bearded monkeys of lust and blood
> Coming to violate woman and child!
> We love liberty; they love storm,
> Riflemen, form! Riflemen, form!
> Riflemen, riflemen, riflemen form! [26]

Intemperate though Tennyson's words now seem, they reflect the fears that led the British government to commission forts on the south coast in reaction to Napoleon III's increased spending on the French navy and coastal defences. British comic literature might perpetuate the notion that the mere mention of the battle of Waterloo was a sufficiently crushing retort to finish any argument with a Frenchman, but France's military power was demonstrated when the two nations fought as allies during the Crimean War. The universal conscription introduced during the French Revolution had been relaxed to allow those who could to pay for substitutes, but the ubiquity of soldiers in France never failed to astonish British visitors. The British Volunteer movement, in response, by 1862 had only managed to recruit some 160,000 men.

Meanwhile, the alleged French penchant for resolving constitutional matters by shedding blood on the streets of Paris continued to be invoked in response to any agitation for British electoral reform. The British government's ineffectual response to the demonstrations and unrest provoked by the failure of the Liberal Reform Bill of 1866 led Matthew Arnold to pose the bleak antithesis of *Culture and Anarchy* (1867–8), and Carlyle to dark prophecies of 'Democracy rampant, as in America, or in France by fits for 70 odd years past'.[27]

---

[24] W. Rossetti, 'Napoleon III, 1870', *Democratic Sonnets* (2 vols, London: Alston Rivers, 1907), xxx.

[25] For a fuller discussion of their writing on this subject see Gridley, *The Brownings and France*, 83–114; and E. Woodworth, 'Elizabeth Barrett Browning, Coventry Patmore, and Alfred Tennyson on Napoleon III: The Hero-Poet and Carlylean Heroics', *Victorian Poetry*, Winter 2006, 543–60.

[26] A. Tennyson, *The Poems of Tennyson*, ed. C. Ricks (3 vols, Harlow: Longman, 1987), iii, 601. This version of the poem was not published during Tennyson's lifetime.

[27] 'Shooting Niagara: and After?', *Macmillan's Magazine*, Aug. 1867, 319–36; repr. in *Critical and Miscellaneous Essays, The Works of Thomas Carlyle*, ed. H. D. Traill (30 vols, London: Chapman & Hall, 1896–1901), xxx,15.

The strangest literary response of the Parisian tendency to violent protest must surely be Ouida's *Tricotrin: the Story of a Waif and Stray* (1869), which must have come to have been seen as almost prophetic within a couple of years of its publication. Since 'Ouida' (the pseudonym of the English-born Marie Louise de la Ramée) was only 9 years old in 1848, she had no immediate memories to draw upon, and indeed the references to revolution made within the novel seem to conflate the affairs of 1798, 1830, and 1848 into examples of an eternal story in which reforming zeal gets out of hand on hot summer nights, and the downtrodden, and their idealist supporters, are led on and tricked by those who simply wish to revenge themselves on their class enemies, or loot the treasures of the rich. The revolutionaries' contempt for human life on the barricades is shown as they increase the height of their defences by slinging their slaughtered comrades on top, all the while singing the Marseillaise. Sacrifice and the endurance of wrongs, the people are told by the author's spokesman, are more heroic than striving for liberty.[28] Such righting of their wrongs as occurs in the novel happens as a consequence of the benevolent intervention of Tricotrin, a Christ-like figure, whose total disaffection from the governing classes from whom he sprang suggests to Ouida's readers that while civil insurrection could only result in increased misery, it was little use looking to earthly rulers for amelioration of their lot.

3.5 THE FRANCO-PRUSSIAN WAR

Francophobia reached new heights at the outbreak of hostilities in the Franco-Prussian war. Tennyson, George Eliot and Matthew Arnold alike voiced criticism of French militarism that extended to embrace generic denunciations of the decadent vanities of the Second Empire, the amoral nature of the French as a nation, and the depravity of contemporary French literature.[29] The German Chancellor's release to the press, in mid-July 1870, of Napoleon's III's cynical attempt to profiteer from the changing balance of power in Europe increased British distrust of the Emperor and his expansionist ambitions. Bulwer Lytton wrote to his son, 'Reflect. France could at this moment and for six months to come destroy us—outnumber our Channel fleet—throw a force into Ireland—and could threw [*sic*] also 50,000 men into England…All I say is Arm, Arm, Arm.'[30] However, his final novel, *The Parisians*, appearing in serial form from October 1872 and covering the last days of the Second Empire through to the spring of 1871, suggests that he had swiftly come to recognize that the French army, for all its numbers, was no match for the well-disciplined Prussians. The novel, while honouring the aristocratic French patriots who joined up to defend their country, had nothing but contempt for the self-serving National Guard.

---

[28] 'Ouida' [M. L. de la Ramée], *Tricotrin: The Story of a Waif and Stray* (3 vols, London: Chapman & Hall, 1869), iii, 351–4 and 389–412.
[29] P. Henderson, *Tennyson: Poet and Prophet* (London: Routledge & Kegan Paul, 1978), 163; *George Eliot Letters*, ed. Haight, v, 113; *Letters of Matthew Arnold*, ed. Lang, iv, 8.
[30] Quoted in L. Mitchell, *Bulwer Lytton: The Rise and Fall of a Victorian Man of Letters* (London: Hambledon Continuum, 2003), 153. Although he published under a series of different names and titles, for consistency this text will employ the form Bulwer Lytton.

Great Britain was officially neutral in this war. Wilkie Collins, staunchly pro-France from the start, claimed that the British government and press conspired to suppress the extent of English working-class support for their French comrades:

> The Lord Mayor (privately instructed, it is whispered, by the Government) has refused to allow a public meeting at the Guild hall to express sympathy with France and to urge the interference of England on the French side—the reason being simply dread of the inflammatory speeches which would be delivered, and of the possible effect of them, in this country as well as abroad.[31]

Seasoned British travellers found that their familiarity with both Germany and France made it hard to know where their allegiance lay. In mid-August 1870, a fortnight before Napoleon III's crushing defeat at Sedan, Margaret Oliphant wrote to John Blackwood, a declared Prussian sympathizer: 'This war is too frightful. I cannot say I sympathise really with either party, but I know much more of the French than of the Germans, and, right or wrong, one's heart goes with the losing side.'[32] Her friend Anne Thackeray Ritchie remarked that her loyalties changed almost daily as she found herself, almost against her will, scanning the papers, 'column after column' for the latest reports in the wake of Napoleon's defeat at Sedan:

> I was French on Saturday, but since their insane flourishing and hurrahing, and embracing on Sunday, I began to think that a despot's was the only rule they were fit for. You will read of their all *keeping* the guard at bridges, and fraternising over the republic... It is all so utterly silly.[33]

By contrast, British republicans such as Swinburne rejoiced over the declaration of a new republic and, though he lamented the blood shed at Sedan, used the occasion to dedicate a lengthy 'Ode on the Proclamation of the French Republic' to Napoleon III's implacable enemy Victor Hugo.[34] Swinburne's friend Eliza Lynn Linton summed up the changing disposition of British opinion thus:

> The war broke out between France and Prussia, and at the first the tide of liberal sympathies went with Prussia, as representing opposition to the Empire. But as time went on, sides changed, and moderates backed up Prussia, while the ultra-Tories and the Republicans went with France; the one hoping to see the Empire restored, the other longing for the establishment of liberty.[35]

Just as the rise and fall of Napoleon I had gripped a previous generation, so the fall from power of the Emperor Napoleon III, who had dominated the European

---

[31] *The Public Face of Wilkie Collins: The Collected Letters*, ed. W. Baker, A. Gasson, G. Law, and P. Lewis (4 vols, London: Pickering & Chatto, 2005), ii, 224.

[32] *The Autobiography and Letters of Mrs M. O. W. Oliphant*, ed. Mrs H. Coghill, intro. Q. D. Leavis (Leicester: Leicester University Press, 1974), 227, 230. Reflecting at a later date on a friend who never wavered in his support for the Germans, she remarked tartly: 'he knew something of the German nation and people, and very little of the French, whom he was thus free to regard with prejudice and disapproval, as so many do': M. Oliphant, *A Memoir of the Life of John Tulloch* (Edinburgh: William Blackwood & Sons, 1888), 261.

[33] *Letters of Anne Thackeray Ritchie*, ed. H. Ritchie (London: John Murray, 1924), 140.

[34] Repr. in A. C. Swinburne, *Songs of Two Nations* (1875).

[35] E. Linton, *The True History of Joshua Davidson, Christian and Communist* (London: Strahan, 1872), 228.

political scene for over a generation, exercised the imagination of the nation where he had once again taken up exile. Robert Buchanan's *Napoleon Fallen: A Lyrical Drama*, published in the *Athenæum* of 7 January 1871, seems to have prompted Robert Browning to return to the outline of a poem about the Emperor that he had first contemplated in 1860[36] and publish *Prince Hohenstiel-Schwangau, Saviour of Society* (1871). Buchanan, surprisingly for a man raised in a radical, freethinking household, shows a degree of sympathy for his chain-smoking, prematurely aged, deposed Emperor. Arraigned by a series of characters, including the ghostly revenants of those mistreated during his reign, Buchanan's defeated Napoleon is shown as a man whose mistake has been to abandon his twenty-year-long pursuit of peace and prosperity for France. The drama's dénouement leaves his fate to Judgement Day and Christ's salvific power.

Not content to leave the verdict on Napoleon to the bar of eternity, Browning's long and complex poem sought to tease out the political philosophy that had really animated this Emperor. At the heart of the poem lies the question of whether the principled pragmatism that Elizabeth Barrett Browning had so admired in this leader was chiefly exercised for the benefit of France or to maintain himself in power. Where Buchanan's Napoleon has lost a fight with objective foes, victims, and critics, Browning's Napoleon, on the brink of war, fences with shadows in a series of ghostly dialogues always focused on his overriding preoccupation with his own reputation. Pursuing so illusory and variable a goal, Browning suggests, must render a man finally unknowable even to himself. Worse still, as Napoleon's last words in the poem, 'Double or quits! The letter goes! Or stays?', reveal (l. 2155) that this posturing in front of history's mirror has formed the leader whose lack of fixed purpose is about to sacrifice France itself. This letter, it seems reasonable to assume, contains the fatal instructions to French diplomats that had led to the Franco-Prussian war.

So topical was Browning's poem that 1,400 copies sold in the first five days. Yet its message was a matter of some dispute. Henry Reeve, editor of the *Edinburgh Review*, considered that the poem delivered a 'eulogium on the Second Empire', while another critic called it 'a scandalous attack on the old, constant friend of England'.[37] It has been customary to attribute this difference of opinion solely to the notorious obscurity of Browning's verse, but these divergent opinions of the poem's bias equally reflected the growing polarization of British opinion about contemporary events in Paris. As the siege had taken hold, so the hostility to France which had marked the early stages of the war had notably softened in some sections of the British press. Matthew Arnold and George Eliot, both initially pro-Prussian, now counterbalanced their reading of W. H. Russell's *Times* reports from the front with Labouchère's accounts in the *Daily News* of the conditions inside the besieged city.[38] The privations of this stage of the war seemed unimaginable to

[36] By 1 Oct. 1871 Browning had written the about 1,800 lines of this poem of 2,155 lines: *Dearest Isa: Robert Browning's Letters to Isabella Blagden*, ed. E. C. McAleer (Edinburgh: Thomas Nelson, 1951), 367.

[37] W. C. DeVane, *A Browning Handbook* (New York: Appleton-Century-Crofts, 1955), 321; *Dearest Isa*, ed. McAleer, 372.

[38] *Letters of Matthew Arnold*, ed. Lang, iii, 452; *George Eliot Letters*, ed. Haight, v, 117.

those accustomed to the opulent displays of the Second Empire: as Anne Thackeray Ritchie wrote in December 1870 to James Fitzjames Stephen, then based in India, 'Paris is farther than India nowadays'. The fate of the consequent new wave of French exiles recently arrived in London, all 'well-bred, high-thinking' women, should, she declared, serve as 'a lesson to all middle class ladies'.[39]

It was this swing of opinion in the British press that prompted John Carlyle to stir his brother, Thomas, to public support for the Prussians: 'I notice the delusions in regard to Prussia which are getting more and more vehement in the newspapers, so that even the *Times* and *Daily News* which have been steadily against the French hitherto, seem to be turning quite round'.[40] Carlyle's ensuing letter to the editor of the *Times*, published on 18 November 1870 under the title 'Mr. Carlyle on the War',[41] started by mocking what he represented as the sentimentality of the British press in recommending magnanimity to Germany in its treatment of fallen and afflicted France. Rather, he argued, history was taking its revenge on a nation which over the course of the last four centuries had proved itself 'insolent, rapacious, insatiable, unappeasable, continually aggressive'; had failed to profit from the reforming spirit of the Revolution of 1789; and was now in need of the 'terribly drastic dose of physic' which the Germans were well placed to administer. His letter concluded:

> That noble, patient, deep, pious and solid Germany should be at length welded into a Nation, and become Queen of the Continent, instead of vaporous, vainglorious, gesticulating, quarrelsome, restless and over-sensitive France, seems to me the hopefullest public fact that has occurred in my time.[42]

It was perhaps as well that Thomas did not respond to his brother's fresh urging, the week after the siege ended, to take up the cudgels on Germany's behalf again.[43]

3.6 THE COMMUNE

Republican triumphalism at Napoleon III's downfall, and humanitarian sympathy for Parisian sufferings, were however a far cry from full-blooded socialist support for the red flag of the Communards. The drama that played itself out in the early spring of 1871, when the provisional French government showed itself incapable of taking the measure of the discontent of the Parisian working classes, once again

---

[39] *Letters of A. T. Ritchie*, ed. H. Ritchie, 144, 142.

[40] MS NLS 1775D, fo. 246, quoted in C. Heyrendt, '"A Rain of Balderdash": Thomas Carlyle and Victorian Attitudes toward the Franco-Prussian War', *Carlyle Studies Annual* 22 (Spring 2006), 245–6.

[41] Repr. as 'Latter Stage of the French-German War, 1870–71', in *Works of Carlyle*, ed. Traill, xxx, 49–59.

[42] Although its publication was long delayed, this outburst seems to have goaded Swinburne into his 'Ballad against the Enemies of France', where he employed a translation of the 15th-c. French poet Villon to curse all those who held Carlyle's political views. This poem, bearing the words 'translated and endorsed' above his signature, appeared in the *Athenæum*, 17 Feb. 1877, 224. See also *The Swinburne Letters,* ed. C. Y. Lang (6 vols, New Haven, Conn.: Yale University Press, 1959–62), iii, 268.

[43] MS, National Library of Scotland 1775E, fo. 15, quoted by Heyrendt, '"A Rain of Balderdash"', 254.

had uncomfortable resonances for British observers. On 20 March 1871, in the wake of the Montmartre fracas, Matthew Arnold worried that 'a socialistic and red republic' will act as 'a perpetual flag to the proletaire everywhere'. A week later, however, he declared that 'Paris does not make me so angry as it does many people': this was partly because he despised 'Thiers and the upper class generally', and partly because thus far 'all the seriousness, clearmindedness, and settled purpose' lay with 'the Reds'. 'There is no person or thing, as you say', he wrote to his mother on 31 May, in the wake of *La semaine sanglante*, 'to give one any satisfaction when one regards France at present', but 'the Paris convulsion' had served to demonstrate 'that fixed resolve of the working class to count for something and *live*, which is destined to make itself so much felt in the coming time, and to disturb so much which dreamed it would last for ever'.[44]

The scale of the internecine chaos and destruction that then engulfed the cultural capital of Europe brought the 1789 Revolution to mind; but since by 1871 very few of the British population had personal memories of the reign of terror, the Commune and its aftermath largely supplanted the symbolic force of the earlier event in the later Victorian mental imaginary. Fictional responses were remarkably swift in appearing. Although Bulwer Lytton had not completed the final chapters of *The Parisians* (1873) before he died, he had already written the 'envoi' in which a bourgeois Parisian prophesies the continuation of the vested interests that had seen his class rise during the Second Empire.[45] The revolutionaries, whose only unifying goal had been the destruction of the Empire, are condemned to collapse into factional fighting, while the lot of the ignorant Paris rabble remains unchanged. The novel's strongest denunciation, however, was reserved for *la trahison des clercs*, in this case the treason of a generation of dissolute Baudelairean figures 'inebriate with brag and absinthe' who had made money out of airing their views in radical papers, but were nowhere to be found when trouble broke out.[46] Victor Hugo, whose romanticization of the working classes Bulwer Lytton regarded as dangerously sentimental nonsense, is singled out for particular opprobrium.

British writers of a socialist disposition found themselves in some difficulty. Radical republican press support for the Commune in publications aimed at a working-class readership understandably made middle-class writers nervous lest their own views should be tainted with unpatriotic, godless anarchy and associated with the executions and firing of buildings that had attended the final rout of the Paris Commune. The question as to how far the values of the Paris Commune were compatible with English socialist ideals exercised them greatly. Ruskin began Letter VII of *Fors Clavigera*, dated 1 July 1871, by confessing that having 'dined out on several times...and done the best I could to find out what people thought about the fighting, or thought they ought to think about it, or thought they ought to say', he remained little the wiser. Nevertheless, he took the bull by the horns and

---

[44] *Letters of Matthew Arnold*, ed. Lang, iv, 25, 27, 37.

[45] Serialized in *Blackwood's Magazine* between Oct. 1872 and Jan. 1874, the novel was completed by his son, Robert, who took up his role as Secretary to the British Embassy in Paris during 1872.

[46] Lord [E. G. E. L. Bulwer-]Lytton, *The Parisians* (2 vols, London: George Routledge, 1875), ii, 364.

declared to the 'workmen and labourers of Great Britain': 'I am myself a Communist of the old school –: reddest also of the Red', before proceeding to explain his own very particular understanding of these terms.[47]

Ruskin had recently bought his home, 'Brantwood', from William Linton, a radical republican and wood engraver, who after the failure of Chartism had become increasingly immersed in European revolutionary movements. Although Eliza Lynn Linton had long separated from William Linton, the hero of her popular one-volume novel, *The True History of Joshua Davidson, Christian and Communist* (1872), bears notable allusions to her husband's life story. Joshua Davidson is a Cornish carpenter's son, born in 1835, who attempts to practise Christ's teaching in contemporary Great Britain. Finding his work among the British rural and urban poor spurned by institutional religion and middle-class philanthropy, he travels to Paris on 19 March 1871 'to help in the establishment of an organised liberty'. The narrator of this tale, a disciple of Joshua's, claims that the Commune's selfless cooperation and self-government wrote 'one of the brightest pages of modern history', undermined though it was by the working classes' ingrained distrust of these very virtues, the conflicting agendas of the foreign revolutionaries who flocked to its cause, and the confusion that took over as the Versaillists entered the city. Intent on its work as moral fable, Linton's story concentrates on the leading British characters, rather than attempting a historical documentary of the events in Paris. Joshua pleads unavailingly that the Communards spare the lives of their hostages, and a reformed English prostitute does sterling work in the ambulance brigade before being mistaken for a *pétroleuse* and shot. On his return to Great Britain, Joshua is killed by a mob worked up by an Anglican clergyman's claim that Joshua's participation in 'that pandemonium of vice and crime—the Paris Commune' is an instance of the essential kinship between atheism and Communism.[48]

Similarly anxious to rebut this bracketing of socialism and atheism, Roden Noel's collection *The Red Flag and Other Poems* (1872) was more obviously targeted at the conventional thinking of the governing classes from whose ranks he came. Roden Berkeley Wriothesley Noel (1834–94) was the son of an Earl, but this Whig family had a history of fierce anti-establishment sympathies: his uncle, the Reverend Baptist Wriothesley Noel, a notable campaigner for London's working classes, had famously seceded from the Church of England to join the Dissenters in 1848. The nephew also found the Establishment, its church, aristocracy, and government culpably indifferent to the plight of the poor. Roden Noel's jeremiad starts by denouncing the extermination of the Communards, achieved 'so/That there in peace her delicate Agags/Might mince once more with high-born courtesans/O'er the dead people', though he takes no more pleasure in the street fighting that had preceded this: 'Now named Mobrule, now Slavery to a King'. The bulk of the poem is devoted to a series of contrasts of the life of rich and poor in London,

[47] *Fors Clavigera: Letters to the Workmen and Labourers of Great Britain*, in *The Works of John Ruskin*, ed. E. T. Cook and A. Wedderburn (39 vols, London: George Allen; New York: Longmans, Green, 1903–12), xxvii, 115–16.

[48] Linton, *Joshua Davidson*, 231, 234, 271.

each prefaced by the ironic statement: 'There is peace in London.' The poem draws to a conclusion with a Carlylean warning that 'England must join the anarchic devil's dance,/That wilders and exhausts delirious France', and a menacing vision of London consumed by fire as the 'towered Thames/Rolls like the Seine, a tide of eddying flames'. Only the interdenominational endeavours of true Christians, Roden argued, in an allusion to Sodom and Gomorrah, could save London from being similarly destroyed: 'For in mine ears one spake with pity,/"If there be ten there, I will spare the city." '[49]

The distance that those known in England for their socialist and republican commitment were apt to put between their ideals and the working out of these principles in France is particularly obvious in Matilda Betham-Edwards's novel *Brother Gabriel* (1878). At one point the narrator enthuses, 'To have heard the Marseillaise in stirring times on French soil is for a moment to be one with France and her aspirations', yet when an enflamed rabble gather on a provincial election day they are described as 'a veritable human scum...a mass of soured, warped, infected humanity' who have been worked upon by political agitators. The French working classes, it transpires, are a mere pawn in the real war fought by the forces of pro- and anti-clericalism. With the fall of Napoleon, Brother Gabriel, an Irish Franciscan monk, disillusioned with his calling and inspired by his desire to free the French from priestly rule, makes his way to Paris where he throws himself into the roles of 'journalist, orator, club-orator, soldier' and takes up arms for the Commune. Gabriel and his creator are convinced that the Roman Catholic Church kept Napoleon III in power and thus lay behind all the 'immorality of the second Empire'.[50] As a foreigner, Gabriel finds it relatively easy to escape the carnage of the last days of the Commune, but this is largely a ploy by the author to remind the reader how strong are the tentacles of a Jesuit education. Despite his political awakening, Gabriel can imagine no other life than living out his days in the shadow of the monastery where he hopes finally to be readmitted for burial. By 1878, in the eyes of a socialist idealist such as Betham-Edwards, the Third Republic looked no more likely than the Second Empire to deliver utopia, and so the other leading protagonists of the novel, also Irish exiles, leave France and head for America.

By the mid-1880s, when the next swathe of imaginative evocations of the Paris Commune appeared, the emphases had subtly changed in keeping both with the way in which it was fast assuming mythical status and with the manner in which the debate surrounding British socialism had also evolved. Mary Elizabeth Braddon's *Under the Red Flag* (1883) employed a scaled-down version of the plot used in *The Parisians* by her literary master, Bulwer Lytton, to address a similarly paternalist agenda. Strong on topographical detail, her novel also demonstrates the provocative role played by journalists and misguided radicals of aristocratic origin in inflaming an uneducated rabble with whom they have little in common—though,

[49] R. Noel, *The Red Flag and Other Poems* (London: Strahan, 1872), 2–5, 33–8.
[50] M. Betham-Edwards, *Brother Gabriel* (3 vols, London: Hurst & Blackett, 1878), ii, 7, 45; iii, 234–6.

short on space, she wraps these categories up in the same character. 18 March 1871 is represented as a dark day when the underbelly of Paris rose up, unleashing scenes of violence and sacrilege reminiscent of the French Revolution: 'and on 19ᵗʰ March began the great orgy of the Commune, the rule of blood and fire. The offal of journalism, the scum of the gaols, sat in the seat of judgement.' The worst of the excesses is led by a she-devil, Suzon Michel, who had 'unsexed' herself by becoming a *pétroleuse*: she escapes capture while other misguided supporters of the Commune die as so much cannon fodder.[51]

Whether *pétroleuses* actually existed, or were simply, as Eliza Lynn Linton had claimed, women, variously acting as nurses, ambulance bearers, or otherwise servicing the barricades, who were then mistakenly identified as arsonists by the government troops, has long continued a matter of debate.[52] The cheap yellowback reprint of Braddon's novel, however, left readers in no doubt: the cover carries a picture in which a woman, bearing aloft a smoking firebrand, stands clearly prepared to fire the street where her comrades have fallen (Fig. 2).[53] Casting Suzon Michel as the villain of the piece suited Braddon's political and gender agenda well in that Louise Michel, Communard, heroine of the barricades and alleged pétroleuse, had returned from her transportation sentence in New Caledonia in 1880, and had become a key attraction on British socialist platforms. Indeed, she eventually became a permanent exile in London.

It seems to have been the fresh wave of anxiety concerning the potential of foreign political refugees to foment disturbances in London that triggered Anne Thackeray Ritchie into integrating her own memories of the earliest days of the Commune into the plot of her novel *Mrs Dymond* (1885). She may well have borrowed the name of her feckless Irish journalist, Marney, possibly also a spy and traitor, from John O'Mahoney, one of the founders of the Fenian movement responsible for bombing incidents in London in 1883 and 1884. The novel's romantic lead, a young socialist of half-French and half-English descent, is aware of the cross-Channel comings and goings of foreign firebrands and redeemed into marriageable material for the heroine by his revulsion, in the last days of the Commune, at the 'wild saturnalia of the streets, where dishevelled women were dancing round the flames'.[54] This prompts him into temporarily imprisoning a band of Communards to prevent them from their policy of firing all around them as they are beaten into retreat.

Where Bulwer Lytton had displayed an aristocratic disdain for writers of a radical disposition, accusing them variously of vain pride, avarice, immorality, and opportunism, Braddon and Ritchie represent their young firebrands, who are well educated and from good families, as idealists, and salvage them for socially responsible futures. The fact that educated men such as H. M. Hyndman (Eton and Cambridge) and William Morris (Marlborough and Oxford) stood in the vanguard of socialist

---

[51] M. E. Braddon, *Under the Red Flag* (Leipzig: Tauchnitz, 1884), 142–3, 163.
[52] See R. Tombs, *The Paris Commune, 1871* (London: Longman, 1999), 132–46.
[53] M. E. Braddon, *Under the Red Flag, and Other Tales* (London: John & Robert Maxwell, 1886).
[54] *Mrs Dymond*, in *Works of Miss Thackeray* (10 vols, London: Smith, Elder, 1890), x, 508.

Fig. 2. Cover design for yellowback edition of M. E. Braddon, *Under the Red Flag* (1883), showing a *pétroleuse* (by courtesy of the Manuscript, Archives and Rare Book Library at Emory University).

demonstrations in Great Britain of the 1880s was unsettling, even if the overall numerical threat of such movements was minimal.[55]

To William Morris, the Paris Commune seemed a tragic but essentially heroic manifestation of the potential inherent in the collaborative efforts of international socialism. Introduced late into his sequence of poems, 'The Pilgrims of Hope', (1887), published serially from 1885 in the *Commonweal*, the Commune episode is thin on documentary detail. Morris used it instead to provide a symbolic resolution to the conflict between liberalism, with its valorization of individual desires, and the collective, communitarian vision.[56] In brief, the love triangle produced when the British narrator's wife falls in love with one of their socialist comrades is eclipsed by the greater collective cause which leads the three to serve together on the barricades in Paris, the wife in the ambulance corps. The selfless nobility demanded by the Commune—'the hope of the world and the seed that the ages had sown'—allows the narrator to bury his wife and her lover in France, as though husband and wife, and return to raise his boy 'that two men there might be hereafter to battle against the wrong'. Nevertheless the narrator, and the poet, recognize the uphill task involved in transforming a British readership's image of this event:

> For few of you now will be thinking of the day that might have been,
> And fewer still meseemeth of the day that yet shall be.

Ultimately, Morris's failure to offer any detailed description of the street fighting, or of the other combatants on the barricades, undermines his ideological drift by concentrating the emotional focus too firmly on the fate of the British trio. Furthermore, in enveloping his own triangular domestic situation within his utopian politics, Morris's was simultaneously asking readers to accept radical departures from both the political and social conventions of his era.

Perhaps the best-remembered account in British literature of the siege and the Commune occurs in the third section of Arnold Bennett's *The Old Wives' Tale* (1908), where the decadent sensuality and financial recklessness of the last days of the Empire play their part in the rapid decline of Sophie Baines's marriage to the bourgeois *flâneur*, Gerald Scales, before she is left alone to turn the chances of the siege and Commune to her own advantage. Bennett claimed that he derived his sense 'that ordinary people went on living very ordinary lives in Paris during the siege, and that to the vast mass of the population the siege was not the dramatic, spectacular, thrilling, ecstatic affair that is described in history' from an elderly working-class French couple, and from historical sources.[57] His greatest debt, however, was probably to Flaubert's *L'Éducation sentimentale* (1869) and the ironic

---

[55] 'The best estimates suggest that the total membership of all known bodies came to some 3,000': K. T. Hoppen, *The Mid-Victorian Generation: 1846–1886* (Oxford: Clarendon Press, 1998), 650.

[56] My reading concurs with the analysis of the broader politics of the poem, but disputes Morris's achievement of his aims as described in A. F. Janowitz, 'The Pilgrims of Hope: William Morris and the Dialectic of Romanticism', in S. Ledger and S. McCracken (eds), *Cultural Politics at the Fin de Siècle* (Cambridge: Cambridge University Press, 1995), 160–83.

[57] A. Bennett, *The Old Wives' Tale*, ed. M. Harris (Oxford: Oxford University Press, 1995), pp. 3–7.

detachment with which that novel had used the events of 1848 as subtext to the degeneration of the hero's romantic aspirations.[58]

For Bennett, the Commune no longer represented the topical political object lesson on class struggle or the potential threat of working-class insurrection that it had for his predecessors. Even under those extreme conditions which had led his predecessors to see Parisians as a race apart, Bennett represents French tradespeople, in their struggle to live 'ordinary lives', as no more feral, dishonest, or prone to violence than their counterparts in the Five Towns. By Bennett's time the repeated abrupt changes of government which had provided topical object lessons on class struggle to the Victorians had settled into the long-lived Third Republic.

————————

The first three chapters have traced the way in which the succession of regime changes that marked the middle decades of the nineteenth century had constituted Paris as the symbolic site of revolution or tyranny for the Victorians. The next two chapters attend to the distinctive materiality of the urban experience Paris offered visiting British writers.

———

[58] Bennett's scene in the Restaurant Sylvain, introducing the reader to a world of surface glamour which slowly disintegrates to disclose over-dressed prostitutes and drunken escorts coming to blows, owes much to the suppers at the Café Anglais and the Maison d'Or in the central portion of Flaubert's novel. Bennett, *Old Wives' Tale*, 323ff. Cf. G. Flaubert, *A Sentimental Education*, trans. D. Parmée (Oxford: Oxford University Press, 2008), 225–33, 237–42.

4

Topographical

I realize that the supposed objectivity of 'maps' is an effective fiction: that their texts and images are as vulnerable to deconstruction as any others...the 'maps' that I discuss here are something more than purely metaphorical devices: their accounts of the inscription of social life in space means that they also have a substantial materiality.[1]

This chapter discusses the way in which British writers approached, experienced and reacted to Paris as a physical site, and how its swiftly changing aspect in turn offered references and metaphors for the different social milieux to be found within the city. Read together with the next chapter, which considers Paris's sensuous affect on British writers, this topographical approach to Paris shows how the city offered an urban experience qualitatively different from that offered by either London or England's newer manufacturing conurbations, causing more thought-ful British writers to reflect on the *dirigiste* policies that brought about such radical reshapings. Through such observations this section further contributes both to a more nuanced understanding of the Victorian conceptualization of the urban, and to the mid-century British debate about the advantages and disadvantages of state intervention.

4.1 THE JOURNEY TO PARIS

Fictional French aristocrat addressing an English nobleman: 'You pay the penalty of your insular position...Your island is a *cul-de-sac*, you lead to nothing—Paris lies on the great highway of Europe.'[2]

Steam and the peace be thanked! London and Paris are becoming one 'great village,' as far as familiar intercourse is concerned.[3]

The journey between the two capitals was sufficiently arduous to sear itself on the imagination as an essential element of the Parisian experience. During a period when embarking on the Channel crossing would form the first taste of 'abroad' for

---

[1] D. Gregory, *Geographical Imaginations* (Oxford: Blackwell, 1994), 217.
[2] C. Gore, *Greville: or, a Season in Paris* (3 vols, London: Henry Colburn, 1841), iii, 170.
[3] [H. Chorley,] *Athenæum*, 25 July 1840, '*The Paris Sketch-Book. By Mr. Titmarsh*', 589.

increasing numbers of Victorian travellers, it would seem that the Victorian public never tired of accounts of the rigours of the journey, rather in the way that horror stories emerging from today's airports and railway stations seem to meet with a welcome undimmed by familiarity. In the late 1860s Arthur Sketchley, already famous for his 'Mrs Brown' comic monologues, even mounted a theatrical presentation of the experience, entitled 'Paris via Newhaven and Dieppe'.[4] Modelled on the phenomenal success, enjoyed a decade before, by Arthur Smith's staging of the ascent of Mont Blanc, Sketchley overreached himself by employing novelty mechanics that included a piano which kept reverting to the National Anthem and thus closing the show prematurely.[5] Sketchley was in any case riding the crest of a wave that had almost exhausted itself, since the topic had long since been a literary set piece, and the most significant changes to the mode and changing rhythms of the journey had happened in the first half of the nineteenth century.

Paddle steamers, which were less dependent on wind and tide, had superseded sailing ships as a means of public transport during the 1820s, but being small affairs, they were still likely to produce motion sickness in any swell. Measuring some 80 foot long by 15 foot wide, by the 1830s they carried an average complement of 300 tightly packed passengers.

On the British side of the Channel it became possible in the mid-1840s to travel by rail rather than coach from London to the Channel ports. Since direct rail connections on the other side still remained scanty, this latter part of the journey could therefore take anything between 24.5 and 39 hours. One of Anne Thackeray Ritchie's abiding memories was of having been punished, as a 3-year-old in 1840, by her father for waking her baby sister by her persistent crying in a crowded diligence to Paris.[6] Such coaches were capable of accommodating eighteen people and their luggage. Within a decade the advent of a continuous rail service transformed the journey: 1851 found Dickens celebrating the paring of the journey from London to Paris to eleven hours.[7]

An 1828 estimate itemizing every expense likely to be incurred on the 'cheapest and most expeditious Route' from London to Paris reckoned that 'being two nights and one day on the road, your expenses cannot be less than £4.4s and 5d.'[8] Thackeray's calculation that the trip could be undertaken in 1837 for 25 shillings[9] almost certainly omitted the incidentals, which included passports, port taxes, the hire of porters for the luggage, rowing boats for transport from steamer to land—in the absence of permanent docking facilities—and couriers for the onward journey,

---

[4] Sketchley was the pseudonym of George Rose (1817–82), Anglican priest turned Roman Catholic tutor to the Norfolk family before becoming a writer and man of the theatre.

[5] A. W. à Beckett, *The à Becketts of 'Punch': Memories of Father and Sons* (Westminster: Archibald Constable, 1903), 261.

[6] *The Works of William Makepeace Thackeray with biographical introductions by his daughter, Anne Ritchie* (13 vols, London: Smith, Elder, 1899), vol. iv, pp. xxix–xxxii.

[7] 'A Flight', *Household Words*, 30 Aug. 1851, 529–32; repr. in *The Uncommercial Traveller and Reprinted Pieces* (London: Oxford University Press, 1958), 474–84.

[8] F. Coghlan, *A Guide to France, or, Travellers their own Commissioners* (London: J. Onwhyn, 1828), 35.

[9] *The Letters and Private Papers of William Makepeace Thackeray*, ed. G. N. Ray (4 vols, Cambridge, Mass.: Harvard University Press, 1945–6), i, 330.

together with food en route. By 1844 Murray's *Hand-book for Travellers in France* suggested eight alternative routes from London to Paris, all using coach travel on the French side, and costing anywhere between 58 and 76 shillings.[10] Since these prices were to change little over the middle decades of the century, poorer passengers, such as governesses and maidservants travelling for work rather than pleasure, sometimes chose the cheaper five- to six-day voyage between Liverpool and France.[11]

Charlotte Brontë, who had herself made her first crossing to Belgium in the company of family and friends, nevertheless captured the fears and prejudices of an unescorted English governess in *Villette* (1853). The heroine's anxieties range from the fear of being cheated to being forced to mingle at close quarters with unknown men and social inferiors and thus subjected to degrading insult. Her apprehensions include potential difficulties in negotiating fares, arranging accommodation, and ordering food without the help of a male intermediary.[12] Even experienced solitary female travellers felt their dignity and possessions threatened: Mary Clarke made the return trip from Paris each year, but this account of a mid-winter journey suggests it still required fortitude:

> Paris, 23 December 1840
> ...I arrived at Boulogne in the dark...and crawled along through a mile of quagmire (mud is too good a name for it) from the customs house to my boarding house, after having one of my cloaks taken from me by rascally customs-house men. I slept in the cabin, making my carpet-bag (containing the tea-kettle) a pillow, and the spout kept getting always in the wrong place, twist the bag as I would. However tea-kettle-spout, quagmire, customs house and martrying diligence did me no harm and I was very well when I got here—when I got a vile toothache and swelled face.[13]

The intrusive behaviour of the French customs officials as they delved through passengers' most intimate belongings, rumpling and crumpling carefully packed clothing, was frequently seen as a personal affront by British travellers, although Sala qualified a lengthy fictional description of a woman and her daughter undergoing this process by claiming that, in the times of Louis-Philippe, every cross-Channel passenger attempted to smuggle something through.[14]

The importunate soliciting of custom conducted by ubiquitous French touts for the various hotels in Calais and for onward transport presented a further, frequently mentioned source of annoyance to cross-Channel travellers. One of the reasons for the success of the Hôtel Meurice in Paris was the seamless service it ran, courtesy of staff who spoke English, from the posting-house the family ran in Calais to their establishment in Paris.

The solitary bachelor generally felt himself less vulnerable than any woman traveller, and more at liberty to examine the world in miniature squeezed into the

---

[10] Quoted in J. Buzard, *The Beaten Track: European Tourism, Literature, and the Ways to 'Culture' 1800–1900* (Oxford: Clarendon Press, 1993), 42.

[11] M. Betham-Edwards, *Brother Gabriel* (3 vols, London: Hurst & Blackett, 1878), ii, 110.

[12] C. Brontë, *Villette*, ed. H. Rosengarten and M. Smith (Oxford: Clarendon Press, 1984), 74.

[13] M. Lesser, *Clarkey: A Portrait in Letters of Mary Clarke Mohl (1793–1883)* (Oxford: Oxford University Press, 1984), 107.

[14] G. A. Sala, *Quite Alone* (3 vols, London: Chapman & Hall, 1864), ii, 54–5.

confines of the cross-Channel packet. The focused intensity of this experience often produced a good guide to a writer's sociopolitical prejudices. The mixed crowd on board should have offered a heaven-sent opportunity to Thackeray, who delighted in thumbnail sketches of character types and discussion of social mores, but his pleasure in capturing his specimens on paper fought with a Swiftian revulsion at the enforced bodily proximity to 'greasy' fellow passengers. His gathering irritation at the discomfort of improvised sleeping arrangements, the unsuitable food brought aboard by the lower classes, the drunkenness of many male passengers, the pestering by French touts is often expended, in his early accounts, on the figure of the wandering Jew. Indeed, in his first attempt at rendering the horrors of this journey to 'Forign Parts' through the eyes of the Cockney servant Yellowplush, a man with an enormous hooked nose, otherwise unmentioned in the accompanying prose text, is introduced in Thackeray's drawing of the group of servants on the deck of this small sailing smack (Fig. 3).[15] Part of Thackeray's enthusiasm for the speedier night-mail service from Dover to Calais, inaugurated in 1849, may well have been that its cost put it out of the reach of all but wealthier travellers. In any event, his subsequent accounts of Channel crossings abandoned their former class-ridden nature.[16]

Sala, whose fictional compositions owed so much to Thackeray's *tableaux vivants* and commentary mode, adopted a defiantly different sociopolitical stance. In his novel *Quite Alone* (1864), the crossing, depicted as taking place in the early 1840s, is seen largely as it strikes a wholly inexperienced 8-year-old girl, travelling with her inattentive mother. The child's friendly curiosity about the foreign couriers, deckhands, and various classes of women to be found in the ladies' compartment below deck is deployed as a contrast with the peremptory, *de haut en bas* manner her mother habitually employs with social inferiors, so that the episode becomes a platform for the narrator to demonstrate his democratic credentials, and regret the disappearance of the easier class relations of yesteryear.[17]

Less overtly political in his responses to this experience than Sala, Dickens with his restless energy seemed peculiarly responsive to a state of perpetual motion.[18]

---

[15] Thackeray, 'Forign Parts', first published in *Fraser's Magazine*, 17 Apr. 1838, 404–8; repr. in *The Oxford Thackeray*, ed. G. Saintsbury (17 vols, London: Oxford University Press, 1910), i, 218–30. For Thackeray's further reprises of the Channel crossing, see 'An Invasion of France', first published in *The Corsair*, 24 Aug.1839, and repr. in *Paris Sketch Book, Oxford Thackeray*, ii, 1–13; 'From Richmond in Surrey to Brussels in Belgium', in *Little Travels and Roadside Sketches*, first published in *Fraser's Magazine*, May 1844, 517–28, and repr. in *Oxford Thackeray*, vi, 469–89; 'Some Continental Snobs', first published in *Punch*, 12 Sept. 1846, 105–6, and repr. in *The Book of Snobs, Oxford Thackeray*, ix, 376–83; W. M. Thackeray, *Vanity Fair: A Novel without a Hero*, ed. J. Sutherland (Oxford: Oxford University Press, 1991), 335.

[16] 'Paris Revisited by an Old Paris Man', first published in *Punch*, 10 Feb. 1849, repr. in *Oxford Thackeray*, viii, 467–72. Cf. *The Newcomes* (1855), *Oxford Thackeray*, xiv, 271.

[17] Sala, *Quite Alone*, ii, 45–7.

[18] Dickens's travel writing has received extensive critical attention. The brief observations made here are based upon: 'A Flight', *Household Words*, 30 Aug. 1851, 529–33; 'Our French Watering Place', *Household Words*, 4 Nov. 1854, 265–70; 'Railway Dreaming', *Household Words*, 10 May 1856, 385–8; 'Travelling Abroad', *All the Year Round*, 7 Apr. 1860, 557–62; and 'The Calais Night Mail', *All the Year Round*, 2 May 1863, 229–33. With the exception of 'Railway Dreaming', repr. in *Dickens' Journalism*, ed. M. Slater (4 vols, J. M. Dent, 1994–2000), iii, 370–76, the remaining pieces can all be found in *The Uncommercial Traveller and Reprinted Pieces*.

Fig. 3. 'The Calais Packet—Mr. Yellowplush's Emotions on First Going to Sea', by W. M. Thackeray (*Oxford Thackeray*, ed. G. Saintsbury (17 vols, London: Oxford University Press, 1910), i, 221).

Just as prepared as Thackeray to complain about the indignity of sea-sickness[19] and the various inconveniences visited on the hapless traveller, he nevertheless took a greater interest in the passing landscape the journey provided, and was prepared to strike up conversation with the motley passengers he encountered en route. Thackeray's sense of superiority to both his fellow travellers and readers is frequently replaced in Dickens by the sheer pleasure of being able to flaunt his recently acquired knowledge. In anticipation of his friend Forster's first trip to France in January 1847, Dickens, signing himself 'Français naturalisé, et Citoyen de Paris', wrote him a detailed account, in French, not only of the various stages of the journey on the French side but of the conversations he would need to have with the passport officials at Boulogne, the hotel touts, and the innkeeper. His bragging was in vain. Commenting on Dickens's advice, Forster sourly noted that such a letter was good practice at writing French correctly for a man 'who never spoke that language very well'.[20]

The finest and most detailed account of this journey, however, is to be found in Thomas Carlyle's 'Excursion (Futile Enough) to Paris; Autumn 1851: thrown on paper, pen galloping, from Saturday to Tuesday October 4–7, 1851', an entertainingly grumpy account, penned in part to persuade his wife that he was not in thrall to his Parisian hostess, Lady Ashburton. Whereas on his only previous trip in 1824 Carlyle had been a relative unknown, he was now able to activate contacts from the *Times* to the Foreign Office to obtain his passport.[21] He secured those seasoned travellers Robert and Elizabeth Barrett Browning as his travelling companions, taking advantage of Robert's bustling expertise with customs officers and coachmen to sit at ease himself, light yet another cigar, and survey the world around him. Carlyle's trenchant telegraphese incorporates mention of a religious tract distributor aboard the ferry who offered his wares in English, French, and German; evocations of the sea-sickness Carlyle seemed almost alone in avoiding; the necessity of advancing watches a quarter of an hour to adjust to French time; accounts of convenient walking tours in Dieppe; architectural details; price lists; descriptions of the passing French landscape; comments on French farming practices; and snatches of conversation with, and appraisals of, the native population.[22]

4.2 A CITY IN TRANSITION

On arrival Carlyle was keen to get his bearings in a city that had undergone substantial change in the quarter of a century since his last visit. He was able to

---

[19] 'The Calais Night Mail', in *The Uncommercial Traveller*, 179–87.

[20] *The Pilgrim Edition of the Letters of Charles Dickens*, ed. G. Storey et al. (12 vols, Oxford: Clarendon Press, 1965–2002), v, 4–5.

[21] In 1846 Thackeray told a Paris correspondent searching for biographical information about Carlyle that, despite the European scope of his writings, Carlyle had 'never been abroad at all': *The Letters and Private Papers of William Makepeace Thackeray: A Supplement*, ed. E. F. Harden (2 vols, New York: Garland, 1994), i, 177.

[22] 'Excursion (Futile Enough) to Paris; Autumn 1851', repr. in *Last Words of Thomas Carlyle* (London: Longmans, Green, 1892), 149–91.

recognize 'the Rue de la Paix and Place Vendôme', but the Rue de Rivoli, where he was staying at that resort of wealthy English travellers, the Hôtel Meurice, had been much extended.[23] In 1824 the Rue de Rivoli had run from the Place de la Concorde to the north wing of the Louvre; Charles X and Louis-Philippe had extended it further eastward, but it was in the wake of the 1848 revolution that the government realized how useful the project of removing the 800 or so houses on the dark streets and filthy lanes stretching into the Marais would be in providing much-needed work for the labouring classes.[24]

The sheer scale of centrally planned demolition and construction work, executed in a relatively circumscribed area, dwarfed the chaotic but piecemeal scars wrought on London's more sprawling territory by such developments as the coming of the railway. In 1851 Carlyle spoke of Paris *intra muros*[25] as comparable in size and activity to Dublin rather than to London's 'huge traffic and groaning wains'.[26] By the end of the century, despite the demolition of 20,000 houses and the building of 43,000 between 1852 and 1869 alone, the French capital was still two and a half times smaller than London. At the same time, the political powers of its rulers allowed them to impose progressively more concentrated social groupings on Paris, whereas the 'intense and fractured localism' that prevailed in London planning led to a more gradual incorporation of villages where rich and poor continued to live in closer proximity.[27]

The creation of new streets and the opening up of new vistas was sufficiently disorientating for returning visitors, but the Parisian habit of giving the city a political makeover at each change of regime was bewildering.[28] The Madeleine, for instance, planned as a church in pre-Revolutionary days, was re-envisaged by Napoleon I as a memorial to the Great Army, then reclaimed as a church under the Restoration, and rededicated as a monument of national reconciliation during the July Monarchy. Briefly considered for use as a railway station in 1837, it was finally consecrated as a church in 1842.

More confusing still were the name changes. What had started as Place Louis Quinze in 1755 was renamed Place de la Révolution when it housed the guillotine, becoming Place de la Concorde as a symbol of the end of the 'reign of terror'. With

---

[23] Ibid. 166.

[24] T. Forester (ed.), *Paris and its Environs: an Illustrated Handbook* (London: Henry G. Bohn, 1859), 45.

[25] A new, defensible fortification, 34 km long, had been built between 1841 and 1846. The area between this and the older, inner Farmers-General Wall, where the charging of the *octroi* or city tax commenced, attracted industries and their workforce, which were particularly concentrated in the northeast from Montmartre (18th arrondissement) down through Belleville (19th) to Ménilmontant (20th). The quarter of a kilometre inside the ramparts, where building was banned and wine escaped the *octroi*, made this a popular suburban belt for Sunday recreation. On 1 Jan. 1860 Napoleon expanded the city limits, so forming 20 arrondissements where there had formerly been 12. The arrondissement numbering in this chapter follows the post-Napoleonic numbering.

[26] Carlyle, 'Excursion', *Last Words*, 166.

[27] J. White, *London in the Nineteenth Century* (London: Jonathan Cape, 2007), 449. Cf. C. Dickens, 'A Monument of French Folly', *Household Words*, 8 Mar. 1851, 553–8, and *The Uncommercial Traveller and Reprinted Pieces*, 589–600, where he compares the self-interest of the City of London with the superiority of state-regulated hygiene in Paris.

[28] 'Street Names in Paris', *Pall Mall Gazette*, 8 Dec. 1868, 9.

the arrival of the Restoration it briefly reverted to Place Louis XV, before becoming Place Louis XVI, while during Napoleon I's 'Hundred Day' recapture of the Empire in 1815 it became Place de la Chartre. Louis-Philippe restored its title of Place de la Concorde in 1830. Trying to identify it in 1851, Carlyle offered both 'Place de la Révolution' and 'Place Louis Quinze', noting how it had been *'altogether* altered' by the installation of the Luxor Obelisk and the general smartening it and the area westward had undergone.

Nor were buildings exempt from the process of name change. The Palais-Royal, renamed Palais de l'Égalité during the 1789 revolution, became the Palais Nationale under Louis-Philippe. Napoleon III symbolized the start of his Empire by reinstituting the name of the Palais-Royal and installing his uncle there. Who could be surprised, therefore, inquired the *Daily News*'s correspondent, that it became a symbolic victim of the inferno in which the Commune ended?[29] Sala's contempt for a nation which set so much store on name changes amid civil disorder emerged when he noted that one of the first acts of the provisional government, in a nation in the throes of Napoleon III's defeat, was to send a workman to the façade of the Grand Opéra to change 'impériale' to 'nationale' in the wording, 'Académie Impériale de Musique'.[30]

These changes required mapping. Literary guidebooks proliferated, becoming (it has been claimed) 'the characteristic genre of post-revolutionary Paris'.[31] Introductions to Paris written from an individual perspective were slowly eclipsed by the more impersonal type of travellers' handbook, first popularized by Baedeker's and Murray's series in the 1820s and 1830s, and there is a growing body of scholarship devoted to travel writing of this nature. This chapter's purpose, however, is to identify the nature of the changes in the areas of the city that particularly interested mid-nineteenth-century British writers.

In their attempts to fix or produce meaningful order and relationship from the bewildering speed of material change in Paris, nineteenth-century British writers frequently froze time to produce the concentrated essence of a Paris which had probably never existed. A brief exchange from Julia Kavanagh's *Bessie* (1872), published in the immediate wake of the Commune's collapse, offers at once an example of and comment upon this process. On her first visit to Paris, the naïve young heroine wakes in a room in a Hotel Meyerbeer, overlooking the Champs-Élysées:

> My young head had got full of some odd fancies, in which chronology was little regarded, and topography ignored. I gathered in a cluster the Bastille and Notre Dame, the Seine and the Boulevards…
>
> 'Oh! Mademoiselle,' I cried, breathlessly, 'do you know where we go today?'…
>
> 'What is the matter, my dear child? The Bastille! Why that has been pulled down ages. The Tuileries are no great distance. (Alas! there were Tuileries then!), and Cours de la Reine is close by. But what can you want with that dullest of dull walks?'[32]

---

[29] *Daily News*, 26 May 1872.

[30] *The Life and Adventures of George Augustus Sala written by himself*, 2nd edn (2 vols, London: Cassell, 1895), ii, 227–8.

[31] P. P. Ferguson, *Paris as Revolution: Writing the Nineteenth-Century City* (Berkeley: University of California Press, 1994), 39.

[32] J. Kavanagh, *Bessie* (3 vols, London: Hurst & Blackett, 1872), i, 74–7.

Kavenagh

Bessie's list of sights conjures up a mythical Paris composed ~~of visitors' reliance on folk memories, rather than a visitable reality.~~ The novel lacks precise historical specificity, but the mention of the Hôtel Meyerbeer places it somewhere between the 1830s, when Meyerbeer first established himself as one of the capital's rising operatic composers, and the burning of the Tuileries palace in 1871. As an English tourist, Bessie is in search of the essence of history, while her down-to-earth French companion's response suggests that to a mid-nineteenth-century bourgeoise the Bastille's symbolic role in the 1789 Revolution is of no more consequence than are Royal gardens and palaces. Furthermore, when the two women agree on their itinerary, choosing the brightly lit galleries of the Palais-Royal, Bessie knows that she has succumbed to 'the weakness of the flesh' and is privileging a Paris of 'unflagging gaiety' and consumerism over the search for the places where 'the sorrowful and illustrious dead' had once trod the city's streets.

A recent claim that Dickens knew nothing of the Faubourg Saint-Antoine, where the scenes of urban poverty and revolution are set in *The Tale of Two Cities*, may or may not be factually correct,[33] but it is surely more to the point that Dickens would have been aware that this area was also off the beaten track of his average British reader and, most importantly, that the much-changed Paris of the 1850s could not serve as template for descriptions of late eighteenth-century Paris.[34]

By contrast, other British novelists sought to achieve historical authenticity by locating their plots 'in the days when' such and such a street had still existed. Although not on a par with Joyce's painstaking recreation of 16 June 1904 in Dublin, novels such as Sala's *Quite Alone*, Braddon's *Under the Red Flag*, and Du Maurier's *Trilby* appear to have prided themselves on their ability to plot their characters' journeys across recently demolished parts of the city.

4.3 PARIS PRE-HAUSSMANN

Carlyle's detailed description of his 1851 visit neatly summarizes the alterations made under Louis-Philippe's regime, while providing a snapshot of Paris two months before Napoleon III and the *soi-disant* Baron Haussmann (1809–91) embarked on their ambitious programme. His systematic explorations of all four compass points leading from his hotel on the Rue de Rivoli; his repeated visits to the Champ de Mars (7th arrondissement), site of military displays and national festivals; his ventures into the suburban villages of Passy and Auteuil (16th), and through the Bois de Boulogne, as yet 'a dirty, scrubby place', suggest a city whose economic and social climate might still change abruptly at a street corner, revealing enclaves of squalid poverty within easy walking distance of the fine buildings and monuments which had been built or refurbished since his last visit. These last

---

[33] A letter of 27 Jan. 1856 records, 'Yesterday I turned to the right when I got outside the Barrière de l'Étoile, walked round the wall till I came to the river, and then entered Paris beyond the site of the Bastille. Today I mean to turn to the left when I get outside the Barrière': *Letters of Charles Dickens*, ed. Storey et al., viii, 37.

[34] A claim made in C. Jones, J. McDonagh, and J. Mee (eds), *Charles Dickens*, A Tale of Two Cities *and the French Revolution* (Basingstoke: Palgrave Macmillan, 2009), 13.

included the July column, the Hôtel de Ville and Palais de Justice in the east, and the Place de la Concorde and Arc de Triomphe de l'Étoile in the west. In the winding, narrow streets behind the Rue Saint-Honoré (1st arrondissement), he noted a 'block of half-demolished buildings still standing' occupied by 'the forlorn of the earth'. He also remarked how to the east and north of the city the 'old houses seemed older and more dilapidated', and how, among the 'crowds of poor-looking people, a bourgeois, in clean linen and coat' only occasionally made an appearance.

The wealth and activity of the city had been slowly migrating towards the northern and western sectors of the city, towards the shops of the *grands boulevards*. In the wake of the banning of gambling houses throughout France on 1 January 1838, the fashionable crowd had deserted the Palais-Royal, until the mid-1830s their favoured haunt for shopping, gaming, and socializing, and it now bore a neglected air.[35] In 1845 Wilkie Collins had already noted that 'the Palais Royal is now encased in denser clouds of tobacco smoke and more crammed with heterogenous crowd of people, every evening, than ever I saw it before'.[36]

By contrast, in the twenty-seven years since Carlyle's previous visit, the arcades, mainly to be found in the first and second arrondissements, had mushroomed. These passageways, covered in iron and glass and lined with shops, which for Walter Benjamin were to epitomize the apex of the capitalist dream and the seductive pursuits of modern consumerism, receive only passing reference from Carlyle: he bought a 'Nero's *collar and string* (gift for my wife), at the top of the Rue de la Paix; cigars a little further on' and used another passageway to avoid a downpour.[37]

In Benjamin's opinion the heyday of the arcades was to be short-lived, as Haussmannization developed the *grands boulevards* to their detriment.[38] If this was so, their heyday almost passed the British by. Perhaps because they were already familiar with the concept from the London arcades, mid-century British writers paid remarkably little attention to them.[39] Frances Trollope, feeling by the midway point of *Paris and the Parisians* (1836) that her female readers might be tiring of her attention to high culture, did allude to the 'Passages' as Paris's latest 'ornamental invention', remarking on the way in which they were adorned by fresh flowers. However, she considered the *grands magasins* of Paris to be smaller, less well stocked, and inferior in the quality of their materials to their London counterparts. Even shopping expeditions, she claimed, carried the risk of veering suddenly into more dangerous precincts. Venturing on foot to a haberdasher just beyond the environs of the Bourse, into the Marché des Innocents, which formed part of the Les Halles market complex, and seeing a crowd of some fifty or sixty people, she instantly feared that it might be the harbinger of some fresh revolution.[40]

---

[35] Carlyle, 'Excursion', *Last Words*, 175, 177.

[36] *The Letters of Wilkie Collins*, ed. W. Baker and W. Clarke (2 vols, London: Macmillan, 1999), i, 27–8.

[37] Carlyle, 'Excursion', *Last Words*, 184, 186.

[38] W. Benjamin, *Charles Baudelaire: A Lyric Poet in the Era of High Capitalism*, trans. H. Zohn (London: NLB, 1973), 35–51.

[39] For further discussion of their relation see M. Hollington, 'Dickens, Sala, and the London Arcades', *Dickens Quarterly* 28(4) (Dec. 2011), 273–84.

[40] F. Trollope, *Paris and the Parisians in 1835* (2 vols, Paris: Baudry's European Library, 1836), ii, 1–10, 227–8.

Neither did the novelist and long-time Paris resident Catherine Gore single out the arcades for attention in her various descriptions of the city, though she was far more appreciative than Frances Trollope of the shopping opportunities presented by Paris's 'boulevarts' [*sic*] where 'even the sun seem[ed] to shine more brightly'.[41] Her 1842 guide was quite specific in pinpointing the Rue de Richelieu, the Rue Vivienne, and the Rue de la Bourse (1st and 2nd) as offering the heartland of Paris's shopping territory, and the rectangle described by the Faubourg Saint-Honoré, the Tuileries Gardens, and the Faubourg Saint-Germain south of the river as the fashionable area of the city much favoured by English visitors.[42]

Carlyle was more interested in socioeconomic contrasts than in the fashionable quarter where he was staying. He merely waited while Lord Ashburton visited his club on the Rue de la Paix ('*Club* of Frenchmen chiefly, and of some *étrangers*, near the boulevards)', and during his one trip to the Comédie Française on the Rue de Richelieu paid more attention to the audience than to the 'worthless racket and cackle' proceeding from the stage.[43] If Paris's legitimate theatre could be so dismissed, it was as well that no one invited Carlyle to attend the melodramas playing on the Rue Saint-Martin or the Boulevard Montmartre, or stroll further east along the Boulevard du Temple (3rd/11th). Gore gave it as her opinion that respectable visitors would do well to venture no further east than the latter boulevard,[44] often known as the 'Boulevard du crime' on account of the tenor of the shocking and violent plays enacted in the many theatres located there.

To the south of the Seine, on the left bank, were two further areas of interest to British writers: the Faubourg Saint-Germain (7th) and the Latin Quarter (6th). In *Greville, or, a Season in Paris* (1841), a novel which Catherine Gore was writing concurrently with her guidebook, *Paris in 1841* (1842), she used the contrast between the tastes of two young Englishmen, the one bourgeois and the other aristocratic, to illustrate the social distance between the very mixed society frequenting the restaurants in the Palais Royal and the far more select company of the Faubourg Saint-Germain, where the aristocracy lived in their *hôtels particuliers, entre cours et jardin*. Comparatively cheaply priced land on the left bank had allowed these grand town houses to incorporate charming courtyards, sometimes to be glimpsed through an open *porte-cochère*, and beyond the mansion itself a quiet, enclosed garden was frequently to be found. This double barrier from the sounds, smells, and sights of street life formed a mark of exclusivity.

Since the Revolution, however, few aristocrats could afford to occupy an entire mansion, and many of the more substantial buildings had been taken over by religious communities, government ministries, charitable endowments, and hospitals.[45] The famous mental asylum La Salpêtrière, lodged in this quarter, afforded Frances Trollope twenty minutes horrified fascination as she watched

[41] Gore, *Greville*, i, 93.
[42] C. Gore, *Paris in 1841* (London: Longman, Brown, Green, and Longmans, 1842), 207, 220.
[43] Carlyle, 'Excursion', *Last Words*, 178, 162–4.
[44] Gore, *Paris in 1841*, 255.
[45] A. T. Ritchie, *Chapters from Some Memoirs* (London: Macmillan, 1894), 7; Gore, *Paris in 1841*, 183–4.

the inhabitants taking their exercise in the courtyard: the asylum would form the setting for many a Gothic tale.[46]

Neither Gore nor Trollope, however, saw fit to discuss the ambience created by the student garrets and boarding houses of the Latin Quarter in their guides to the city: instead they confined their observations to the architecture of the churches and colleges spanning the left bank between the Faubourg Saint-Germain to the west (7th arrondissement) and the Jardin des Plantes, or zoological gardens, to the east (5th). Perhaps they were too painfully conscious of the truth of Bulwer Lytton's remark: 'At Paris, how slender is the line that divides the authoress from the *Bohémienne*.'[47]

Many a young British male, studying medicine, law, or art by day and attempting to supplement his income by journalism at night, chose the cheap lodgings available in the neighbourhood of the Sorbonne and the Panthéon, but the Latin Quarter's bohemian excess seem, as this book's final chapter will demonstrate, to have been as much a matter of literary myth as of lived experience. Thackeray, for instance, who would proudly refer to a period of his life in the early 1830s when he 'was as poor as Job: and sketched away most abominably, but pretty contented: and we used to meet in each others' little rooms and talk about Art and smoke pipes and drink bad brandy & water',[48] was careful to established the credentials of his fictional alter ego, Michael Angelo Titmarsh, by domiciling him 'up a hundred and thirty-seven steps in the remote quarter of the Luxembourg'.[49] In reality Thackeray had done little more than flirt with the bohemian life of the left bank, having been obliged, throughout much of his artistic phase, to return each night to his demanding and critical British grandmother's more respectable rental accommodation on the right bank.[50]

4.4 HAUSSMANNIZATION

Napoleon III and Haussmann's work in remodelling the city was based upon the notion of easier circulation of air, traffic, and troops—that is to say, improved health, better communications, and a rule of law and order more readily imposed on the clear vistas of wide boulevards than in narrow winding alleys.[51] For British writers, such developments represented a major change in the way in which they experienced the city. As a male, and a keen walker, Carlyle faced few bars to his explorations, but during Louis-Philippe's reign unescorted women's opportunities were far more limited, if they were reluctant to make themselves conspicuous by

---

[46] F. Trollope, *Paris and the Parisians*, ii, 163–4. Cf. 'The Self-Devoted', a two-chapter tale inset within G. W. M. Reynolds, *Pickwick Abroad: or, The Tour in France* (London: Sherwood, Gilbert, & Piper, 1839), 283–94.

[47] Lord [E. G. E. L. Bulwer-]Lytton, *The Parisians* (2 vols, London: George Routledge, 1875), i, 320.

[48] *Letters of Thackeray*, ed. Ray, ii, 503.

[49] 'A Caution to Travellers', in *Paris Sketch Book*, Oxford Thackeray, 24.

[50] *Letters of Thackeray*, ed. Ray, i, 286–91.

[51] An accessible, well-illustrated summary can be found in M. Gaillard, *Paris Sous le Second Empire au temps de Charles Baudelaire* (Étrépilly: Presses du Village, 2002).

resorting to journeys either on foot or in an open cabriolet.[52] The explosion of state-regulated transport options under the Second Empire elicited an article by Blanchard Jerrold particularly praising the growth of the omnibus service, which, having started with ten routes in 1828, by 1855 boasted 400 omnibuses and waiting-rooms to ensure women's safety at changeover points.[53]

Starting from the west, the Arc de Triomphe offered a hub to which Haussmann added further spokes. Anne Thackeray Ritchie recalled played at the base of this monument as a child in the days of Louis-Philippe, coming there daily from her grandparents' apartment in an old hôtel on the Avenue Sainte-Marie, a road leading from the Faubourg du Roule (renamed the Faubourg Saint-Honoré after 1847). The faded glory of this hôtel, with its central courtyard and Italian garden, was swept away, as was the convent opposite, in the course of the city's refashioning.[54] This development, together with the extension and broadening of the Rue de Rivoli from the Palais-Royal to the Marais, and thence, via the Rue Saint-Antoine, to the Place de la Bastille, involved wholesale demolition of the housing on the small streets behind these major thoroughfares, and so inevitably diminished the accommodation previously available to the poorer members of an English colony who had typically lodged in the narrow back streets between the Champs-Élysées and the Place Vendôme.

A more northern radial from the Arc de Triomphe would eventually form the Boulevard Haussmann, ending at the renovated eastern Place du Château d'Eau (subsequently to become Place la République.) Meanwhile the creation of the Boulevard Malesherbes, leading from the Madeleine to the Parc Monceau, not only destroyed further cheap housing but attracted visitors who would formerly have chosen the Chaussée d'Antin as a fashionable address.

The rebuilding of Paris's central marketplace, Les Halles, to encompass the city's overflowing and chaotic food supplies under vast roofs constructed of iron and glass, was a microcosmic version of the entire Haussmannian project, in its aim of imposing order and countering health hazards. In its turn, Les Halles, or 'the Belly of Paris' as Émile Zola dubbed it in his novel, *Le Ventre de Paris* (1873), became symptomatic of the Second Empire: a spectacle of flagrant materialism, a hotbed of gossip and a site of surveillance.

Nor did Haussmann neglect the left bank. Boulevard Saint-Michel now formed the southwards continuation of the Boulevard de Sébastopol, and was intersected by the Boulevard Saint-Germain, which paralleled the Rue de Rivoli across the river and so cut straight through the heart of the traditionally subversive Latin Quarter. The remodelling of the Île de la Cité as a river-crossing site for official buildings drove many of the poor, the criminal classes, and those who had worked along the *quais* out to the suburbs in search of accommodation. Nevertheless, some narrow alleyways of higgledy-piggledy, much subdivided houses, often dating back to the medieval period, did survive on the left bank, and it was increasingly here that British novelists placed their poorer characters. Mary Braddon, for instance, in *Under*

---

[52] H. S. Edwards, *Personal Recollections* (London: Cassell, 1900), 5.

[53] B. Jerrold, 'Paris upon Wheels', in *Imperial Paris; including new scenes for old visitors* (London: Bradbury & Evans, 1855), 227–38.

[54] Ritchie, *Chapters*, 33.

the Red Flag has her two poor, convent-educated Irish girls make their way into Paris of the 1860s via the 'wilderness of stone and plaster' that characterized the construction of the northern boulevards, before they come upon the central cafés, fountains, gardens, and monuments, and finally cross to the left bank and find Rue Gît-le-Coeur, 'a shabby little street' near the Quai des Augustins (5th arrondissement).[55] Here they live in a small neighbourhood of artisans, shopkeepers, journalists, and labourers. It was this community, well outside the square mile known to English tourists, which, in Braddon's version of events, fostered the political resentment that produced the Commune.

Similarly, the northern and eastern outskirts of the city were a closed book to British visitors, and when the journalist Henry Vizetelly set out to examine the doss-houses, shanty-towns, and tunnels of the gypsum quarries, housing the city's the refuse sorters, water carriers, foreign factory workers, thieves, and prostitutes, he hired an off-duty policeman for his protection.[56]

4.5 BRITISH REACTIONS TO HAUSSMANNIZATION

When Thackeray looked at the home his mother and stepfather had moved to by 1851, he wrote, 'somehow it's a dismal end to a career. A famous beauty and soldier who has been in 20 battles and led a half dozen of storming parties to end in a garret.' He added that it was not so much their poverty that upset him, but 'the undignified dignity' in which these remnants of a former age were now forced to conduct themselves in a society which, as the Second Empire progressed, would become ever more based upon wealth and the appearance of wealth.[57] The previous December, Dickens had found another impecunious exile, the once famous British dramatist John Poole, narrowly avoiding starvation by 'trembling and staggering over a small wood fire' in a fifth-storey room in a house 'in the Rue Neuve Luxembourg'.[58] Such a haunt, along with the furnished rooms or 'garnis' for 15 sous a night, or the all-night wine shops of Les Halles to which Sala claimed Englishmen down on their luck repaired,[59] would soon disappear in the Haussmannian remoulding of the heart of the city.

Nevertheless, Dickens was inclined to a positive view of these developments. In October 1853 he wrote to his wife:

> Paris...wonderfully improving, Thousands of houses must have been pulled down for the construction of an immense street now making from the dirty old end of the Rue de Tivoli,[*sic*] past the Palais Royal, away beyond the Hotel de Ville. It will be the finest thing in Europe. The quays are Macademized and as clean, as Regent Street. Indeed the general improvement in the essential articles of what is to be seen and what is to be smelt, is highly remarkable.[60]

[55] M. E. Braddon, *Under the Red Flag* (Leipzig: Tauchnitz, 1884), 20.
[56] [H. Vizetelly,] 'Night Rambles in Paris', *Pall Mall Gazette*, 3, 5, 6, 9 and 13 June 1868.
[57] *Letters of Thackeray*, ed. Ray, ii, 732–3.
[58] *Letters of Charles Dickens*, ed. Storey et al., vi, 239–40.
[59] Sala, *Quite Alone*, ii, 223.
[60] *Letters of Charles Dickens*, ed. Storey et al., vii, 163.

Nine years later he exclaimed to W. H. Wills, his subeditor on *Household Words*, 'I couldn't find my way to the Poste Restante, without looking at a Map!—I suppose I have been there, at least 50 times before. Wherever I turn, I see some astounding new work, doing or done.'[61] Given that Dickens's first visit to the city was in 1847, he had scarcely had time to develop nostalgia, and Wills dutifully toed the party line by celebrating 'Paris Improved' in the magazine in November 1855, comparing the rapidity with which solid change had been brought about to the planners' blight that affected London.[62]

Admittedly, the rubble, plaster dust, and earth thrown up as old buildings were razed and new ones erected, sewers laid, and gas lighting installed caused grumbling. Only a year after Wills's panegyric Dickens was complaining, 'It is difficult to picture the change made in this place by the removal of the paving stones (too ready for barricades) and macadamisation...We are again in a sea of mud. One cannot cross the road of the Champs Elysées here, without being half over one's boots.' Roaming further afield simply guaranteed that this 'sea' turned into 'oceans of mud': 'In desperation I went outside the Barriers last Sunday on a headlong walk, and came back with topboots of mud on, and my very eyebrows smeared with mud. Georgina is usually invisible during the walking time of the day. A turned-up nose may be seen in the midst of a heap of splashes—but nothing more.'[63]

As pavements were created along the new wide boulevards, so the lot of the hapless pedestrian, previously subject to the mud churned up in narrow streets never designed for coaches, began to improve. Surveying the changes that had taken place between 1856 and 1862, Elizabeth Gaskell recalled that in the Latin Quarter, where there was now a 'broad new artery', there had formerly been scarcely room 'for one uncrinolined person to walk', and passing carriages had created a 'dado of mud' on the houses of its narrow streets, though the inhabitants of the grander hôtels had always been protected by their porter's lodges and stables from the filth of the streets.[64] The insouciance of the aristocracy in the bad old days is well illustrated by Lady Blessington's displeasure at 'the negligence and bad management of the persons whose duty it is to remove the snow or mud from the streets', thus rendering them 'exceedingly disagreeable to those who have carriages', and her consequent thrill when the snow lay thick enough to permit her set to use their highly decorated sledges.[65] Dickens would caricature such aristocratic indifference to the plight of poorer inhabitants in the incident in *A Tale of Two Cities* where the Marquis St Evrémonde finds it 'rather agreeable...to see the common people dispersed before his horses', and kills a child in the 'wild rattle and clatter' with which his carriage proceeds.[66]

Looking back from the late 1880s over fifty years of visiting Paris, Frances Trollope's son, Thomas Adolphus Trollope, could only marvel at what had been

---

[61] Ibid., Oct. 1862, x, 151.
[62] [W. H. Wills,] 'Paris Improved', *Household Words*, 17 Nov. 1855, 361–5.
[63] *Letters of Charles Dickens*, ed. Storey et al., viii, 33,15.
[64] E. C. Gaskell, 'French Life', first published in *Fraser's Magazine* 69 (Apr.–June 1864), 435–9, 575–85, 739–52, and repr. in *The Works of Elizabeth Gaskell*, ed. J. Shattock et al. (10 vols, London: Pickering & Chatto, 2005–6), i, 359.
[65] The Countess of Blessington, *The Idler in France* (2 vols, London: Henry Colburn, 1841), ii, 130.
[66] C. Dickens, *A Tale of Two Cities*, ed. A. Sanders (Oxford: Oxford University Press, 2008), 105.

achieved in his own lifetime: he detected a transformation 'far more radical' in nature than any London could boast:

> [T]o those who remember the streets of Louis Philippe's city, the change in the whole conception of city life, and the manière d'être of the population, is far greater. With the exception of the principal boulevards in the neighbourhood of the recently completed Madeleine, and its then recently completed flower market, the streets were still traversed by filthy and malodorous open ditches, which did more or less imperfectly the duty of sewers, and Paris still deserved its name of 'Mudtown'. Wretched little oil lamps, suspended on ropes stretched across the streets, barely served to make darkness visible. Water was still carried at so much the bucket up the interminable staircases of the Parisian houses.[67]

The introduction of an efficient sewerage system and the supply of running water to houses, arranged on a grid coordinated with the new street plan, contributed— at least for those who frequented the wealthier parts of the right bank—to the sense of Paris as a healthier city, no longer contaminated by heaps of rotting rubbish, and less subject to the ravages of typhoid and recurrent outbreaks of cholera. 'No sooner do I get to Paris than the cough vanishes... the lightness of the air here makes the place tenable,' wrote Elizabeth Barrett Browning late in the autumn of 1851.[68] When Napoleon III hosted Queen Victoria's state visit in August 1855, she was based in the semi-rural surroundings of Saint-Cloud, and her carriage progress through this 'most beautiful and the gayest of cities, with its high handsome houses, in every one of which there is a shop' was of course confined to the spruced-up areas; but she was repeatedly struck by the way in which the absence of the industrial smog that bedevilled London not only made 'everything white and bright' and produced 'a brilliancy of effect that is indescribable', but by 'the air' which 'is so light and so clear, and so devoid of our baneful coal smoke, that everything in the greatest distance is seen quite clearly and distinctly'.[69]

So ingrained in the British cultural imagination is the concept of the Victorian city as harbouring pestilence that tributes to nineteenth-century Paris's recuperative powers strike a surprising note. Dante Gabriel Rossetti decided to splash out in 1860 by spending the first week of his honeymoon in the Hôtel Meurice and a second week in nearby cheaper lodgings, because Lizzie always seemed healthier in Paris; and it was Bulwer Lytton's decision to recuperate in Paris from a severe illness that afforded the long, hard gaze at the last days of the Empire which resulted in his last novel, *The Parisians*.[70] Nevertheless, in sweltering weather, conditions in the old apartments on the left bank could still prove unpleasant. Elizabeth Gaskell told a friend that during July 1861, when she stayed with the Mohls, who lived on

---

[67] T. A. Trollope, *What I Remember*, ed. H. van Thal (London: William Kimber, 1973), 84–5.

[68] *The Letters of Elizabeth Barrett Browning*, ed. F. G. Kenyon, 2nd edn (2 vols, London: Smith, Elder, 1897), ii, 23.

[69] *Queen Victoria: Leaves from a Journal: A Record of the Visit of the Emperor and Empress of the French to the Queen, and of the Visit of the Queen and H.R.H the Prince Consort to the Emperor of the French*, 1855, intro. R. Mortimer (London: André Deutsch, 1961), 76, 87, 94.

[70] *The Correspondence of Dante Gabriel Rossetti*, ed. W. E. Fredeman et al. (8 vols, Cambridge: D. S. Brewer, 2002–9), ii, 298–9. Bulwer Lytton, *Parisians*, vol. i, pp. v–vi.

the fourth and fifth floor of 120 Rue du Bac (7th), 'Paris altogether was abominable; noisy, hot, close, smelling of drains—*and*—perpetual cooking, &c; and we were none of us well there.'[71]

British visitors, made happy by their improved physical surroundings, were less likely to share the economic and political scepticism of Parisian residents who variously feared compulsory purchase, inflationary prices, and an influx of the labouring classes, or saw in the whole programme an attempt to mask poverty and curb insurrection. Bulwer Lytton's *The Parisians* was exceptional in describing a city where the bitterness and envy of the dispossessed is held at bay only by the government's capacity to continue to pay the labouring masses for building work. With the benefit of hindsight, he recognized that the speculative investment in new building by the financier classes had been a bubble bound to burst. Nevertheless, despite these political reservations, he dismissed sentimental nostalgia for the old Paris as tiresome affectation: the regrets of an Orléanist Vicomte are pilloried as the self-indulgence of a man constantly lamenting an illusory Golden Age:

> 'I miss the dear Paris of old—the streets associated with my *beaux jours* are no more. Is there not something drearily monotonous in these interminable perspectives? How frightfully the way lengthens before one's eyes! In the twists and curves of the old Paris one was relieved of the pain of seeing how far one had to go from one spot to another— each tortuous street had a separate idiosyncrasy; what picturesque diversities, what interesting recollections—all swept away!'[72]

Elizabeth Gaskell might regret the 'great loss to memory and that kind of imagination which loves to repeople places', but on balance felt that such nostalgia was outweighed by the 'clear passage for air and light' effected in the 'picturesque, historical, dirty, and unhealthy' Latin Quarter.[73]

John Ruskin might have been expected to mount an impassioned campaign in favour of retaining the old medieval quarters, but he was surprisingly ambivalent about the Haussmannian project: he was in any case reluctant to align himself with Victor Hugo's tendency to glamorize the criminal life and poverty associated with former working-class enclaves such as Île de la Cité.[74] His fear lest other cities should be redesigned as copies of the Champs-Élysées was prompted more by fear for fine European Gothic cathedrals than by any desire to save dilapidated medieval alleyways.[75] He might disapprove aesthetically of the 'stout handkerchief knot' motif on the columns in the Rue de Rivoli, but felt nevertheless that 'Paris in its own peculiar character of bright magnificence had...everything to gain, from the gorgeous prolongation of the Rue Rivoli'.[76] It is true that Gustave Doré's illustrations to Émile de La Bédollière's *Le Nouveau Paris* (1860), which began with a

[71] *The Letters of Mrs Gaskell*, ed. J. V.Chapple and A. Pollard (Manchester: Manchester University Press, 1966), 925.

[72] Bulwer Lytton, *Parisians*, i, 121.

[73] 'French Life', in *Works of Elizabeth Gaskell*, ed. Shattock et al., i, 359.

[74] *The Works of John Ruskin*, ed. E. T. Cook and A. Wedderburn (39 vols, London: George Allen; New York: Longmans, Green, 1903–12), xxxiv, 277.

[75] Ibid. xii, 426.   [76] Ibid. ix, 257.

frontispiece (Fig. 4) depicting labourers cheering as Paris's medieval towers and spires were carted away, provoked Ruskin to a diatribe about the 'interminable lines of massy streets, wearisome with repetition of commonest design, and degraded by their gilded shops, wide-fuming, flaunting, glittering, with apparatus of eating or of dress', but this was as much a denunciation of the consumerism of the Second Empire as of the boulevards' architectural aesthetic. He disapproved of the hotch-potch created on the riverside where the gleaming flanks of the palace now abutted a river cumbered with barges and swimming baths, but these contrasts were part of the fascination Paris held for him as 'a fiend-city with fair eyes; for ever letting fall her silken raiment so far as that one may "behold her bosom and half her side"'.[77]

After Napoleon's defeat, Ruskin conceded that the Emperor's architectural pro-gramme had consisted of 'pulling down lovely buildings, and putting up frightful ones carved all over with L.N.s', but the decline in standards at the Hôtel Meurice in the early years of the Third Republic, when sugar tongs were no longer provided and sugar derived from sugar beet had replaced brown sugar derived from sugar cane, seemed to concern him almost as much.[78]

4.6 ACCOMMODATION

Then as now, securing suitable accommodation in Paris was a major concern for the British visitor, and especially for those who made their living by writing. Living centrally, for instance, was important for foreign correspondents, but carried asso-ciated disadvantages. Joseph Crowe remembered the hard work involved in carry-ing supplies to their apartment on the fifth floor when his father decided in 1834 to move the family in from the village of Les Batignolles to the Rue deu Vingt-Neuf-Juillet, immediately north of the Rue de Rivoli.[79] Since the Parisian diet of pre-Haussmannian days was largely based upon takeaways from *traiteurs*, or cook-shops selling prepared ingredients, both the food and the fuel necessary for its reheating had to be hauled up endless stairs to the apartment.

Higher land prices in central Paris led to tall buildings with accommodation arranged horizontally; so the higher the apartment, the cheaper the rent and the poorer the occupant. As Frances Trollope commented:

> It would not be easy, perhaps, to find any city in which the price of a dwelling is more accurately proportioned to its value, than Paris. Everything seems taken into consid-eration. The common blessings of light and air; the comparative vicinity to all points of favourite or necessary resort; the number of stairs to be climbed up and scrambled down—all and everything is brought to account.[80]

The capacity to move, uncomplainingly, one flight higher indeed becomes symp-tomatic of the altruism of the heroine of her novel *Fashionable Life* (1856).

[77] Ibid. xix, 114–15.   [78] Ibid. xxvii, 171; xxviii, 209.
[79] J. Crowe, *Reminiscences of Thirty-Five Years of My Life* (London: John Murray, 1895), 8.
[80] F. Trollope, *Fashionable Life; or, Paris and London* (3 vols, London: Hurst & Blackett, 1856), ii, 259.

Fig. 4. Frontispiece by Gustave Doré for Émile de La Bédollière, *Le Nouveau Paris: histoire de ses vingt arrondissements en 1860* (by courtesy of the Getty Research Institute, Los Angeles (3004–924)).

Women writers tended to show a particular interest in the social implications of these arrangements. Elizabeth Gaskell reflected that the system of having concierges and their families on twenty-four-hour duty, and servants living as well as working alongside their mistresses, had much to commend it in terms of security, economy, and the servants' moral welfare. Eliza Lynn Linton felt that the inevitable contact between the various conditions and classes as they passed each other on the staircases of these buildings must inevitably have a beneficial effect in refining the habits of the Parisian lower classes.[81] Hers was an unusual attitude: for the most part, British novelists tended to emphasize the multiple perils arising from various social strata living at such close quarters. The entire plot of Henrietta Jenkin's novel *Once and Again* (1865) springs from the tiered arrangements of the house in the Rue de Varennes (7th), in which a widowed Englishwoman and her 8-year-old daughter take up residence at the start of the novel. The lonely child makes friends both with the Marquis who lives in the grandest apartment beneath them and with the family and student lodger of the drunken, wife-beating French professor who lodges on the top floor. The class tensions, conflicts, and misunderstandings set afoot here will determine the future trajectory of the girl's life, loves, marriage, and early widowhood. Worse still, it is suggested, such chance communities offer little by way of structures of deference or mutual loyalty. The down-on–his-luck professor in the attic regions introduces a confidence trickster, picked up at a café in the Palais Royal, to the household, and this conman then passes off his mistress as maid to the widow and her daughter on the second floor, while simultaneously attempting to secure the widow's affections and money.

In the days before lifts and elevators, hotel accommodation was similarly tiered, with wealthier guests occupying the lower floors. Carlyle was distinctly peeved to find that he had been placed in a 'naked, noisy room' on the fourth floor of the Hôtel Meurice, with a balcony overlooking the noisy Rue de Rivoli, while Lord and Lady Ashburton occupied a 'sumptuous' suite; he demanded to be transferred to a room facing the interior courtyard on the following night.[82] But then Lord Ashburton travelled in style: when he fell ill in Paris in October 1863 he occupied the *entresol* [mezzanine level] for some months at the nearby Hotel Bristol (Rue du Faubourg Saint-Honoré), accompanied by ten servants, including his own physician and cook. Such was the prestige of *entresol* rooms that in Jenkin's *Once and Again*, when the widow returns to Paris, anxious to obtain a fashionable match for her daughter, the two women starve themselves in order to take rooms on that level, while a more knowing French family, with whom they have been travelling, by taking fifth floor rooms in the same hotel save sufficient money to allow them to eat out.[83]

Hotels in the English quarter were notoriously expensive. Margaret Oliphant recalled how she had been had saved from embarrassment when, as an impecunious widow, travelling back with her small children from Italy where her husband had died in 1859, she had naïvely taken her sister-in-law's advice, received 'at second, or third hand, through Mr. Pentland', to opt for the Hotel Bristol:

---

[81] [Linton,] 'French Domesticity', *Household Words*, 24 June 1854, 434–8.
[82] Carlyle, 'Excursion', in *Last Words*, 162–7.
[83] [H. Jenkin,] *Once and Again: A Novel* (3 vols, London: Smith, Elder, 1865), ii, 5–7.

The rooms were delightful, but so were the prices...I faltered, and said we had been sent there by Mr Pentland—but—The name acted like magic. Mr Pentland—ah! that was another thing—the rooms were just half the price to a friend of Mr. Pentland. He was the editor of Murray's Handbooks—but of that important fact I was not aware.[84]

Writers intent on staying for any length of time, especially when accompanied by their families, usually found renting the best option. The extensive descriptions of the various apartments Lady Blessington and her husband viewed in the summer of 1828 formed a veritable snobs' guide for rich British visitors. Deciding that one house they had already viewed twice was too small to accommodate their needs, the Countess haughtily observed: 'In England, a person of the Maréchal's rank who had a house to let would not show it *in propriâ personâ*, but would delegate that task, as also the terms and negotiations, to some agent.' A second house in 'the Rue St. Honoré, *entre cour et jardin*, a few doors from the English embassy' failed to please because the entrance led through the dining room and so 'the odour of dinner must enter the *salons*'. Finally, they considered themselves lucky in securing an hôtel in the Faubourg Saint-Germain, offering views over the Seine to the Tuileries gardens. Although unfurnished, its décor conveyed 'the splendour that marked the dwellings of the imperial *noblesse*, and some notion of it may be conceived from the fact that the decorations of its walls alone cost a million of francs'. The problem of finding appropriate furnishings was solved when Lady Blessington discovered not only that they could be rented 'by the quarter, half, or whole year' but that the rental sum would be taken into account should they decided to purchase the furniture at the end of the year.[85] How she would have admired Queen Victoria's prudence in deciding to take back to England, as one of the perks of costly state travel, the toiletry items decorated with her initials, which had been provided by the Emperor for her stay at the palace of Saint-Cloud.[86]

The crowning glory of the Hôtel Ney, however, which Lady Blessington eventually decided upon, was its historical pedigree. She was thrilled by the notion that it was in the principal drawing room that the news had been broken to the Princesse de la Moskowa of her husband Marshal Ney's death sentence at the hands of a Restoration firing squad in 1815. True, Lady Blessington had momentarily been so moved that she had briefly considered refusing the hôtel, but then she 'remembered that such is the fate of mankind; that there are no houses in which scenes of misery have not taken place.' Her only remaining worry was 'how, after it, shall we ever be able to reconcile ourselves to the comparatively dingy rooms in St. James's Square, which no furniture or decoration could render any thing like the Hôtel Ney?'[87]

Dickens was equally desirous to impress with the apartment he took in the winter of 1846 at 48 Rue de Courcelles, Fauborg Saint-Honoré. Not only was it owned by the Marquis de Castellane but, as he told virtually all his correspondents, it was 'a gentleman's house, and not one furnished to let': it had formerly been occupied

[84] *The Autobiography of Margaret Oliphant*, ed. E. Jay (Oxford: Oxford University Press, 1990), 88.
[85] Blessington, *Idler in France*, i, 90, 91, 98, 109.
[86] *Queen Victoria: Leaves from a Journal*, intro. Mortimer, 140.
[87] Blessington, *Idler in France*, i, 105–7, 117.

by Henry Bulwer, a senior diplomat at the British Embassy. Unfortunately, the extreme cold that winter made it costly to heat the draughty house where no door or window seemed to fit properly. By the beginning of December this was even beginning to have a detrimental effect on his work:

> [I] have been most hopelessly out of sorts—writing sorts; that's all. Couldn't begin, in the strange place; took a violent dislike to my study. And came down into the draw-ing-room; couldn't find a corner that would answer my purpose; fell into a black contemplation of the waning month; sat six hours at a stretch, and wrote as many lines, &C. &c. &c.... Then, you know what arrangements are necessary with the chairs and tables; and then what correspondence had to be cleared off; and then how I tried to settle to my desk, and went about and about it, and dodged at it, like a bird at a lump of sugar.[88]

During his next prolonged stay with his family in the winter of 1855–6, the fact that the *entresol*, together with the first floor, a 'slap-up' kitchen, and servants' quarters, at the top of No. 49 Avenue des Champs-Élysées afforded plenty of room for moving the furniture around acted as an additional inducement for preferring it to a more elegantly furnished residence on the Rue Faubourg Saint-Honoré. However, his sister-in-law and right-hand woman, Georgie, complained that her bedroom was so dirty that it smelt, so Dickens summoned 'the porter, the porter's wife, the porter's wife's sister, a feeble upholsterer of enormous age from round the corner, and all his workmen (4 boys)' and insisted on a thorough clean-ing and the replacement of all the carpets and hangings before the rest of his family moved in.[89]

French interior arrangements were sufficiently distinct from the dark, cluttered décor that characterized many Victorian rooms that they merited comment: Gaskell and Linton, for instance, discoursed at length on the comparative sparsity and formality of the furniture in the main room of French apartments; the prefer-ence for highly polished tiles or parquet flooring, supplemented by the occasional rug, and the obligatory 'garniture de cheminée', or mantelpiece adornments of mirror, ornamental, clock and candelabra. The French penchant for satin uphol-stery was also noted by visiting British women. Queen Victoria was charmed by the light green satin with which her sitting room at Saint-Cloud had been freshly kitted out for her 1855 state visit; but, judging by Elizabeth Barrett Browning's grumbling that same year when she found herself lodging in 'a pit' of an apartment in the Faubourg Saint-Germain, at 102 Rue de Grenelle, the heavy usage in rental apartments quickly took its toll on this material. The 'yellow satin furniture' attracted her particular dislike, and she was not happy until she and Robert had relocated to 3 Rue du Colisée, off the Champs-Élysées, which was '[c]lean, car-peted; no glitter, nothing very pretty—not even the clocks—but with sofas and chairs suited to lollers'.[90]

By the time of the Second Empire, the vicinity of the Champs-Élysées seems to have become the preferred British rental location. The apartment blocks, bordering

[88] *Letters of Charles Dickens*, ed. Storey et al., iv, 668, 675.
[89] Ibid. vii, 720, 724.
[90] *Letters of Elizabeth Barrett Browning*, ed. Kenyon, ii, 212, 219, 221.

an avenue broad enough to expose them to the sunlight, were family-friendly, in a city where landlords were normally hostile to receiving either children or pets.[91] Furthermore, as a main arterial route, along which the Emperor and Empress made their way back and forth between Saint-Cloud and the Tuileries, its comings and goings afforded free entertainment. Dickens was much amused by his wife's constant 'flying to the window' of their Champs-Élysées apartment for fear of missing any departure from the Tuileries, while also congratulating himself on its offering their children a window from which to look out on the busy life outside.[92] Even Margaret Oliphant, grieving for the loss of her 10-year old daughter, was cheered by the temporary home she created for her remaining children in the winter of 1864 on 'the sunny side', or northern aspect, of this avenue.

> It was at the height of the gaiety and prosperity of the Empire, and I used to say that the sight of all that gay stream of life from the windows, all the fine people coming and going, the brightness and the movement, were a kind of salvation to me in that dark and clouded time.[93]

To what extent the apartment buildings favoured by the new boulevard architecture, with its complex negotiations of private and public space, were a product of, or conduit for, nineteenth-century Parisian bourgeois behaviour, and to what degree these spaces were gender-aligned, continues to be hotly contested.[94] Typically, these neoclassical blocks boasted six storeys, the first floor above ground level having an elaborate balcony and the top floor an undecorated balcony the length of the building. The balconies afforded occupants on these levels an almost theatrical proximity to the social spectacle of the streets below; and women who lived in such apartments experienced a gain in their viewing privileges, albeit more limited and passive than those enjoyed by male *flâneurs*.[95]

The social significance of Haussmannian boulevard architecture did not escape British writers: Dickens admired the way in which balconies enabled the Parisian workman to take pleasure in the life of the city, untroubled by what his neighbours might think of him.[96] Eliza Lynn Linton's belief that top-floor accommodation was more likely to be rented by government clerks than artisans seems plausible: she attributed something of the strength of the family ties, which she felt distinguished French from English society, to the way in which even relatively poor French families were provided with means of enjoying their 'innocent pleasures' together, so that a government clerk might prefer to smoke on the balcony after

---

[91] H. Vizetelly, *Glances Back through Seventy Years: Autobiographical and Other Recollections* (2 vols, London: Kegan Paul, Trench, Trübner, 1893), ii, 122.

[92] *Letters of Charles Dickens*, ed. Storey et al., viii, 87; vii, 719.

[93] *Autobiography of Margaret Oliphant*, ed. Jay, 110.

[94] S. Marcus, *Apartment Stories: City and Home in Nineteenth-Century Paris and London* (Berkeley: University of California Press, 1999), 27–50.

[95] For a discussion of the balcony's contribution to 'uncontaminated' viewing, see M. Kessler, 'Dusting the Surface, or the Bourgeois, the Veil, and Haussmann's Paris', in A. D'Souza and T. McDonough (eds), *The Invisible Flâneuses? Gender, Public Space, and Visual Culture in Nineteenth-Century Paris* (Manchester: Manchester University Press, 2006), 49–64.

[96] C. Dickens, 'Insularities', *Household Words*, 19 Jan. 1856, 1–4; 2, repr. in *Dickens' Journalism*, ed. Slater, iii, 343.

dinner in his wife's company rather than immediately repairing to his male drinking companions, as his English counterpart might do.[97]

––––––––––

The windows and balconies that formed so pronounced a feature of Haussmann's reconfiguration of Paris offered a framing device through which to see and be seen in this most spectacular of European cities. Indeed, Haussmann's French critics were inclined to accuse him of having made a theatrical show of Paris, by producing a meretricious façade for the benefit of visitors, rather than attending to its inhabitants more urgent needs. It is to the notion of Paris as a theatre of the senses that the next chapter will turn.

[97] [Linton], 'French Domesticity', *Household Words* (24 June 24 1854), p. 435.

5

Sensational Paris

They cannot live without artificial excitements, without *sensations agréables*.
Their houses are not homes, but places where they sleep and dress; they live in
cafés and promenades and theatres; and ten thousand dice are set a-rattling
every night in every quarter of their city. Every thing seems gilding and filigree,
addressed to the eye not the touch.[1]

For most British travellers, Paris embodied not only France's history but its quintessence. Arriving tired and disorientated, they first experienced Paris as a
mélange of strange sights, sounds, smells, and tastes from which even the decision to keep to the English quarter could not entirely insulate them. First impressions variously mention the sound of ostlers hailing each other in French; the
smells of garlic, lemon sherbert, and inadequate drains; and encounters with
French cuisine. British visitors who decided to embrace this alien sensory environment sometimes exhibited their Francophilia in somatic terms. Arthur
Hugh Clough complained that when his friend Matthew Arnold returned to
Oxford in early 1847, 'full of Parisianism; theatres in general, and Rachel in
special: he enters a room with a chanson of Beranger's on his lips[2] ... his carriage shows him in fancy parading the Rue de Rivoli;—and his hair is guiltless
of English scissors.'[3]

Sight-seeing—a compound coinage dating from the 1820s—formed the conscious priority for most first-time visitors; but as they mulled over what they had
seen, their reflections often revealed a complex mixture of aesthetic, emotional and
moral response. As the quotation at the head of the chapter suggests, the British
were very alive to the danger that the Parisian fondness for stimulating the senses
could only come at the expense of blunting moral judgement. This chapter focuses
on the fresh sensory stimulI simultaneously savoured and distrusted by British visitors to Paris.

---

[1] *The Collected Letters of Thomas and Jane Welsh Carlyle*, ed. C. R. Sanders, K. J. Fielding, et al. (40
vols, Durham, NC: Duke University Press, 1970–2012), iii, 180.
[2] Béranger's lyrics, set to popular folk tunes, had made him a republican hero and thus a provocation to Oxford's conservative denizens.
[3] *The Correspondence of Arthur Hugh Clough*, ed. F. L. Mulhauser (2 vols, Oxford: Clarendon Press,
1957), i, 178–9.

5.1 SPECTACULAR PARIS

Conceived from the seventeenth century as an *axe historique*, offering a series of vistas and perspectives, Paris was above all a city of spectacle, whose appeal transcended linguistic barriers: the pre-1830 Galignani guides to Paris carried a section entitled 'A Plan for Viewing Paris in a Week', accompanied by a pull-out map, entitled 'Panorama of the Curiosities of Paris' (See Map, pp. xiv–xv). The city offered a series of carefully sited vantage-points, sometimes envisaged in fiction, as a moment in time and space to reflect on the hero's progress. Famously, Balzac's *Père Goriot* (1835), set in the Paris of 1819, ended with its main character, the provincial arriviste Eugène de Rastignac, being able, from the heights of the Père Lachaise cemetery, to identify the space between the column of the Place Vendôme and the cupola of Les Invalides as containing the glittering heart of the Parisian social world he intended to conquer. An inversion of this scene occurs in G. W. M. Reynolds's novel *Alfred de Rosann; or, the Adventures of a French Gentleman* (1839), where the bourgeois hero, wrongly sentenced to a chain-gang bound for the galleys, reaches comparable high ground on the city's outskirts from which he looks back on a 'panoramic view of Paris', to mourn everything he has lost.[4] These prospects would have proved all the more striking to the British because of the contrast they offered to London, with its seemingly haphazard developments clustered around lines of communication not much altered since Roman times.

5.1.1 The panoramic experience

When Dickens told Count d'Orsay that he had not been 'prepared for' the 'immense impression' Paris would make upon him on his first visit in 1844, the remark was slightly disingenuous.[5] Few visitors in this period would have arrived wholly uninformed about the spectacle Paris would provide. Guidebook illustrations supplemented artists' impressions, and, in the late 1820s the dioramas produced in Paris by Louis Daguerre and Charles Bouton travelled across the Channel: these illusions of three-dimensional, life-size scenes, produced by light shining on and through movable diaphanous paintings, played to an audience who themselves moved through 73 degrees.[6]

In May 1848, the Colisseum on the east side of Regent's Park saw the launch of another virtual tour of Paris. This circular picture of Paris by moonlight, painted by Danson and viewed by an audience from a central revolving dais, was particularly popular because it profited from the ability to show in detail the sites made notorious by the latest regime change. As one guidebook to Paris enthusiastically

---

[4] G. W. M. Reynolds, *Alfred de Rosann: or, the Adventures of a French Gentleman* (London: J. W. Southgate, 1839), 25–6.

[5] *The Pilgrim Edition of the Letters of Charles Dickens*, ed. G. Storey et al. (12 vols, Oxford: Clarendon Press, 1965–2002), iv, 166.

[6] Bouton's diorama of 'Environs de Paris, St Cloud' was shown at the diorama in Park Square, Regent's Park, London, from June 1826 to spring 1828; then in Liverpool from May 1831 to Jan. 1832, and Edinburgh from Nov. 1836 to Dec. 1837. Daguerre's 'Vue de Paris, prise de Montmartre' came to London soon after its 1830 display in Paris.

exclaimed, panoramas and dioramas 'show us the whole wide world... without trouble or expense', while simultaneously whetting the appetite for the actual encounter.[7]

Dickens favoured an apartment on the Champs-Élysées, precisely because it provided comforting proximity to that 'moving panorama always outside, which is Paris itself'. Yet, during an earlier visit, his self-imposed division of spending two weeks each month at his desk, followed by two weeks' wholesale immersion in the spectacular, produced a troubling sensation of disjuncture: 'I have been seeing Paris—wandering into Hospitals, Prisons, Dead-houses, Operas, Theatres, Concert Rooms, Burial-grounds, Palaces, and Wine shops. In my unoccupied fortnight of each month, every description of gaudy and ghastly sight has been passing before me in a rapid Panorama.'[8] Martin Meisel has drawn attention to the way in which 'panoramic and dioramic modes affect the style, the form, and the scope of Dickens's fiction', but the part they played in his representation of Paris deserves closer inspection.[9]

Repeatedly the reader of Dickens's Parisian pieces is invited to participate in a state of suspended reality, to collude in 'the delicious traveller's trance which knows no cares, no yesterdays, no tomorrows, nothing but the passing objects and the passing scents and sounds!'[10] The articles, 'Railway Dreaming', 'Travelling Abroad', and 'A Flight', all work, in the mode of the spectacular illusion, to convince readers that they are observing an actual scene through the narrator's eyes, only to be 'disillusioned' when finally confronted with the truth that the place where they have conceived of themselves as present, at least by proxy, has only ever been an imaginative recreation by a narrator already far distant from Paris. For Dickens, foreign travel seems to have both intensified and legitimated his sense that his art, rather than being mimetic, was an act of animating or ventriloquizing figures who must always remain unknowable. It was the start of a cross-Channel journey that prompted this piece of authorial musing:

> A wonderful fact to reflect upon, that every human creature is constituted to be that profound secret and mystery to every other. A solemn consideration, when I enter a great city by night, that every one of those darkly clustered houses encloses its own secret; that every room in every one of them encloses its own secret; that every beating heart in the hundreds of thousands of breasts there, is, in some of its imaginings, a secret to the heart nearest it!... In any of the burial places of this city through which I pass, is there a sleeper more inscrutable than its busy inhabitants are, in their innermost personality, to me, or than I am to them.... So with the three passengers shut up in the narrow compass of one lumbering old mail coach; they were mysteries to one another.[11]

In this respect Dickens was more like Thackeray, the puppet master, than has sometimes been admitted. If Thackeray's patrician attitude to his fellow travellers,

---

[7] B. Hofland, *Emily's Reward, or the Holiday Trip to Paris* (London: Grant & Griffith, 1844), 142.

[8] *Letters of Charles Dickens*, ed. Storey et al., vii, 724; v, 19.

[9] M. Meisel, *Realizations* (Princeton, NJ: Princeton University Press, 1983), 63–4.

[10] C. Dickens, 'A Flight', in *The Uncommercial Traveller and Reprinted Pieces* (London: Oxford University Press, 1958), 484.

[11] C. Dickens, *A Tale of Two Cities*, ed. A. Sanders (Oxford: Oxford University Press, 2008), 16.

referred to in the previous chapter, depends upon maintaining a narrative distance from them, so Dickens employed the conceit of the panorama to mount representations of Paris that emphasize their nature as the deliberately engineered product of a theatrical impresario. In the theatre of Dickens's own mind Paris might at times play as 'ghastly and gaudy', but to the readers of *Household Words* he was determined to present 'the gigantic-moving-panorama or diorama mode of conveyance' as a positive example of the 'new and cheap means [that] are continually being devised, for conveying the results of actual experience, to those who are unable to obtain such experiences for themselves; and to bring them within the reach of the people—emphatically of the people'. Such spectacles exposed viewers to 'new worlds…beyond their little worlds' and served to 'widen their range of reflection, information, sympathy, and interest. The more man knows of man, the better for the common brotherhood among us all.'[12] As author therefore, Dickens could persuade himself of his ability to work a magic which at other times he acknowledged to be philosophically impossible.

The ingenuity with which Dickens sought to heal this division between the solipsistic, yet intensely present, inner life of the imagination and the evidence of a wider external world, which could suddenly seem illusory, is nowhere better displayed than in 'Railway Dreaming'. First, the narrator works to construct the theatre which will demonstrate the public social life of Paris to be essentially egalitarian; then he adopts the role of passive spectator at the performance he has himself set up: taking his post-prandial coffee and cigar in a street-front café, the narrator of 'Railway Dreaming' observes, 'The place from which the shop-front has been taken makes a gay proscenium; as I sit and smoke, the street becomes a stage, with an endless procession of lively actors crossing and recrossing.' An extensive cast list crosses the stage, carefully selected to range, socially speaking, from 'lounging exquisites' to 'pickers-up of refuse', before the street and café lights are turned on to remind us that the show is over. In moralizing the experience, however, Dickens gives the game away: the bilious distrust of the writer in the solitary place can never be entirely placated by a spectacle always under suspicion of being an illusion in which he has proved an all-too-willing collaborator:

> It is surely better for me, and the family group, and for the two old ladies, and for the workman, to have thus much of community with the city life of all degrees, than to be getting bilious in hideous blackholes, and turning cross and suspicious in solitary places! I may never say a word to any of these people in my life, nor they to me; but we are all interchanging enjoyment frankly and openly—not fencing ourselves off and boxing ourselves up.[13]

5.1.2 Seeing and being seen in public spaces

Dickens was of course right to interpret the opening up of vistas along the widened boulevards as evidence of deliberate political and social engineering. Each

---

[12] 'Some account of an extraordinary traveller', *Household Words*, 20 Apr. 1850, 77; repr. in *Dickens' Journalism*, ed. M. Slater (4 vols, London: J. M. Dent, 1994–2000), ii, 202–11.
[13] 'Railway Dreaming', in *Dickens' Journalism*, ed. Slater, iii, 370–6.

fresh regime change seemed to renew the fear of disaffected sections of the population 'getting bilious in hideous blackholes', and consequently a heavy police presence, especially notable under the Imperial regime, made Paris a site of vigilant surveillance.

During Louis-Philippe's reign, the phenomenon of the *flâneur*, or urban stroller, observing and categorizing the people in the streets around him,[14] flourished alongside a variety of literary forms offering to anatomize the city's inhabitants.[15] The reasons for this marked interest in reading the Parisian social order have been much debated, and often attributed to a sense of the city's uncertain or contested identity, provoked by such factors as the aristocratic left-bank contempt for, and distrust of, the growing commercial power of the occupants of the right bank; the rearrangement of the city's topography; and confusing changes in the names and usage of its public spaces.

Government reactions to the dangerous atomization of city life took a more positive turn in the creation of parks as shared spaces where the different classes were encouraged to enjoy in common the pleasures of seeing and being seen. In exile, Napoleon III had been impressed by London's green spaces, stretching from Hyde Park in the west to Victoria Park, 'planted' in a poor working-class area of the East End. Consequently, between 1850 and 1870, under the direction of Haussmann and his chief civil engineer, Alphonse Alphand, the parkland of Paris was expanded from 47 to 4,500 acres.[16] Established parks received elaborate makeovers: the Bois de Boulogne, formerly largely composed of natural woodland and clearings, and known for its riding tracks and as a place of assignation for amatory or duelling adventures, was landscaped to afford serpentine pathways, stretches of open lawn, and large-scale water features. These developments went far to address the previous complaints of British visitors, such as Barbara Hofland's fictional family, who deplored the impossibility of finding an equivalent to leafy Hampstead or Richmond in the dusty central Paris of 1844.[17]

Contemporary British commentary suggests that to an extent Napoleon III's policy worked. By 1854 Eliza Lynn Linton observed that, unlike their British counterparts, French fathers felt 'no degradation' in accompanying their wives and children for a stroll in a Parisian park.[18] The walks and arbours of these parks provided safe spaces for nursemaids and their charges, otherwise confined to gardenless apartment blocks. Henry James's depiction of the Luxembourg gardens, viewed

---

[14] M. Rose, *Flaneurs and Idlers* (Bielefeld: Aisthesis, 2007); M. Lauster, *Sketches of the Nineteenth Century: European Journalism and its Physiologies, 1830–50* (Basingstoke: Palgrave Macmillan, 2007); M. Gluck, 'The Flâneur and the Aesthetic: Appropriation of Urban Culture in Mid-Nineteenth-Century Paris', *Theory, Culture and Society* 20 (Oct. 2003), 53–80; all emphasize the error of conflating the earlier happy 'sociable presence' of the inquiring city stroller with the Baudelairean *flâneur* of the second half of 19th c.—by turn one of the crowd, an observer, and an artist—or with Walter Benjamin's more complicated interpretation of this figure. Contemporary commentators sometimes claimed that Haussmann's rationalization of the city substantially detracted from the *flâneur*'s previous opportunities for enjoying the unexpected.

[15] For further discussion of these genres, see Ch. 11.

[16] C. Prendergast, *Paris and the Nineteenth Century* (Oxford: Blackwell, 1992), 9.

[17] Hofland, *Emily's Reward*, 30–31.

[18] [E. Linton,] 'French Domesticity', *Household Words*, 24 June 1854, 437.

through the eyes of his harried hero, Lambert Strether, suggests the magical sense of 'time out' afforded by these miniaturized landscapes, simulating the intimate spaces of private gardens:

> In the Luxembourg gardens he pulled up; here at last he found his nook, and here, on a penny chair from which terraces, alleys, vistas, fountains, little trees in green tubs, little women in white caps and shrill little girls at play all sunnily 'composed' together, he passed an hour in which the cup of his impressions seemed truly to overflow.[19]

Such sociable proximities could also provoke anxiety. Even in the days of the Restoration monarchy, when class distinctions had been more marked, Lady Blessington had thought it advisable to warn her readers of Parisian customs in matters of public conduct, lest 'an ignorance might lead to give offence':

> In England, a lady is expected to bow to a gentleman before he presumes to do so to her, thus leaving her the choice of acknowledging his acquaintance, or not; but in France it is otherwise, for a man takes off his hat to every woman whom he has ever met in society, although he does not address her, unless she encourages him to do so.

Casual encounters in spaces such as the Tuileries gardens, supposedly the haunt of aristocrats, were fraught, for the uninitiated Englishwoman, with intimations of familiarity: 'the hat is held a second longer off the head, the bow is lower, and the smile of recognition is more *amiable*.'[20]

By the time of the Second Empire the protocol for public spaces had diverged even more sharply between Paris and London. The British, Bulwer Lytton noted, were used to the London parks providing amusement for either the very rich or the poor, while the middle classes preferred the privacy and sobriety of the suburbs. The heroine of Bulwer Lytton's *The Parisians*, already compromised from the author's point of view by her role as a professional singer, is introduced walking alone in the Bois de Boulogne. Although it is swiftly revealed to the reader that she undertakes these daily constitutionals for her health, the young *flâneurs* who observe her are seen as justified in their momentary uncertainty as to whether she can be quite '*comme il faut*', and their further speculation as to whether she is some rich man's mistress.[21] Post-Commune novels, by contrast, tended to emphasize sedition rather than impropriety as the danger of indiscriminate mingling in the parks: the casual intimacy of café concerts or feast-day celebrations provided perfect cover for the hastily exchanged word or note.

Days when Paris was *en fête* saw an influx of itinerant jugglers, stall-holders, travelling fairs and circuses to the Champs-Élysées, where criminals and pickpockets could find rich pickings among the distracted spectators. The annual July festivities celebrating Louis-Philippe's ascent to the throne demonstrated a 'bread and circuses' pandering to the populace that middle-class Britons found disturbing in its suggestion that the good humour of the masses might, if not placated, change

---

[19] H. James, *The Ambassadors* (2 vols, 1909; New York: A. M. Kelley, 1971), i, 80.
[20] Countess of Blessington, *The Idler in France* (2 vols, London: Henry Colburn, 1841), i, 275.
[21] Lord [E. G. E. L. Bulwer-]Lytton, *The Parisians* (2 vols, London: George Routledge, 1875), i, 51, 54.

at any moment to a darker mood.[22] While Shrove Tuesday's carnivalesque parades, led by a garlanded fat ox, provided the local colour beloved by visiting writers, and gave *flâneurs*, both real and fictional, the opportunity to ogle young Parisian shop-girls dressed in their finest attire, these fictional accounts repeatedly suggest that just beneath the surface colour and gaiety lay a murkier, more threatening underworld.[23]

Sala's *Quite Alone* captures the intoxicating mixture of fear and fascination felt by a young girl rapt by the spectacle as she wanders from booth to booth at the July *fête*, before being suddenly kidnapped at knife-point and dragged down to the hovels on the banks of the Seine where the show-people have their lodgings. Her naïve eye serves to accentuate the troubling features of a spectacle where the cheap and tawdry masquerade as the precious and authentic. The experience is encapsulated in a freak show exhibiting 'La Femme Sauvage'. Reputedly from Madagascar and allegedly fêted by the royal houses of Europe, this scantily clothed exhibit lives on a diet of raw meat and is prone to violence.[24] As the novel develops, 'La Femme Sauvage' is shown to be but one of multiple self-reinventions of a Parisian actress and socialite, turned vaudeville artiste, circus bareback rider, and drunken virago. Simultaneously titillating and disgusting, prized exotic and uncivilized alien, to the British demi-mondains who wine and dine her, this woman comes to represent the allure of Paris, a city without restraint, which they hope to ogle and flirt with while remaining themselves unharmed.

Where Parisian parks and fairgrounds were mainly a matter of spectacle, its public balls, open to all who could afford a ticket, offered a riskier prospect. G. W. M. Reynolds illustrated the doubly transgressive nature of the rowdy masked ball at the Hôtel de Ville, which inaugurated the pre-Lenten revelry, by having his Pickwickians encounter Sam Weller, disguised as a gipsy woman: a violation of both the class and gender divide.[25] Thackeray spoke with horror of having been caught up in a mad dance of the Carnival Ball as it careered through the English quarter, with 'all the ranks in the empire, all the he and she scoundrels of the capital, writhed and twisted together'.[26] A visit to Le Bal de l'Opéra, where, from midnight, men in evening dress mingled with women sporting black masks and hooded cloaks, was represented in Catherine Gore's fiction as the *ne plus ultra* for upper-class women bent on playing with erotic fire (Fig. 5). From the relative safety of a box women might survey the wild abandon taking place beneath, but venturing onto the ballroom floor, too crowded to admit of dancing, they would find themselves mingling with courtesans and were in any case (she explained) inevitably exposed to the

---

[22] e.g. Thackeray, 'The Fêtes of July', *The Corsair*, 5 Oct. 1839; repr. in *Paris Sketch Book, The Oxford Thackeray*, ed. G. Saintsbury (17 vols, London: Oxford University Press, 1910), ii, 33–41; G. A. Sala, *Quite Alone* (3 vols, London: Chapman & Hall, 1864), iii, 7–9.

[23] e.g. Thackeray, 'Shrove Tuesday in Paris', in *Loose Sketches, Oxford Thackeray*, iii, 461–507; [H. Jenkin,] *Once and Again: A Novel* (3 vols, London: Smith, Elder, 1865), i, 1–2.

[24] Sala, *Quite Alone*, iii, 16–36.

[25] G. W. M. Reynolds, *Pickwick Abroad: or, The Tour in France* (London: Sherwood, Gilbert, & Piper, 1839), 395–403.

[26] Thackeray, 'On some French fashionable novels', in *Paris Sketch Book, Oxford Thackeray*, ii, 102.

Fig. 5. 'La sortie du bal masqué de l'opéra', engraving from *La Semaine illustrée*, 24 February 1860.

appraisal of male libertines who would then retire to the Café de Paris to boast of their exploits over dinner. Only French *lionnes*,[27] or fashionably eccentric women, were sufficiently worldly-wise, or careless of appearances, to manage an escapade so fraught with social peril.[28]

5.1.3 Spectating in the Louvre

Some of Paris's more eye-catching attractions were designed to focus the eye—and thus, it was hoped, the mind and heart—on all that France had achieved; yet their very Frenchness, taken together with the opportunities they provided for mixed viewing, could also produce disquiet in a British breast.

   Napoleon I had ransacked the artistic treasures of the lands he had conquered to adorn the Louvre, and despite the return of some of these after his downfall, successive rulers continued to augment the collection in self-aggrandising fashion. thereby also ensuring that this former palace formed a symbolic object of attack during times of political unrest in the city. When the Louvre and the Tuileries were set on fire in 1871, Ruskin was quick to point out the irony that this should have been done under the aegis of 'Parisian notions of Communism':

---

[27] Although *lionne* had made its way into Anglo-French usage by the time of the July Monarchy to denominate a woman who wished to be seen as a fashionable spectacle, there had been since the 17th c. a degree of ambiguity surrounding the meaning of 'lions' and the cognate verbal noun, 'lionizing', the first of which could refer either to a thing worth seeing, and hence a much-sought-after celebrity, and the second to the pursuit of either of these.

[28] C. Gore, *Greville: or, a Season in Paris* (3 vols, London: Henry Colburn, 1841), iii, 245–57, and *The Ambassador's Wife* (3 vols, London: Richard Bentley, 1842), iii, 183–4.

For we Communists of the old school think that our property belongs to everybody, and everybody's property belongs to us; so of course I thought the Louvre belonged to me as much as to the Parisians, and expected they would have sent word over to me, being an Art Professor, to ask whether I wanted it burnt down.[29]

Yet such a monument to French nationalistic pride also prompted frequent British reflection. As an English father in Barbara Hofland's *Emily's Reward* (1844) tells his young son, while they survey the obelisk and other accoutrements with which Louis-Philippe had recently furnished the Place de la Concorde, 'we have never been blessed by a government zealous for the possession or protection of the fine arts'. When his wife mildly rebukes him by mentioning that the British have not been 'cursed with one anxious to despoil their neighbours', no mention is made of the Elgin marbles.[30]

Even the most patriotic Briton acknowledged that the Louvre's rich accumulation of nationalized treasures dwarfed that of their own National Gallery, founded as recently as 1824.[31] G. W. M. Reynolds proclaimed the British edifice a 'monument of bad taste and ill-judged economy', while Thackeray excoriated the facilities it offered: 'Artists from England, who have a national gallery that resembles a moderate-size gin-shop, who may not copy pictures, except under particular restrictions, and on rare and particular days, may revel here [the Louvre] to their hearts' content.'[32] Seeking to recapture the heady thrill of his own first encounter with the 'half a mile of pictures' on offer in the Louvre, Thackeray later has the young painter Clive Newcome pen an ecstatic letter home, qualified on this occasion by the admission 'that there are a score [of pictures] under the old pepper-boxes in Trafalgar Square as fine as the best here'.[33]

The Louvre's collection served as a veritable revelation for Victorian artists and writers: Dante Gabriel Rossetti spoke of rushing from one gallery to the next in the excitement of his 1849 visit. On subsequently revisiting the Louvre in 1855 with Robert Browning, he remarked upon finding his companion's encyclopedic knowledge of early Italian art exceeded that of Ruskin himself.[34] Queen Victoria and the young Henry James were visitors in the same year. Victoria, who was 'dragged' through the galleries in a small chair, to keep her fresh for the ball at the Hôtel de Ville that night, recorded that it took 'full three hours and a half going through them—unfortunately very, very hurriedly. One ought to go there two hours every day for a week.'[35] G. W. M. Reynolds, however, probably judged both his characters and readership aptly when, after 'an agreeable couple of hours' in the Louvre,

---

[29] Ruskin, *Fors Clavigera: Letters to the Workmen and Labourers of Great Britain*, in *The Works of John Ruskin*, ed. E. T. Cook and A. Wedderburn (39 vols, London: George Allen; New York: Longmans, Green, 1903–12), xxvii, 116.

[30] Hofland, *Emily's Reward*, 33.

[31] e.g. A. Trollope, 'The National Gallery', *St James's Magazine* 2 (Sept. 1861), 163–76.

[32] Reynolds, *Pickwick Abroad*, 244; W. M. Thackeray, 'On the French School of Painting', *Fraser's Magazine*, 20 Dec. 1839, 679–88; repr. in *Paris Sketch Book, Oxford Thackeray*, ii, 55.

[33] *The Newcomes, Oxford Thackeray*, xiv, 273.

[34] *The Correspondence of Dante Gabriel Rossetti*, ed. W. E. Fredeman et al. (8 vols, Cambridge: D. S. Brewer, 2002–9), i, 109, 113; ii, 80.

[35] *Queen Victoria: Leaves from a Journal: A Record of the Visit of the Emperor and Empress of the French to the Queen, and of the Visit of the Queen and H.R.H the Prince Consort to the Emperor of the French*, 1855, intro. R. Mortimer (London: André Deutsch, 1961), 106.

he despatched Pickwick and his companions to the Palais-Royal, 'to refresh themselves with ices and fresh air'.[36]

The 12-year-old Henry James was bowled over in the Galerie d'Apollon by 'a general sense of *glory*' which he later took to stand for 'not only beauty and art and supreme design, but history and fame and power, the world in fine raised to the richest and noblest expression'. For James, the Louvre represented the quintessence of 'the Second Empire, which was (for my notified consciousness) new and queer and perhaps even wrong, but on the spot so amply radiant and elegant'.[37]

For James's fictional characters, a visit to the Louvre became a touchstone of their capacity to appreciate both the aesthetic and moral calibre of the Old World. His early novel *The American* (1877) begins with an extended sketch of the eponymous hero visiting the Louvre in May 1868, and watching a female copyist at work, learning her trade by imitating the Old Masters. The way in which she uses the gallery for a self-conscious performance of her art and trades her small talent in pursuit of her financial and social ambition helps to explain the convention by which women, and especially women artists, required a chaperone in Parisian art galleries.

The Louvre's rich collection of classical sculpture had already become a trope for eroticism. Thackeray's earlier mockery of the French admiration for the neo-classical is laid aside as Clive Newcome warms to the charms of Greek sculpture. Clive's breathless encomium singles out the generous beauty of the Louvre's Venus de Milo to contrast with the chilly hauteur of the huntress Diana, whom the girl he loves more nearly resembles.[38]

It was therefore scarcely surprising that Thackeray's daughter's first work of fiction should use the galleries and paintings of the Louvre as the setting for the initial steps in a connoisseur's seduction of a naïve young English girl.[39] Thackeray could not, however, have foreseen how his daring exploitation of the Louvre's marmoreal splendours to express Clive's sexual frustration might act as licence for Swinburne, for whom *The Newcomes* was allegedly a favourite novel.[40] Swinburne's 'Hermaphroditus'(1866) used the Louvre's sculpture of the sleeping Hermaphrodite as the occasion for a sonnet sequence on bisexual love.

5.1.4 *Expositions universelles*

As if permanent exhibitions and edifices were insufficient, Napoleon III mounted the *expositions universelles* of 1855 and 1867 as demonstrations of Paris's claim to

[36] Reynolds, *Pickwick Abroad*, 244.
[37] H. James, *A Small Boy and Others* (London: Macmillan, 1913), 361.
[38] 'On the French School of Painting', in *Paris Sketch Book*, *Oxford Thackeray*, ii, 47. *Newcomes*, *Oxford Thackeray*, xiv, 272.
[39] A. T. Ritchie, *The Story of Elizabeth*, in *The Works of Miss Thackeray* (10 vols, (London: Smith, Elder, 1890), vi, 80–83.
[40] C. Maxwell, 'Swinburne and Thackeray's *The Newcomes*', *Victorian Poetry*, Winter 2009, 733–46.

model the ideal of the modern city. A couple of months before the 1855 exhibition was due to open, Dickens reported that Paris hoteliers were anticipating 'a prodigious influx' of people, and the figures suggest they were right to do so.[41] Ambivalent as always about such triumphalist celebrations of nationhood, Dickens left his visit until near the end of the exhibition. Moreover, apart from an aside in an article the following January in which he contrasted the daring and drama of the French art on show there with the staidness of contemporary British art, Dickens apparently did not consider the 1855 exhibition appropriate for discussion in *Household Words*.[42] Thomas Cook's failure to achieve group concessions from the Paris-bound railway companies to enable excursions for the lower middle and working classes to the 1855 event suggests that Dickens was right in judging that this exhibition would prove beyond the reach of the greater part of his readership.

By the 1867 Exposition, however, Cook was successful in arranging a £5 inclusive ticket, including accommodation out in the suburb of Passy.[43] The opening up of the event to a broader class range justified increased newsprint coverage while also provoking a good deal of snobbery. George Rose's 'Mrs Brown at the Paris Exhibition', first published in *Fun Magazine* (1867), poked fun at lower class British trippers, rather as Dickens's character Mrs Lirriper had done.[44] Sala, the *Daily Telegraph*'s lead writer, ensconced himself for the duration in a suite of rooms in the Hotel Windsor on the Rue de Rivoli, expressly in order not to have to mix with English trippers at the hotel's table d'hôte, and sent home reports, subsequently collected as *Notes and Sketches of the Paris Exhibition* (1868).[45] Eneas Sweetland Dallas covered the exhibition for the *Times*, while Blanchard Jerrold's pieces were collected in *Paris for the English* (1867).

Although the 1855 event had shared something of a transnational genesis with London's Great Exhibition of 1851—Prince Albert had visited the French commercial exhibition of 1849 on four occasions, while Louis-Napoleon diplomatically acknowledged Albert as his inspiration—British writers were often prompted to reflect on national differences.[46] Particularly in the case of the 1867 Exposition, neither the lavish state funding nor the Emperor's unpopularity went unnoticed: Henry Vizetelly, Paris correspondent of the *Illustrated London News*, possibly embittered by the picture rights being granted to a popular French photographer, claimed that the crowd gathered to welcome Napoleon III to the opening event

---

[41] P. Gerbod, 'Voyageurs et résidents britanniques en France en XIXᵉ siècle: une approche statistique', *Acta Geographica* 76 (1988), 19–36.

[42] C. Dickens, 'Insularities', *Household Words*, 19 Jan. 1856, 1–4; repr. in *Dickens' Journalism*, ed. Slater, iii, 339–46. Cf. *Letters of Charles Dickens*, ed. Storey et al., vii, 742–5.

[43] J. Buzard, *The Beaten Track: European Tourism, Literature, and the Ways to 'Culture' 1800–1900* (Oxford: Clarendon Press, 1993), 63.

[44] Dickens, 'Mrs Lirriper's Legacy', in *All the Year Round*, Christmas 1864, 573–600; repr. in *Christmas Stories* (London: Oxford University Press, 1956), pp. 405–32.

[45] G. A. Sala, *The Life and Adventures of George Augustus Sala written by himself*, 2nd edn (2 vols, London: Cassell, 1895), ii, 141–2.

[46] *Queen Victoria: Leaves from a Journal*, intro. Mortimer, 96.

had to be augmented by a rent-a-mob of cheering Parisian *ouvriers*, and overseen by an inadequately disguised, heavy police presence.[47]

Expositions were, however, exceptional events, while Paris's theatres were a more constant source of spectacular entertainment.

5.1.5 The Parisian theatres

Such was British enthusiasm for attending the theatre in Paris that by mid-century some British papers carried regular reviews of the season's plays in the neighbouring capital, and a number of British dramatists turned their viewing to good account by imitating, translating, adapting, or pilfering from French models of the day.[48] Wilkie Collins's first play, for example, was a translation from the French, and some British residents in Paris, among them Henry Addison (1805–76) and William Thackeray's cousin Tom (1796–1877), discovered that selling their translations to the English stage formed a useful supplement to their army half-pay.

Although Paris offered a nightly diet of comedies, melodramas, operas, and circus spectaculars,[49] a visit to the classical drama performed at the Théâtre Français, judged dull stuff by Thackeray and Dickens alike, was considered an obligatory proof of respectability.[50] By 1840 Thackeray declared classical tragedy dead. The great tragedienne Rachel had only just begun to perform there, and even she, Thackeray considered, 'can only galvanize the corpse not revivify it'. Famous actresses such as Madame Rachel (1821–58) and Mademoiselle Mars (1779–1847), the latter specializing in ingénue and comic roles, in fact developed a devoted following. In the winter of 1846–7 Matthew Arnold allegedly attended every one of Rachel's performances; his last volume of poems (1867) contained three elegiac sonnets in her honour, and he would brook no comparisons: '[N]ever did I come so close to quarrelling with "Uncle Matt"', wrote Mrs Humphry Ward after her first trip to Paris in 1874, 'as when, on our return, after having heard my say about the genius of Sarah Bernhardt, he patted my hand indulgently with the remark—"But, my dear child—you see—you never saw Rachel!".'[51]

For those who found French classical conventions and the rhythms of the alexandrine daunting, the opportunity for observing the audience could prove as entertaining as the spectacle on stage. Carlyle, who was afforded a seat in Lord

[47] H. Vizetelly, *Glances Back through Seventy Years: Autobiographical and Other Recollections* (2 vols, London, Kegan Paul, Trench, Trübner, 1893), ii, 188.

[48] J. Bishop, '"They Manage Things Better in France": French Plays and English Critics 1850-55', *Nineteenth-Century Theatre* 22(1) (Summer 1994), 5–29.

[49] The theatre culture of 19th-c. Paris is too vast a subject to be summarized here. Further aspects of the topic can be pursued in J.-C. Yon, *Les spectacles sous le Second Empire* (Paris: Armand Colin, 2010); and *Le théâtre français à l'étranger: histoire d'une suprématie culturelle* (Versailles: Université de Versailles Saint-Quentin-en-Yvelines, 2008), which includes discussion of the influence of the French theatre in Anglophone countries. F. W. J. Hemmings, *The Theatre Industry in Nineteenth-Century France* (Cambridge: Cambridge University Press, 1998) contains sections on the audience, the actors, and playwrights.

[50] 'French Dramas and Melodramas', in *Paris Sketch Book*, Oxford *Thackeray*, ii, 291; *Letters of Charles Dickens*, ed. Storey et al., viii, 35.

[51] Mrs H. Ward, *A Writer's Recollections 1856–1900* (London: William Collins, 1918), 157–8.

Normanby, the English ambassador's, draughty box at the Théâtre Français, judged the 'clever energetic set of faces visible' in the *parterre* 'far superior to such as go to Drury Lane'—one of the two patent theatres in London capable of offering comparable drama—and devoted more space to describing General Changarnier, victor of many foreign campaigns, whom he spotted in the stalls, than to the 'worthless racket and cackle' of the two pieces performed on stage.[52]

The lively sense of the audience being as much under surveillance as the performance itself lent the act of attending controversial plays such as Dumas *fils'* *La Dame aux camélias* a scandalous edge. This tale of the courtesan with the heart of gold, which opened at the Vaudeville in 1852, divided English viewers. Elizabeth Barrett Browning refused to 'allow that it is immoral' even if the intensity of the experience 'almost killed me out of my propriety'. She and Robert both wept openly as the pathetic tale unfolded, while Thackeray walked out, so disgusted was he with the ethics espoused by the tale.[53] Over a decade before he had already expressed himself heartily ashamed of 'the hideous kind of mental intoxication' that six years of regularly viewing 'the fictitious murders, rapes, adulteries, and other crimes' on offer on the Parisian stage had induced in him. Yet he was forced to admit that they had both 'interested and excited' him at the time.[54]

It was these plays' undoubted affective quality that troubled British viewers. Annie Thackeray Ritchie's *The Story of Elizabeth* pivots upon a Parisian performance of *Faust*, where an English girl attending the theatre without parental permission finds herself amidst 'hundreds of people, silent, and breathless too, with interest, with excitement'. This collective suspension of moral judgement concerning the seduction taking place on stage helps to cloud her own moral compass with regard to the potential seducer who sits beside her. Worse still, in her eagerness, she leans forward, unveiled, in the box, and so becomes the subject of gossip. The delirious nervous fever to which she instantly succumbs in the aftermath of this escapade includes the figures of Faust and Mephistopheles, 'crowding upon her and glaring furiously'.[55] The physiological impact of Elizabeth's night at the theatre helped to secure the tale's place in reviews devoted to the new English genre of 'the sensation novel', a genre which would frequently locate the murders upon which their plots hung in the theatres of Paris.[56]

If English viewers could prove so susceptible, Lady Blessington could only wonder at the folly of the French authorities in permitting plays such as Scribe's *Avant, pendant, et après* (1828), a three-act account of the French Revolution to be performed 'to so inflammable a people as the French...I confess I felt uneasy when I witnessed the deep interest and satisfaction evinced by many in the *parterre* during the representation.' She remained undecided as to whether the 'frivolity and

---

[52] T. Carlyle, 'Excursion (Futile Enough) to Paris; Autumn 1851', in *Last Words of Thomas Carlyle* (London: Longmans, Green, 1892), 163.

[53] R. Gridley, *The Brownings and France: A Chronicle with Commentary* (London: Athlone Press, 1982), 124–8; *Letters of the Brownings to George Barrett*, ed. P. Landis and R. E. Freeman (Urbana: University of Illinois Press, 1958), 181; *The Letters and Private Papers of William Makepeace Thackeray*, ed. G. N. Ray (4 vols, Cambridge, Mass.: Harvard University Press, 1945–6), iii, 618.

[54] 'French Dramas and Melodramas', in *Paris Sketch Book, Oxford Thackeray*, ii, 293.

[55] *The Story of Elizabeth*, in *Works of Miss Thackeray*, vi, 96–8, 112.

[56] For further discussion of the alleged immorality of French actresses, see section 14.3.

vices' attributed to the *ancien régime*, the verisimilitude with which the sanguinary mob of the Reign of Terror were depicted, or the promise of swift promotion to the status of Revolutionary hero would prove most inflammatory. Of another play, Mélesville's *La Maison du rempart* (1829), depicting an armed mob of an earlier era, she wrote: 'Sparks of fire flung among gunpowder are not more dangerous. Shewing a populace what they can effect by brutal force is a dangerous experiment; it is like letting a tame lion see how easily he could overpower his keepers.'[57] Dickens's account to her of a melodrama playing at the Cirque Olympique in January 1847 may have helped to inform *A Tale of Two Cities*, but can have done little to reassure the Countess: 'there is a new shew-piece called the French Revolution, in which there is...a series of battles (fought by some five hundred people who look like fifty thousand) that are wonderful in their extraordinary vigor and truth'; as he told another correspondent, 'there is a power and massiveness in the Mob, which is positively awful.'[58]

5.2 THE CITY OF DEADLY FRISSONS

> We live in an age, *ma bonne Augusta*, when none but exciting subjects have an interest. Tears are now only shed when great crimes are their source; domestic feelings are *passés de mode*; and those who would awaken sympathy, must dare guilt. Look at the theatres in France—here horror on horror accumulates, and plaudits 'loud and deep' follow every scene of guilt, and every sentiment of reckless daring! Look at the crimes every day committed in that land of passion, where naught sleeps save—reason; and where events, public and private succeed each other so quickly, that the mind is kept in a continual and delightful state of excitement...[I]n France a woman's head can embrace simultaneously many more subjects than ours can contain in succession, during the lapse of a twelvemonth. And hence their general freedom from concentrated or violent affections, a freedom that renders them *toujours gai, et toujours aimable*.[59]

If the Parisian stage proved the French to be addicted to scenes of crime and passion, the streets outside provided a theatre of violent history where the English visitor could sup full of horrors. British writers often seemed to feel that their own capacity for deep feeling was guaranteed by the way in which they deplored their neighbours' cold-heartedness and shallow ability to ignore or erase the evidence of their recent history. They rarely reflected on the ghoulish disposition that repeatedly led them in search of a shudder of appreciative terror in the presence of so much death and destruction.

---

[57] Blessington, *Idler in France*, i, 169–73, 249.
[58] *Letters of Charles Dickens*, ed. Storey et al., Jan. 1847, v, 14, 20.
[59] Countess of Blessington, *The Victims of Society* (3 vols, London: Saunders & Otley, 1837), i, 22–4.

5.2.1 Following the revolutionary trail

Planning his friend John Forster's first visit to Paris, Charles Dickens naturally assumed that he would wish to see 'all the spots made memorable by the first revolution'.[60] As soon as it was possible to visit French shores again, after the embargo in operation during the Napoleonic Wars, British tourists flocked to inspect the sites of the 1789 revolution. The Barrett Brownings saw nothing incongruous in 1815 in combining a shopping trip with a tour, accompanied by their children, of the major sites of the recent revolution. Barbara Hofland's child's guide to Paris has the paterfamilias begin his instructive survey of the magnificent and well-assorted objects displayed in the remodelled Place Louis XV [Place de la Concorde] with the reminder, 'yet, in this very place, was the horrible guillotine first set up! Here has royal, virtuous, and innocent blood flowed like water!'[61] The 14-year-old Matthew Arnold's journal recorded with some gusto the 'Place de la Concorde where Louis Seize was guillotined', as one of the sites included in his first visit with his parents in 1837. Forty years later, however, in the wake of the Commune, he was quick to denounce 'the national vulgarity' of 'English sightseers who...have begun to flock over to the show of fallen Paris'.[62] To his mind this fresh wave of tourism was quite different in nature from the 'historically-informed' trip he had undertaken with his family in 1837, or his expeditions to Paris to worship at the feet of Rachel.

Arnold would surely have been appalled by Carlyle's souvenir hunting. On his 1851 trip Carlyle made a pilgrimage to the Temple prison (3rd arrondissement), where Marie Antoinette had been incarcerated. Shorn of its towers by Napoleon I, who was anxious to prevent its becoming a royalist shrine, it was to be completely demolished in 1860 by Napoleon III, but for three francs Carlyle persuaded the concierge to cut off 'a bit of room-paper for souvenir' from the Queen's *oratoire*, providing 'a memorable scene in one's archives' for the author of *The French Revolution*.[63]

Some British visitors' reactions to the sites of revolution were sharply inflected by their personal convictions or circumstances. Dante Gabriel Rossetti, for instance, marked his republican sympathies by apostrophizing the 'Place de La Bastille' in a sonnet, rather than the Place de la Concorde. Queen Victoria was all too conscious, during her 1855 visit to Paris, that 'Everywhere one walks on classical (Historical), alas! too often bloody ground.' Her monarchical nervousness in driving across 'the Place de la Concorde, most magnificent, where poor Louis XVI, Marie-Antoinette, and so many others were guillotined' was understandable; as was a later moment in the Tuileries Palace, where she thought of the blood that had flowed, a whole

[60] *Letters of Charles Dickens*, ed. Storey et al., v, 13, n. 4.
[61] Hofland, *Emily's Reward*, 32.
[62] *The Letters of Matthew Arnold*, ed. C. Y. Lang (6 vols, Charlottesville: University of Press of Virginia, 1996–2001), i, 28; iv, 25.
[63] 'Excursion', in *Last Words of Thomas Carlyle*, 179.

dynasty swept away, and all now depending on the 'too precious life' of her host, Napoleon III.[64]

Until 1871 it was the 1789 Revolution, rather than the intervening regime changes, that proved the major attraction: indeed, most visitors were quick to mention how swiftly a semblance of normal life returned to the streets of central Paris in the wake of the events of 1830, 1848, and 1851. By comparison with these, the destruction wrought during the Commune, in a city so recently regarded as 'the Seat of the Graces, the School of the Arts, the Fountain of Reason, the Eye of the World',[65] was on a more devastating scale.

As much as the actual damage done, it was the folk memories of the mass executions and violence of 1793 that lent contemporary events their power to shock. Henry James's hero, Lambert Strether, imagines that he can hear the very 'voice of Paris' from an open window in the Faubourg Saint-Germain: 'Thus and so, on the eve of the great recorded dates, the days and nights of revolution, the sounds had come in, the omens, the beginnings broken out. They were the smell of revolution, the smell of the public temper—or perhaps simply the smell of blood.' For Strether, the 'irremediable void' left by the destruction of the Tuileries palace triggers a sensitivity to personal loss and to his own country's experience of civil war that 'winces like a touched nerve'.[66] Touring Paris in December 1871, Margaret Oliphant was moved to a sense of the apocalyptic which would resurface in her supernatural tale *A Beleaguered City* (1880), where the ghosts of the dead return to challenge the nineteenth century's complacent rationalism and materialism:

> The shining city, clean as a bride in her general aspect as one had always seen her, was almost impassable, like grimy London in a thaw, every corner heaped with slush and mud; and here and there, as the slow cab...crept along at a footpace, gaunt ruins rising into the wintry morning light, the Tuileries, the Hôtel de Ville, the Ministry of War, and many others, terrible tokens of what had been....[T]he sight of these roofless and windowless piles of building, lifting their charred walls in the very centre of the movement of the great city, was strangely overwhelming and impressive.[67]

The skeletal ruins of a city so recently renowned for its spectacle and gaiety attracted previous visitors anxious to judge the scale of the devastation for themselves and fresh waves of English tourists attracted by their accounts. As Arnold Bennett commented, 'The articles which George Augustus Sala wrote under the title "Paris herself again" ought to have been paid for in gold by the hotel and pension-keepers of Paris. They awakened curiosity and the desire to witness the scene of terrible events'.[68]

This rush to marvel at and report upon Paris's tableaux of violence and death, as at some medieval *danse macabre*, was so unembarrassed and repetitive that a brief satire on the subject, *Forty-Eight Hours in Paris Amidst the Ruins* (1871), has repeatedly

---

[64] *Queen Victoria: Leaves from a Journal*, intro. Mortimer, 140, 86, 108.
[65] Lytton, *Parisians*, ii, 160.   [66] *The Ambassadors*, i, 79; ii, 274.
[67] M. O. W. Oliphant, *Memoir of the Life of Laurence Oliphant and of Alice Oliphant, his wife*, 6th edn (2 vols, Edinburgh: William Blackwood & Sons, 1891), ii, 82.
[68] A. Bennett, *The Old Wives' Tale*, ed. M. Harris (Oxford: Oxford University Press, 1995), 455.

been misclassified as documentary journalism.[69] The title gives the clue to the contempt of its author, Henry Addison, for the kind of war tourism which easier travel had made a weekend affair. Making deliberate play of the contrast between his title page appellation as 'Lieut-Col.' and the narrator's timorous character as one of the many English who 'travelled over from pure curiosity wetted and increased by the strong consciousness that there was considerable danger mixed up with the undertaking', the tale mocks the narrator's appetite for scenes of carnage, his credulity, and his attention to his own bodily comfort. In the course of one day he manages to take in the instant execution of a *pétroleuse*, firing squads gunning down Communards at opposite ends of the city in the Bois de Boulogne, and the cemetery of Père Lachaise, while also making sure he has time to repair to his hotel for food prepared to please English palates. Alarmed by the danger to which pedestrians could be exposed, he takes a carriage 'to arrange my ideas in my favourite resort when resident in Paris, the lovely and smiling little "parc de Monceaux"'. Once arrived there, it is 'the lovely trees cut down, the rare Indian plants torn up, the whole of the grass dug up' that make him declare 'I looked around, I almost screamed with horror', before he even notices corpses being exhumed from their temporary graves. Determined to experience revolutionary intrigue to the full by attending a Communist meeting, he falls easy prey to a French master of disguise and duplicity, and the story ends by revealing the narrator as another specimen of the English tourist dupe long familiar from the tales of G. W. M. Reynolds and Thackeray.

5.2.2 Theatres of death

The efficiency with which the guillotine in the Place de la Révolution sheared heads from bodies in the final two years of the 1789 Revolution, combined with the rapid manner in which the corpses scattered in the boulevards in subsequent engagements were cleared away to permit normal life to resume, persuaded the British, whose memories of civil war were two centuries old, that the French were naturally bloodthirsty and callous. As someone opposed to the death penalty, Amelia Opie felt it necessary to explain the hypnotic attraction the 'notorious engine of death' held for her: 'I do not believe that in my own country I should have gone to look at the gallows; but there was something new, curious and historical in the sight of the guillotine on the Place de Grève, which caused every repugnant feeling to be swallowed up in intense curiosity.'[70] Thackeray, who famously wrote of the 'terror and shame' he experienced at an English hanging, was equally appalled by the carnivalesque atmosphere surrounding French executions.[71]

[69] H. R. Addison, *Forty-Eight Hours in Paris Amidst the Ruins* (London: C. H. Clarke, 1871), 3–32, 4–5, 8. The Bodleian Library's copy is bound in a collection entitled 'Historical Pamphlets', while *ODNB* refers to it as though it were an eyewitness account.
[70] A. Opie, 'A Morning at Paris in 1829', in *The Aurora Borealis, a Literary Annual*, ed. The Society of Friends (Newcastle upon Tyne, 1833), 235.
[71] 'The Case of Peytel', in *Paris Sketch Book, Oxford Thackeray*, ii, 251–79. Cf. 'Going to see a man hanged', *Fraser's Magazine*, Aug. 1840, 15–58; repr. in *Oxford Thackeray*, iii, 189–205.

G. W. M. Reynolds and Dickens were rather more equivocal in their approach to the public performance of capital punishment. Given that Reynolds translated Victor Hugo's plea against the death penalty, his stance might appear unambiguous,[72] but in his fiction the sober realism involved in offering the exact dimensions of the guillotine, or describing the executioner's preparation of his victim, tends to give way all too soon to a certain enthusiasm for the macabre. A full-page illustration accompanied a French policeman's tale of the execution of a parricide in *Pickwick Abroad* (Fig. 6), and the reader is offered a ringside seat at the event: 'I saw the executioner apply his hand to the cord—the knife, already reeking with blood, fell—and the gory head of the parricide rolled into a basket beneath!' The fact that the gendarme, his story told, 'tossed off the remainder of his wine . . . and departed with a promise to call at Meurice's hotel' is doubtless intended to attribute the grisly enjoyment to French hard-heartedness, but Reynolds had already managed to reap full authorial advantage from his morbid recital.[73]

Despite deploring the behaviour and disposition of the crowds at public executions, Dickens responded to the inherent theatricality of the guillotine. Discovering that it was possible to hire the machine for a private demonstration, he told Wilkie Collins that he thought such an event would be 'like Punch's Show'.[74] Barely a year later, he made his first mention of *A Tale of Two Cities*, whose dramatic denouement would depend upon the inexorable operation of the guillotine. The novel's final scene may cast the determining vote in Dickens's account of the French Revolution by picturing it as essentially an act of working-class vengeance, but the long-drawn-out prose rhythms conveying the tumbrils' approach to the place of execution ensure that readers are partially implicated in the gruesome anticipatory pleasure of the *tricoteuses* as they count the heads crashing in front of them. The hiatus that occurs between the drop of head Twenty-Three and the last thoughts posthumously given to Carton opens up the gap in the last chapter's logic. However hard Dickens worked at the sentimental transformation of a mistaken execution into a redemptive sacrifice, the tenor of his novel was against him. Just as Carton's notion that Lucy's child can live the life his better self would have wished for is mere wish-fulfilment (Dickens would subsequently repudiate such pipe-dreams in the last chapter of *Great Expectation*, where Pip's similar hopes for his namesake are rebuffed by the child's mother), so Dickens fails to establish any real connection between the suffering and brutality of eighteenth-century France and the prophecy of the emergence of a 'beautiful city' and 'brilliant people'.[75] Successive French governments might pride themselves on erasing the signs of death from the site of mass execution, but for Dickens's readers and British tourists in Paris, the thrill would always lie in visualizing it as a theatre of death.

Acts of imagination were necessary to recall the bloody beheadings that had taken place in the Place de la Concorde, but Paris also offered more material displays

---

[72] V. Hugo, *Le dernier jour d'un condamné* (1829). G. W. M. Reynolds's translation, *Last Day of a Condemned Man* (1837), carried Reynolds's own preface, protesting against capital punishment.
[73] Reynolds, *Pickwick Abroad*, 108–9.
[74] *Letters of Charles Dickens*, ed. Storey et al., viii, 30.
[75] *A Tale of Two Cities*, ed. Sanders, 360.

Fig. 6. 'The Execution of the Parricide', steel engraving by Alfred Crowquill for G. W. M. Reynolds, *Pickwick Abroad; or The Tour in France* (London: Sherwood, Gilbert and Piper, 1839).

of the dead. One of the inset tales with which G. W. M. Reynolds sought to make his readers flesh creep in *Pickwick Abroad* concerned 'that loathsome tenement of death', the Catacombs, an ossuary dating from the late eighteenth century. A duped lover of the Napoleonic period, whose husband has been murdered by her seducer, lures her former lover to 'that place of skulls—in that vast sepulchre for the relics of millions of individuals—in the presence of hideous skeletons—surrounded by myriad of fleshless bones—at the lone hour of midnight—far beneath the reach of succour in case of danger'. Five days later she is discovered dead, her lover a gibbering maniac 'playing with the fleshless sculls [*sic*] around him!' The hysterically breathless tones in which Reynolds recounts this tale is unfortunately somewhat undermined by an accompanying woodcut, clearly not tailored to this story, showing a family party being escorted on a tour of the tastefully arranged bones and tombstones of Paris's long-departed dead.[76] By the mid-1850s it had apparently become more difficult to gain entry to the Catacombs, though Dickens assured Wilkie Collins that his name would act as an 'Open Sesame'.[77]

By 1830, Père Lachaise cemetery, the best-known of three new Paris cemeteries opened by Napoleon I, contained some 33,000 burials, amongst them long-term British residents, since interment there was open to all regardless of race or religion. Originally located beyond the city limits, it was some distance from the usual English stamping grounds, but swiftly became a site for British pilgrimages: in 1838 Thackeray mentioned his intention of taking an omnibus out there.[78] Although not officially Roman Catholic, the nature of some of the monumental statuary erected there excited the disapproval of staunch Evangelicals such as Mary Martha Sherwood, who deplored 'the secret infidelity' which led so many to adorn the graves with eloquent tributes to the departed, rather than simple reflections on Biblical teaching.[79]

The democratic nature of Paris's citizens' entitlement to burial also intrigued the British. Blanchard Jerrold considered the Second Empire's municipal regulation of all funerals sufficiently remarkable to devote an entire essay to it: the downside of the city's monopoly was the prohibitive tax which rose steeply with any refinement to the basic service.[80] Alice Corkran, who had been raised in Paris, made a magnificent funeral and the purchase of a family plot in Père Lachaise the yardstick of respectability in her short story 'Père Perrault's Legacy': it tells how one of the despised *chiffonniers*, or rag-and-bone men, of Paris spends the whole of a small legacy on a plot for himself and his wife rather than suffer interment in the communal fosse. When the magnificent cortège passes, the Emperor and Empress themselves accord respect by commanding their carriage to be drawn aside.[81]

[76] Reynolds, *Pickwick Abroad*, 431–48.
[77] *Letters of Charles Dickens*, ed. Storey et al., viii, 30.
[78] *Letters of Thackeray*, ed. Ray, i, 356.
[79] M. M. Sherwood, *Père La Chaise* (Wellington, Salop: F. Houlston & Son, 1823), 90.
[80] B. Jerrold, 'Departed this Life in Paris', in *Imperial Paris; including new scenes for old visitors* (London: Bradbury & Evans, 1855), pp. 43–62.
[81] A. Corkran, *The Young Philistine and Other Stories* (London: Burns & Oates, 1887), 89–126.

A further Parisian display of the dead, which fascinated partly because it had no direct English equivalent, was provided by the Morgue. Here the public was granted free access to unidentified dead bodies displayed on marble slabs, semi-naked and doused by a constant stream of water, their clothes hanging nearby as an added clue to their identity. Exhibited to all and sundry behind a glass window, as if 'Holbein should represent Death, in his grim Dance, keeping a shop, and displaying his goods like a Regent Street or Boulevard linen-draper', these corpses lured Dickens by an 'invisible force'.[82]

For Dickens the pathos of the Morgue lay in its ultimate objectification of human beings into things incapable of returning the onlookers' gaze.[83] The extent to which his own comic vision relied upon a not dissimilar reduction of his characters to objectified automata, often identifiable chiefly by their clothing, may have been partly what discomforted him. The thought of the processes of decomposition seeping into the water, food, and smells of Paris sickened and haunted him, and he found it unintelligible that French women and children seemed emotionally unaffected by this proximity to the reality of death.[84] Though Dickens does not dwell upon this aspect, the fact that these corpses provided viewers of both sexes with an uninterrupted view of semi-nude bodies added a further spectacular frisson to the experience, and may explain the nature of the distinction Thomas Hardy's wife, Emma, essayed after her visit to the Morgue: '*not offensive* but repulsive'.[85]

The Gothic appeal of the Morgue was heightened by its site on the Quai du Marché Neuf, near Notre-Dame on the crowded Île de la cité. The contrast of the 'artificial excitements' offered by the 'jugglers and quacks and cooks and barbers and dandies and gulls and sharpers', hoping to make money from the crowds who flocked to the Morgue, across the Pont Neuf, and the grim sight of a 'poor outcast stretched in silence and darkness forever' caused Carlyle, during his 1824 visit, to record, 'I think I never felt more shocked in my life'.[86]

In 1863 Haussmann advertised his intention of tidying a new and enlarged Morgue away behind the cathedral, onto the Quai de l'Archevêché—a move that provoked Robert Browning, in his poem 'Apparent Failure' (1864), to prompt his British readers into considering whether suicides might not be embraced within God's redemptive scheme.[87] George du Maurier used the relocation of the Morgue to indicate the passage of time in his Paris-centred novel *Trilby* (1894),[88] while John O'Shea clearly placed his tale *Mated from the Morgue* (1889) in 1866 so that his opening scene, involving the spectacle of a prostitute suicide soon to be transported to the dissecting-room—'Gruesome journey and grim destiny!'—could

[82] 'Railway Dreaming', in *Dickens' Journalism*, ed. Slater, iii, 375; 'Travelling Abroad', in *The Uncommercial Traveller and Reprinted Pieces*, 64.

[83] 'Some Recollections of Immortality', in *The Uncommercial Traveller and Reprinted Pieces*, 192.

[84] 'Travelling Abroad', in *The Uncommercial Traveller and Reprinted Pieces*, 65–7.

[85] M. Millgate, *Thomas Hardy: A Biography* (Oxford: Oxford University Press, 1982), 165.

[86] *Collected Letters of Thomas and Jane Welsh Carlyle*, ed. Sanders et al., iii, 181.

[87] Only after the 1880 Burial Act was it permitted to conduct a Christian service at the burial of a suicide in an English churchyard.

[88] G. du Maurier, *Trilby*, intro. E. Showalter, ed. D. Denisoff (Oxford: Oxford University Press, 1995), 26, 196.

reuse a previous piece of his journalism offering a full description of the new facility.[89]

Tourists were inherently unlikely to be able to identify the bodies on display, but these anonymous corpses, who had frequently died by their own hand or as victims of foul play, challenged spectators to invent the previous life histories that had led to this bleak conclusion. Most obviously they served as a grim moral warning of the madness and indigence awaiting those, particularly women, who had lost their way in this heartless city. The adolescent heroine of Ouida's *Tricotrin* (1869), for instance, is taken by her protector to see a young female suicide laid out there, as part of a monitory tour designed to alert her to the dangers lurking behind the dazzle and allure of Paris. Sala, anxious to wring the maximum affect from the Morgue in his novel *Quite Alone*, created what was in effect a split theatrical set. Upstairs the innocent young heroine sits chatting to the Morgue Keeper's daughter, while her roué, gambler father, is, unbeknownst to her, being stripped and displayed downstairs as a suicide—a procedure described in ghoulish detail.[90]

The Morgue also became closely associated with the invention of crime fiction, a genre itself often loosely based on the tales of that infamous French villain turned policeman, Vidocq.[91] By giving his first detective story the title 'The Murders in the Rue Morgue' (1841), Edgar Allan Poe economically signalled its genealogy. Sam Weller's tale, in Reynolds's *Pickwick Abroad*, of a drunken Englishman, left for dead by the thieves who mug him and taken to the Morgue by the night-police, is merely a comic variant on the standard tales of horror: this corpse is 'resurrected' when the water playing over the bodies cures his hangover, but in coming to life he causes the Morgue's concierge to have a heart attack.[92] The Thames corpses who float the narrative mysteries of both *Our Mutual Friend* and *Great Expectations* may well have drawn upon Dickens's memories of the drowned and disfigured victims, hooked from the Seine, that he had returned to again and again. Wilkie Collins's laconic 1845 report to his mother that he had 'looked in at the Morgue'[93] was to bear fruit in *The Woman in White* (1859), where the villainous Count Fosco, whose origin lay in 'a sort of French Newgate calendar' Collins had picked up on a Paris bookstall, ends his days in the Paris Morgue, 'unowned, unknown; exposed to the flippant curiosity of a French mob!'[94]

British commentators were frequently fascinated as much by the spectators at the Morgue as by the cadavers themselves. Time and again writers such as Dickens, Collins, and O'Shea dissected the nature of the audience. Taken in conjunction with the *tableau mort*, the viewers seemed to represent a Paris in miniature. Often ignoring their own narrative complicity in the experience, British writers portrayed

[89] J. O'Shea, *Mated from the Morgue: A Tale of the Second Empire* (London: Spencer Blackett, 1889), 103.

[90] *Quite Alone*, ii, 262–89.   [91] See section 13.5 for further discussion of Vidocq.

[92] *Pickwick Abroad*, 99.

[93] *The Letters of Wilkie Collins*, ed. W. Baker and W. Clarke (2 vols, London: Macmillan, 1999), i, 32.

[94] W. Collins, *The Woman in White*, ed. H. Sucksmith (London: Oxford University Press, 1975), 581, 599; *The Public Face of Wilkie Collins: The Collected Letters*, ed. W. Baker, A. Gasson, G. Law, and P. Lewis (4 vols, London: Pickering & Chatto, 2005), ii, 224.

the Morgue as a theatre, whose stage illuminated the harsher extremes of the city's life while the viewers, young and old, bourgeois and artisan, male and female, solitary and in family parties, conveyed the cold-hearted curiosity of the ultimately unknowable French.

———————

The previous two chapters, devoted to the materiality of the urban experience, have concentrated on Paris as a spectacle available to all British visitors, regardless of their ability to communicate in French. The final two chapters of the book's opening section focus on the type of social experience open to British writers and the degree to which they were able to penetrate Paris's cosmopolitan *salon* culture.

6

Socializing in Paris

A round of sightseeing, concerts, opera and theatre might suffice to fill briefer visits but a stay of any length, especially if accompanied by family members, raised the question of finding a wider social life in Paris. Getting to meet and talk to the city's resident population, other than by way of conversations with waiters and shop assistants, demanded access to a variety of networking systems which might vary in kind from the familial, through widely available public institutions, to the more private yet formal intellectual, artistic, and political world of the *salons*. In a period when a trip to Paris was to become a possibility for the lower middle classes, social cachet was increasingly attached to gaining access to French society, and satire accordingly directed at British visitors who clung to the company of their compatriots. The extent to which any particular British writer was able to penetrate Paris's Francophone social circles depended upon a variety of factors, including the length of their stay, their linguistic facility, their class, gender, marital status, preferred pastimes, and previous circle of acquaintance. Talent, or rather a reputation, backed by good letters of introduction, counted most in gaining entry to the intellectual and artistic world of the Parisian *salons* to which the next chapter will be dedicated.

6.1 SOCIABILITY AND GENDER

In the slightly curmudgeonly guise of an 'Old Paris Man' returning to former haunts after an absence of four years, Thackeray informed his *Punch* readership of the plans he had made: 'I will not tell any of my friends that I am here, thought I.' However, within five minutes, 'and before I had crossed the Place Vendôme, I had met five old acquaintances and friends, and in an hour afterwards the arrival of your humble servant was known to all our old set....I was not allowed to see a single Frenchman, save one...whom I saw at a Club in London last year, who speaks English as well as you.' Anxious to resume his French gastronomic experiences, Thackeray claimed to have been inundated by dinner invitations to tables groaning with viands imported from Fortnum and Mason and menus entirely dictated by British tastes.[1] The date of this short piece, in spring 1849, is significant.

---

[1] 'On some Dinners at Paris', first published in *Punch*, 3 Mar. 1849; repr. in *The Oxford Thackeray*, ed. G. Saintsbury (17 vols, London: Oxford University Press, 1910), viii, 479–81.

The February revolution the previous year, followed by the bloodshed on the city's streets during the 'June Days' when the provisional government took on the discontented working classes, had (for a while at least) scattered the inhabitants of the English colony.² Thackeray's article might therefore be interpreted as offering reassurance that Paris was once again a safe destination for the British, and, moreover, that there was a fair chance of reaping the rewards of having befriended the French exiles of the last regime.

As a solitary male, possessed of good French, familiar with the city, and now boasting a reputation as the author of *Vanity Fair*, Thackeray enjoyed considerable freedom of choice. He could accept an invitation to dine in the home of English acquaintance, take a seat at the table d'hôte of his hotel (which involved eating from the set menu sitting cheek by jowl with fellow guests), or make for one of the restaurants in the vicinity of the Palais-Royal, such as Véry, Véfour, or Les Trois Frères, all much frequented by the British. Sala, a keen trencherman, observed that, since the English of every class were notoriously unwilling to assimilate, equivalent establishments had grown up in the back streets of Paris, prepared to serve English cheeses, beer, and beef to down-at-heel British travellers and the English servant classes.³

The route of Thackeray's stroll, from a hotel packed with English and American visitors, through the heart of the English quarter towards the Place Vendôme facilitated the impromptu manner in which he was able to make his social arrangements. Dickens, praising Paris as 'the place for lonely men to dwell in', wrote of the ease with which, unaccompanied, he had frequented its restaurant and café culture during the winter of 1856. Conveniently forgetting the various members of his family who had accompanied him to Paris, he adopted a solitary fictional persona, partly in order to boast his own status as accomplished *flâneur*, and partly to contrast his bachelor role with what he wished to characterize as the typically French *familiale* enjoyment of the capital's parks and public places.⁴

Some kinds of jaunt were generically male. Dickens preferred the company of a compatriot or two for his night-time sallies into the world of louche Parisian dancing halls, but finding himself alone, described for Wilkie Collins an episode in the 'Don Giovanni' or 'Haroun Alraschid' style adventures they often undertook together:

> On Saturday night, I paid three francs at the door of that place where we saw the wrestling, and went in, at 11 o-Clock, to a Ball. Much the same as our own National Argyll Rooms. Some pretty faces, but all of two classes—wicked and coldly calculating, or haggard and wretched in their worn beauty. Among the latter, was a woman of thirty or so, in an Indian shawl, who never stirred from a seat in a corner all the time I was there. Handsome, regardless, brooding, and yet with some nobler qualities in her

---

² Lady Chichester (1801–76), an army widow who had endured the vicissitudes of military life in the West Indies and Quebec, was so fearful on 16 Feb. 1848 that she threatened to retreat to her cellar for the duration: *ODNB*.

³ G. A. Sala, *Quite Alone* (3 vols, London: Chapman & Hall, 1864), ii, 246–54.

⁴ 'Railway Dreaming', *Household Words*, 10 May 1856, 385–8; repr. in *Dickens' Journalism*, ed. M. Slater (4 vols, London: J. M. Dent, 1994–2000), iii, 370–6.

forehead. I mean to walk about tonight, and look for her. I didn't speak to her there, but I have a fancy that I should like to know more about her.[5]

Writing home in 1849 from Paris, where he had gone on an all-male trip, Dante Gabriel Rossetti explicitly instructed his brother not to show his scatological sonnet inspired by the cancan and the whores he and his companions had visited at the popular dance-hall, Le Bal Valentino—or, if William were to be obliged to pass the letter around the family, to be sure to 'scratch out' the poem before doing so.[6]

By contrast with the options open to single men, novels, short stories, and articles repeatedly stressed the very lonely lot of the solitary English female, confined to viewing Paris from the windows of a secluded room or apartment while waiting for an invitation or visit from a potential hostess. Such women otherwise ventured into the streets only on charitable missions, or to attend one of the Protestant churches or chapels to be found in the capital: although even then, according to Henrietta Jenkin, they might find themselves spurned by British congregations who had brought their home-grown snobberies with them.[7] The *flâneur*, in any event, simply had no female equivalent. Even the history of the word *flâneuse* as a feminized form of the sauntering male, carries something of the notion of the passive and immobile: Émile Littré's dictionary of 1863 cited its use in an advertisement to mean 'chaise longue'.[8] It is a measure of Elizabeth Barrett Browning's defiance of convention, and perhaps of her own frustrated desire for physical independence, that she should have portrayed her young gentlewoman Aurora Leigh 'walking', 'musing', and 'loitering' alone on the streets and quays of Paris.[9]

Although married women, widows, and elderly spinsters enjoyed a greater capacity for organizing their own social life, their arrangements tended to be less casual than those of Dickens or Thackeray. Visiting women writers or writers' wives were more dependent upon networks begun at home. When Elizabeth Gaskell determined on a break in Paris for herself and her daughter, Meta, she acquired an introduction through Unitarian circles: Florence Nightingale sent her to the famous *salonnière* Mary Mohl. This enabled them to meet far more 'rather famous people in Paris' than a married woman, unaccompanied by her husband or other male relative, could normally have expected to do.[10] Even before Robert's father and sister moved to Paris, Elizabeth Barrett Browning became an expert at tasking English women friends already in Paris, such as Anna Jameson or Thackeray's mother, with such matters as inspecting potential accommodation prior to their arrival, and taxed London acquaintance for introductions to the best

---

[5] *The Pilgrim Edition of the Letters of Charles Dickens*, ed. G. Storey et al. (12 vols, Oxford: Clarendon Press, 1965–2002), viii, 96, 623.

[6] *The Correspondence of Dante Gabriel Rossetti*, ed. W. E. Fredeman et al. (8 vols, Cambridge: D. S. Brewer, 2002–9), i, 115.

[7] [H. Jenkin,] *Once and Again: A Novel* (3 vols, London: Smith, Elder, 1865), i, 34.

[8] É. Littré, *Dictionnaire de la langue française*, vol. 3 (Paris: Pauvert, 1863), 1631; cited in P. P. Ferguson, 'The Flâneur On and Off the Streets of Paris', in K. Tester (ed.), *The Flâneur* (London: Routledge, 1994), 32.

[9] E. B. Browning, *Aurora Leigh*, bk 6, ll. 206, 282.

[10] *The Letters of Mrs. Gaskell*, ed. J. V. Chapple and A. Pollard (Manchester: Manchester University Press, 1966), 712.

salons. The newly married Emma Hardy, by contrast, had no such connections to exploit when she and her husband reached Paris in 1874 for their honeymoon, and since he had only recently begun to socialize with the London literati, Thomas Hardy had no introductions to the *salons.* Worse still, Emma Hardy's taste in gaudy, girlish clothes, unbecoming to a 34-year-old bride, made her a subject of comment and laughter in the Parisian streets.[11]

It is perhaps surprising to realize how circumscribed even a married woman's ventures into the public domain were. Dickens wrote to Wilkie Collins, as of a special event, of having taken 'Mrs Dickens, Georgina, and Mary and Kate, to dine at the Trois Frères. Mrs Dickens nearly killed herself, but the others hardly did that justice to the dinner that I had expected.'[12] Whereas such restaurants constituted the default option for bachelors in need of sustenance, women required a close male relative in attendance. Catherine Gore, the silver-fork novelist, always anxious to educate her readers in *comme il faut* behaviour, held it to be axiomatic that a married woman should not eat in a public restaurant unattended by her husband.[13] The reason for this prohibition is made clear in Flaubert's *Éducation Sentimentale* (1869), where dining in popular restaurants or displaying oneself in an open carriage is the privilege of the mistress rather than the wife. Little had changed by the early years of the twentieth century, when *A Woman's Guide to Paris* (1909) lamented that unaccompanied female travellers still found themselves eating dull hotel meals rather than eating out or attending the theatre.[14]

Margaret Oliphant recalled the stir she had caused in the 1860s when, having settled a party composed entirely of women and children in their hotel for the night, she had ordered 'an innocent champagne, St. Peray', followed by 'meat and wine', rather than 'teas or coffee meals'.[15] The custom of patronizing pastry shops, Henrietta Jenkin observed, effectively confined women to eating in the expensive tourist haunts of the right bank, because the left bank was ill-supplied with such places so that unaccompanied women risked finding themselves placed in unfortunate proximity to the predominantly male clientele frequenting the quarter's restaurants.[16]

The nearer to distressed gentility women approached, the greater the importance of preserving respectability. Even the presence of their fiancés is insufficient protection from dubious company, for Braddon's two convent-educated Irish sisters when their menfolk propose adjourning for Tortoni's famous ices after a trip to the theatre.[17] At the opposite end of the social spectrum, dining out appealed as a déclassé novelty. Having dined on oysters and fish at the restaurant *Au Rocher de Cancale*, Lady Blessington confided to her journal:

[11] M. Millgate, *Thomas Hardy: A Biography* (Oxford: Oxford University Press, 1982), 165–6.
[12] *Letters of Charles Dickens*, ed. Storey et al., viii, 95.
[13] C. Gore, *The Ambassador's Wife* (3 vols, London: Richard Bentley, 1842), iii, 183–4.
[14] Quoted in R. Mullen and J. Munson, *'The Smell of the Continent': The British Discover Europe* (Basingstoke: Macmillan, 2009), 40.
[15] *The Autobiography of Margaret Oliphant*, ed. E. Jay (Oxford: Oxford University Press, 1990), 107.
[16] *Once and Again*, ii, 7.
[17] M. E. Braddon, *Under the Red Flag* (Leipzig: Tauchnitz, 1884), 76.

A *diner de restaurant* is pleasant from its novelty. The guests seem less ceremonious and more gay; the absence of the elegance that marks the dinner-table appointments in a *maison bien monté*, gives a homeliness and heartiness to the repast; and even the attendance of two or three ill-dressed *garçons* hurrying about, instead of half-a-dozen sedate servants in rich liveries, marshalled by a solemn-looking *maître-d'hôtel* and groom of the chambers, gives a zest to the dinner often wanted in more luxurious feasts.[18]

For all their freedom to frequent Parisian cafés and restaurants, British men were sometimes a little inclined to feel themselves deprived of their homosocial London clubs, where the system of approving or blackballing potential members made it likely that one would be assured of meeting social peers. In the Parisian portion of his novel *The Martins of Cro' Martin* (1857), Charles Lever has a British member of the 'Cercle' spell out the social contract to his countrymen when one of them has suggested nominating a moneylender of uncertain origin to the 'Cercle':

A club is a democracy, where each man, once elected, is the equal of his neighbor. Society is, on the other hand, an absolute monarchy, where your rank flows from the fountain of honor—the host. Take him along with you to her grace's 'tea,' or my lady's reception this evening, and see if the manner of the mistress of the house does not assign him his place, as certainly as if he were marshalled to it by a lackey. All his mock tranquillity and assumed ease of manner will not be proof against the icy dignity of a grande dame; but in the Club he's as good as the best, or he'll think so, which comes to the same thing.[19]

To such unfortunate 'clubless dandies' Forester's guide recommended particular cafés such as those of the Passage de l'Opéra, also frequented, since 1848, by 'minor speculators of the Stock Exchange.... To the gay world all the rest is terra incognita.'[20] As an English-language paper, the *Paris Satirist*, inquired in 1836, tongue firmly in cheek, where were the Parisian equivalents of cricket and the boat race? 'The British Newsroom at Galignani's', the English Jockey Club together with 'Pigeon-shooting at Mr Bryon's establishment at Tivoli', were all it could recommend as substitutes.[21]

When it had opened in 1801 at 18 Rue Vivienne, Galignani's had been part of Paris's comparatively small clubland, in the area between the Rue Richelieu and the Place de la Madeleiene and adjoining the French and Italian Operas. Its reading room, giving onto an attractive garden, offered some 200 or more European and American newspapers, and operated in concert with a circulating library on the first floor which by 1836 contained some 30,000 books. The addition of a room, open from 8.00 a.m. to 11.00 p.m. for the sole purpose of 'conversation', contrived to turn the firm's premises into a gentlemen's club for British male residents and visitors. In describing the young Thackeray's disruptive behaviour, the garrulous

---

[18] Countess of Blessington, *The Idler in France* (2 vols, London: Henry Colburn, 1841), ii, 79–80.

[19] C. Lever, *The Martins of Cro' Martin* (2 vols), in *The Novels of Charles Lever*, ed. by his daughter (36 vols, London: Downey, 1897–9), ii, 17.

[20] T. Forester (ed.), *Paris and its Environs: An Illustrated Handbook* (London: Henry Bohn, 1859), 92.

[21] 'English Amusements', *Paris Satirist*, 14 Apr. 1836, 3.

memoirs of Frederick Locker-Lampson help to explain the firm's decision to separate serious readers from mere browsers:

> Some years ago—I met a man somewhere—I forget where, or who he was—who told me that in past times he used to pay annual visits to Paris; that he often looked into Galignani's reading room (now defunct), and there was to be seen a very tall young man, with black hair and spectacles, who used to *rôder autour de la chambre*, with his hands in his pockets and his shoulders up to his ears, in a shivery, restless, uncomfortable sort of way. This young man occasionally would take up a paper, glance at it, and then fling it back on the table, over the heads of the readers.[22]

Galignani's move in 1856 to 224 Rue de Rivoli set the seal on the firm's social credentials: wealthy visitors had only to take a very short stroll from the fashionable Hôtel Meurice at 228 to inscribe their name and address in Galignani's Visitors' Book, whence it was transcribed to the pages of the *Messenger*, serving as a formal announcement of availability for social invitations.

The English Jockey Club, though it boasted two French Dukes as founder members, had been primarily designed, from its inception on the Rue Blanche in 1825, to cater for the British. Nevertheless it also attracted Anglophile Frenchmen, who, according to Gore's novel *Greville: or, a Season in Paris*, took it in their stride when the racing was moved in 1836 from the Bois de Boulogne to Chantilly, 25 miles north of Paris, and even partook in such English sporting events as Cowes week.[23] Meanwhile the Club's city quarters became as much the home of a dandified demimonde as of the racing fraternity. Its relocation at the apogee of the Second Empire to the Boulevard des Italiens, next to the newly commissioned Opéra, to which members enjoyed access through a stage door, served to confirm the slightly louche air it had by then acquired. Vizetelly, who took up the rôle of a Paris correspondent in 1865, recalled how horse-racing had come to dominate the fashions: men sported scarf pins, shirt fronts, cuffs, collars, and ties emblazoned with jockeys, horses, saddles, stirrups, spurs and whips, and hunting paraphernalia, while the *demi-mondaines* 'bedecked themselves with massive earrings shaped of horse-shoe form, from which stirrups dangled as drops'.[24]

The roped-off swimming pools on the Seine were a further location where club-like facilities, such as an elegant houseboat, a garden, or a reading-room and a dining-room, could be found.[25] Dickens wrote of one hot day when he had joined the 'male population in striped drawers, of various gay colours, who walked up and down arm in arm, drank coffee, smoked cigars, sat at little tables, conversed politely with the damsels who dispensed the towels, and every now and then pitched themselves into the river head foremost, and came out again to repeat this social rou-

[22] F. Locker-Lampson, *My Confidences: An Autobiographical Sketch Addressed to my Descendants*, ed. A. Birrell (London: Smith, Elder, 1896), 302.

[23] C. Gore, *Greville: or, a Season in Paris* (3 vols, London: Henry Colburn, 1841), ii, 141.

[24] H. Vizetelly, *Glances Back through Seventy Years: Autobiographical and Other Recollections* (2 vols, London: Kegan Paul, Trench, Trübner, 1893), ii, 125.

[25] Edward Planta, *A New Picture of Paris or, the Stranger's Guide to the French Metropolis* (London: Samuel Leigh and Baldwin & Cradock, 1831), 389, 285.

tine', noting that he had only participated 'in the water part of the entertainments'.[26] For more sedate visitors Forester's guide proposed Le Cercle des Échecs,[27] although a novel of the time implied that chess was yet another game through which professional confidence tricksters could strike up acquaintance with unsuspecting British amateurs over the café tables of the Palais-Royal.[28] There remained the alternative for those like Joseph Crowe, thoroughly accustomed since childhood to the French way of life, of joining a French institution such as the Cercle des Arts, which he did in the early 1850s, noting that it provided both a useful bachelor pied-à-terre and a vital route to the information he needed as a foreign correspondent.[29]

6.2 SOCIALIZING WITH THE FRENCH

It was entirely possible to attend theatres, visit museums, shop, swim, ride, or shoot, observing but never mixing with the French. Moving beyond the confines of the English colony or the fellow English-speaking guests in one's hotel demanded an effort, for, as Lady Blessington told her readers, 'Parisian society is very exclusive, and is divided into small coteries, into which a stranger finds it difficult to become initiated.' The Parisian social system, she explained, was organized on different principles from its London equivalent, preferring frequent gatherings among a restricted circle to the less selective gatherings of their British neighbours. 'To preserve the charm of these unceremonious *réunions*, strangers are seldom admitted to them, but are invited to the balls, dinners, or large parties, where they see French people *en grande tenue*, both in dress and manner, instead of penetrating into the more agreeable parties to which I have referred.' The more intimate society, however, she opined, 'is precisely the sort of one that literary men would, I should suppose, like to mingle in, to unbend their minds from graver studies, and yet not pass their time unprofitably; for in it, politics, literature, and the fine arts, generally furnish the topics of conversation.'[30]

When 'mere tourists' began to arrive in increasing numbers, an English writer's ability to boast acquaintance with Frenchmen and women of note sounded a note of cultural superiority. As Elizabeth Barrett Browning wrote rather smugly to her sister Henrietta in 1850:

> We shall have art and literature in Paris, and Robert being a member of the Historical Institute, and another literary society, (for which they sent him diplomas) we shall be able to know the best people we like to know. So that's our scheme! We shall avoid the English and live our own free lives.[31]

[26] 'Travelling Abroad', in *The Uncommercial Traveller and Reprinted Pieces* (London: Oxford University Press, 1958), 65.

[27] Forester, *Paris and its Environs*, 92.   [28] [Jenkin,] *Once and Again*, i, 63.

[29] J. Crowe, *Reminiscences of Thirty-Five Years of My Life* (London: John Murray, 1895), 85.

[30] Countess of Blessington, *The Idler in France*, i, 268–9.

[31] *Elizabeth Barrett Browning: Letters to her Sister, 1846–1859*, ed. L. Huxley (London: John Murray, 1929), 124.

By contrast, 'The Family that goes abroad because it is the thing to do', caricatured by Anthony Trollope in 1865, was looked down on precisely because it made 'no preparation...for social intercourse. Letters of introduction are not obtained, nor is there time for any sojourn that would make an entrance into society possible.'[32]

Even with the necessary introductions, the 'real, rougeless, *intime*' of French sociability would, Thackeray insisted, forever remain impenetrable to British visitors.[33] Although as an adult he visited Paris almost annually, shortly before his death he claimed that 'he had never in his life been intimate in a single French family'.[34] His youthful experiences had led him to he declare that if an English gentleman lived in Paris for ten years he was likely, at best, to enjoy 'say three dinners, and very lucky too' in a 'French private house'.[35] When Thackeray's wife's mental instability left him bereft, the French engraver Louis Marvy and his family welcomed him, but in the main his socializing with Frenchmen took place in a professional capacity and a public venue.[36] The success of *Vanity Fair* seems to have secured his admission to the home of renowned Parisians such as the theatre critic Jules Janin, or the painter Théodore Gudin.[37] Thackeray's account of dinner at the Gudins in 1851 suggests obligatory entertaining: the motley assortment of French and British assembled around their table included another painter, a French general, a Prince, an entrepreneurial British railway engineer and his wife, and 'one of the stupidest and handsomest women I ever saw in my life' who proceeded to ignore her immediate neighbour, Thackeray, in favour of talking over his back to a handsome Frenchman.[38] Dickens wrote enthusiastically of lavish dinners given in their homes by French hosts in his honour, but their very grandeur confirms the view of Paris habitués such as the Lady Blessington and Thackeray that such occasions were formal events rather than expressions of intimate friendship.

It is possible that the bourgeois tone characterizing the leading circles of the Third Republic produced a change in social mores. The impression given by the memoirs of that socially protean journalist Richard Whiteing contrive to suggest that he had found himself equally welcome at 'Sunday-at-homes' with Gustave Doré's family and at tea parties in the Batignolles given by a female stationer's assistant, later denounced as having been a *pétroleuse* during the Commune.[39] The suspicion that these occasions may have been written up in such a way as to suggest a greater familiarity with the domestic lives of interesting Parisians than their nature really warranted is augmented by a remark made by Henriette Corkran, who had met Whiteing in her mother's *salon*: she claimed that 'strange

---

[32] A. Trollope, *Travelling Sketches*, ed. A. Briggs (New York: Arno Press, 1981), 10.

[33] 'On Some French Fashionable Novels', in *Paris Sketch Book, Oxford Thackeray*, ii, 97.

[34] G. N. Ray, *Thackeray: The Uses of Adversity (1811–1846)* (London: Oxford University Press, 1955), i, 171.

[35] 'On Some French Fashionable Novels', 94.

[36] 'A St Philip's Day in Paris', first published in *Britannia*, 15 and 22 May 1841; 'Shrove Tuesday in Paris', first published *in Britannia*, 5 June 1841; both repr. in *Loose Sketches, Oxford Thackeray*, iii, 461–507.

[37] *The Letters and Private Papers of William Makepeace Thackeray*, ed. G. N. Ray (4 vols, Cambridge, Mass: Harvard University Press, 1945–6), ii, 500; iii, 460.

[38] Ibid. ii, 732.

[39] R. Whiteing, *My Harvest* (London: Hodder & Stoughton, 1915), 240–2, 89–90.

contrasts and class inequalities interest him more far more than politics or even literature'.[40]

For those without professional avenues for broaching Parisian society, there remained one other route for meeting the cosmopolitan array of talented men and women to be found in mid-nineteenth-century Paris: the ambassadorial receptions.

6.3 THE BRITISH EMBASSY

Purchased in 1814 on behalf of George III by the Duke of Wellington from Pauline Borghese, Napoleon Bonaparte's sister, the British Embassy, in the Hôtel de Charost, at 39 Rue du Faubourg Saint-Honoré, formed a rallying-point for the English colony clustered in the surrounding streets. It was also the symbolic location for expressions of changing French attitudes to the English. Lady Blessington, who had remained in the house next door to the Secretary of the Embassy during *les Trois Glorieuses* of July 1830, in early August recorded, 'The English are very popular in Paris at this moment, and the ready recognition of Louis-Philippe by our government has increased this good feeling. A vast crowd escorted the carriage of Mr Hamilton, the Secretary of the Embassy, to his door, as he returned from his first accredited audience of the new monarch, and cries of *Vivent les Anglais!* filled the air.'[41] A decade later, Sala recalled a similar outburst of public opinion, only in this case it took the form of Anglophobia. Louis-Napoleon's use of English shores for launching an abortive coup had combined with the national sentiment occasioned by the return of Napoleon I's remains for reburial in Paris, to foment bad feeling. Crowds would gather every evening outside the Embassy, baying for the blood of Granville, the Ambassador, and even for that of a Mr Patten, an Embassy physician who was unfortunate enough to live opposite. Sala's mother was so alarmed that she removed her children from their schools and hurried back to England.[42]

As Great Britain's premier Embassy, in days when the diplomatic service was a genteel occupation rather than a profession, it attracted ambassadorial grandees who often showed very little enthusiasm for returning to England when rudely dislodged from their stints at the apex of Parisian society by a change of British government. Viscount Granville (George Leveson-Gower), who served from 1824 to 1828; December 1830- to mid-March 1835; and again from 5 May 1835 to mid October 1841, toured Europe for two years after this final posting rather than return home. Lord Cowley (Henry Wellesley), after a very brief first posting (30 March–4 May 1835) returned for a second stint (16 October 1841–June 1846), then retired to a house in the Place Vendôme. He died the following year during the Marquess of Normanby's tour of office (1846–52) and so did not live long

---

[40] H. Corkran, *Celebrities and I* (London: Hutchinson, 1902), 356.
[41] Countess of Blessington, *The Idler in France*, ii, 246.
[42] *The Life and Adventures of George Augustus Sala written by himself*, 2nd edn (2 vols, London: Cassell, 1895), i, 135.

enough to see his eldest son, the second Baron Cowley, enter the Embassy, where he served from 1852 to 1867.

The mores of England's upper classes tended to make these Ambassadors sympathetic to the moral tone of the French court and the scandalous ménages exiled from London high society. A happy family man when he took up this posting, Granville was married to the niece of his former lover, and one of the two illegitimate children borne to him by the Countess of Bessborough worked as his Private Secretary. Though remarried, the first Lord Cowley had been involved in a spectacular divorce case when his first wife eloped; and while in post the Marquess of Normanby indulged in a liaison with Louise-Agathe Beaudouin, better known by her stage name, 'Atala Beauchêne'. At the height of the Second Empire, the Embassy staff included at least two legendary womanizers: Julian Fane and Wilfrid Scawen Blunt. The latter kept a diary itemizing sexual conquests that included, in quick succession, Lord Cowley's daughter, Feodorowna, and the English courtesan Catherine Walters, or 'Skittles' as she was known, who *inter alios* also enjoyed the favours of Napoleon III and the Prince of Wales.

Yet Fane and Blunt's reputations as minor poets also suggest the cultured background from which such appointees often came. Thackeray's creation, the dapper young poet-attaché Walsingham Hely, is cut from their mould: his less than onerous life at least pleases his mother, who is anxious that he avoid becoming 'a victim to too much money, pleasure, idleness' as his older brother, who died a rake, had done.[43] Great Britain's mid-century representative, the Marquess of Normanby, had four romantic novels to his name, and an interest in amateur theatricals that extended well beyond his extramarital liaisons. Such personal interests caused the Embassy staff to welcome illustrious British writers to their dining table.

By the time that Dickens decided to winter in Paris in 1846 he was sufficiently famous to be confident of such an invitation from Lord Normanby. On his side, Dickens benefited from being able to give the impression to correspondents at home of being intimately acquainted with the fraught state of Franco-British relations, provoked by the marriage of the Queen of Spain's sister to a son of Louis-Philippe, and the annexation of Cracow by the Austrians. After his first dinner at the Embassy, Dickens felt entitled to report to Forster that Normanby seemed to have 'an anxious haggard way with him, as if his responsibilities were more than he had bargained for'. A couple of days later he was referring to him as 'the Markis' and giving it to be understood that his discussions with Normanby of possible 'theatricals' had a bearing on the political situation, since the Ambassador had explained that French plays might, at the current juncture, act 'as a bit of a conciliation, and a popular move'.[44] In January 1863, during Baron Cowley's period of office, Dickens agreed to give readings from *David Copperfield* at the Embassy to raise money for charity. According to his own account, 'such a hit was never made here' and 'gorgeous beauties all radiant with diamonds, clasped their fans between their two hands, and rolled bout in ecstasy' even if they did not understand

[43] *Adventures of Philip, Oxford Thackeray*, xvi, 347.
[44] *Letters of Charles Dickens*, ed. Storey et al., iv, 663, 669, 672.

English.[45] Lady Cowley's report, however, suggests that, although he was suffi-ciently famous to be invited to Embassy dinners, his status was more that of actor than distinguished visitor: she apparently came upon Dickens changing behind a pillar and considerably embarrassed by his trouserless state.[46]

The aristocratic note struck by Embassy appointments helped to remind those who attended the Embassy's levées that they were in the presence of those who rep-resented Her Britannic Majesty. George Sala recalled how Lady Granville came with a temporary throne embellished with the royal coat of arms when patronizing func-tions outside the Embassy.[47] This first lady of the Embassy, who conceived of herself as a home-loving person, unlikely to impress the Paris *élégantes*, had considerably overspent the Foreign Office budget during her husband's first term in office by commissioning glazed galleries from the fashionable French architect Louis Visconti, and thought nothing of ordering a lackey to produce the effect of an instant orang-ery for an event in January 1826 by tying individual fruits to the trees.[48]

Thackeray, who had been young and impecunious during Granville's reign, depicted the semi-autobiographical hero of *The Adventures of Philip* as mortified by the shabby figure he cut at the Queen's birthday celebrations among the Embassy's 'saloons, galleries, supper-rooms, and halls of gilded light' and its gardens, deco-rated with 'a beautiful row of illuminated lamps, lighting up a great coronal of flowers'.[49] The success of *Vanity Fair* transformed him into a welcome guest of the Embassy set: writing to Jane Brookfield in January 1851, he mentioned attending Lady Sandwich's ball: 'Everybody was there—Thiers Molé and the French Sosiatee: and lots of English. The Castlereaghs very kind and hearty... Ld Normanby & wife exceeding gracious—Lady Waldegrave—all sorts of world—and if I want the reign of pleasure it is here it is here.'[50] Nevertheless, he did not forget the slights he felt his social equals had meted out to him in his penniless youth. Contrasted to that manly pen-pusher Philip Firmin, hero of *The Adventures of Philip*, the poet-attaché Walsingham Hely, is shown as an effete dandy, and, the surname, Phipps, the Marquess of Normanby's patronymic, is bestowed upon a humble journalist col-league of Firmin's.

Compatriots with more radical sympathies than Thackeray's had always affected to despise an institution representing the English crown. The Irish Lady Sydney Morgan seized the opportunity to air her political antipathy to the English by contrasting the stuffy formality of Embassy receptions with the less pretentious elegance to be found in the French *salons*.[51] G. W. M. Reynolds devoted a chapter

---

[45] Ibid. viii, 210–11.

[46] Ibid. viii, 202–3; C. Gladwin, *The Paris Embassy* (London: Collins, 1976), 102.

[47] Sala, *Life and Adventures*, i, 129–31.

[48] K. Hickman, *Daughters of Britannia: The Lives and Times of Diplomatic Wives* (London: Flamingo, 2000), 121; C. MacCallum, 'Visconti et l'ambassade de Grande-Bretagne', in B. De Andia and D. Fernandes (eds), *Rue du Faubourg St Honoré* (Paris: Délégation à l'action artistique de la ville de Paris, 1994), 147.

[49] *Adventures of Philip*, 358.   [50] *Letters of Thackeray*, ii, 731.

[51] Lady S. Morgan, *France* (London: Henry Colburn, 1817), i, 405–6. On a later occasion, having accepted an invitation to celebrate the 'English' King's birthday, she transferred her radical critique to the person of the Austrian ambassador, representative of a regime that had recently proscribed her writings: *France in 1829–30*, 2nd edn (2 vols, London: Saunders & Otley, 1831), 148–9.

of *Pickwick Abroad* to venting his spleen against an institution that offered, in miniature, a picture of all he held to be wrong with English society: an engraving of the Embassy façade is surrounded by text representing it as the heartland of the English swindler. The ambassador, Lord Pompus, and his wife, residing at the 'British Legation Hotel', are impostors disguised in fine clothing, who host *salons* where stout-hearted Britons like Pickwick find themselves mingling in the crush with notorious rogues. Worse still, the Embassy replicates Great Britain's inequitable society: a later chapter shows the British Consul, housed in the Embassy, obsequiously supplying an absconding aristocrat with a passport while simultaneously dispatching an impoverished English workman to a French debtors' prison, 'where he died of a broken heart in the course of three or four months, leaving a wife and large family without the means of obtaining a morsel of bread'. Always ready to settle a few personal scores amidst his class warfare, Reynolds used the Embassy assembly to introduce a series of thinly disguised portraits of long-time foreign residents in Paris, starting with the 'somewhat stout and dumpy... celebrated Mrs. Goffe, the authoress'. 'A quiet, domesticated woman, fond of her children, and devotedly attached to literary pursuits', she is accompanied by her husband, 'good-looking, but somewhat wild' and 'on the whole... much liked by the English in Paris'. Having thus disposed of Catherine Gore and her husband, Charles, an Embassy attaché from 1832 to 1840, Reynolds sketched the Embassy lawyer, various military figures, and Baron Rothschild, who appears as the pock-marked 'Baron James Rochiel, the great banker... talking with a degree of emphasis that betrays consciousness of superiority... and... boasting of favours which were never accorded him'.[52]

Since the Embassy's admission criteria were less stringent than those for Queen Victoria's drawing-room, it allegedly became the route by which English *parvenus* obtained their entrée to society. In her 1842 travel guide, Catherine Gore identified this loophole: 'Persons, of whatever nation, provided with letters of introduction, especially if diplomatic, are sure of being warmly welcomed; and once established in French society, are fixed there for life.' Her fiction also dwelt heavily upon the contrast between the exclusivity of Carlist receptions in the Faubourg Saint-Germain and official celebrations such as the Queen's birthday 'at the Ambassade d'Angleterre; where, as in every foreign circle, all parties, sects, and opinions, are of necessity admitted'. Although a later chapter defends this eclecticism as offering a venue unsullied by party politics, Gore was at repeated pains to point out that Ambassadresses regularly also hosted 'private parties' or weekly *salons* with far more select guest lists.[53] She would doubtless have approved of Lady Cowley's attempts to weed her guest list by receiving only those who had first been presented at the English court; but if the social satirists are to be believed, Lady Cowley's embargo only intensified the stratagems of social climbers. In 1846, just as Lady Cowley concluded her reign, Thackeray

[52] G. W. M. Reynolds, *Pickwick Abroad: or, The Tour in France* (London: Sherwood, Gilbert, & Piper, 1839), 100, 255–6, 111, 115.

[53] C. Gore, *Paris in 1841* (London: Longman, Brown, Green, & Longmans, 1842), 234; *Greville*, i, 183; iii, 69; i, 234. Cf. *The Ambassador's Wife*, ii, 265–7.

and Frances Trollope—who, like many English novelists of the day, used bankers as their marker of social insecurity—concurred in identifying the British Embassy in Paris as the weak link in the maintenance of English class barriers. In his *Punch* series 'The Snobs of England', Thackeray described a banking family with the surname of Muggins:

> It was abroad that they learned to be genteel. They pushed into all foreign courts, and elbowed their way unto the balls of Ambassadors. They pounced upon the stray nobility, and seized young lords travelling with their bear leaders. They gave parties at Naples, Rome, and Paris. They got a royal prince to attend their soirées at the latter place, and it was here that they first appeared under the name of De Mogyns.[54]

Frances Trollope, who in 1846 was repackaging her knowledge of Paris and its ways into a how-not-to-embark-on-Continental-travel novel entitled *The Robertses on their Travels*, concentrated on the specifics by which such 'elbowing' was achieved. The novel begins with the banker's wife congratulating herself on having used the family apothecary to obtain a letter of introduction from one of his titled patients to secure the Robertses' introduction to the Embassy. Once in Paris, Mrs Roberts is thrilled to find that admission to Embassy events allows the family to form acquaintance without being at the expense of hosting their own dinner parties. Unfortunately, given her enthusiasm for trumpeting her own social successes, Trollope had managed to time her research trip for *Paris and Parisians 1835* during the ambassadorial interregnum.[55]

Upon one thing many travel guide writers agreed: the hospitality offered at the balls thrown by the British Embassy seemed parsimonious. Reynolds's Pickwick and friends remark upon the 'prudential and economical arrangements' which neglect to offer dinner, and the journalist Henry Vizetelly claimed that the second Lord Cowley, forced to give an exceptionally grand ball for visiting dignitaries to the 1867 Exposition Universelle, employed the service of a bagpiper to ensure that his French guests went home supperless, adding: 'It was an old joke that smoke was rarely seen to issue from the ambassador's kitchen chimney.'[56] Gore, in honour bound to defend the institution for which her husband worked, was a lone voice of loyal support. Indeed, the statistics praising the Embassy's lavish provision that she offers in her novel *Greville* sound as if they have been extracted from an official report: 'the hospitalities during the last quarter of a century have exceeded fourfold, those of any other household in Paris, during four times the same number of years.'[57] In point of fact, the Embassy probably assumed that many of their guests would have followed Parisian habits, dining early and speedily so as to leave time for an evening at the theatre or attending a *salon*.

---

[54] 'On Some Respectable Snobs', in *The Book of Snobs, Oxford Thackeray*, ix, 292.
[55] F. Trollope, *The Robertses on their Travels* (3 vols, London: Henry Colburn, 1846), i, 4, 24, 66–8; *Paris and the Parisians in 1835* (2 vols, Paris: Baudry's European Library, 1836), i, 7.
[56] Reynolds, *Pickwick Abroad*, 116; Vizetelly, *Glances*, ii, 193–4.
[57] *Greville*, i, 232.

As this chapter has indicated, the range of Parisian social events and milieux open to visitors was limited, which helps to explain why British accounts of the city's attractions trod such a repetitively narrow round. Nevertheless, there was a further formal social institution, perceived as characteristically Parisian, where British writers bearing appropriate credentials could hope to meet with those who counted in this cosmopolitan city; and it is to the *salon* that the next chapter is devoted.

7

The *salons*

The salon is an abstract circle in which male and female, like mathematical ciphers, are equal and interchangeable; personality becomes a sexually undifferentiated formal mask. Rousseau says severely of the eighteenth-century salon, 'Every woman at Paris gathers in her apartment a harem of men more womanish than she.' The salon is politics by coterie, a city-state or gated forum run on a barter economy of gender exchange.

Elegance, the ruling principle of the salon, dictates that all speech must be wit, in symmetrical pulses of repartee... The salon, like the object-realm venerated by the esthete, is a spectacle of dazzling surfaces—words, faces, and gestures exhibited in a blaze of hard glamour.[1]

From time to time French exiles attempted to transport the *salon* culture, but it never became entirely indigenized in Great Britain. This chapter examines the British fascination with an institution they regarded as characteristically Parisian, even while acknowledging that its days of its cultural pre-eminence and power-brokering were in decline. In the earlier years of the period with which this book deals, so essential were the *salons* to Parisian sociability that British residents also adopted the formula. The concluding section of the chapter discusses the part played by the *salons* in the professional lives and self-esteem of many a British writer visiting or working in Paris for any length of time.

7.1 THE CULTURAL PRACTICES OF THE *SALON*

After careful study, under expert tutelage, of the rites and rituals of the *salon*, Elizabeth Gaskell concluded, 'the agreeableness of these informal receptions depends on many varying circumstances, and I doubt if they would answer in England'.[2] Having experienced a little of Parisian *salon* life, Margaret Oliphant came to much the same conclusion and returned to England to write her comic masterpiece *Miss Marjoribanks* (1866), based upon the heroine's preposterous idea of transplanting the *salon* to the English provinces. The novel's heroine, while acknowledging 'that

---

[1] C. A. Paglia, 'Oscar Wilde and the English Epicene', *Raritan* 4(3) (Winter 1985), 85–109.
[2] 'French Life', in *The Works of Elizabeth Gaskell*, ed. J. Shattock et al. (10 vols, London: Pickering & Chatto, 2005–6), i, 384.

there was a great difference between the brilliant society of London, or Paris... where women have generally the best of it, and can rule in their own right; and even the best society of a country town, where husbands are commonly unmanageable', nevertheless determines to indigenize the *soirée*.[3]

Not the least of Miss Marjoribanks' problems was the need to disrupt the gender segregation that prevailed in British society, where women were expected to leave their menfolk to linger over post-prandial port and cigars, rather than proceeding together to mingle with further guests in the *salon*. Nor were the gatherings in large London houses, reigned over by political hostesses, truly comparable because their focus was narrower and yet their invitation list large and indiscriminate, while London's lionizing literary parties, or Unitarian Manchester's evenings of rational discussion, seemed a little tame by contrast with the exotic mix to be found in Parisian *salons*.[4]

The distinctiveness of the *salon* was partly a matter of urban geography: mid-nineteenth-century Paris was far more compact than the undisciplined sprawl of villages and suburbs that characterized contemporary London. British visitors would remark how a *salonnière* based in the aristocratic quarters of the Faubourg Saint-Germain, could easily slip across the river for a breakfast visit to invite new arrivals in the British quarter on the right bank to her forthcoming *salon*.[5] The impossibility of replicating such arrangements in a middle-class suburban villa 'in Pocklington Square'—a name reminiscent of the remoter reaches of Yorkshire—is the comic point of Thackeray's 1847 Christmas story, *Mrs Perkin's Ball*.[6]

Parisian hostesses named a regular time when they let it be known to a select number that they received at home. The intimacy associated with an apparently casual arrangement was thus a hallmark of the *salon*. Rarely catering for more than fifteen to twenty guests, who might drop in and out during the course of an evening, the *salons*' exclusiveness inevitably made them hotbeds of gossip. Catherine Gore's novel *The Ambassador's Wife* (1842) put to good effect her years as a Parisian *salonnière* by painting a picture of the snares which these gatherings held for an ingénue diplomat's wife, unaware of, or indifferent to, the political ripples lying below the surface of contending parties' *salons*.

Some *salonnières* received six days out of seven. The Comtesse de Circourt continued this punishing routine for another eight years after receiving terrible burns

[3] M. O. W. Oliphant, *Miss Marjoribanks*, ed. E. Jay (London: Penguin, 1998), 15, 49. I have traced the development of this theme more fully in 'British Women Writers and the Mid-Nineteenth-Century Parisian Salon', in H. Brown and G. Dow (eds), *European Connections: Readers, Writer, Salonnières* (Oxford: Peter Lang, 2011), 145–62.

[4] 'Company Manners', in *Works of Elizabeth Gaskell*, ed. Shattock et al., i, 296.

[5] M. C. M. Simpson, *Letters and Recollections of Julius and Mary Mohl* (London: Kegan, Paul, Trench, 1887), 81.

[6] Pearson's argument that this derives from an earlier piece, 'The Party at Willowford', written for the *Paris Literary Gazette* 9 (22 Dec. 1835) and larded with French phrases designed to appeal to its Paris-based Anglophone audience, makes even more plausible the supposition that Thackeray once again has a Parisian social scene in mind: R. Pearson, *W. M. Thackeray and the Mediated Text: Writing for Periodicals in the Mid-Nineteenth Century* (Aldershot: Ashgate, 2000), 30, 31, 229–31.

from catching her hair in a candle flame. When she died in 1863, her friend and fellow *salonnière*, Madame Mohl, found herself pondering whether the effort had been worth it:

> I had some thought of trying to set up a *salon* every night, and in time it would be furnished; but it's a great restraint to stay at home always, yet I am quite sure it is the only way. I have not patience, however, to bear with the tiresome people that I see come to all the ladies that have one. Many years ago I had people every evening, but they were few in number, and I remained at home because my mother's health would not let her go out. It was then I first knew all the people who have since grown celebrated. They were young and unknown—Thiers, Cousin, the Thierrys, Ampère, Merimée, and many more who are dead. They are now grown old, and lazy, and rich, and fashionable; and in those days, when tiresome people came, I did not mind as I do now. I now always prefer seeing people anywhere but at my own house; I am so much freer, and can go away when I am tired of them.[7]

Despite these reservations, she continued her Wednesday and Sunday afternoon and Friday evening *salons* well into her 80s; indeed, she was said to have wanted to die on a Saturday so as to manage just one more Friday night.

As a domestic institution the *salon* was in fact well-suited to the frail, as Elizabeth Barrett Browning was swift to recognize. She told her sister Henrietta that for her these small gatherings had acted as 'the shop-windows of the world as well as of the boulevards', for 'though the Paris salons seem very calm you can't turn your head without seeing or hearing something interesting—and I, you know, have had such a shut-up life, that it is natural I should be more than usually interested.'[8] Madame Mohl's own *salon* had developed from her landlady, Madame de Récamier (1777–1849), adopting the habit of bringing guests from her higher apartment to the lower rooms of the convent building, Abbaye-aux-Bois, on the Rue du Bac, to entertain the invalid mother of 'Clarkey', as Madame Mohl was then known. By 1835 Clarkey was sufficiently embedded in this set to be able to lay on a one-off performance by Chateaubriand (1768–1848), the traveller, historian, politician, diplomat, Catholic apologist, founding father of French Romanticism, and star exhibit of Récamier's *salon*, for the benefit of Frances Trollope and her daughters: he gave them one of his celebrated readings from his autobiographical work-in-progress, *Mémoires d'outre-tombe* (1848–50).[9]

Managing the guest-list was a *salonnière*'s first challenge. Madame Mohl and her husband, Julius, told Elizabeth Gaskell that in the golden days of Mesdames Duras and Récamier, 'All who wished to be admitted, had to wait and prove their fitness by being agreeable elsewhere; to earn their diploma, as it were, among the circle of these ladies' acquaintants; and, at last, it was a high favour to be received by

[7] Simpson, *Julius and Mary Mohl*, 209, 128.

[8] *Elizabeth Barrett Browning: Letters to her Sister, 1846–1859*, ed. L. Huxley (London: John Murray, 1929), 163.

[9] F. Trollope, *Paris and the Parisians in 1835* (2 vols, Paris: Baudry's European Library, 1836), ii, 147–62; T. A. Trollope, *What I Remember*, ed. H. van Thal (London: William Kimber, 1973), 88–9; Simpson, *Julius and Mary Mohl*, 86, 21, 128–9.

them.'[10] For a first-time guest, obtaining an invitation to a *salon* could prove a complicated business. Elizabeth Barrett Browning's enthusiasm for admission to George Sand's *salon* led her in a circuitous route which involved asking Thomas Carlyle to approach Mazzini, whose work Sand had recently been involved in translating, for a letter of introduction to the 'Highpriestess of anarchy'.[11] Carlyle himself, having experienced a pre-*salon* dinner at which he was expected to 'manufacture French', vowed that he would burn all his introductions to the *salons*, preferring sightseeing to listening to the disagreeable 'clatter-clattering' and 'talkee-talkee' of the *salons*.[12]

It was a *salonnière*'s duty, as Madame Mohl put it, to tend her *salon* so that, however distinguished, no man could hog the fireplace and harangue the rest of the company.[13] The *salon* thus allowed women to stake out a sophisticated space which, not being exclusively feminine in nature, could not be dismissed as a trivial gathering to be cancelled at the whim of a man's convenience.

The *salon* held a particular attraction for female writers in that it offered evening socializing without the need to engage in the prior round of time-consuming morning calls which would have been de rigueur in Great Britain. 'How much preferable is the French system of evening visits, to the English custom of morning ones, which cut up time so abominably!' wrote Lady Blessington in her Parisian journal. 'Few who have lived much abroad could submit patiently to have their mornings broken in upon, when evening, which is the most suitable time for relaxation, can be enlivened by the visits that are irksome at other hours.'[14] Taking Meta, to Paris with her in 1863, Elizabeth Gaskell delighted in the fact that the *salons* involved 'no preparation' for her, while providing a social round for her daughter, whom she recalled 'saying with great delight, "we need never be an evening at home"'.[15]

Better still, in the world of the *salon* women writers were not made to feel awkwardly 'clever' or 'unladylike' in displaying their talent, whereas in Great Britain, Frances Trollope tartly observed, 'most English girls would rather be thought an idiot than a BLUE'.[16] Instead, intelligent discussion between the sexes of matters of mutual interest was actively encouraged. As Lady Blessington remarked, 'Conversation is, with the French, the aim and object of society. All enter it prepared to take a part, and he best enacts it who displays just enough knowledge to show that much remains behind.' Neither over dinner nor in the *salon*, she added, did French men assume that women wished to hear them discourse of their sporting exploits:

This is a great relief, for in England many a woman is doomed to listen to interminable tales of slaughtered grouse, partridges, and pheasants; of hair breadth "scapes by flood

[10] 'Company Manners', in *Works of Elizabeth Gaskell*, ed. Shattock et al., i, 297–8.

[11] *The Collected Letters of Thomas and Jane Welsh Carlyle*, ed. C. R. Sanders, K. J. Fielding, et al. (40 vols, Durham, NC: Duke University Press, 1970–2012), xxvi, 201.

[12] 'Excursion (Futile Enough) to Paris; Autumn 1851', repr. in *Last Words of Thomas Carlyle* (London: Longmans, Green, 1892), 181, 186.

[13] Simpson, *Julius and Mary Mohl*, 86.

[14] Countess of Blessington, *The Idler in France* (2 vols, London: Henry Colburn, 1841) i, 128–9.

[15] 'French Life', in *Works of Elizabeth Gaskell*, ed. Shattock et al., i, 384.

[16] F. Trollope, *Paris and the Parisians*, ii, 96.

and field,' and venturous leaps, the descriptions of which leave one in doubt whether the narrator or his horse be the greater animal of the two, and render the poor listener more fatigued by the recital than either was by the longest chase.[17]

'Nowhere', Frances Trollope triumphantly declared 'are the higher efforts of the female mind more honoured than in France.'[18] As a middle-aged wife and mother, married to a melancholic recluse, she could see distinct advantages in sociable gatherings where experience and wit rather than nubile youth and beauty were at a premium. Lady Blessington went so far as to declare:

> France is the paradise for old women...but England is the purgatory...In France a woman may forget that she is neither young nor handsome; for the absence of these claims to attention does not expose her to be neglected by the male sex. In England, the elderly and the ugly 'could a tale unfold' of the *naïveté* with which men evince their sense of the importance of youth and beauty, and their oblivion of the presence of those who have neither.[19]

Even George Eliot, who disliked the little she had seen of Paris during a two-day trip there with the Brays in 1849, was prepared to use the *salons* of seventeenth-century France for an oblique condemnation of contemporary British society. Claiming that, 'In France alone the mind of woman has passed like an electric current through the language...in France alone, if the writings of women were swept away, a serious gap would be made in the national history', she attributed French women's superior development to 'being admitted to a common fund of ideas, to common object of interest with men; and this must be the essential condition at once of true womanly culture and of true social well-being.' By 1854, when she wrote this essay, Eliot had met Madame Mohl in London, through the good offices of the Bonham Carters, with whom her friend Sophia Hennell had been a governess.[20] Although her initial impressions were unfavourable—her '*make-up* was certainly extraordinary, but I suppose she is a superior woman'—a decade later she was very appreciative of the 'most interesting' breakfast gathering of sculptors and writers that Mohl had arranged for the benefit of Lewes and herself.[21]

Thackeray, who was frequently disparaging about the Parisian cult of the *salon* as providing rather tamer fare than a gentlemen's London club, nevertheless recognized that its success depended upon a stylized ritual that enabled men and women to mingle freely. Writing to his friend Jane Brookfield in January 1851, he told her that he had been to a 'swoary at M. Duchatel's' in a 'splendid hotel in the Fbg St. Germain: magnificent droaring room: vulgar people I thought.' A one-time financial journalist, then a minister in Guizot's administration, by 1851 Count Duchâtel (1803–67) had retired from politics to care for his substantial art collection. These

---

[17] Countess of Blessington, *The Idler in France*, i, 188, 243.
[18] F. Trollope, *Paris and the Parisians*, ii, 101.
[19] Countess of Blessington, *The Idler in France*, i, 85–6.
[20] George Eliot, 'Woman in France: Madame de Sablé', in T. Pinney (ed.), *Essays of George Eliot* (London: Routledge & Kegan Paul, 1968), 54.
[21] *The George Eliot Letters*, ed. G. S. Haight (9 vols, New Haven, Conn.: Yale University Press, 1954–6, 1978), ii, 39; iv, 334.

credentials alone, however, could not guarantee a correctly run *salon*. Thackeray reported, 'The men as they arrived went up & made their bows to the lady of the house, who sate by the fire talking to other 2 ladies, and this bow over the gentlemen talked standing to each other. It was uncommonly stewpid.'[22]

A *salonnière's* chief concern was not to foster individual friendships, nor to act as a marriage broker, but to orchestrate a conversation noted for elegance, wit, and critical acumen. Têtes-à-têtes, indeed, were considered bad form.[23] The supreme importance attached to elegant expression was sometimes a cause of considerable anxiety for British visitors. Frances Trollope noted how the French, even when fluent in English, refused to compromise their reputation for *salon* wit by using English with their guests. Meanwhile, the English, who frequently read and appreciated French literature, contrived to mangle their spoken French, which was irritating when they could so easily (she opined) pick up a passable French accent from a maid or valet.[24] Lady Blessington believed that this expectation of fluency in each others' language was a relatively recent phenomenon, and presumably a consequence of the easing of cross-Channel travel restrictions in the wake of the Napoleonic wars. After entertaining a Mr Cuthbert together with M. Charles Lafitte, she noted in her journal for 1829:

> The advance of civilization was evident in both these gentlemen—the Englishman speaking French with purity and fluency, and the Frenchman speaking English like a born Briton....But it is not alone the languages of the different countries that Mr. Cuthbert and M. Charles Laffitte have acquired, for both are well acquainted with the literature of each, which renders their society very agreeable.[25]

Many of the statesmen, journalists, and historians who frequented the *salons* in the 1830s had perforce spent prolonged periods of exile in England. Chateaubriand, who had supported himself by giving French lessons during one impoverished stay in London and who later served as French Ambassador there, seems to have been particularly fond of baiting his hostess's Anglophone guests. Frances Trollope was provoked by his declaration that no English person was capable of truly understanding French literature. Her son Thomas, an arrogant Oxford undergraduate at the time, seemed entirely impervious to the fact that Chateaubriand was almost certainly mocking him in asking him to explain 'the construction of the sentence, "Let but the cheat endure, I ask not aught beside"—a task in which I entirely failed during the best part of half an hour'.[26] Less ambitious to star in fashionable intellectual circles than either his mother or brother had been, Anthony Trollope prosaically advised the unhappy English tourist, 'To be able to be happy and at rest among the mountains is better than a capacity for talking French in saloons [*sic*].'[27]

[22] *The Letters and Private Papers of William Makepeace Thackeray*, ed. G. N. Ray (4 vols, Cambridge, Mass.: Harvard University Press, 1945–6), ii, 731.
[23] M. C. M. Simpson, 'Some Personal Recollections of Madame Mohl', *Macmillan's Magazine* (Sept. 1883), 424.
[24] F. Trollope, *Paris and the Parisians*, i, 195–7.
[25] Countess of Blessington, *The Idler in France*, i, 250.
[26] F. Trollope, *Paris and the Parisians*, i, 195; T. A. Trollope, *What I Remember*, 88.
[27] A. Trollope, *Travelling Sketches*, intro. A. Briggs (New York: Arno Press, 1981), 112.

Margaret Oliphant attributed her own reluctance to make the most of the standing invitation she enjoyed to the aristocratic Montalembert *salon* to a couple of occasions when the Count held up her French to 'gentle ridicule'. Her humiliation was all the greater because she had already translated several volumes by this man, whose English, she discovered when she finally met him, was 'perfect in accent and idiom': he had spent his formative years in England.[28] George Sala, having had the advantage of an early education in a Francophone Parisian school, observed with a strong whiff of snobbery that Oliphant's 'Parisian was of the school of Stratford-atte-Bowe...it smacks strongly of boarding-school French at two guineas a quarter.'[29]

It may well have been Dickens's fear of such snubs, as much as his work patterns, that led him to avoid the *salons*, fond though he was of boasting to friends back home of the compliments he had received on his French. Lamartine (1790–1869), the distinguished man of letters and statesman, for instance, apparently told him at a dinner party one night that he spoke French 'easily' for a foreigner, which may have been intended to cast a subtle slight on an accent unacceptable in the *salons*. (Lamartine was married to an Englishwoman and had spent the almost statutory period of exile in London.) Notably, although Dickens was referred to Madame Mohl by Elizabeth Gaskell, so that she might explain French translation rights to him, there is no record of his having attended her *salon*.[30] Being able to enjoy the *salons* was far easier for the likes of the Brownings, both of whom had had intensive French teaching in their childhood, Elizabeth even spending seven months in a school in Boulogne to perfect her spoken French.[31]

Dickens had at least enjoyed the opportunity of prolonged stays in Paris. British writers on shorter visits continued to be surprised by how little their education in modern languages had prepared them for the testing-ground of the *salons*. Mary Augusta Ward, for instance, lamented how poorly she had performed at Madame Taine's *salon* in 1874: Paul Bourget, the young French *littérateur* she had been so anxious to meet, 'did not then speak English, and my French conversation, which had been wholly learnt from books had a way at that time—and alack, has still—of breaking down under me, just as one reached the thing one really wanted to say.'[32]

Conversation may have been the *salon*'s chief purpose, but this did not preclude other forms of entertainment being offered. Frances Trollope's account noted that the *salons* she visited each had a characteristic note: where one hostess would offer a prominent French politician of the day, another would offer a foreign revolutionary, a philosopher, a metaphysician, or a musician.[33] Her son Thomas would later

[28] *The Autobiography of Margaret Oliphant*, ed. E. Jay (Oxford: Oxford University Press, 1990), 111–13.

[29] George Augustus Sala, 'The Cant of Modern Criticism', *Belgravia* 4 (Nov. 1867), 53.

[30] *The Pilgrim Edition of the Letters of Charles Dickens*, ed. G. Storey et al. (12 vols, Oxford: Clarendon Press, 1965–2002), viii, 4.

[31] R. Gridley, *The Brownings and France: A Chronicle with Commentary* (London: Athlone Press, 1982), 3.

[32] Mrs H. Ward, *A Writer's Recollections 1856–1900* (London: William Collins, 1918), 154.

[33] F. Trollope, *Paris and the Parisians*, i, 196–8.

provide a vivid recollection of a musical soirée the Trollopes had attended in the
salon of Italian-born Princess Cristina Trivulzio di Belgiojoso (1808–71).[34]

> The amusement of the evening consisted in hearing Liszt and the princess [Belgiojoso]
> play on two pianos the whole of the score of Mozart's *Don Giovanni*! The treat was a
> delightful one; but I dare say that I should have forgotten it but for the finale of the
> performance. No sooner was the last note ended than the nervous musician swooned
> and slid from his seat, while the charming princess, in whom apparently matter was
> less under the dominion of mind, or at least of nerve, was as fresh as at the
> beginning![35]

Some *salonnières* would lay on dancing when younger guests were expected.[36] The
17-year-old Meta Gaskell wrote home of the polishing of floors and general bustle
taking place in Madame Mohl's rooms to prepare for such an occasion that coming
evening. She was more daunted by the thought that she and her mother would
'afterward go on to the Geoffroi St. Hilaires'—where I am afraid we shall have to
talk zoologically—'and, her mother inserted parenthetically, 'be kissed'. If Meta
found the prospective scientific focus of the conversation at this famous
Lamarckian naturalist's house a little daunting, Elizabeth had found the 'very political' hue of the Thierry salon the previous night frankly bewildering: 'such a commotion about a pamphlet'.[37,38] Perhaps the fact that she deemed the Parisian *salon*
fit matter for the readers of *Household Words* was one indication that the polished
exclusivity of this world was already in decline.[39]

7.2 THE DECLINE OF THE *SALONS*

Historians of the *salon* argue that it was the Second Empire that dealt a series of
death-blows to this Parisian cultural phenomenon.[40] The ostentatious entertaining
favoured under this regime was fundamentally at odds with the modest fare on
offer in earlier days, when preparing elegant contributions to the conversation
had counted for more than planning extravagant dress to attract attention. In 1835
Frances Trollope had noted that, while great balls differed little in London and
Paris, the informality of the dress permitted in the *salons* and the 'habitual absence
of ceremony and parade' were very agreeable.[41] In 1851 Elizabeth Barrett Browning
still found this lack of pomp at an evening entertainment a decided attraction. 'You
go in a morning dress, and there is tea. Nothing can be more *sans façon*,' she wrote

---

[34] T. A. Trollope, *What I Remember*, 95.
[35] Ibid.   [36] Simpson, *Julius and Mary Mohl*, 86.
[37] *The Letters of Mrs. Gaskell*, ed. J. V. Chapple and A. Pollard (Manchester: Manchester University
Press, 1966), 332.
[38] Amédée Simon Dominique Thierry (2 Aug. 1797–27 Mar. 1873), French journalist, historian,
and subsequently senator.
[39] Gaskell, 'Company Manners', in *Works of Elizabeth Gaskell*, ed. Shattock et al., i, 295–310.
[40] e.g. S. Kale, 'The Decline of Salons, 1830–1848', in *French Salons: High Society and Political
Sociability from the Old Regime to the Revolution of 1848* (Baltimore: Johns Hopkins University Press,
2004), 165–99.
[41] F. Trollope, *Paris and the Parisians*, i, 36.

home to Mary Mitford. She expanded on the theme to her sister, Henrietta: 'a cup of infinitesimally weak tea is the extent of hospitality. Lady Elgin was prodigal and gave us bread and butter: but that was an exception. You wear white gloves, and your hair is neatly dressed—gowns up to the throat. There's no fuss.'[42]

Those accustomed to this older style of *salon*, like Julius Mohl, the German orientalist who married Mary Clarke in 1847, 'used to be very sarcastic if any lady arrived smartly dressed, which was often the case, as Madame Duchâtel received on the same evening all the rank and fashion of the Orléanist party'. Back in the *salon*'s Restoration heyday Lady Blessington had singled out the social solecism of a benighted Englishwoman, Mrs Hare, who turned up in full rig for the theatre, apparently ignorant that this would usually be followed by a visit to a *salon*, 'where the graceful *négligé* of a *demi-toilette* prevails':

> [N]ot aware that at Paris people never go *en grande toilette* to the theatres, [she] came so smartly dressed, that, seeing our simple toilettes, she was afraid of incurring obser-vation if she presented herself in a rich dress with short sleeves, a gold tissue turban with a bird-of-paradise plume, and an *aigrette* of coloured stones; so she went to our house, with a few of the party, while I accompanied the rest to the theatre.[43]

It was to the rise of the very mixed social economy patronized by the wealthy of the Chaussée d'Antin that Sala attributed the change of the *salon* culture in his novel *The Seven Sons of Mammon* (1862). His fictional *salon*, described as taking place in 1849 in an apartment of lavish splendour, is marked not only by the hostess's neg-ligence in failing to invite compatible guests but by her own withdrawal from the *mêlée*, which she leaves to her servants' attention.[44]

By the mid-1860s Mary Mohl was complaining, 'There is an imitation of London— large parties, luxury and expense.' Furthermore, the general rise in prices meant that English visitors, who had formerly been able to spend half a year or more in Paris getting to know people, now found they could only afford a couple of months.[45] Mary, whose dress had always been simple to the point of eccentricity, found her-self increasingly retreating to the *salons* of an older generation. 'It is the sort of going into company I like—no dress, no invitation,' she wrote of the gathering at the de Broglie *salon*; 'it grows very scarce here now.'[46] However, the scant supply of goods and money in the wake of the Commune briefly lent a new impetus and lease of life to her *salon*:

Paris, 20 January 1872
I have a dinner party pretty regularly, once a fortnight, on Friday—twelve or thirteen people. The intervening Friday people come in the evening without invitations...

I have made a point, even when this winter I was at my worst, of cultivating society —which, being my especial talent, I will not bury, for in the present state it is far more useful than giving away money....And every little does a little good, were it only to

[42] *Elizabeth Barrett Browning: Letters to her Sister*, ed. Huxley, 145.
[43] Countess of Blessington, *The Idler in France*, i, 194.
[44] G. A. Sala, *The Seven Sons of Mammon* (London: Tinsley Brothers, 1862), i, 57–115.
[45] Simpson, *Julius and Mary Mohl*, 217–18.
[46] Ibid. 82, 209, 217–18, 244.

feed the poor horses and hackney coachmen; it is far better to give them employment than [charitable] help.[47]

But, by the era of the Third Republic, her *salon* was a faded echo of its former glory. When the recently married Mary Augusta Ward, who had sought an invitation to this legendary *salon* from her Oxford neighbour, Max Müller, attended in 1874, she was distinctly disappointed by the arrangements, and by her 81-year-old hostess, whom she compared to Thackeray's disillusioned fairy godmother in *The Rose and the Ring*:

> [In] the corner was the Spartan tea-table, with its few biscuits, which stood for the plain living whereon was nourished the high thinking and high talking which had passed through these rooms. Guizot, Ampère, Fauriel, Mignet, Lamartine, all the great men of the middle century had talked there; not—in general—the poets and the artists, but the politicians, the historians, and the *savants*. The little Fairy Blackstick, incredibly old, kneeling on the floor, with the shabby dress and tousled grey hair...If only one had heard her talk! But there were few people in the room, and we were none of us inspired. I must sadly put down that Friday evening among the lost opportunities of life.[48]

Annie Thackeray Ritchie dated the symbolic moment of the *salon*'s death rather more precisely, to 18 March 1871, the date that, for her, represented the triumph of mindless working-class brutality over the cultured liberal atmosphere of the *salons*. In the closing scenes of her novel *Mrs Dymond*, an elderly Frenchwoman bids farewell to her oldest friend, a socialist idealist, who lives in a house on the Rue du Bac, 'well known to the world...Chateaubriand had lived there...Madame Recamier has lived there and her friend and disciple...there had come the Ampères and Mathieu de Montmorency.' The scene is both 'haunted by those familiar ghosts of the first half of the century' and pregnant with the violent 'awakening' to be experienced by the peaceful inhabitants of the Abbaye. As the Commune takes hold, the old man loses faith in the people who turn out to be 'irrational and ignorant', the absolute antithesis of all that the *salon* in the Rue du Bac had stood for, and he finally dies at the hands of the drunken leader of a rabble pursuing a wounded gendarme.[49]

In reality the death of the Parisian *salon* had little connection with the forces of anarchic violence and more to do with a slow shift of power from one elite to another that was already under way during the Second Empire. Bulwer Lytton's *The Parisians*, in which the complex plot works its way between Parisian rich and poor, Saint-Germain and Montmartre, the old aristocracy, the press, and the world of high finance, suggests that by the Empire's dying days *salon* culture was fragmenting in ways that foretold its end. In this novel, writers and well-to-do foreigners continue to attend the *salons*, but these gatherings are dominated by politics, and

---

[47] M. Lesser, *Clarkey: A Portrait in Letters of Mary Clarke Mohl (1793–1883)* (Oxford: Oxford University Press, 1984), 197.

[48] Ward, *A Writer's Recollections*, 159.

[49] *Mrs. Dymond, The Works of Miss Thackeray* (10 vols, London: Smith, Elder, 1890), x, 461, 503–6.

writers are valued only in so far as their talent can be harnessed for party purposes. Legitimist aristocrats still shun opposition *salons*, but some of their number have learned to accommodate themselves to the *salons* held in court circles, hoping to perpetuate the Emperor's rule as the closest to monarchy the times allow and a hedge against the threats of republicanism or democracy. The old families of the Faubourg Saint-Germain are being eclipsed by financiers who host their gatherings in restaurants.

As the century wore on, the professional classes were as likely to discuss politics in press offices or at the Bourse, and the savants increasingly congregated in *académies*, or learned societies. Removing the *salon* from the privacy of the home to public spaces hired by men destroyed the illusion of intimacy and deprived the *salonnières* of their organizing powers. Meanwhile, the democratizing force of mass circulation newspapers, proliferating political parties, and voluntary associations gradually eroded the importance of the leisured class, so that by the time of the Third Republic to say that something was of importance 'in the *salons*' was tantamount to declaring it of merely academic interest.

The picture drawn by Richard Whiteing of a *salon* run by the French journalist Juliette Adam, née Lambert (1836–1936), pays interesting testament to the destruction of the delicately balanced 'barter economy of gender exchange' which occurred as Republicanism gained ground.[50] She discouraged women as guests, concentrating instead on assembling the leading political and literary figures of the gathering opposition to the Emperor in her drawing-room in the Boulevard Poissonnière, and later in the Boulevard Malesherbes. The tactics of this wealthy bourgeoise *salonnière* entirely overturned the received wisdom of the left bank: 'The legitimists said you could never have a *salon* without an aristocracy; the Orléanists, that you could never have it without wealth as well; and of course both implied that you need not look for wealth or birth outside their ranks.'[51]

Salons that retained their focus on literary or artistic attainment rather than partisan politics were better able to outlast changes of regime, but Henry James's novel *The Ambassadors* (1903), a finely calibrated picture of the social geography of post-1870s Paris, suggests that the *salons* of this era spoke to a ghostly past and observable shifts in power as much as to any present social arrangement. The hand-picked guest list at Madame de Vionnet's *salon* in her first floor apartment in the Rue de Bellechasse, Fauborg Saint-Germain, and its furnishings, inherited rather than newly purchased, speak of an aristocratic line of transmission. Deliberately juxtaposed with this is the picture of another *salon*, instantly recognizable to those who had known the Mohls by its location in a courtyard garden adjoining a former convent. James had visited Madame Mohl at the Abbaye-aux-Bois during the year of 1875–6, but he was well aware that he was only in time to catch the shadow of former glories.[52] Julius Mohl had died early in the January of 1876, and George Eliot told a correspondent that she had heard sad reports of 'the dear old lady

[50] Paglia, 'Oscar Wilde and the English Epicene', 85.
[51] R. Whiteing, *My Harvest* (London: Hodder & Stoughton, 1915), 141.
[52] *The Complete Notebooks of Henry James*, ed. L. Edel and L. H. Powers (Oxford: Oxford University Press, 1987), 542.

sobbing bitterly in her solitude'.[53] In James's novel, a young American explains the composition of the *salon*, now run by the elderly sculptor Gloriani:

> Oh they're everyone—all sorts and sizes; of course I mean within limits, though limits down, perhaps rather more than limits up. There are always artists—he's beautiful, inimitable to the *cher confrère*; and then *gros bonnets* of many kinds—ambassadors, cabinet ministers, bankers, generals; what do I know? even Jews. Above all always some awfully nice women—and not too many; sometimes an actress, an artist, a great performer—but only when they're not monsters; and, in particular, the right *femmes du monde*…he has some secret…He's the same to everyone. He does n't ask questions.'[54]

James's analysis of the new *salons* of the Third Republic detected the transference of cultural agency from a woman to a man, and observed a sociability founded on the deliberate avoidance of the discussion of potentially divisive issues.

7.3 THE *SALON*'S MORAL AMBIENCE

Salonnières seeking an eclectic mix of talent indeed knew better than to ask intrusive questions. Madame Mohl stoutly admitted, 'I don't pick out my acquaintance for their morality, but for the quality of their minds in general', though it should be noted that this had not prevented the Nightingale parents from seeking her help in launching the young Parthenope and Florence in the winter of 1838–9, and seeking her social skills again in 1853 when they had reached impasse with Florence's mounting resentment at their conventional vision for her future.[55,56]

The unashamed worldliness of the *salon* culture, its elegance and surface *politesse*, had long fascinated the English. Lady Blessington, famed for her moral unorthodoxy, observed:

> few English shine in conversation with the French. There is a lightness and brilliancy, a sort of touch and go, if I may say so, in the latter, seldom, if ever, to be acquired by strangers. Never dwelling long on any subject, and rarely entering profoundly into it, they sparkle on the surface with great dexterity, bringing wit, gaiety, and tact, into play.[57]

An ambience where a certain flirtatiousness was almost part of a *salonnière*'s job specification and making oneself agreeable a guest's primary duty had the potential to confuse the uninitiated: Frances Trollope gave a fictional description of at least one young Englishman who, having misinterpreted a *salonnière*'s welcome as an invitation to greater intimacy, swiftly finds himself and his family banned from further attendance.[58]

[53] *George Eliot Letters*, ed. Haight, vi, 363 (Apr. 1876).
[54] H. James, *The Ambassadors* (2 vols, 1909; repr. New York: A. M. Kelley, 1971), i, 199.
[55] Lesser, *Clarkey*, 102–3, 138–9.
[56] With her hostess's connivance, Florence spent her time in Paris studying its hospitals and receiving nursing training with the Sisters of Charity.
[57] Countess Blessington, *The Idler in France*, i, 187–8.
[58] F. Trollope, *The Robertses on their Travels* (3 vols, London: Henry Colburn, 1846), i, 90–106.

Some Parisian *salons* were indeed run by foreigners whose presence in Paris had initially been prompted by finding themselves exiled from 'good society' at home. Princess Cristina Trivulzio di Belgiojoso managed to attract a mixture of Italian revolutionaries together with European writers and musicians to her *salon*, despite it being generally known that the daughter born to her in 1838 had not been fathered by the Princess's husband, from whom she had long been amicably estranged.

Equally notorious was the Russian-born Princess de Lieven (1785–1857). She had accompanied her husband to England in 1812 when he took up his position as the Russian ambassador. Her forte was entertaining politicians, and she was rumoured to have slept, *inter alios*, with each successive British Prime Minister, save Canning, before her husband was recalled to Russia in 1834.[59] Finding that Russia's climate no longer suited her, she made her home in Paris, where through her *salon* she continued to manipulate her conquests and engage in diplomacy: the twice-widowed Guizot, her *salon*'s leading attraction, was commonly believed to be her lover. Her exploits made good fictional copy. Catherine Gore's caricatures of this dazzling rival became increasingly transparent. In the *Diary of a Désennuyée* (1836) she appeared as Princess Dragonitski, a decaying beauty, who, 'having figured as ambassadress at half the courts in Europe, fancies she has held half the sovereigns in Europe, like a pouncet box, between her fore finger and thumb', and in *Greville* (1841) as the Countess Kersakoff, 'who left her husband to do duties in the Imperial household', and, while constantly complaining of ill-health, was 'tireless in doing the social round, on the arm of any good-looking foreigner she could recruit'.[60] Nor is Bulwer Lytton's ploy of absenting her fictional proxy from Paris likely to have prevented contemporaries from identifying the Princess de Lieven as the original behind the bewitching Russian *salonnière* who had begun her lifelong enslavement of the Marquis de Rochebriant in London:

> [W]hile he was yet very young, he had lived a frank libertine life until he fell submissive under the yoke of a Russian princess, who, for some mysterious reason, never visited her own country and obstinately refused to reside in France. She was fond of travel, and moved yearly from London to Naples, Naples to Vienna, Berlin, Madrid, Seville, Carlsbad, Baden-Baden—anywhere for caprice or change, except Paris.... She was very rich, she lived semi-royally. Hers was just the house in which it suited the Marquis to be the *enfant gâté*...Not that he was domiciled with the Princess; that would have been somewhat too much against the proprieties, greatly too much against the Marquis's notions of his own dignity.[61]

Looking back in old age with some amusement at the various 'queer' couples she had met as a young widow in 1864, Margaret Oliphant wondered how to describe the 'elderly romances' between *salonnières* and their male companions, whose

---

[59] A rather more defensive account in which she is credited with only three great loves in her life is provided by J. L. Cromwell, *Dorothea Lieven: A Russian Princess in London and Paris, 1785–1857* (London: McFarland, 2006).

[60] C. Gore, *Greville: or, a Season in Paris* (3 vols, London: Henry Colburn, 1841), iii, 136, 158. *The Ambassador's Wife* (3 vols, London: Richard Bentley, 1842), ii, 310.

[61] Lord [E. G. E. L. Bulwer-]Lytton, *The Parisians* (2 vols, London: George Routledge, 1875), i, 30.

devotion, having outlasted the *grande passion* of youth, now seemed to place them somewhere between the categories of relatives, guests, and lovers.[62] The examples Oliphant offered came from a world of minor literary figures, journalists, artists, and actresses who found Paris sympathetic to the unorthodox living arrangements of exiles, but the necessarily close relations between the *salonnière* and her chief attraction perhaps made it inevitable that such rumours would circulate. Madame Récamier may have provided herself with the figleaf of propriety by living in a *pension* where only women could rent apartments, but Chateaubriand, who moved nearby, was with her daily whilst his unhappy wife languished at home.

British writers with pretensions to cosmopolitan culture found themselves torn between the desire to gain entry to these charmed circles and the need to express moral revulsion. Elizabeth Barrett Browning managed the neat trick of maintaining her reputation for moral probity with her English correspondents by providing a brief coda of disapprobation to her salacious inventory of gossip. Alfred de Musset, poet, dandy, and darling of the salons, provoked the following tidbit to send to Mary Mitford in the spring of 1852:

> Alfred de Musset was to have been at M. Buloz', where Robert was a week ago, on purpose to meet him... Do you know his poems? He is not capable of large grasps, but he has poet's life and blood in him, I assure you. He is said to be at the feet of Rachel just now, and a man may nearly as well be with a tigress in a cage. He began with the Princess Belgiojoso—followed George Sand—Rachel finishes, is likely to 'finish' in every sense. In the intervals, he plays at chess. There's the anatomy of a *man*![63]

Whether or not to attend George Sand's *salon* proved the ultimate challenge for the British literary visitor. Frances Trollope's guide to Paris devoted her account of George Sand (as Baroness Aurore Dudevant was known) to her literary oeuvre, claiming she knew little of her private history, although it seems likely, from her son Thomas's recollections of the period he spent with his family in Paris in 1836, that she gained admission to her *salon*. Thomas claimed to have seen Sand on a number of occasions, and decided from her physiognomy that, although she was at that period of her career both acting and writing and had attracted the attention of Louis-Philippe's police, she was nevertheless 'a lady':

> 'She was decidedly attractive.... the features were unmistakable refined in character and expression, and the mouth—the most trustworthy evidence-giving feature upon that point—was decidedly that of a high-bred woman.'[64]

When Matthew Arnold set out in July 1846, aged 23, on his pilgrimage from Oxford to visit his idol, she was still in her early 40s, and he hastened to tell a later generation of readers that, when she admitted him to her country estate at Nohant, 'the main impression she made was... of simplicity, frank, cordial simplicity', adding: 'There was at that time nothing astonishing in Madame Sand's appearance.

---

[62] *Autobiography of Margaret Oliphant*, ed. Jay, 115–16.

[63] *The Letters of Elizabeth Barrett Browning*, ed. F. G. Kenyon, 2nd edn. (2 vols, London: Smith, Elder, 1897), ii, 64.

[64] F. Trollope, *Paris and the Parisians*, ii, 267; T. A. Trollope, *What I Remember*, 91.

She was not in man's clothes.' It was perhaps just as well that he narrowly missed her when a second opportunity presented itself in Paris in 1859. Visiting Sand in her country setting had allowed him to turn her into a sort of latter-day Wordsworthian, in close contact with the healing powers of nature, and valuing the simple life and pleasures of the peasant.[65]

Elizabeth Barrett Browning had written a couple of embarrassingly adulatory sonnets to this 'true genius, but true woman', and modelled the attic lodgings in London where Aurora Leigh begins her poetic career on Sand's writer's eyrie on the Quai Saint-Michel, before she sought an introduction to her *salon*.[66] So enthusiastic was she that she declared to her friend, Mary Russell Mitford, 'I won't die, if I can help it, without seeing George Sand.' Accounts of her two visits in the spring of 1852 to George Sand's Sunday *salon* in the Rue Racine suggest that it was the chance of viewing Sand amidst her entourage as much as the likelihood of a heart-to-heart exchange that attracted Elizabeth.[67] Given Sand's scandalous reputation, derived as much from her high-profile lovers, cross-dressing, and cigar-smoking as from her novels, even such a staunch defender of a woman's right to self-determination as Elizabeth admitted that Robert was a 'prince of husbands' for making this pilgrimage twice. When reporting the first visit, she asked Mitford to note that 'We didn't see her smoke'. In a later letter to the same correspondent, Elizabeth leapt to the defence of at least two notorious aspects of her idol's behaviour:

> Her usual costume is both pretty and quiet, and the fashionable waistcoat and jacket (which are a spectacle in all the 'Ladies' Companions' of the day) make the only approach to masculine *wearings* to be observed in her. She has great nicety and refinement in her personal ways, I think, and the cigarette is really a feminine weapon if properly understood. Ah, but I didn't see her smoke. I was unfortunate.

However, Sand's 'priestess'-like behaviour amidst a circle of deferential men did not please Robert, who 'observed that "if any other mistress of a house had behaved so, he would have walked out of the room"'. Elizabeth dealt with her own misgivings by transferring Robert's distaste from Sand to her acolytes:

> She seems to live in the abomination of desolation, as far as regards society—crowds of ill-bred men who adore her *à genoux bas*, betwixt a puff of smoke and an ejection of saliva. Society of the ragged Red diluted with the lower theatrical. She herself so different, so apart, as alone in her melancholy disdain! I was deeply interested in that poor woman, I felt a profound compassion for her. I did not mind much of the Greek in Greek costume who tutoyéd her, and kissed her, I believe, so Robert said; or the other vulgar man of the theatre who went down on his knees and called her 'sublime'. 'Caprice d'amitié,' said she, with her quiet, gentle scorn. A noble woman under the mud, be certain.[68]

[65] 'George Sand', in *Essays Religious and Mixed, The Complete Prose Works of Matthew Arnold*, ed. R. H. Super (11 vols, Ann Arbor: University of Michigan Press, 1960–77), viii, 216–36.
[66] The sonnets appeared in Elizabeth Barrett Browning's 1844 collection.
[67] *Letters of Elizabeth Barrett Browning*, ed. Kenyon, ii, 50, 55–7, 59–60, 62–4.
[68] Ibid. 60, 63.

Elizabeth had decided that 'there could never have been a colour of coquetry in that woman'. However, the appearance of a woman in her 50s rather than the iconic *femme fatale* of the Sand legend was clearly a disappointment to many English male visitors. Robert Browning wrote to Carlyle, even before he had met Sand, 'We heard quantities about her the other night... how she had grown visibly aged of a sudden (like Mephistopheles at the Brocken when he says he finds people ripe for the last day)'. British writers with a keen sense of their own reputations did not expect to be treated with 'gentle scorn' by an ageing *salonnière*. Dickens's demeaning dismissal contrives to suggest that Sand's distinction is both character-istically and uniquely French:

> Just the kind of woman in appearance whom you might suppose to be the Queen's monthly nurse. Chubby, matronly, swarthy, black-eyed. Nothing of the blue-stocking about her, except a little final way of settling all your opinions with hers, which I take to have been acquired in the country where she lives, and in the domination of a small circle. A singularly ordinary woman in appearance and manner.[69]

Over and above more personal reasons for distrusting their moral atmosphere, anti-feminism forms a distinctive thread in British novelists' pictures of the *salons*. G. W. M. Reynolds housed his *salonnière* in the Rue Taitbout, the street where Balzac was to lodge the mistresses of his rich financiers, and compares her to the actress-singer Madame Vestris (1797–1856), whose sexual conquests were legendary.[70]

Thackeray repeatedly represented the *salon* as the playground for wicked women using their intelligence and sexual charm to wreak damage on unsuspecting men. Becky Crawley is received, during the winter of 1815–16, 'with much distinction' in the *salons* of the duchesses of the Faubourg Saint-Germain and Louis XVIII's splendid new court, while in the concluding paragraphs of *Pendennis* Blanche Amory is consigned to her appropriate level of Dantean hell when she marries the Comte de Montmorencie de Valentinois, and runs *salons* 'amongst the most *suivis*' in Paris.[71] The reverence accorded in left-bank *salons* to aristocratic titles was inher-ently no more obnoxious to Thackeray than its English equivalent, for, as he pointed out in the *Book of Snobs,* it was easy for the English to sneer at 'a French Marquis of twenty descents' while bending a sycophantic knee to their home-bred equivalents.[72] Rather, it lay in the *salon*'s approbation of morally worthless surface attributes. His *salons* prove equally welcoming to meretricious female charm and mere wealth: the vulgar Lady Clavering's inheritance, enabling her to take an hôtel in heart of the Faubourg Saint-Germain for the Paris season, suddenly redeems her, in the eyes of the *salonnières*, from her East Indian parentage.[73] It is hard not to suspect that Thackeray, who was sensitive to his own Anglo-Indian background,

---

[69] *Letters of Charles Dickens*, ed. Storey et al., viii, 33 (20 Jan. 1856).
[70] Reynolds, *Pickwick Abroad*, 181; H. de Balzac, *Splendeurs et misères des courtisanes* (1838).
[71] W. M. Thackeray, *Vanity Fair: A Novel without a Hero*, ed. J. Sutherland (Oxford: Oxford University Press, 1991), 454; W. M. Thackeray, *The History of Pendennis: His Fortunes and Misfortunes, His Friends and His Greatest Enemy*, ed. J. Sutherland (Oxford: Oxford University Press, 1994), 259–61.
[72] 'English Snobs on the Continent', *The Book of Snobs, Oxford Thackeray*, ix, 388.
[73] *Pendennis*, ed. Sutherland, 259–61.

was reflecting on the way in which Parisian doors, previously closed to him as a jobbing journalist, had suddenly opened to him following the success of *Vanity Fair*.

Even at the end of the century, when it might be imagined that the extravagance of the Belle Époque would have dimmed the image of the Second Empire, these earlier *salons* and their *salonnières* continued to be used by novelists to suggest a whiff of sulphur. When rationalist Squire Wendover introduced Mrs Humphry Ward's eponymous hero, Robert Elsmere, to Madame de Netteville, whose Second Empire Parisian *salon* he had attended, it is hinted that free-thinking and free love had been closely allied there: 'One suspects her of adventures just enough to find her society doubly piquant.' The stuff of Wendover's recollections of 'a talk at Nohant with George Sand,—scenes in the Duchesse de Broglie's salon' are enough to make Ellesmere yearn for the intellectual life of the continent; but when he and his wife attend Madame Netteville's cigarette-perfumed London *salon*, its racy conversation, ranging from contemporary scandals to Renan's latest theologically unorthodox book, forms a further measure of the distance he is travelling from his Evangelical wife's moral code.[74]

A further test of the *salon*'s moral ambience, which became something of a fictional cliché, was whether it might 'bring a blush into the cheek of the young person'.[75] The repeated device in Henry James's European novels of placing an *ingénue* of marriageable age in the midst of the cynical manoeuvrings of her seniors, the better to suggest their corrupting influence, was by no means innovatory. Tales of real *salons* suggests that it was not only young girls that an anxious parent needed to worry about. Coventry Patmore (1823–96), who had been sent to a school in Paris at the age of 16, spent his Sundays at Catherine Gore's fashionable *salon* in the Place Vendôme. The lonely Patmore, who spent his weekdays in solitary splendour in an apartment in his headmaster's house, away from the other boys, reacted to the sophisticated, flirtatious atmosphere of the *salon* by falling in love with the Gores' 18-year-old daughter, Cecilia, famous for her 'wasp-like' waist. Fortunately she scoffed at her young admirer, but he preserved a picture of her, which he placed within a shuttered frame on the drawing-room walls of his own marital home, pointing it out to visitors as 'the very first Angel'.[76]

It would seem to have been the more permissive culture of the Second Empire that led Frances Trollope to expose the moral risks the *salons* posed to the young and inexperienced, whereas during her 1835 visit she had clearly believed these to be outweighed, in the case of her own sons and daughters, by the *salons*' social and intellectual advantages. *A Fashionable Life* (1856) contains a chapter devoted to *lionnes*, or celebrity *salonnières*: pride of place is given to a certain Lady Hilberton's *salon*, where the majority of the women, including their hostess, smoke. Flanked by two lounging men, Lady Hilberton reclines on an ottoman, puffing away at a cigar. Her English visitors conclude that they have been in the presence of 'a typical

---

[74] Mrs H. [M. A. Ward, *Robert Elsmere*, ed. C. de Ryals (Lincoln: University of Nebraska Press, 1967), 338, 308, 420–5.

[75] C. Dickens, *Our Mutual Friend*, ed. A. Poole (London: Penguin, 1997), 132.

[76] D. Patmore, *The Life and Times of Coventry Patmore* (London: Constable, 1949), 36–41.

lionne…the sort of woman now met *driving a pair* of horses on the Bois de Boulogne, than, as in former times, *riding one*', a picture suggesting that the *lionne* of the July Monarchy, famed for being 'a woman of fashion of the most pre-eminent kind', had given way under the Second Empire to a *lionne* more famed for 'oriental' laxity of sexual behavior.[77] Lady Hilburton's deliberate flouting of convention leads her English visitors to conclude it better to deny the *salons* entirely to their young companion, a girl on the verge of coming out.

The fictional Lady Hilburton's nationality is significant. Where the French associated the *lionne*'s 'surrogate masculinity…expressed in her love of strenuous physical exercise such as horse-riding…eating with a hearty appetite…and her manly habits such as drinking and smoking' with Anglophile eccentricity, the British detected the corrupting influence of the French on Paris's English *salonnières*.[78] Although Lady Hilburton's name recalls that of the first Lady Ashburton (1805–57), whose cossetting of male writers and indifference to female guests may at some time have given offence to Frances Trollope, the original for Lady Hilberton was very probably Lady Theodosia Monson (1803–91) who had become an intimate in George Sand's *salon* and affected smoking and male dress by way of homage to her idol. An ardent feminist and reputedly bisexual—Monson had early separated from her husband, the fifth Baron, who had died in 1841—she possessed obvious credentials for mediating the Sand aura to a circle of English acquaintance which included Dickens and Eliza Lynn Linton as well as Monckton Milnes and the Brownings.

7.4 BRITISH *SALONNIÈRES*

As will be indicated by the following thumbnail sketches of those British *salonnières* most frequently mentioned by British writers, these women, like their foreign equivalents, hosted gatherings in Paris that, despite sharing favoured guests, managed to retain an individually distinctive flavour. In common with other Parisian *salons* they also spanned a wide gamut in terms of their social, cultural, and moral ambience.

In the case of Sarah Austin (1793–1867), for instance, it was the cosmopolitan composition she achieved that was most remarked: it was claimed that three languages could often be heard in use at any one time, in her *salon*.[79] A writer and translator in her own right, she had moved to Paris in 1843 with her husband, John Austin (1790–1859), the legal philosopher. Here the gregarious, energetic Sarah compensated for the reclusive propensities of her permanently ailing, depressive husband by becoming a *salonnière*. Her very success in attracting the Parisian elite may

---

[77] Gore, *Greville*, i, 143.
[78] F. Trollope, *Fashionable Life; or, Paris and London* (3 vols, London: Hurst & Blackett, 1856), i, 272; M. Gill, *Eccentricity and the Cultural Imagination in Nineteenth-Century Paris* (Oxford: Oxford University Press, 2009), 87.
[79] Quoted in L. Hamburger and J. Hamburger, *Contemplating Adultery: The Secret Life of a Victorian Woman* (London: Pan, 1994), 217.

indeed have led to the Austins' sudden decision to make England their permanent residence again in the spring of 1848: among her regular guests had been Prime Minister Guizot, whose ban on a popular demonstration in January 1848 precipitated the February Revolution.[80]

Wealthier British *salonnières* tended to come and go annually between Paris and London, assembling their gatherings from whichever of their protégés happened to be in town. Links forged in Paris's more promiscuous chains of acquaintance could sometimes have embarrassing consequences back in England. Arthur Stanley, Dean of Westminster, and his wife, Lady Augusta, daughter of the *salonnière* Lady Elgin, and Queen Victoria's favourite companion, had initially been introduced to one another in Madame Mohl's *salon*, where they were thoroughly accustomed to meeting religious progressives such as Florence Nightingale and Ernest Renan. Another Elgin daughter, who had met George Eliot and G. H. Lewes in Paris at Madame Mohl's *salon* during their visit over the New Year of 1867, thought it would be a happy idea to join the stray links of the chain together by inviting Eliot and Lewes to dinner to meet her sister Augusta and the Dean in London. Defending their decision many years later, the host recalled: 'When we first became acquainted we were told that she and Lewes had been married in Germany, and that they were reluctant to move out of their own immediate circle, or to enlarge it... [Stanley] was considerably taken aback when he found that Mrs Lewes was in no way Mr. Lewes's wife.'[81]

In the earlier part of my period, the glittering Blessington *salon* encompassed Bulwer Lytton, Benjamin Disraeli, and Dickens among its habitués; however, the hostess's reputation meant that male writers' wives were often left at home as hostages to propriety: Dickens, for instance, only permitted his wife to call on the Countess's journalist niece once the Countess was dead.[82] Marguerite Gardiner had led an early life that bore little close inspection, involving, as it did, separation from the husband she married at 14½ and five years living with an officer from the light dragoons, before her first husband's death enabled her second marriage, four months later, in 1818, to the Earl of Blessington. When in 1822 she met the French Count d'Orsay, twelve years her junior, she became instantly enamoured. Their affair continued despite the marriage of her 15-year-old stepdaughter, Lady Harriet Gardiner, to Count d'Orsay in 1827. The Earl died in 1829, and by 1831 Harriet had left the Blessington household and her marriage. The Countess's published account of the interesting two and half year period spent in Paris, from June 1828 to November 1830, makes no overt mention of this domestic turmoil. Instead, her husband's uxorious devotion is emphasized, his death duly acknowledged as 'the heaviest trial of my life'; d'Orsay is swiftly thereafter insinuated into the text as her regular companion, and his blood relations as her deepest concern. With d'Orsay

---

[80] In widowhood she seems to have relocated to Paris again, being on hand to receive her cousin Mrs Rossetti together with two of her children, Christina and William, on Christina's first trip abroad in 1861: J. Marsh, *Christina Rossetti: A Literary Biography* (London: Pimlico, 1995), 273.

[81] A memory from F. Locker-Lampson, *My Confidences* (1896), quoted in *George Eliot Letters*, ed. Haight, v, 227–8n.

[82] *Letters of Charles Dickens*, ed. Storey et al., vii, 736.

at her side, she continued to write and to run *salons* in Paris and London until finally, in 1849, mounting debts forced the couple to leave their goods to be sold up in London, and return to Paris, where they hoped that Louis-Napoleon, a frequent guest during his exile in London, would provide a position for the Count.

Meanwhile, Harriet d'Orsay had set up on her own on a refreshingly different tack, becoming famous in the English colony for her piety and philanthropy. Sala recalled accompanying his mother in the winter of 1840 to Harriet's soirées in the Rue Tronchet, and recorded the story, then going the rounds, that she had sold one of her ringlets at a charity fair to Louis-Philippe's heir for the princely sum of 5,000 francs.[83] Her second marriage, in 1852 to Spencer Cowper (1816–79), networked her back into the heart of respectable English society, where she could boast that leading Evangelical, Lord Shaftesbury, as a relative by marriage.

Like Lady Blessington, the improbably named Scottish novelist, essayist, and *salonnière* Baroness Marie Pauline Rose Blaze de Bury (1813–94) was equally at home in Paris and London. Although her maiden name was Stuart, she was widely believed to be an illegitimate daughter of Lord Brougham (1778-1868), which was presumably why she chose as one of her pseudonyms 'Arthur Dudley', the name of a man who had laid claim to being an illegitimate son of Elizabeth I. Married in 1844 to a French writer with a German title, she was fluent in French and German, and had been contributing literary essays to *Revue des deux mondes* since the age of 18: when she reviewed Matthew Arnold's poetry in its pages in 1854, he paid tribute to the cosmopolitan identity she had achieved by referring to her as 'ma compatriote, dans sa qualité d'Anglaise'.[84] A successful *salonnière*, however, had to offer more than intellectual attractions. A letter written to his wife by the ponderous Scots theologian John Tulloch, Principal of St Andrews, who was visiting Paris in December 1858, conveys at the same time her desire to please and his slight suspicion that this too is part of an act:

> I have seen Madame Blaze de Bury: she is evidently what Sir David would call 'a very *char*ming woman,' speaks like a book…Scotch, and yet thoroughly French in her manners,—but also with very clear intelligence and winning and eloquent ways. She was very kind, regretted my leaving so soon, and promised when I returned to introduce me to Montalembert and other distinguished people, of whom she obviously considers herself a centre.

On home ground in London, Tulloch found her less impressive: though she was wearing 'a charming dressing-gown' ('not as engaging as yours', he hastened to reassure his wife), she spoke 'with the most perfect ignorance' when they came to debate *Essays and Reviews* in 1862.[85] The desire to find herself at the heart of affairs developed in her a legendary fervour for the drama of political intrigue. In 1862

[83] *The Life and Adventures of George Augustus Sala written by himself*, 2nd edn (2 vols, London: Cassell, 1895), i, 132.

[84] *The Letters of Matthew Arnold*, ed. C. Y. Lang (6 vols, Charlottesville: University of Press of Virginia, 1996–2001), i, 292.

[85] M. Oliphant, *A Memoir of the Life of John Tulloch* (Edinburgh: William Blackwood & Sons, 1888), 140, 152.

Robert Browning confided to Isa Blagden that he was in fear of Madame de Bury after having watched the contemporary historian Kinglake seated next to her at a dinner party, 'sucking in authentic news about new cessions of territory & so on' which she was bearing hotfoot from Vienna, where she had allegedly communed daily with the diplomat Henry Lytton. Elizabeth Barrett Browning's estimate of their hostess had been far more pragmatic: in 1855 she confided to a friend:

> Madame Blaze de Bury has called on me; and tho Madame Mohl hates her, I am glad because of the access she gives to characteristic French Society. For the rest, I don't much mind whether she has a mind (or not) to be Lord Brougham's daughter, or a descendant of the Scottish kings.[86]

The Baroness's theatrical self-invention did not diminish with age. 1875 found Anne Thackeray Ritchie writing from Paris to her husband-to-be:

> Yesterday I went to call at a most horrible literary stuffy sham Faubourg St. Germain salon. Madame Blaze de Bury was exactly like a character in *Tourgenieff*, and welcomed an Alexis Alexandrovitch, and gave him tea with shrieks of surprise and rapture, and then asked me with a scream of delight how I wrote such charming books?

Anne Thackeray Ritchie, however was already *parti pris* in the rivalry between Madame Blaze de Bury and Madame Mohl. Despite the fact that she found Julius Mohl and his academic colleagues 'like a set of old grammars walking about', she concluded, 'It's much nicer there than at Madame Blaze de Bury's, with her shrieks and heraldic fuss.'[87]

Madame Julius Mohl (née Mary Clarke, 1793–1883), whose *salon* for so long played a leading part in introducing English writers to Parisian cultural life, had little beyond her personality to trade on when she and her mother left Great Britain for good in 1813. They soon formed friendships among the liberal intelligentsia of Paris who were opposed to the oppressive censorship operating under the Restoration monarchies of Louis XVIII and Charles X. A series of men, including the philosopher-historian Charles Fauriel, the philosopher Victor Cousin, and the historian-politician Adolphe Thiers, were supposed to be romantically attached to their spirited hostess, and although she experienced the occasional anxiety about rumours reaching her Evangelical sister and MP husband back in England, her standing in Paris seemed unaffected. 'I married late, and was rather given to sentimental flirtation for a good many years—all with the most honourable intentions, of course,' she later averred.[88] Her French circle reflected her heterogeneous interests. Artists and sculptors spoke to her own training as a portrait painter in the ateliers of Paris. In providing the young Louisa Mackenzie with an introduction to Madame Mohl, as she set out on her first trip to Paris in 1851, Parthenope Nightingale told her, 'She knows a great deal about art, and would tell you all

[86] Robert Browning to Isa Blagden, 21 July [1862]; and Elizabeth Barrett Browning to Mrs Martin, 28 Dec. 1855, transcript (BC\X62\62065-00) held in Armstrong-Browning Library, Baylor, Texas.
[87] *Letters of Anne Thackeray Ritchie*, ed. H. Ritchie (London: John Murray, 1924), 163–4.
[88] Lesser, *Clarkey*, 116.

manner of books, and show you artists and help you in every way.'[89] The education clearly 'took': in marrying the widowed Lord Ashburton, Louisa was to become as famous a *salonnière* as his first wife.

Savants, whose lectures Madame Mohl enthusiastically attended, graced her gatherings, where they might meet actresses, writers, or musicians. Her eventual marriage to Julius Mohl in 1847 added a network of orientalists to this scholarly band, and ensured that each fresh election to the Académie Française was keenly debated in her *salon*. By inheriting Madame Récamier's guest-list, Mary Mohl also added aristocratic friends from the Faubourg Saint-Germain to her collection. Her British acquaintance spanned a wide circle, from long-established Unitarian families such as the Nightingales to the liberal thinkers she encountered during her annual visits to England, where she found a warm welcome at such pieds-à-terre as the Deanery at Westminster. It was the prospect of meeting guests drawn from across Europe, frequently sourced through the network she shared with fellow *salonnières* such as the Italian Princess di Belgiojoso, or the Comtesse de Circourt and Madame Swetchine, both Russians, that continued to make her modest rooms so attractive to British visitors.

Anticipating her first appearance there as a guest, Elizabeth Barrett Browning wrote to Mary Mitford, 'We go on Friday evening to a Madam Mohl's where we are to have some of the "celebrities," I believe, for she seems to know everybody of all colours, from white to red.'[90] Consequently, as the years passed, and guests drawn from the ever- richer strata of her life mingled in her rooms, embarrassing chance meetings could occur. The Comte de Montalembert, a leading liberal Catholic and a near neighbour, promptly left the *salon* with his wife when he saw Ernest Renan, Julius Mohl's freethinking colleague, enter.[91]

The sheer longevity of her reign as a *salonnière* gave successive generations the impression of a direct line of access to the Paris of their parents, or even grand-parents. When John Tulloch met her in 1858 he already saw her as 'a funny old woman', yet she was to run her *salon* for almost another twenty years.[92] Within a couple of years of her death, Madame Mohl's *salon* had become the stuff of com-peting legends, as a variety of her acquaintance struggled to assert pre-eminence amongst her vast circle. Kathleen O'Meara, a long-time Paris resident, was first into print in 1885 with *Madame Mohl: Her Salon and her Friends: A Study of Social Life in Paris*; the same year witnessed Anne Thackeray Ritchie's recollections of Mohl's home in the Rue du Bac in her novel *Mrs Dymond*. In 1887 Mary Simpson, Nassau Senior's daughter, enlarged upon a previous article, and produced *Letters and Recollections of Julius and Mary Mohl* in which she took particular issue with O'Meara's account of Mohl's relations with London friends.[93] By 1888, Margaret

[89] V. Surtees, *The Ludovisi Goddess: The Life of Lady Ashburton* (Salisbury,Wilts.: Michael Russell, 1984), 35.
[90] *Letters of Elizabeth Barrett Browning*, ed. Kenyon, ii, 26.
[91] Simpson, *Julius and Mary Mohl*, 210.
[92] Oliphant, *Life of John Tulloch*, 139.
[93] M. C. M. Simpson, 'Some Personal Recollections of Madame Mohl', *Macmillan's Magazine* (Sept. 1883), 424–36.

Oliphant was confident in asserting, Madame Mohl had become something of a household name.[94]

By no means every British *salon* in Paris offered so cosmopolitan an ambience. The narrator in Thackeray's *Adventures of Philip* describes the soirées hosted in the English colony as 'parties where there are forty English people, three Frenchmen, and a German who plays the piano'.[95] When he had become famous, Thackeray would occasionally gratify his mother by accompanying her to humdrum 'tea-parties', amidst grander engagements such as a presidential ball or a soirée given by d'Orsay's sister, the Duchesse de Gramont. Letters to Jane Brookfield written in early 1851 recorded humble affairs such as 'a pretty little English dance' hosted by the wife of an English railway engineer, or a visit to a Madame Colmache, 'a good woman who writes books, [and] keeps a select boarding house for young ladies who wish to see Parisian society'. Yet even such modest gatherings afforded further introductions. Madame Colmache introduced him to Virginie Ancelot, wife of the dramatist Jacques Ancelot, who was allegedly dying to add him to her *salon* collection, though Thackeray self-mockingly noted that, when he spoke to her, she clearly had no idea who he was. The next night, he continued, 'my mother had her little T and they danced and it was not at all unpleasant quand on y etait [*sic*]'.[96]

It was *Vanity Fair's* success that secured Thackeray a welcome in the *salons* of the wealthy. The first Lady Ashburton (née Harriet Mary Baring, 1805–57), who boasted of not reading, liked nothing more than 'collecting' writers and hastened to add Thackeray to her hoard in 1848. It was her fondness for Thomas Carlyle's company that excited Jane Welsh Carlyle's wrath, possibly, as Ella Hepworth Dixon was to suggest, because 'With money', Jane too 'could have run a salon, given dinner parties, and shone as she ought'.[97] It was Lady Ashburton's invitation to Carlyle to join her and her husband in Paris for a week in September 1851 that prompted his detailed but disenchanted accounts of the guests he met in her *salon* in her suite at Hotel Meurice, and of Lady Sandwich's *salon* at 2 Rue Saint-Florentin.[98]

Another wealthy British *salonnière* who opened her doors to Thackeray was Ellen Julia Hollond (1822–84), wife of a Liberal MP and herself a writer. Thackeray, who shared an Anglo-Indian background with this couple, attended their gatherings at 63 Portland Place, and when after 1848 they decided to winter in Paris, attended their richly appointed Parisian *salon* in the Rue Basse-du-Rempart, and later in the Rue d'Astorg. Ellen Hollond seems to have been equally at home writing in English or French. Under her own name she published travel writings, while her anonymous publications in Paris were mainly devoted to explaining the ecumenism and religious tolerance advocated by such movements as Quakerism and Unitarianism; she would have found many of these interests embodied in Elizabeth

[94] Oliphant, *Life of John Tulloch*, 139.
[95] *Adventures of Philip*, Oxford Thackeray, xvi, 325.
[96] *Letters of Thackeray*, ed. Ray, ii, 734, 747–8.
[97] Quoted in N. Clarke, *Ambitious Heights: Writing, Friendship, Love—the Jewsbury Sisters, Felicia Hemans, and Jane Welsh Carlyle* (London: Routledge, 1990), 4.
[98] Carlyle, 'Excursion', in *Last Words*, 168–72, 181–2.

Gaskell, whom Madame Mohl arranged for her to meet in 1855.[99] Ellen Hollond's championship of freedom also inflected the tone of her *salon*, where those opposed to Napoleon III and all his works were especially welcome—an intensity of political focus that wearied guests such as Madame Mohl who preferred 'variety'.[100] Robert Hollond, whose immense wealth funded his wife's lust for entertaining talented conversationalists, apparently had little French and was apt to retreat to keep company with a bottle of whisky.

Neither a husband nor immense wealth was essential to the running of a *salon*. Lady Elizabeth Elgin (1790–1860), or the 'widow of the marble man', as Elizabeth Barrett Browning initially referred to her, settled as a widow in a ground-floor apartment in a grand *hôtel* on the Rue de Varennes (7th arrondissement), where she allegedly ran one of the 'best houses' in Paris.[101] In October 1851 Elizabeth mentioned that she and Robert were going to attend and hoping to 'see Balzac's duchesses and *hommes de lettres* on all sides... which is just our reason for going'.[102] In the event, she told Mary Mitford, she and Robert 'saw some French, but nobody of distinction'.[103] When old-age and ill-health had confined Lady Elgin to a wheel-chair, Matthew Arnold and John Tulloch were still drawn to her *salon*, confident that her well-connected daughters would continue to add new guests to their mother's list.[104]

Some ten months before Elizabeth Barrett Browning's first visit, Thackeray had escorted his mother to one of Lady Elgin's *salons* and reported finding her 'an honest grim big clever old Scotch lady, well read and good to talk to—dealing in religions of many denominations, and having established in her house as a sort of Director, Mr. Caird, one of the heads of the Irvingites; a clever shifty sneaking man'.[105] W. R. Caird had clearly played on two of Lady Elgin's enthusiasms: 'Scotch matters in general' and new religious movements.[106] This Scots clerk had married one of the young Campbell sisters, whose claim to divinely inspired glossolalia had helped ruin the Carlyles' old friend, the credulous Revd Edward Irving. After his wife died in 1840, Caird managed to parlay her fame into a role for himself. Funded by wealthy Irvingites, he acquired a roving brief evangelizing on behalf of the movement in Europe, before being appointed an Irvingite 'apostle' in 1860. It was quite possibly his encounter with Caird which occasioned Thackeray's long satirical interlude in *Pendennis* (1850) on the mixture to be found in the Parisian *salons* of the genuinely pious with religious charlatans, milking the purses of British women, 'renowned for austerity, and of a quite dazzling moral purity'.[107]

Lady Elgin indeed had a well-developed penchant for 'all sorts of supernatural-isms'. In January 1852 she brought the abolitionist George Thompson to visit the

[99] *Letters of Mrs. Gaskell*, ed. Chapple and Pollard, 332.
[100] Simpson, *Julius and Mary Mohl*, 128.
[101] *Elizabeth Barrett Browning: Letters to her Sister*, ed. Huxley, 144. Cf. A. T. Ritchie, *Chapters from Some Memoirs* (London: Macmillan, 1894), 7–10.
[102] *Elizabeth Barrett Browning: Letters to her Sister*, ed. Huxley, 144.
[103] *Letters of Elizabeth Barrett Browning*, ed. Kenyon, ii, 26.
[104] *Letters of Matthew Arnold*, ed. Lang, i, 427; Oliphant, *Life of John Tulloch*, 139.
[105] *Letters of Thackeray*, ed. Ray, ii, 749.
[106] Oliphant, *Life of John Tulloch*, 139.   [107] *Pendennis*, ed. Sutherland, 260–1.

Brownings; he 'knew all about the "Rappists", had heard the spirits "rap," knew how a spirit gave a kiss to one lady, and an autograph to another.' This rage for séances and table-rapping evoked the kind of impassioned debate between believers and sceptics which was inimical to the cool, witty repartee for which French *salons* had been famed. Elizabeth Barrett Browning reported a soirée that she herself held in May 1852 almost ruined by such a falling-out:

> When [Lady Elgin] talked of a communion of souls, Mrs. Jameson began to talk of private madhouses—in a way which made my blood run cold.—I really thought there would have been an explosion between the two women, & that Robert & I, who agree so admirably with Lady Elgin, (for whom I bear quite an affection) would never carry the evening to an end safely. Lady Elgin *did* say—"Perhaps you think me mad."[108]

His wife's credulous enthusiasm for table-turning became, in Robert's poem, 'A Lover's Quarrel', one of the disagreements that threatened to sour the lovers' springtime. By October 1852 Elizabeth and Robert were so divided on the matter that Henriette Corkran, then a small child, claimed to remember the explosion that had greeted her mother's expression of interest in spiritualism at a gathering in the Corkrans' fifth-floor apartment.[109] It sounds, from Anne Thackeray Ritchie's memoirs, as if she and her sister Minnie were also present at this gathering 'in a little high-up room': her first recollection of the Brownings was of her father, who was 'always immensely interested by the stories of spiritualism and table-turning', attempting to mediate between the believing wife and sceptical husband.[110]

By the summer of 1856 Robert Browning's bête noire, the American Daniel Dunglas Home, was firmly ensconced in the *salons* of Paris, eventually penetrating the Imperial court itself (possibly through the good offices of Arethusa Gibson (1814–85), an English *salonnière* who had befriended Louis-Napoleon during his exile in London). Frances Trollope, who had herself come under Home's sway in England and Florence that summer, swiftly recognized that he would provide good copy for providing a more contemporary gloss to her writings about Paris. The heroine of *Fashionable Life; or, Paris and London* (1856) duly consults her old schoolmaster mentor in England, asking him to countenance or discourage her attendance at a séance conducted by a visiting American medium in the *salon* of Madame de Charmont, a Swedenborgian. The exchange of letters reaches no definitive conclusion, thus avoiding offending readers in either camp. It did, however, afford Trollope the opportunity to voice her concern about the possible exploitation of the recently bereaved, to recount the phenomena which rapidly escalated from tables moving to a creepy séance at which the hands of the dear departed appeared and inscribed a message for their living loved ones.[111]

---

[108] *Letters of the Brownings to George Barrett*, ed. P. Landis and R. E. Freeman (Urbana: University of Illinois Press, 1958), 165, 181.

[109] H. Corkran, *Celebrities and I* (London: Hutchinson, 1902), 34.

[110] A. T. Ritchie, *Records of Tennyson, Ruskin and Browning* (London: Macmillan, 1892), 191–2. For Thackeray's continuing interest in spiritualism, see G. Dawson, 'Stranger than Fiction: Spiritualism, Intertextuality, and William Makepeace Thackeray's Editorship of the *Cornhill Magazine*, 1860–62', *Journal of Victorian Culture* 7(2) (2002), 220–38.

[111] F. Trollope, *Fashionable Life*, ii, 105–58.

7.5 THE SIGNIFICANCE OF THE *SALON* FOR BRITISH WRITERS

The way in which men like Caird and Home had managed to make their way into the heart of *salon* society threatened the *salons'* reputation as a mechanism for monitoring the constant influx of new arrivals to Paris with a view to replenishing the exclusive groups at its heart. Although fame and achievements were as much passports to the *salons* as ancient lineage it is important not to underrate the social cachet provided by being known to have rubbed shoulders with the glitterati of Europe.

Lady Sydney Morgan and Frances Trollope, who harboured anxieties about their reputation for gentility, both used their access to the *salons* to bolster their estimation with the reading public at home. Morgan, rumoured to be the daughter of a bankrupt Irish actor and even to have trod the boards herself, also had strong radical political sympathies that made her suspect in London's Tory circles and press. She therefore assured readers of her guide to Paris, 'We had above twenty houses open to us, on different nights in the week, during our residence in Paris, where we were always sure of being graciously received, and of finding good society.' Emphasizing that the French are 'at all times circumspect in their societies, and averse from large and indiscriminate assemblies', she underscored her own acceptability by declaring, 'The *obscure*, the *unknown* and the *unnoted*, have therefore but little chance of obtaining admissions into good French houses, of any party or faction, if not *particularly recommended*, by letters or personal introduction.' Her manoeuvre paid off: Paris provided a convenient cultural stepping-stone from her Irish origins to acceptance in London literary circles.[112]

Frances Trollope was recovering from the personal and literary scandal caused by her *Domestic Manner of the Americans* (1832), which had been illustrated by a young French émigré, Auguste Hervieu, whom she had been unwise enough to take on her trip to America while leaving her husband at home in England. Her ploy for re-establishing herself via the medium of the Paris *salons* was identical to Morgan's:

> Joyfully, therefore, have I welcomed the attention and kindness that have been offered in various quarters; and I have already had the satisfaction of finding myself on terms of most pleasant and familiar intercourse with a variety of delightful people, many of them highly distinguished....And here let me pause to assure you, and any other of my countrymen and countrywomen whose ears I can reach, that excursions to Paris, be they undertaken with what spirit of enterprise they may, and though they may be carried through with all the unrestrained expense that English wealth can permit, yet without the power by some means or other of entering into good French society, they are nothing worth.

The elegant exclusivity of Parisian *salons*, she triumphantly observed, 'can only be guessed at by those, who by some happy accident or other, possess a real and effec-

---

[112] Lady S. Morgan, *France* (London: Henry Colburn, 1817), i, 405, 399.

tive "open seseme [*sic*]!" for the doors of Paris'.[113] Frances Trollope's conviction of
the social credentials her efforts had secured might well have been shaken had she
lived to read her snobbish son Thomas's memoirs, in which he dismissed Guizot as
carrying himself like a schoolmaster, Thiers as having the air of a stockbroker, and
Chateaubriand as an insincere old humbug.[114]

Elizabeth Barrett Browning was not above letting it be known back home that
she had mingled with France's political and artistic movers and shakers. The following excerpt from a letter betrays a slight anxiety lest her correspondent fails to
appreciate the star quality of those with whom she is mixing:

> Tonight we are going to Ary Scheffer's to hear music and to see ever so many celebri-
> ties. Oh, and let me remember to tell you that M. Thierry, the blind historian, has sent
> us a message by his physician to ask us to go to see him, and as a matter of course we
> go. Madame Viardot, the prima donna, and Leonard, the first violin player at the
> Conservatoire, are to be at M. Scheffer's.

Some British writers, however, were also alive to the peculiar professional opportunities available in a city where the printed word was so highly prized. For their
1851 trip, Elizabeth Barrett Browning made sure that Robert was equipped with
an introduction 'to Emile Lorquet of the "National," and Gavarni of the "Charivari,"
so that we shall manage to thrust our heads into this atmosphere of Parisian journalism, and learn by experience how it smells'. She was particularly keen that
Robert should become an habitué of Madame Buloz' *salon*. Madame Buloz was
married to the proprietor of *Revue des deux mondes*, a paper which had begun to
show 'an ardent admiration of the present English schools of poetry', and which
had published a laudatory article on Robert by Joseph Milsand, who was to become
his lifelong friend.[115] In 1848 Buloz had also been appointed chief administrator
of the Comédie-Française, so the *salon* received a mixture of France's most famous
contemporary cultural icons.

Anglophone journalists working in Paris could consider themselves fortunate if
they possessed a wife capable of running a *salon*. Eyre Evans Crowe's wife's Saturday
salon included English and Irish artists and journalists, together with many of the
French writers and politicians who were active agents in the 1830 revolution and
so provided invaluable government contacts for him when Louis-Philippe came to
the throne.[116] The journalist Frazer Corkran's wife was described by a colleague as
'a woman of stately beauty and wide literary culture, [who] had in her *salon*, taken
charge of the social part of his work'.[117] In their fifth-floor apartment, on the Rue
Basse du Rempart, in the fashionable area of the Boulevard des Italiens, they
received Victor Hugo, de Vigny, Lamartine, and Balzac, along with Thackeray,
the Brownings, and even (their daughter Henriette alleged) Dickens.[118] In a later

[113] F. Trollope, *Paris and the Parisians*, i, 36.
[114] T. A. Trollope, *What I Remember*, 92–3.
[115] Letters of Elizabeth Barrett Browning, ed. Kenyon, ii, 75, 26, 30.
[116] *Letters of Thackeray*, ed. Ray, i, 334; J. Crowe, *Reminiscences of Thirty-Five Years of My Life*
(London: John Murray, 1895), 6–10.
[117] Whiteing, *My Harvest*, 136.
[118] Corkran, *Celebrities and I*, 31, 34, 40, 52.

generation Emily Crawford was to keep both her own and her husband's careers as foreign correspondents afloat by recruiting to her *salon* eminent French politicians of the likes of Thiers, Gambetta, Carnot, and Georges Clemenceau.

The opportunity for socializing with publishers, often regarded as little better than bookseller tradesmen in England, could also prove valuable. Madame Mohl notably included publishers and translators as well as writers within her extensive acquaintance, and seems to have become something of an unpaid literary agent in her own right, attempting, unsuccessfully, to persuade George Eliot to break with her old Swiss friend, d'Albert Durade, and use one of her own friends as her French translator.[119] She acted as intermediary between the French publisher Louis Hachette and Madame Belloc, an invalid friend of hers, about translating *Cranford*; and was later dispatched by Elizabeth Gaskell to make contact with Dickens, then in Paris, to secure for her the translation rights of 'my stories published in Household Words'.

Elizabeth Gaskell, customarily thought of as entrusting her business affairs to her husband, when in Paris took her cue from Madame Mohl. Gaskell was eventually to describe herself to Hachette as having become 'the journalist you have employed to keep you "au courant" in English literature'. Writing to recommend contemporary British fiction he might consider publishing in French, she nominated only women novelists, and constituted herself the network facilitator should he wish to make contact with her friends, Mrs Nicholls (better known to us as Charlotte Brontë) or Miss Jewsbury. She was less sanguine about the translatability of Charlotte Yonge's work (though Yonge was to find a much-sought-after translator in Guizot's daughter, Henriette de Witt).[120]

Yet the encounters and networks facilitated by the Parisian *salons* were probably more valuable in ways that are harder to measure than these commercial opportunities. The *salons* offered British writers first-hand contact with European literature and thought, thus offering a counterweight to the provincialism which dedicated Europhiles like Matthew Arnold or John Stuart Mill believed to be the besetting sin of an island race. Moreover, the networks spanned by these hostesses' assiduous letter-writing frequently extended well beyond Europe. Frances Trollope managed to make fictional capital out of this habit in her *The Old World and the New* (1849), in which a British *salonnière's* letters to relatives embarked on a pioneering adventure in Ohio, keep them up to date with the swiftly changing Parisian political situation of 1848–9.

The *salons* also served to encourage the notion of literary work as performance: von Humboldt's readings from his thirty-volume account of his travels in the Americas with Aimé Bonpland had been a claim to fame of Helen Maria Williams's Parisian *salon* at the start of the century,[121] just as Chateaubriand's readings from

[119] *George Eliot Letters*, ed. Haight, iv, 367.
[120] *Further Letters of Mrs Gaskell*, ed. J. Chapple and A. Shelston (Manchester: Manchester University Press, 2003), 131, 147; *Letters of Charles Dickens*, ed. Storey et al., viii, 4.
[121] N. Leask, 'Salons, Alps and Cordilleras: Helen Maria Williams, Alexander von Humboldt, and the discourse of Romantic travel', in E. Eger, C. Grant, C. ó Gallchoir, and P. Warburton (eds), *Women, Writing and the Public Sphere, 1700–1800* (Cambridge: Cambridge University Press, 2001), 217–35.

his forty-two volume *Mémoires d'outre-tombe* formed the mainstay of the *salon* which Madame Récamier passed to her British protégée, Madame Mohl. Dickens's public readings were doubtless largely a product of his taste for 'the boards', but it is notable that his first private reading to a group of friends of a current work, *The Chimes* (1844), took place during a flying visit to London from Europe; and in the aftermath of his first European tour, which concluded with a prolonged stay in Paris, Swiss friends identified the readings from *Dombey and Son* to which he invited them as 'A Soirée'.[122]

As this chapter has indicated, the Parisian *salons* hosted by women, and where women were admitted as much on their own as their spouses' reputation, served to provide many European women writers, including the British, with a sense of the legitimacy of their own calling. Meanwhile, male Victorian writers, who were notoriously sensitive to the double contempt for a feminized domestic occupation and mere hand labour to which their vocation exposed them in England, returned from the *salons* with a sense of the esteem in which writing was held in the neighbouring capital.

As we shall see in the next part of this book, devoted to the part Paris played in the development of nineteenth-century Anglophone journalism, the social cachet and political influence some of their French colleagues achieved was to make a profound impression on many British journalists.

---

[122] *Charles Dickens: The Public Readings*, ed. P. Collins (Oxford: Clarendon Press, 1975), p. xix.

PART II

ANGLOPHONE JOURNALISM
IN PARIS

The second part of the book is concerned with the significance of Paris for mid-nineteenth-century Anglophone journalism and journalists. Although the term 'journalist' had existed since the late seventeenth century to describe those who kept private journals, and was swiftly extended to cover those who earned money by contributing to published journals, the cognate noun, 'journalism', was a comparative latecomer. The *OED* records its first usage in January 1833: in the course of the discussion of a French work, *Du journalisme*, the reviewer for the *Westminster Review* remarks upon the word as a useful invention, emanating as it did from France, 'where the power of journalism is acknowledged to be enormous'. The development of 'journalism' as a back-formation via French suggests how closely related the product and the producer were becoming, especially at a time when 'journalism', lacking entry qualifications or specific training, hardly counted as a profession. Whereas a briefless English barrister was still entitled to account himself a lawyer, a journalist only existed to the extent to which he practised his 'trade', which—at least in the early stages of a career—was usually paid as piecework.

During this period, when the press in both Great Britain and France was changing rapidly both in its modes of production and content, 'journalism' necessarily proved a capacious category, capable of describing factual reporting, commentary, opinionated observation, and the semi-fictional account. The four chapters in Part II concentrate on work initially destined for periodicals and newspapers, and pay greater attention to writers whose primary source of income came at some time in their lives from working as a Paris correspondent for a London-based paper, or for the Anglophone press published in Paris, than to those established British writers who opportunistically used the occasional visit to Paris to generate fresh copy.

Since the source material used here draws heavily upon memoirs, biographies, autobiographies, and correspondence, it is difficult to draw an absolute distinction between the lineaments of the history of journalism and the personalities involved. Nevertheless, Chapter 8 will focus on the press conditions which won for nineteenth-century Paris the soubriquet of the 'city of ink'[1] and in consequence made it a honeypot for both tyro writers and speculative British investors in the Anglophone periodical press in Paris. Chapter 9 investigates the class, education, and gender of the British journalists working in Paris over this period. Chapter 10 concentrates on their working lives and the qualities that made for success in this competitive world. Chapter 11 exploits this picture of the opportunities and snares presented by Anglophone journalism in Paris, to demonstrate the lasting significance of his Paris years to the career of William Makepeace Thackeray as both writer and illustrator.

---

[1] See 'City of Ink 1830–48', in P. Mansel, *Paris Between Empires, 1814–52: Monarchy and Revolution* (London: Phoenix, 2001).

8

Press conditions

This chapter considers the conditions in the rapidly changing print industry of the mid-nineteenth century; the appeal of Paris as a city where journalists occupied a respected position; the practical problems Anglophone journalists encountered, in peacetime and under war conditions, in getting their material to Great Britain, and finally, the swift expansion and decline in the first half of the century of an Anglophone journalism specifically targeted at the British in Paris.

8.1 THE PRINT TRADE

During the 1830s and 1840s a rapid expansion in print media occurred almost simultaneously in a number of European cities. For the most part London and Paris kept pace with one another developmentally in matters such as technological innovation; changing price structures; the emergence of the publisher as a distinct category from the printer-bookseller; the appearance of the modern wide-circulation newspaper; and the advent of the *feuilleton*, or fiction in serialized form.[1]

Occasionally a specific route by which a particular phenomenon travelled from one capital to another can be traced, as in the case of the keepsake book introduced to France by a small number of identifiable British editors.[2] However, this is merely part of the more complex tale of the commercial flow in engraving between neighbouring capitals. From the late 1820s to the early 1840s, editors of fashionable keepsakes and annuals, such as Alaric Watts (1797–1864), were prepared to travel to Paris to acquire engravings prepared by lithography, a process in which engravings were made by the artist directly onto the stone or steel plate, rather than by transferring an original onto a plate or block. Whereas in Paris lithography was widely esteemed and valued as much in the comic and cheaper press as in the fine

[1] For a succinct summary see J. S. Allen, *In the Public Eye: A History of Reading in Modern France, 1800–1940* (Princeton, NJ: Princeton University Press, 1991), 27–54.

[2] See A. Glinoer, 'Collaboration and Solidarity: The Collective Strategies of the Romantic Cenacle', in S. Whidden (ed.), *Models of Collaboration in Nineteenth-Century French Literature: Several Authors, One Pen* (Farnham: Ashgate, 2009), 37–54.

fashion plates of a Jules David,[3] in Great Britain, anxieties about the contamination of the highbrow press by its cheaper relation tended to restrict lithography to the opposite ends of the market. Ambitious young English engravers such as the Thomas brothers, George (1824–68) and William (1830–1900), therefore sought their training in Parisian workshops, and then made their way to America, where lithography was proving a success in the illustrated press. Meanwhile London engraving firms made up for the deficiencies in home-grown expertise by recruiting foreign engravers.[4] Gavarni, Doré, and Daumier found plentiful work in England, and Thackeray believed that his Parisian friend the engraver Louis Marvy, who had joined the stream of exiles created by the European revolutions of 1848, would easily find employment in London. The cross-Channel commerce in engraving became sufficiently well known to be used as a plot device for moving the hero from one capital to another in such novels as Wilkie Collins's *The Woman in White* and Anne Ritchie's *Mrs Dymond*.[5]

During the period covered by this book, the print trade was an industry with permeable national boundaries and fluid internal structures, depending on highly portable skills and offering flexible routes between artisanal, commercial, and literary endeavour. Three careers will suffice to illustrate this point. The printer Sydney Waterlow (1822–1906), subsequently Lord Mayor of London, having completed a seven-year English apprenticeship, instantly headed for Paris, where he spent the winter of 1843 producing a bilingual catalogue for Galignani's lending library. The German-born Bernard Quaritch (1819–99), in pursuit of his aspiration to become the Napoleon of booksellers, employed his stint in Paris (1844–5) with the bookseller and publisher Théophile Barrois, to pick up an expertise in the burgeoning French school of oriental studies. Carrying this specialism with him to London, he was to become the publisher of the *Rubáiyát of Omar Khayyam* (1859).

The third example, Henry Vizetelly (1820–94), born into a London printing family, served an apprenticeship as a wood engraver, and worked with the caricaturist John Leech on his first successful drawings, *Paris Originals*, for *Bell's Life*. By the early 1840s he recognized the possibilities of the illustrated press and was involved in founding a series of illustrated weeklies. Whether he overreached himself in these ventures, or whether falling in with the set ruled over by that notorious drinker and gambler George Augustus Sala was responsible, is unclear, but in 1865, with his affairs in disarray, Vizetelly and his family left for Paris. For the next five years he was a salaried foreign correspondent for the *Illustrated London News*, supplementing this income with articles placed elsewhere, and the odd translation of French fiction: it is of this mid-century period in journalism that his memoirs offer their racy anecdotal account. The Franco-Prussian war saw Vizetelly and his 17-year-old son become war correspondents, but the experience also seemed to

---

[3] Sought out by Isabella Beeton to illustrate her reports on the Paris fashion shows in the British press.
[4] R. Whiteing, *My Harvest* (London: Hodder & Stoughton, 1915), 27, 30.
[5] W. Collins, *The Woman in White*, ed. H. Sucksmith (London: Oxford University Press, 1975), 578; A. T. Ritchie, *Mrs Dymond*, *The Works of Miss Thackeray* (10 vols, London: Smith, Elder, 1890), x, 167–77.

mark a turning-point in his career. After a brief venture into oenophilia, he decided to set up in London again as a publisher specializing in translations of contemporary French and Russian literature. It was his championship of the work of Émile Zola, seventeen of whose novels he published in translation, that landed him a three-month prison sentence in 1889.

Vizetelly's versatility was probably exceptional, but his view that an engraver's training was no bar to becoming a wordsmith was not: Thackeray and Sala, for instance, took formal instruction in engraving while they were also writing for magazines and newspapers. Journalists in Paris commonly found themselves supplementing their salaries with translation, adaptation, or simple theft of others' work. As fiction became a staple ingredient of newspapers, so many a journalist tried his hand at a genre by which he might establish an independent name. Balzac, and after him Thackeray and Flaubert, made this figure of the young man with literary ambition, essaying a series of genres and slowly evolving in the course of subsequent novels, into a characteristic figure of the print milieu. Reflecting on the long and varied lives of his contemporaries in the print fraternity, Vizetelly concluded that they proved the French axiom which declared that journalism 'leads a man to everything, provided he has the wit to abandon it at the proper moment'.[6]

There was however a facet of the Parisian life of print which differentiated it from London: the status, wealth and prestige accorded to the press in France made Paris a more attractive place to earn a living as a journalist, and indeed persuaded many a young Briton to consider journalism as a career, whatever his first reason had been for coming to Paris.

8.2 THE PRESTIGE OF THE PRESS

When Thackeray wrote of France in December 1839 as 'the paradise of painters and penny-a-liners', he had already spent some six years in Paris trying to establish himself as either one or the other. The statistics of the 1830s, which saw a striking reversal in the male:female ratio of Paris's population from a historical norm of approximately 100:117 to 110:95,[7] suggest that he was by no means alone in seeing Paris as the city where a young man could seek his living, and in his own chosen métiers the potential rewards seemed exceptional:

> [W]hen one sees M. Thiers's grand villa in the Rue St. George (a dozen years ago he was not even a penny-a liner, no such luck); when one contemplates, in imagination, M. Gud'n, the marine painter, too lame to walk through the picture gallery of the Louvre, accommodated, therefore with a wheelchair, a privilege of princes only, and accompanied—nay, for what I know, actually trundled—down the gallery by majesty itself, who does not long to make one of the great nation, exchange his native tongue

---

[6] H. Vizetelly, *Glances Back through Seventy Years: Autobiographical and Other Recollections* (2 vols, London: Kegan Paul, Trench, Trübner, 1893), ii, 189.

[7] C. Jones, *Paris: Biography of a City* (London: Penguin, 2006), 324.

for the melodious jabber of France . . . ? Noble people! they made Tom Paine a deputy; and as for Tom Macaulay, they would make a *dynasty* of him.[8]

Ingres' famous portrait of Louis-François Bertin (1832), depicting the press baron as an imposing bourgeois colossus whose steely menace dominates the canvas, contrives to convey the combined fear and fascination with which the power of the press was contemplated in France. When Henry Cole, the British Commissioner for the Paris *Exposition Universelle* of 1867, alighted on a display mingling the last quarter of a century's British literature and journalism as the exhibit most likely to appeal and to impress the French, George Augustus Sala saluted it as a master stroke.[9]

Journalism's prestige in Paris was closely linked to its attendant dangers. Those who used the press to satirize the government, of whatever shade, frequently found themselves imprisoned. The recurrent bouts of press censorship that occurred under each of the mid-nineteenth-century French regimes spoke to the power of a press which was seen as 'both a symbol of and a means for the construction of a regenerated society'.[10] Catherine Gore was merely repeating the *on dit* of the Parisian diplomatic circles in which she mixed in attributing the regime change of 1830 to the work of 'freedom-of-the-press-mongers' who had fomented the working classes to action.[11] In the aftermath of *les Trois Glorieuses* journalists acquired heroic status. It had been the protest, signed by forty-four journalists, against Charles X's ordinance of 25 July 1830 subjecting newspapers to pre-publication authorization, and the subsequent enforced closure of several newspapers, that brought the crowds to the barricades.

The journalist as hero was immortalized in an immediately posthumous portrait of Jean-Georges Farcy (1800–1830), a journalist on *Le Globe*, one of the proscribed papers, who was killed in street combat on 29 July.[12] The painter Alexandre-Marie Colin (1798–1855), from whom Farcy had borrowed his weapons, presented his friend as a figure, at once dashing and noble, in the act of grinding the offending ordinance underfoot. Farcy is equipped with the symbols of both the warrior and the young man about town: he is armed with a rifle and sword, two pistol butts peep from his breast pocket, while a recently discarded top hat and opera scarf lie to one side. As if to enrol him in France's honourable historic line of those prepared to take up arms to defend the nation, Farcy is posed against a background of further symbolic weaponry, by way of a display of knives and daggers, and an antique cuirass and helmet.

Forty years later, as the Second Empire writhed in its death throes, Bulwer Lytton's novel *The Parisians* (1872) offered a more sinister British reading of the

---

[8] 'On the French School of Painting', in *Paris Sketch Book, Oxford Thackeray*, ed. G. Saintsbury (17 vols, London: Oxford University Press, 1910), ii, 45.

[9] *The Life and Adventures of George Augustus Sala written by himself*, 2nd edn (2 vols, London: Cassell, 1895), i, 302.

[10] J. D. Popkin, 'Press and "Counter-Discourse" in the Early July Monarchy', in D. de la Motte and J. M. Przylblyski (eds), *Making the News: Modernity and the Mass Press in Nineteenth-Century France* (Amherst: University of Massachusetts Press, 1999), 15–42.

[11] C. Gore, *The Ambassador's Wife* (3 vols, London: Richard Bentley, 1842), iii, 278.

[12] The painting hangs in the Musée Carnavalet in Paris.

power of the Parisian press. One of the novel's leitmotifs is the way in which various interests, from those of high finance to the stealthy revolutionaries of Montmartre, use the press to manipulate public opinion. In the eyes of Bulwer Lytton's fictional visiting American colonel, himself the son of an earlier revolution, the Parisian press is an alarming phenomenon because its skilled rhetoricians are little better than irresponsible demagogues:

> [L]ike all people who are *blasés*, the Parisians are eager for strange excitement, and ready to listen to any oracle who promises a relief from indifferentism. This it is which makes the Press more dangerous in France than it is in any other country. Elsewhere the press sometimes leads, sometimes follows, public opinion. Here there is no public to consult, and instead of opinion the Press represents Passion.[13]

It was not necessary for a French writer to apply himself directly to contemporary political commentary in order to achieve political influence. Eugène Sue (1804–57), had been elected as a socialist to the Chamber of Deputies in 1850, riding on the back of the fame he had won as author of the immensely popular serial *Les mystères de Paris* (1842–3), in which a superhero metes out justice and exacts retribution on behalf of the poor and oppressed in a world of low life criminality. The dangers attendant on winning fame in a populist cause became clear when his next blockbuster, *Les mystères du peuple* (1849–57), expressing his egalitarian sympathies and disappointment at the death of the Republic, led to Sue's exile and the proscription of his work. The former 'penny-a liner' Adolphe Thiers (1797–1877), by whose 'grand villa' Thackeray had been so impressed in 1839, had previously won acclaim as author of a ten-volume history of the French Revolution, before helping to found, *Le National*, one of the newspapers involved in toppling Charles X. Serving as premier under the July Monarchy of Louis-Philippe, his anti-imperialist stance won him imprisonment and exile during the days of the Second Empire, but in 1871 he became President of the Third Republic.

For British writers the heights to which their French peers could rise was truly remarkable. 1831, the year after spectacular triumphs of the Parisian press, found Thiers' contemporary, Thomas Carlyle, telling his brother that in London 'Magazine work is below street sweeping as a trade'.[14] As Louis-Philippe gave way to Louis Bonaparte in February 1848, Charlotte Brontë wrote:

> How strange it appears to see literary and scientific names figuring in the list of Members of a Provisional Government! How would it sound if Carlyle and Sir John Herschel and Tennyson and Mr. Thackeray and Douglas Jerrold were selected to manufacture a new constitution for England?[15]

Political power could prove short-lived, but the material evidence of these literary men's wealth seemed incontestable. Eugène Sue's socialist sympathies did not

---

[13] Lord [E. G. E. L. Bulwer-]Lytton, *The Parisians* (2 vols, London: George Routledge, 1875), ii, 27.

[14] *The Collected Letters of Thomas and Jane Welsh Carlyle*, ed. C. R. Sanders, K. J. Fielding, et al. (40 vols, Durham, NC: Duke University Press, 1970–2012), v, 272.

[15] *The Letters of Charlotte Brontë, with a Selection of Letters by Family and Friends*, ed. M. Smith (3 vols, Oxford: Clarendon Press, 1995–2004), ii, 35.

prevent him from living in considerable style on the fruits of his earnings. The antiques, hothouses, and fountains of his Paris residence might make the axiom attributed to him that 'No one has the right to superfluities while anyone is in want of necessities' ring a little hollow in some Parisian ears, but they impressed the likes of Charles Dickens, as did the protestations of another acquaintance, the wealthy dramatist Eugène Scribe (1791–1861), that he too had started as a humble law clerk.[16] Dickens was also probably aware that successful though he was in British terms, the sales figures achieved by popular French authors regularly outstripped his own.[17] When he dined at the home of Émile de Girardin (1802–81), novelist, journalist, press baron, and five times elected to the Chamber of Deputies, the English writer confessed himself 'speechless with wonder' at the scale of the lavish banquet thrown on his behalf.

> No man unacquainted with my determination never to embellish or fancify such accounts, could believe in the description I shall let off when we meet, of dining at Emile Girardin's—of the three gorgeous drawing-rooms with ten thousand wax candles in golden sconces, terminating in a dining-room of unprecedented magnificence with two enormous transparent plate-glass doors in it... On the table are ground glass jugs of peculiar construction, laden with the finest growth of Champagne and the coolest ice. With the third course is issued Port Wine... which would fetch two guineas a bottle at any sale. The dinner done, Oriental flowers in vases of golden cobweb are placed upon the board. With the ice is issued Brandy; buried for 100 years. To that succeeds Coffee, brought by the brother of one of the convives from the remotest East, in exchange for an equal quantity of Californian gold dust. The company being returned to the drawing-room—tables roll in by unseen agency, laden with Cigarettes from the Hareem of the Sultan, and with cool drinks in which the flavour of the Lemon arrived yesterday from Algeria, struggles voluptuously with the delicate Orange arrived this morning from Lisbon.... All this time the host perpetually repeats 'Ce petit dîner-ci n'est que pour faire la connaissance de Monsieur Dickens; il ne compte pas; ce n'est rien.' And even now I have forgotten to set down half of it.[18]

It was not just Girardin's stupendous wealth that impressed Dickens but the 'unseen agency' that allowed him access to foreign parts. Paris offered British journalists a gateway to cosmopolitan Europe and the sense of proximity to networks of secret power.

At times of political tension, Paris also offered journalists the sensation of not merely reporting upon but partaking in the perilous civil warfare being played out on its streets. Stories of journalists availing themselves of the privileged viewing platform of the Parisian balcony, but involuntarily getting caught up in the fighting taking place below, entered the mythology of journalism, and eventually

[16] U. Pope-Hennessy, *Charles Dickens, 1812–1870* (London: Reprint Society, 1947), 333, 364.

[17] Although not presented in directly comparable form, useful statistics are provided in R. D. Altick, *The English Common Reader* (Chicago: Chicago University Press, 1957), 381–90; M. Lyons, 'In Search of the Bestsellers of Nineteenth-Century France, 1815–1850', in *Reading Culture and Writing Practices in Nineteenth-Century France* (Toronto: University of Toronto Press, 2008), 15–42.

[18] *The Pilgrim Edition of the Letters of Charles Dickens*, ed. G. Storey et al. (12 vols, Oxford: Clarendon Press, 1965–2002), viii, 34–5.

became a recognized fictional trope.[19] Turnbull, the *Times* correspondent, prefaced his account of the July 1830 barricades with the tale of an Englishman summarily shot because the troops believed he had been throwing stones from the balcony of his hotel room.[20] Henry Sutherland Edwards (1828–1906) recalled that a later *Times* employee, the music critic J. W. Davison, hoped to take advantage of the fact that he happened to be holidaying there when Napoleon III seized imperial power. Intent on sounding out his Parisian contacts, he was breakfasting with a French music publisher in the Rue de Richelieu when the soldiers below, believing a shot had come from inside his windows, tore up the stairs, killed a remonstrating servant, and ordered the guests at gunpoint onto the boulevard. They were spared only because the commanding officer recognized Adolphe Sax, inventor of the saxophone, as one of their party. Moments after they had fled, the soldiers 'swept' the boulevard with musketry fire.[21] During the Commune, a third *Times* employee, the war correspondent Laurence Oliphant, interpreted the graze from a bullet entering through the window of the house in which he was temporarily sheltering as the sign that his divine protection had been removed, and promptly returned to his cultic community on the shore of Lake Eyrie.[22]

8.3 GETTING NEWS OUT OF PARIS

French belief in the power of the press encouraged successive governments to keep almost as keen an eye on foreign language newspapers as on their own. The Second Empire was repeatedly attacked for exercising a censorship far worse than that which had toppled previous regimes. Elizabeth Barrett Browning, a staunch defender of Louis-Napoleon as a Carlylean strong leader, was outraged by a misleading report in the *Athenæum* to the effect that Parisian compositors were being thrown out of work by the Emperor's heavy censorship. She claimed: 'In respect to literature nothing can be more mendacious than to say there are restraints upon literature. Books of freer opinion are printed now than would ever have been permitted under Louis-Philippe.' Nevertheless, even she had to she concede, 'There is restraint in the newspapers.'[23]

Henry Vizetelly recalled the daily scrutiny of foreign papers arriving at the Hôtel des Postes by the ministry of the interior during the Second Empire, from which the *Times* and *Daily Telegraph* seemed to enjoy a 'special immunity'. Sometimes the paper would be released on condition that a paragraph offensive to the government

[19] See e.g. 'Ouida's' account of the June Days Uprising of 1848 in *Tricotrin: The Story of a Waif and Stray* (3 vols, London: Chapman & Hall, 1869) or M. E. Braddon's of the Commune in *Under the Red Flag* (Leipzig: Tauchnitz, 1883).

[20] D. Turnbull, *The French Revolution of 1830* (London: Henry Colburn & Richard Bentley, 1830), vii.

[21] H. S. Edwards, *Personal Recollections* (London: Cassell, 1900), 26, 72.

[22] M. O. W. Oliphant, *Memoir of the Life of Laurence Oliphant and of Alice Oliphant, his wife*, 6th edn (2 vols, Edinburgh: William Blackwood & Sons, 1891), ii, 81.

[23] Elizabeth Barrett Browning to Anna Jameson, 2 May [1856], transcript (BC\x56\56063-00) held in Armstrong-Browning Library, Baylor, Texas.

was cut out of each copy, but no explanation would be proffered for excisions, cancelled sheets, and blackouts. Even *Galignani's Messenger*, a Paris-based Anglophone paper particularly renowned for its impartial reporting of Franco-British material, found itself censored in the immediate wake of Napoleon's assumption of absolute powers.[24] By the latter days of the Second Empire, the censorship of the English papers by the French ministry of the interior was in the hands of the Paris corre-spondent of London's *Evening Star*, a man born in France to English parents. The irony of the fact that its readers regarded this as a paper of democratic sympathies did not go unnoticed by the British journalist fraternity.[25]

Despite the periodic censorship of national news, Paris's pre-eminence as the mid-nineteenth-century hub for international news had been assured in 1835 when Charles-Louis Havas, a Parisian translator and advertising agent, established the first international newsagency there: it swiftly became a resource for foreign correspondents and for subeditors making up the pages of anglophone papers in Paris. Two of Havas's former employees, Paul Julius Reuter and Bernhard Wolff, acquired the newsagency part of the business in 1852, and it was Reuter who grad-ually transformed the slow process of taking the news by surface over land and sea. At first he rented carrier pigeons to span the 100-mile gap between the Belgian and German telegraphs. In 1851 he turned his attention to the new Dover–Calais undersea cable as a means of transmitting commercially valuable information between the London and Paris stock exchanges: Galignani's *Messenger* swiftly availed itself of the telegraph to offer its readers the latest London prices on the same day.[26]

Although Queen Victoria was comforted during her 1855 visit to Paris by telegraphic reports about the children she had left at home, and the next year Dickens declared 'it was impossible not to be moved and excited' by the novelty of the electric telegraph being used as a device in the dénouement of a Parisian play celebrating the return of the troops from the Crimea,[27] Reuter found it hard to persuade the British press of the benefits of his telegraphic service.[28] When the distance from London to Paris remained the shortest of the major connections between European capitals, it seemed difficult to justify the considerable expense of the telegraph's bare factual report against the benefits of a fuller account from a journalist on the spot. So, in October 1858, Reuter was driven to offering his ser-vice on a fortnight's free trial.

It took the outbreak of the Franco-Prussian war for a British newspaper to instruct its foreign correspondents to send their entire copy by telegraph. The *Daily News*, flush with a fresh injection of money from the new part-owner, Henry

---

[24] *Harper's New Monthly Magazine* 21(4) (Feb. 1852), 399.

[25] Vizetelly, *Glances*, ii, 204–7; Whiteing, *My Harvest*, 82.

[26] D. Cooper-Richet and E. Borgeaud, *Galignani*, trans. I. Watson (Paris: Galignani, 1999), 11.

[27] *Queen Victoria: Leaves from a Journal: A Record of the Visit of the Emperor and Empress of the French to the Queen, and of the Visit of the Queen and H.R.H the Prince Consort to the Emperor of the French*, 1855, intro. R. Mortimer (London: André Deutsch, 1961), 89; *Letters of Charles Dickens*, ed. Storey et al., viii, 11–12.

[28] D. Read, *The Power of News: the History of Reuters* (Oxford: Oxford University Press, 1992), 5–30.

Labouchère, stole a march on its rivals. Archibald Forbes (1838–1900), the paper's war correspondent, took advantage of its policy to scoop his veteran rival, W. H. Russell of the *Times*: Forbes would ride all night from the war zone to Luxembourg, where the wires were free from military censorship.[29] The expense paid off: the *Daily News*'s circulation jumped from 50,000 to 150,000 in the course of the war.[30] Even the suspension of private telegrams during the Commune did not prove insurmountable for the *Daily News*. During some twenty years working as the paper's Paris correspondent, George Morland Crawford (1812–85) had developed a network of friendships with France's leading politicians, and Thiers gave Crawford access to his special wire for his dispatches.

Looking back some fifteen years later, John Augustus O'Shea (1839–1905) of the *Standard* remained a sceptic: if sent direct from the front, these costly telegrams had been subject to censorship, and got through only thirty-six hours in advance of a full report. But then O'Shea hankered after the more relaxed reporting style of his earliest days in Paris, some ten years before the war, when 'the reckless competition for the earliest intelligence had not yet set in; the pen of the ready writer was not handicapped by that pestilent wire, which is utterly destructive of style and too often lends itself to inaccuracy.'[31]

In truth, prior to regular telegraphic communications being established, getting news from Paris to London had been a laborious business requiring dispatches to be sent first to Boulogne, then by ferry to Dover, and finally by road or rail to London. Non-pressing dispatches went by post, first by mail-coach and later by train. O'Shea's contemporary Richard Whiteing (1840–1928), who felt that 'the first great period' of the Paris correspondent had ended with the collapse of the Second Empire, described the arrangements of his predecessors thus:

> They wrote long letters hot with the impression of things seen and lived, and where there was need of haste, they hired post-chaises, and set off for Calais on their own account, to catch the mail boat. It was a matter of days and nights of ceaseless travel, of reckless and lavish bargains with the post-houses on the road, of neck-and-neck races in genial rivalry for the chance of a first bid for the last relay left in the stable, each flourishing a mocking farewell to the other with his packet, as he forged ahead. On the road back they shared the victor's chaise, with frequent halts for an omelette and a bottle in the old inns of old towns—the best chums in the world. In this way they beat the official couriers from the embassies, and gave Downing Street itself first news.[32]

Sir Joseph Crowe (1825–96) recalled an occasion in 1849 when he had been acting as the Paris correspondent for the *Daily News*, and learned, just after the post had departed, that the Hungarian war of independence had failed; so he personally took the news to Dover, managing to return to his Paris desk within the space of twenty-four hours—the fastest time in which such a return trip could then be

[29] Whiteing, *My Harvest*, 282.

[30] L. Brown, 'The Treatment of the News in Mid-Victorian Newspapers', *Transactions of the Royal Historical Society*, 5th ser., 27 (1977), 33.

[31] J. A. O'Shea, *Leaves from the Life of a Special Correspondent* (2 vols, London: Ward & Downey, 1885), 235, 260, 120.

[32] Whiteing, *My Harvest*, 136–7.

made. In the mid-1830s his father, Eyre Evans Crowe, Paris correspondent for the *Morning Chronicle,* had kept carrier pigeons on the terrace of the family's fifth-floor apartment on the Rue du 29 Juillet as an alternative to employing hard-riding couriers to send the news on the first leg of its journey to Boulogne.[33] Pictures recording daily life during the siege of Paris celebrated the return of the pigeon post and the use of the hot-air balloon—both capable of soaring high above the Prussian guns to land in unoccupied territory—as symbols of the city's resistance.

The development of microscopic photography theoretically allowed pigeons to carry substantial information on a collodion film—ten times lighter than paper—which could then be magnified, projected onto a screen, and transcribed by teams of secretaries. Trained pigeons, however, were at a premium, and likely as not to have been eaten as the siege progressed, so the provisional French government organized a 'balloon-post' made available to journalists for their dispatches. The weight limitations imposed a laborious routine: O'Shea recalled writing a lengthy report on foolscap before passing it to a 'devil' to transcribe in minute calligraphy onto the 'onion-skin' tissue paper permitted.[34] As the siege tightened its grip, the foreign correspondent's duty to get the news home became increasingly arduous. After a balloon despatch of sketches intended for the *Illustrated London News* had landed within the German lines, and promptly been used by the German press, Henry Vizetelly resorted to sending an original and three copies by separate balloons; but after Paris had consumed all its horseflesh, this meant a walk of between six and eight miles to a launchpad.[35]

Even the Paris correspondents who made it to the war zone rarely managed to get anywhere near the front line, because Napoleon III was convinced that William Russell's reporting during the Crimean War had revealed the allies' thinking to the war office in St Petersburg.[36] Meanwhile some of the French papers, such as *Le Gaulois,* fanned the flames by running an increasingly hostile campaign against British journalists still in Paris, claiming them to be at best disclosing the state of the besieged city to the Prussians and at worst acting as their spies.[37] In the febrile atmosphere of September 1870 any foreigner in Paris, or in the war zone, who spoke either poor French or good German was apt to be taken for a Prussian spy. Vizetelly got into the habit of carrying old bills and receipts about his person around Paris as a safer proof of residence than a British passport, but this did not prevent him and his son being repeatedly imprisoned.[38] Sala recalled how, leaving the Café du Helder at midnight, he was surrounded by a mob and flung, as a spy, into a police cell in the Rue Montmartre, where he was promptly attacked by his fellow prisoners as an enemy of France. Hauled off on the Sunday morning to the prefecture near to the Palais de Justice, he managed to get a message to the

[33] J. Crowe, *Reminiscences of Thirty-Five Years of My Life* (London: John Murray, 1895), 88, 8.

[34] O'Shea, *Leaves,* ii, 310–11.

[35] Vizetelly, *Glances,* ii, 426. Vizetelly had already provided a highly detailed, illustrated description of the various aerial means of communication in operation by Nov. 1870 in *Paris in Peril* (2 vols, London: Tinsley Brothers, 1882), ii, 140–51.

[36] Sala, *Life and Adventures,* ii, 199.

[37] [H. Labouchère,] *Diary of the Besieged Resident in Paris, reprinted from the* Daily News *with Several New Letters and Preface* (London: Hurst & Blackett 1871), 274.

[38] Vizetelly, *Glances,* ii, 424.

British Embassy, who secured his freedom at midday. In retrospect he congratulated himself on escaping in the nick of time: two hours later, he claimed, crowds who viewed the Emperor and the Prussians with equal loathing had taken possession of the city, and had they found him in a prison cell might well have murdered him as a Prussian spy.[39] O'Shea recalled getting deliberately drunk in order to face the execution which he believed awaited him as a suspected spy.[40]

Over the course of years these survivors' tales had plenty of opportunity for embellishment, whereas Labouchère's contemporary reports from the besieged city carried a more measured account of the daily difficulties he encountered as a foreign correspondent. So hidebound were the French by bureaucracy, he claimed, that French postmen would sit on the boxes of their carts, by now devoid of both horses and mail, until they were given instructions to dismount by officials who seemed to be making no attempt to find alternative ways to run the blockade after access by train had become impossible. Labouchère took to sending his dispatches by balloon although he had no way of telling how many would get through to the coast, and by 21 September he was forced to assume that the English would know more than besieged Parisians about the progress of the war. Nevertheless the Parisians' hunger for news of any sort, Labouchère noted, encouraged the launching of forty-nine new papers in the city in the course of the siege.[41]

While the Prussian high command were reasonably hospitable to journalists, the French Emperor's edicts meant that British reporting of French military activities was largely reliant on official bulletins, gossip amongst the officers at headquarters, and rumours circulating at the rear of the army's lines. Besieged Paris correspondents had little option other than to offer a commentary on French reporting of the war, contrasting its specious rhetoric with the evidence of their own eyes. Both Labouchère and Sala denounced the way in which French journalists, from the safety of their offices, urged working men to heroic military sacrifice. Sala produced a particularly fine illustration of the mental dissociation from the realities of war involved in the celebration of *la gloire* when he noted the lengthy philological debate that had developed in the press over whether the verb *amener* or *emmener* should have been used in reporting the Emperor's decision to take his son to the front with him.[42]

It took the siege to detach the city of Paris from its position at the heart of European politics, and to turn its press to such local concerns; but there had long existed within Paris an Anglophone press largely directed to the very parochial concerns of the city's English residents.

8.4 THE ENGLISH NEWSPAPER BUSINESS IN PARIS

Shipping multiple copies of British newspapers from London to Paris was a costly business. When Thackeray bought the *National Standard* in 1833 he wrote from

[39] Sala, *Life and Adventures*, ii, 218–26.
[40] O'Shea, *Leaves*, ii, 263–84.
[41] [Labouchère,] *Diary of the Besieged Resident*, 291.
[42] Sala, *Life and Adventures*, ii, 201.

Paris to his mother: 'I cant get subscribers for it here, the postage being so enormous that it quite overbalances the cheapness of the paper.'[43] He should perhaps have thought harder about the established local competition. In the wake of Napoleon I's eleven-year blockade of the English Channel in 1814, at least two immigrant printers had swiftly recognized the opportunity of catering for residents of the newly reconstituted English colony in Paris.

In 1815 it seemed a natural development for James Smith, John Hurford Stone's successor at the 'English Press', established during the French Revolution by the radical émigré community in Paris, to advertise a bi-weekly paper, *The Paris and London Chronicle*, which would be 'like the journals of England'.[44] The other immigrant venture was run by an Italian bookseller, Giovanni Galignani (1757–1821), who had moved to Paris with his father-in-law, an English printer, in 1801, attracted by the capital's flourishing print trade. On 2 July 1814 they had launched the first Paris-based English-language newspaper, Galignani's *Messenger, or the Spirit of English Journals*, as a thrice-weekly affair. By August 1815 it was being published every day except Sunday, and in 1825 the firm launched *The London and Paris Observer* as their offering for the seventh day of the week.[45] The fact that stamp duty on newspapers continued in England until 1855 curbed the competition from the proliferation of British daily papers which was to occur when this tax was lifted, and in any case, untrammelled by copyright considerations, the *Messenger* prided itself on the speed with which it passed on political, cultural and financial news. At the close of the Second Empire, Bulwer Lytton was to picture the *Messenger* as forming essential reading for the international revolutionaries haunting the cafés of Montmartre.[46]

From 25 Jan 1830 the *Messenger* issued two editions a day—an early morning edition for Parisians and an afternoon one for distribution to the French provinces and the rest of Europe. The paper's comforting recipe of studied political neutrality, combined with a useful advertisement section and accounts of the comings and goings of fashionable society, served to keep British expatriates and travellers in touch with the news from home. Courtesy of reviews reprinted in the *Messenger*, Dickens was not only able to maintain an *au courant* correspondence with the likes of Wilkie Collins about the latest offerings of the London theatre, during his winter stay of 1856, but also, having identified them in pirated form, to berate W. H. Wills, his assistant editor at *Household Words*, for letting articles first submitted to their paper go to rival publications.[47] The wide circulation of its later edition also made the paper a convenient device for novelists wondering how to reunite far-flung characters. Accompanying his widowed sister abroad, Thackeray's Indian

[43] *The Letters and Private Papers of William Makepeace Thackeray*, ed. G. N. Ray (4 vols, Cambridge, Mass.: Harvard University Press, 1945–6), i, 262.

[44] M. B. Stern, 'The English Press in Paris and its Successors, 1793–1852', *Papers of the Bibliographical Society of America* 74 (1980), 307–59.

[45] *ODNB*; Cooper-Richet and Borgeaud, *Galignani*.

[46] Lord Lytton, *Parisians*, i, 235.

[47] *Letters of Charles Dickens*, ed. Storey et al., viii, 11, 20, 28.

nabob Jos Sedley is pictured as reading 'every word of Galignani's admirable newspaper'.[48]

The *Messenger* became a fixture, surviving political vicissitudes and changes in Parisian print economy until 1890, when it moved to London and became the *Daily Messenger*.[49] Working for the *Messenger* could therefore be relied upon for a regular income, but the way in which it was assembled made the pay low and the work unexciting for aspiring writers. When O'Shea responded in about 1860 to their advertisement for 'a gentleman of University education who was qualified to contribute original articles on French subjects and write dramatic criticisms on French plays', a fellow Irishman, Captain Bingham, the Paris correspondent of the *Pall Mall Gazette*, told him, 'Half the English writers in Paris have had a sickening of that factory.' Once in post, O'Shea discovered that all the paper really required was a translator who could turn French news into readable condensed form.[50]

From the start, Galignani's employees sought additional work from London-based newspapers. Cyrus Redding (1785–1870), for instance, who worked for the paper from 1815 to 1818, doubled as correspondent for the *London Examiner*. When Thackeray good-heartedly agreed for a few days in March 1838 to deputize for Battier, a fellow journalist unable to support his wife and four children during a bout of illness, he found himself also committed to the *Morning Advertiser*. He wrote to his wife, 'I have promised to write his letter for him, as well as to do his Galignani work—the whole may occupy 4 hours every day, but 2 of these must be from 8 to 10 in the morning, w^h hours are usually spent by me in bed.'[51] By the early 1860s, under the regime of the tyrannical Irish editor, 'Pomposo', his three or four employees found the work more onerous. O'Shea's account of the paper's petty economies suggest that by then it found itself in an altogether more competitive market. He recalled that the Paris morning papers would be borrowed from the firm's popular reading room below before the subscribers arrived, so that the editor could mark the articles to be translated: 'these were not cut out, that would be too wasteful; pins were simply stuck into them, diagonally if they were to be abbreviated, perpendicularly, if they were to be given in full'. Once the first edition had been put to bed, there was a short break at 1.30 p.m., followed by an afternoon of translation, before agreeing the next day's programme with the editor. On average a subeditor would endure this treadmill existence for about two months. O'Shea's successor, a barrister by the name of Davin, lasted only three weeks.[52]

Such newspapers seem in any case to have been subsidized by other activities open to Parisian printer/publishers. Stone, of the 'English Press', had, for instance, teamed up with Théophile Barrois (Senior), already established as a bookseller

---

[48] W. M. Thackeray, *Vanity Fair: A Novel without a Hero*, ed. J. Sutherland (Oxford: Oxford University Press, 1991), 788.

[49] G. Barber, 'Galignani's and the Publication of English Books in France from 1800 to 1852', *The Library*, 5th ser., 16(5) (1961), 283–4.

[50] O'Shea, *Leaves*, i, 109–10.

[51] *The Letters and Private Papers of William Makepeace Thackeray: A Supplement*, ed. E. F. Harden (2 vols, New York: Garland, 1994), i, 31.

[52] O'Shea, *Leaves*, i, 109–12.

specializing in English works, to supply Paris's English-speaking colony with 'a Collection of Best English Novels'. Galignani's launched 'La Librairie Française et Étrangère', and the 1831 edition of Edward Planta's *New Picture of Paris, or the Stranger's Guide to the French Metropolis* identified M. Dennis's establishment at No. 55 Rue Neuve Saint-Augustin as a further bookseller specializing in British literature, and like Galignani also offering a reading room.[53] In their Restoration heyday, there were some 520 such *cabinets de lecture* offering one-off sessions or more extended membership packages,[54] but Sala represented them as already, in the early 1840s, forming little more than musty retreats for the elderly of Paris.[55]

A further competitor, 'La Librairie des Étrangers', launched in the Rue de Tournon in 1824 by Martin Bossange (1766-1865), seems to have given Galignani's a run for its money. By 1831 Bossange, Père et fils had moved to more 'splendid' premises at 60 Rue de Richelieu[56] and by the mid-1830s also had a base in the Rue Neuve Saint-Augustin.[57] The young G. W. M. Reynolds, who had come to Paris in the immediate wake of the 1830 revolution, already radicalized by reading Tom Paine's *The Rights of Man* (1791–2), was simultaneously working in 1835 for Bossange's bookshop and as literary editor for the *Paris Literary Gazette* (1835–6), a paper aimed primarily at Paris's English colony. *The Paris Advertiser and Journal of English and Foreign Literature* (17 January–3 July 1836) was also advertised as under the direction of George W. M. Reynolds, and issuing from La Librairie des Étrangers. He was further involved that same year in the affairs of the *London and Paris Courier*, discussed in greater detail below. It is uncertain whether the failure of the former or the collapse of the latter was more responsible for Reynolds being forced to declare himself bankrupt in 1836 and settle with his French creditors from London the following year. What is clear is that Reynolds believed he had scores of his own to settle with various proprietors, and a tale to tell about the unhealthy state of the Anglophone newspaper industry in Paris.

In his immensely popular novel-cum-travel guide *Pickwick Abroad* (1837–8), Reynolds set a scene in a hotel in the heart of the English quarter, where a newly arrived guest asks the waiter for the names of the fashionable people currently to be found in Paris. By way of answer, the waiter summons a representative of the Circulating-Library Department, of the establishment in the Rue Neuve Saint-Augustin, who happens to be dining in an adjoining room. When this fawning clerk, Mr Matthew Tunks, duly appears, he brandishes the list of 'Fashionable Arrivals' published in the *Paris Advertiser*, only to admit, under question, that it lists only its own subscribers, not those who subscribe to Galignani. His claim for the superiority of his own establishment is backed up by quoting directly from the prospectus: 'We have forty thousand volumes in the Circulating-Library alone,

[53] E. Planta, *A New Picture of Paris or, the Stranger's Guide to the French Metropolis* (London: Samuel Leigh and Baldwin & Cradock, 1831), 389.

[54] F. Parent-Lardeur, *Lire à Paris au temps de Balzac: les cabinets de lecture à Paris* (1815–1830) (Paris: EHESS, 1982), 10.

[55] G. A. Sala, *Quite Alone* (3 vols, London: Chapman & Hall, 1864), iii, 11–15.

[56] Planta, *New Picture of Paris*, 390.

[57] Barber mentions locations in Rue de Tournon and 60 Rue de Richelieu in 'Galignani's and the Publication of English Books', 270–1.

and we take four hundred newspapers every day.' As Tunks leaves, the waiter asserts that he is 'considered to be the greatest liar in Paris; and the Frenchman, who is the sleeping proprietor of the establishment to which he belongs, is the most notorious villain in existence. His name is Jules Rénard—he lives in the Rue de Tournon—and the way in which he treated a young English gentleman in respect of that library, was shameful in the extreme.' Reynolds' process of naming and shaming also took in the 'immortal M. Bennis' (a barely disguised M. Dennis), who presides over the 'circulating library in the Rue Neuve Saint Augustin'.[58]

The intricate web of investment, carried out through a variety of active and sleeping partnerships, that seems to have characterized the Paris print trade at this period is suggested by the fact that Planta's 1831 guide singles out for particular commendation M. Rénard's two circulating libraries, at 1 Rue Caumartin and 16 Rue de l'Université, without any sense of their being connected with Bossange's enterprise.[59] Reynolds' novel meanwhile asserts the supremacy of the firm of Galignani by making its newspaper, *The Messenger*, first port of call both when the villain seeks to rent rooms and when the hero wants to announce his forthcoming nuptials.[60]

Despite the rewards that newsprint seemed to offer during a period when the population of Paris continued to grow—in 1830 it numbered nearly 800,000, in 1851 nearly a million, and it reached 1.9 million by 1872[61]—the regular market for Anglophone dailies remained comparatively small. In 1831 the resident British population in Paris was about 4,500, accounting for some 10 per cent of the foreigners in Paris. By 1851 this number had scarcely risen: now numbered at 5,053, the British formed 9.28 per cent of foreign residents. Although British expatriate growth over the middle years of the century was roughly commensurate with that of the city's population as a whole, it was more markedly susceptible to political disruptions. During the opulent days of the Second Empire, it expanded from 7,028 in 1861 to 8,015 in 1866, dipping, unsurprisingly, in the aftermath of the Commune to 7,490 in 1872, but climbing thereafter to 9,268 in 1876.

Admittedly, the number of British travellers passing through Paris for other French or European destinations grew more rapidly: in 1846, 15,000 were recorded as staying in the capital's hotels, *pensions*, and furnished accommodation, and by 1852, despite the recent revolution of 1848 and Napoleon's coup of December 1851, this number had risen to 26,500 and accounted for some 40 per cent of transient foreigners. However, it seems likely that such visitors, if they bought a newspaper at all, would have chosen the *Messenger*, on account of its well-established name and wider European circulation. There is no reason to believe that the advent of mass tourism in the wake of the first Paris Exposition in 1855, or the democratizing effect of Thomas Cook's early group tours to Paris in the 1860s, substantially altered the position, since such visitors typically stayed for briefer

---

[58] G. W. M. Reynolds, *Pickwick Abroad: or, The Tour in France* (London: Sherwood, Gilbert, & Piper, 1839), 339–40, 423.
[59] Planta, *New Picture of Paris*, 389.
[60] Reynolds, *Pickwick Abroad*, 228, 379.   [61] Jones, *Paris*, 324–5.

periods than the wealthy, and escorted sightseeing meant that travellers had less need to glean their information from the local press.

Overall, then, there seems little reason to doubt Paul Gerbod's conclusion that during the period 1830–75 the socioeconomic composition of the resident British enclave changed little, comprising mainly professionals, merchant, bankers, industrialists, artists, journalists, the retired, and those of private means.[62] A consistent market of this type was unlikely to reward novelty, and the close-knit nature of this community was likely to foster the practice of passing one copy of a newspaper through the hands of several readers before it was discarded. In the face of these facts, it is difficult to account for the seemingly boundless optimism to be found among the waves of young British journalists and their backers in Paris in the 1830s, other than by assuming that they hoped that the good fortune and glamour of their French counterparts would somehow rub off on them.

Something of the cut-throat competition that these British newspaper men experienced can be glimpsed in the opening salvo of *The Paris Satirist: a weekly journal*, which in the event only survived for two numbers, appearing on 14 and 21 April 1836. James Acland (1799–1876) announced himself as editor of the first number, while the second number claimed to be compiled by Acland and son. Acland senior was by turn clerk, actor, electoral statistician, and a journalist whose radical weekly paper, denouncing the impositions and misdemeanours of Bristol's public servants in the late 1820s, had already landed him in an English prison more than once. In an article entitled, 'State of the British Press in Paris', which formed the main business of the *Satirist*'s first edition, Acland asserted, 'We have already three daily newspapers, three weekly Journals of Literature; and some monthly publications, speaking in our mother tongue, in the capital of France.'

Acland's main target revealed itself in a continuation of this article in the second number, this time under the new title, 'The Anglican and Parisian Press'. Galignani's *Messenger*, he claimed, had exercised a fifteen-year monopoly, unchallenged until the advent in December 1829 of the *London Express and Advertiser*, started by William Dickenson, Colonel Henry, Major-General Armstrong, and Mr St Quentin. This ill-fated venture had lasted only seven months, closing down on 28 July 1830. Its failure was a by-product of *les Trois Glorieuses* which had temporarily dispersed the frightened British colony that formed its major readership. Nevertheless, the threat of competition provided by this short-lived paper had prompted Galignani, as from 1 February 1830, to increase the size of the *Messenger* by some 200 lines—an act of liberality swiftly withdrawn once its rival had sunk. Indeed, on 12 September 1832 the firm halved its offering, only restoring the paper to its previous size two and a half years later because two further Anglophone newspapers appeared on the scene to challenge its pre-eminence. The real reason for Galignani's parsimonious practices, claimed Acland, was a lengthy tussle with their printers, who were paid less and were harder-worked than their London equivalents: rather than employ a

---

[62] The statistics quoted here for the British presence in France are derived from P. Gerbod, 'Voyageurs et résidents britanniques en France en XIXe siècle: une approche statistique', *Acta Geographica* 76 (1988), 19–36.

regular printer, the firm operated a competitive bidding system among rival Paris printers. Meanwhile, Galignani had been profiteering by withholding stamp duty while awaiting the outcome of the political turbulence of the 1830 Revolution. The last in the list of dirty practices of which Galignani stood accused by Acland was the rejection of advertisements that might interfere with the paper's monopoly. As an Anglophone paper, the *Messenger* had followed British press practices in printing advertisements, whereas the French press had not introduced them until 1827, and was not to exploit them fully until Émile de Girardin founded his paper *La Presse* in 1836.

Galignani's letter rejecting an advertisement for the first number of the *Paris Satirist* had referred dismissively to this new paper as only one among a host of attempted contemporary press flotations. In this context, Thackeray's 1833 purchase of the *National Standard*, and the decision in 1836 of his stepfather, Major Carmichael Smyth, to underwrite the *Constitutional and Public Ledger*, appear slightly less naïve ventures than they have formerly done. From his dwelling in Paris's English quarter, Carmichael Smyth's investment would have seemed an appropriate response to an industry visibly flourishing around him, a method of topping up his half-pay pension, and a way of supporting his stepson's career. Nor do the papers' respective demises—the *National Standard* lasted from May 1833 to February 1834; and the *Constitutional* from April 1836 to July 1837—seem proof positive of financial and editorial incompetence when set in the context of Acland's further disclosures about the state of the press in Paris, the paramount city of the print dream.

Among the other new papers disparagingly referred to in the letter Acland received from Galignani had been an evening paper, the *Paris Herald*, floated on 20 December 1835, shortly followed, on 1 January 1836, by the *London and Paris Courier*. The *Paris Herald*, Acland inferred from the name of one of its directors, came out of the same stable as the defunct *London Express and Advertiser*. He praised its independent political stance, but feared for the success of this 'sort of Hermaphrodite Newspaper', which, by appearing as a bilingual publication, automatically halved its news content. (The short-lived runs and re-launches of a number of bilingual papers in this decade would seem to prove Acland's point.) 'Philo Veritas', as Acland signed himself, reserved his real invective for the slowly unfolding scandal of the *London and Paris Courier*, which from its earliest days had professed itself in competition with the *Messenger*.

Acland offered chapter and verse of the financial swindle practised on investors by John Wilks (1793–1846), who had been acting in conjunction with a Joint Stock Company. Their shenanigans included dismissing men from their posts without good reason; reselling these posts; and the failure to produce proper accounts for their investors in order that they might mulct them of further contributions. Acland rightly denounced Wilks as a well-known fraudster, who had previously used the device of acting in concert with a joint stock company peopled with the names of the great and the good to defraud investors. The *Oxford Dictionary of National Biography* offers a catalogue of such crimes perpetrated by Wilks in Great Britain between 1822 and 1828, the year in which his family offered him an annuity on condition he live abroad. Moving to Paris, he then acquired the post of Paris Correspondent for the *Standard*, and proceeded to float false rumours on the Bourse, resulting in his being banned from its precincts and threatened with deportation. His success as a confidence trickster seems to have rested on the sheer scale of his effrontery: in England he had at one time been the proud possessor of three large houses, driving between them in a coach and four, accompanied by outriders. His Parisian residence was identified by Acland as a villa in the newly fashionable village of Auteuil on the western outskirts of the city. Wilks's master stroke on many occasions, however, had been to ally himself with religious and charitable interests: in England in 1826, for instance, needing to gain exemption from being prosecuted for his latest swindle, he had stood for parliament as Sudbury's candidate for religious liberty, only to renege on paying his expenses once elected. According to Acland, Wilks maintained this odour of sanctity in Paris by worshipping on the 'softest hassocks in Paris'—presumably at the chapel of the British Embassy—while cheating the *Courier's* overworked proofreader (perhaps Acland's fellow radical, Reynolds) of his rightful earnings.

Announcing the news that Wilks had bolted, leaving his employees high and dry, Acland then set out his own proposals for a successful relaunch. In brief, he advised that the current expenses of 1,000 francs per month should be cut back to 900; and that this could be met by a circulation of 500 in combination with daily advertisements to the tune of 200 francs, or a circulation figure of 700 topped up by advertising revenue of 182 francs. Moreover, Acland opined, the *Courier* would need to up its game: currently, whether because it was relying on the *Messenger* or drawing on the same sources, the *Courier's* morning edition often offered what had appeared the previous day in the *Messenger's* afternoon edition. The hapless investors would appear to have been unimpressed by Acland's rallying call urging them to recoup their losses and fight the monopoly of Galignani's *Messenger*. Nevertheless, in a new venture of his own, launched later in 1836, Acland was able to announce that the *Courier* had ceased to trade under Wilks's name on 8 September, but that a new society had been founded within the old one, intending to build upon the ruins of the former paper under the new editorship of one George Reynolds.

Still bent on challenging the *Messenger's* monopoly—more as a matter of principle, he admitted, than from any sense that the *Messenger* was in the habit of behaving irresponsibly—on 26 September 1836 Acland launched the *Paris Sun*, a daily paper of 'liberal and enlightened political principles', from offices at 7 Rue Vivienne, just along the way from Galignani's. The inducement he offered to readers included free copies until the end of the month and greater coverage of Continental news than that offered by other papers, because he believed this to be as of least as much interest to those settled in Paris as news from Great Britain. There would be less of a time-lag in obtaining such news, he averred, but gathering it would be more expensive. The first issue contained two pages of news from Spain, Switzerland, Portugal, Russia, Greece, and Norway. He set the political agenda of the first issue by taking a side-swipe at the *Morning Chronicle*, which not only shared the typical British prejudices against Louis-Philippe but had managed to traduce Daniel O'Connell by omitting thirteen lines from a recent speech printed in full in the *Messenger*. In other respects the paper's coverage was little different from its competitors, starting with a page and a half of advertisements, a Visitors' Guide to Parisian attractions, and finishing with a medley of British news, featuring juicy murder cases, politics, and items from the provincial press, followed by a report on 'The Funds'. The notable decline in the number of adverts in the issue for 19 January 1837 suggests why the paper folded after five months.

Undeterred, on Friday 5 March 1837 Acland launched the *Paris Sun-Beam*, a title intended to reflect a ray carried over from the 'partial eclipse' of the previous venture; the intervening delay between the two was attributed to unforeseen problems connected with the legal position of the *Sun*. Intriguingly, the fact that this paper would be employing entirely new type was emphasized as an attraction to subscribers, who would on this occasion enjoy a free first issue. The paper still appeared as from 7 Rue Vivienne, but this time Acland was in partnership with Richard Anthony Dugdale. Nevertheless, the new format of a thrice-weekly publication, with morning and evening editions on each of these days, on pages half the size of its predecessor, suggest a certain reining in of Acland's ambitions, as do its contents. All signs of a liberal, let alone a radical, political agenda had disappeared. Instead, after the obligatory advertisements, which targeted the Parisian British colony with offerings such as a hairdresser operating 'near Galignani's courtyard', or a firm of undertakers promising to transport corpses back to Great Britain together with 'a fit person to accompany the same', a section on Parisian culture was followed by the British Court Circular, which included an account of a rabbit hunt on the Frogmore estate where the gentlemen had retired to the Hope Inn and 'conviviality was kept up until a late hour'. The paper then attempted to capture all shades of British resident interest with literary extracts suitable for family entertainment and sections covering commerce, the racing results, and news pertaining to the clergy, the navy, the army, and the acting profession. Perhaps the appointment of Ambrose Cuddon as editor, a man with considerable experience in England as editor, publisher, and printer of Roman Catholic journals, and of running a circulating library, helped to counterbalance Acland's radical agenda.

Four months later, on 18 June, the *Sun-Beam*'s pages were being used to announce the forthcoming attractions of yet another new daily newspaper, entitled *Dugdale's Messenger*, to be published on 1 August, using 'fine paper, with entirely new type' and employing the same size of sheet as its rival, Galignani's *Messenger*. Despite the title, Acland's voice is still to be heard in the guise of a letter to the Editor: signed 'George Drancier', the letter claims to come from 'a newly arrived British traveller', welcoming the new paper's stand against press monopoly and lamenting the lack of interest displayed by the *Paris Observer* in French manners and society. This however, was Acland's last shot in Paris. In 1838 he returned to England to take up another career as an Anti-Corn Law lecturer.

Retrieving the evidence of the working lives led in Paris by English newspapermen suggests a degree of cross-Channel migration in the print trade, largely lost to history. The *Oxford Dictionary of National Biography*, for instance knows nothing of Cuddon after he disappeared from London, recording him as *fl.* 1822–1828, while the five or more years Acland spent working in Paris are passed over without further detail. It was probably debt rather than government repression of the radical press that led Captain J. B. Holland, the radical owner-editor of *The Monthly Magazine* (1833–6), to change places with Reynolds: 1838 found his erstwhile contributor Charles Dickens forwarding 'poor Holland at Paris' 12 guineas.[63] The jobs they took and the political stance of the organs in which they published suggest that the early careers of a Reynolds, an Acland, or a Holland were virtually interchangeable. What distinguished men like Acland and Reynolds from 'poor Holland' was their capacity to fend off destitution by constantly reinventing themselves. The accounts of careers such as theirs render Thackeray's fictional Colonel Altamont seem slightly less preposterous. The various guises of this forger, blackmailer, and bigamist included time as a newspaper editor as well as a spell 'in irons': when in funds he considers putting up the capital of £200 for a satirical paper sure to be worth £1,000. As Chapter 11 will reveal, Thackeray had kept a close professional eye on the complex twists and turns of Reynolds's career, but even Altamont, a man fashioned in Reynolds's mould, could provide no match (Thackeray contended) for the duplicitous rogues he encounters in Paris.[64]

Whatever its alleged shortcomings, Galignani's *London and Paris Observer: Journal of English and Foreign Literature, Science, and the Fine Arts* seems to have long outlived the *Sun-Beam*. Its reprintings of articles and reviews from *Fraser's* and the *New Monthly*, together with extensive borrowings from *Punch's* material, was bulked out by the pirated reissue of the latest English fiction. Thackeray's reference to the paper as a 'piratical print' in the concluding chapters of *Vanity Fair* would have been prompted by his realization that it was publishing his novel a chapter at a time, devoid of the original illustrations, and without any acknowledgement of the novel's British publishers.[65]

Over the years other newspapers made efforts to establish themselves by supplementing Galignani's coverage. In 1842, for example, 'La Librairie des Étrangères' launched *Paris et Londres: revue de la littérature des beaux-arts* from Rue Neuve Saint-Augustin. This fortnightly was very deliberately targeted at a readership with a European outlook, rather than catering for the home-based interests among the British residents: in particular it boasted the services of Jules Janin (1804–74), Paris's leading theatre critic.

The mushrooming of Anglophone newspapers that Paris witnessed in the second, third, and fourth decades of the nineteenth century noticeably slowed in the second half of the century.

----

[63] *Letters of Charles Dickens*, ed. Storey et al., i, 434.

[64] W. M. Thackeray, *The History of Pendennis: His Fortunes and Misfortunes, His Friends and His Greatest Enemy*, ed. J. Sutherland (1850; Oxford: Oxford University Press, 1994), 294–6; 547–52; and 773.

[65] *Vanity Fair*, ed. Sutherland, 788.

The almost immediate effects of the 1855 abolition of the stamp tax on newspapers in Great Britain, together with the more gradual impact of the copyright laws,[66] meant that the English newspaper business in Paris no longer seemed such a good investment by the later years with which this book is concerned. As the short-lived local papers, offering piece-rate, cheap labour to casual employees, disappeared, so the role of the 'Paris correspondent' became more professionalized; and it is to the changing nature of this role that the next chapter will turn.

---

[66] The Anglo-French Copyright Treaty of 1851 established reciprocal rights for authors in the respective national courts, but the copyright position in regard to news remained more problematic. Provided the original source was acknowledged, the Berne Convention of 1852 specifically excluded from copyright protection 'articles extracted from newspapers or periodicals'. From 1886 the Berne Convention permitted the reproduction of newspaper articles 'unless the authors or publishers have expressly forbidden it', and it was not until 1960 that the right to reprint entire articles verbatim was removed. These caveats about authorial permission might well have been thought to embrace serial fiction, but possibly the publicity gained for further publication in volume form outweighed the tiresome process of pursuing piracy through the courts—a supposition supported by the fact that it was not until 1896 that an amendment to the Berne Convention specifically excluded 'serial stories and tales' from the freedoms from copyright permitted to the press. The date of this exclusion can perhaps be explained by the fact that 1894 had seen the toppling of the expensive three-decker as the first post-serialization publication option for novels in Great Britain.

9

Who were 'the Paris correspondents'?

It is traditionally assumed that literary careers depend upon solitary, highly individualistic work. Journalism, however, for all its competitive impulse, involves a degree of interaction with fellow labourers. Whereas female correspondents typically lived within a family circle, the male Anglophone journalists of the 1830s and 1840s frequently arrived in Paris without family connections or a permanent salaried position, and so had an added incentive for clustering together. Often living in a single room in the bohemian student quarter on the left bank, these newsmen would cross the river daily to work and gossip in the cafés, and hope to gain admission to the *salons* run by the wives of more stably domiciled colleagues. Combing the same French newspapers for news, reviewing the same plays, and attending the same events, while striving to establish an individual voice that would lodge itself in the readers' and employer's consciousness, meant that these writers would have read each others' newsprint closely. Something of the largely good-humoured competitiveness that characterized the time spent in Paris as freelance journalists in 1830s by many of the founder members of *Punch* survived in the magazine's weekly dinners, and companionable French family holidays.

The journalists of the earlier decades indeed fulfil many of the criteria for collaborative creative groups instanced by the sociologist Michael P. Farrell: such occupational networks of generational peer groups, he claims, tend to be formed by ambitious professional novices, attracted to the same 'magnet space'—usually a city—where they are dislocated from familial and other local circles.[1] Considered individually, the careers of those who were entitled to the byline of 'Paris correspondent' are necessarily diverse; but despite the changing role and conditions of employment over the period 1830–75, this chapter will demonstrate that it is possible to identify various shared characteristics in these generations of Paris correspondents. The value of producing such a taxonomy lies in augmenting our knowledge of the history of journalism in the first half of the nineteenth century, revealing Paris as a significant catalyst in the process by which freelance reporters, often stumbling into journalism in a part-time capacity, came to see it as a full-time profession, and uncovering the creative friendships and tensions which would characterize the world of magazine and newspaper production in mid-nineteenth-century London.

---

[1] M. Farrell, *Collaborative Circles: Friendship Dynamics and Creative Work* (Chicago: University of Chicago Press, 2001). See also S. Whidden, 'On Collaboration', in S. Whidden (ed.), *Models of Collaboration in Nineteenth-Century French Literature: Several Authors, One Pen* (Farnham: Ashgate, 2009), 1–18.

9.1 DEFINING A 'PARIS CORRESPONDENT'

The unfolding drama of the French Revolution gave birth to the phenomenon of the modern foreign correspondent. James Perry (1756–1821), who provided on-the-spot accounts from 1791 to 1792 for the *Morning Chronicle,* of which he had recently become part-owner, is generally held to be the first of this new breed of journalist. In taking up residence abroad in the deliberate pursuit of breaking political news, Perry was innovative, but the role of foreign correspondent did not immediately displace the habit of more casual 'letters home' by travellers and stringers anxious to place their wares where they could. As this chapter will demonstrate, women's contributions to the evolution of foreign reporting has hitherto been considerably undervalued.[2]

If the ability to produce an eyewitness account, rather than the mode of publication, is taken as the crucial, defining feature of the foreign correspondent, a case could be made for Helen Maria Williams (1759–1827) as Perry's progenitor. Inspired by the fall of the Bastille the previous year, Williams went to Paris in 1790, and her *Letters Written in France in the summer of 1790 to a friend in England, containing various anecdotes relative to the French Revolution* (1790) was succeeded by a further seven volumes, known as the *Letters from France* (1790–96) in which she detailed the changing fortunes of her friends in the Girondin party and the growing violence of the reign of terror. After periods of imprisonment as an enemy alien, and of enforced exile, Williams welcomed the advent of Napoleon in *Sketches of the state of manners and opinions in the French Republic* (1801), but was forced to turn to the less contentious work of translation, when she became disillusioned with Napoleon and her *salon* fell under police scrutiny. When Napoleon abdicated in 1814, however, she resumed her foreign reporting, with the publication of her *Narrative* of his hundred days in power (1815), and her *Letters* (1819) on the French Protestant Church and on the Bourbon Restoration. Meanwhile her naturalization as a French citizen, in 1817, gave early evidence of the tendency (with which British newspaper editors would become familiar) of the foreign reporter 'going native'.

Prompted by Williams's example, Maria Wollstonecraft set out for Paris in December 1792 intending a six-week visit to report, in epistolary form, on the progress of the Revolution to the British public. The outbreak of war between Great Britain and France in February 1793 and the beginning of the Reign of Terror threatened the safety of expatriates and disrupted cross-Channel communication, and so Maria embarked upon *An Historical and Moral View of the Origin and Progress of the French Revolution* (1794), a narrative tracing events only as far as 1789.

The appeal of the epistolary and narrative modes to female reporters, whatever politics they espoused, lay in their proximity to the private correspondence and journals considered appropriate for their gender: in describing her Parisian routine

---

[2] e.g. M. Conboy, 'Women's Journalism from Magazines to Mainstream', in *Journalism: A Critical History* (London: Sage, 2004), 128–48.

in the late 1820s, Lady Blessington clearly regarded these various genres as almost interchangeable: '[I] write letters or journalise from one until four.'[3]

The development of a fully-fledged cadre of in situ salaried appointees of British newspapers took place slowly and unevenly. In the 1830s some British daily papers boasted a resident correspondent while others continued to translate or paraphrase articles from the foreign press.[4] In 1833, when Thackeray bought the *National Standard and Journal of Literature, Science, Music Theatricals and the Fine Arts,* he told his mother 'It looks well... to have a Parisian correspondent', but planning to return from Paris and base himself in London, he added, 'I think that in a month more I may get together stuff enough for the next ten months.'[5] For a paper more concerned with cultural matters than politics, a resident foreign correspondent was a luxury: even *The Times* did not establish a permanent Paris bureau until 1848.

There also seems to be less evidence in the earlier decades of the shifting between newspapers by salaried Paris correspondents that the *Dictionary of Nineteenth-Century Journalism* suggests was typical of the 'foreign correspondent'.[6] Given the popularity of Paris as a posting, shifts between papers tended to be occasioned more by the fortunes of the employer than by the volition of the correspondent. Archibald Forbes (1838–1900), for instance, transferred to the *Daily News* in time to report the siege only because, in an effort to save money, the *Morning Advertiser* had abruptly dispensed with his services as a war correspondent the year before, while the *Daily News* had recently received a fresh injection of money.

There seem to have been three major routes to becoming a resident salaried correspondent. In the earlier period, word-of-mouth recommendation by an old Paris hand was what counted: this is scarcely surprising at a time when many public appointments were equally dependent on patronage. The second method was to work as assistant or 'devil' for a resident correspondent—reporting on more far-flung events, sifting and translating the foreign press, acting as a substitute during the chief correspondent's vacations, and hoping eventually to step into his shoes. This became a more viable pathway to permanency towards the end of the period, when increasing numbers of British newspapers were prepared to invest in the role of the foreign correspondent. The third route was proven talent: a man who had been sent out as a reporter to cover a specific event, such as a turbulent change of regime, might be asked to stay on for a longer stint as a foreign correspondent if his work provided local colour that found favour with the London office.

In the 1830s and 1840s there is little evidence of the distinction between the reporter recording events and the foreign correspondent, left relatively free from editorial intervention, interpreting them. On the one hand, the resident correspondent was expected to turn his hand to reporting when a crisis arose and no journalist

---

    [3] Countess of Blessington, *The Idler in France* (2 vols, London: Henry Colburn, 1841), i, 128.

    [4] For a succinct account of this process, see R. Pearson, *W. M. Thackeray and the Mediated Text: Writing for Periodicals in the Mid-Nineteenth Century* (Aldershot: Ashgate, 2000), 52–3.

    [5] *The Letters and Private Papers of William Makepeace Thackeray*, ed. G. N. Ray (4 vols, Cambridge, Mass.: Harvard University Press, 1945–6), i, 262.

    [6] L. Brake and M. Demoo (eds), *Dictionary of Nineteenth-Century Journalism in Great Britain and Ireland* (London: British Library, 2009), 224–5.

sent from home could be expected to arrive for a day or so. On the other, some of the so-called 'interpretation' amounted to little more than shaping reports gleaned from the French press into a tale suiting the political opinions of the British newspaper concerned. Whatever their comparative autonomy, Paris correspondents continued to complain of insufferable interference from subeditors.[7] Moreover, the relatively free hand afforded to eyewitness reports during peacetime could be sharply reined in during controversial events or periods of political upheaval. George Sala, who had gone across in December 1851 as a freelance, recalled that the article he sent to *Household Words* was heavily doctored by Dickens and Wills before they were prepared to publish it, so great was their distrust and dislike of Louis-Napoleon. The report became an ungainly hybrid, in which grim information about injustice, shootings, military brutality, and press censorship in Paris was interspersed with light-hearted, comic character sketches.[8]

For much of the period covered by this book, freelance journalists, whose work (when it appeared in the British press) was often described as that of a 'Paris Correspondent', far outnumbered the salaried cohort. Thackeray offers a detailed portrait of such a life in *The Adventures of Philip* (1862): for the hero it consisted of placing articles wherever possible in the British press, substituting for fellow journalists temporarily absent from Paris, and working as a subeditor in a Paris-based Anglophone newspaper. John O'Shea's memoirs, deploring 'the curse of the English system' where 'labour and genius' were swallowed up 'in the omnivorous maw of anonymous journalism', assert that this way of scraping a living from a portfolio of casual contracts and freelance work persisted well into the late 1850s. French journalists, by contrast, were legally obliged to sign their articles, speaking to their government's fear of a press criticism untrammelled by the fear of reprisal.[9]

9.2 PARIS, CITY OF TRANSFORMATIONS

The fleeting nature of the temporary contracts, made either simultaneously or in quick succession, with one or more newspapers suited young men who were looking about them, ostensibly training for a profession in the law or medicine, but always happy to earn ready money and a reputation by writing. The volatile political and social atmosphere of the decade of the Great Reform Bill produced a generation of young English men who no longer saw their future necessarily laid out in the patterns of their forefathers. The success of the generation who had taken their chances in Paris in the 1830s encouraged a fresh generation of young men to rush across to Paris in 1848 and 1851, 'hoping to turn the exciting events of the day to account'.

---

[7] J. A. O'Shea, *Leaves from the Life of a Special Correspondent* (2 vols, London: Ward & Downey, 1885), i, 130.

[8] *The Life and Adventures of George Augustus Sala written by himself*, 2nd edn (2 vols, London: Cassell, 1895), i, 304–5; [Sala,] 'Liberty, Equality, Fraternity, and Musketry', *Household Words*, 27 Dec. 1851, 313–17.

[9] O'Shea, *Leaves*, i, 127–8.

One such, George Hodder, accompanied Douglas Jerrold, owner-editor of a news-paper, on his brief 1848 visit and stayed on as a freelance after his employer's return. He later recorded that, without a commission, he was 'twice reduced to nothing but a butterless roll and watered down *sal volatile* as a stimulant for dinner', and that it was only the generosity of Thomas Frazer, the Paris correspondent of the *Morning Chronicle,* in inviting him to dinner and showing his articles to his own editor that saved him from starvation.[10] The 23-year-old Sala, although not reduced to such penury, ruefully recalled that he had lost money by his enterprise in rushing across to Paris uncommissioned to report on Naploeon's seizure of power in 1851: the trip had cost him £20, but *Household Words* had paid him only the usual rate of £5 for his article.[11]

Hodder and Sala had already embarked on journalism, but Paris's heady mix of print and politics proved potent in shaping the futures of young men uncertain as to the next step in their career. In 1851 Walter Bagehot (1826–77), unsettled by the prospect of his imminent call to the Bar, decided on a vacation in Paris. His visit coincided with Louis-Napoleon's coup and, in a series of seven articles, he argued a line (unlikely to prove popular with Great Britain's liberal intellectuals) that the Emperor had been right to quash incipient anarchy on the streets of Paris. The experience was transformative: within the year he had abandoned the law and fallen back on the family occupation of banking as a means of supporting himself, while he pursued his enduring enthusiasm for political and economic commentary by founding and becoming co-editor of the *National Review*.

The story of Edward Blount (1809–1905) offers another version of the effect of Paris's addiction to print as a career catalyst. The second son of a staunch Catholic landowner and banker, in 1829 he acquired an appointment as an attaché in the British Embassy in Paris. His father's part in co-founding an Irish bank with Daniel O'Connell would have ensured that he was swiftly networked into Paris's strong contingent of Irish Catholic journalists. A brief spell in the consulate at Rome convinced him that diplomacy was not for him and he returned to Paris, on a family allowance, to make his fortune. Arriving back in Paris in 1831 when the French press was flushed with its triumph in effecting regime change, it was perhaps almost inevitable that, looking about him, the first of the two new specu-lative bubbles he explored was journalism. His spell writing for the *Railway Chronicle* would also lead within a few years to his becoming, with his French banking partner, Charles Lafitte, the major financier behind the development of the French railways.

The worlds of journalism and diplomacy frequently overlapped in Paris's cosmo-politan atmosphere, although when it was discovered that the British Embassy chaplain had been acting as the paid correspondent of the *New York Herald* during Victoria and Albert's 1855 state visit it caused a minor scandal, slightly mitigated by the chaplaincy being an unsalaried, honorary post.[12] When the resident English

---

[10] G. Hodder, *Memories of My Time* (London: Tinsley Brothers, 1870), 123–5.
[11] Sala, *Life and Adventures*, i, 304.
[12] C. Gladwin, *The Paris Embassy* (London: Collins, 1976), 102.

population was relatively small, sociable relations between junior Embassy staff and the British press fraternity were almost inevitable, despite the discrepancy at the heart of their respective enterprises. The Embassy's need to privilege political calculation over personal bravery during the siege, for instance, led to denunciations of its pusillanimous evacuation of staff by journalists who stayed in Paris throughout. The cover of a Paris correspondent's search for the latest information, on the other hand, seems to have provided a handy cover for spying.

Few journalists proved themselves such a potential liability to their country as Lewis Goldsmith (1763–1846), a chancer who seems to have been able to make substantial contributions to international misunderstanding through his sensational reports, many of them invented, in the course of a lurid career in which he embraced both radicalism and ultra-conservatism, acted as a spy for the French, and finally managed to inveigle his way into an appointment with the British Embassy. Although he had trained as a lawyer, the start of the century found him in Paris editing a pro-Napoleonic Anglophone newspaper subsidized by the French government. Even at this stage the French authorities recognized that the inflammatory anti-monarchist material he included did not prevent his making overtures to the British Ambassador when he faced deportation, so they promptly employed him to spy on the correspondence of the exiled Bourbons. Characteristically, Lewis changed sides and from 1811 to 1816 ran a paper in London promoting the Bourbons. Back in Paris again in 1825, he now moved in ultra-royalist circles, ingratiated himself with the British Ambassador, probably leaked material to Tom Bowen, editor of the *Times*, and launched another short-lived paper, the *Monitor* (1831). Perhaps the British Ambassador thought to rein in these activities when he appointed Lewis as Embassy solicitor and put him in charge of handling expatriates' post.

Although his was a very different character, the complicated career profile of Laurence Oliphant, encompassing spells as diplomat, politician, and journalist, and acting as *Times* correspondent during the Franco-Prussian war, gave rise to rumours that he was a government spy. This may have had much to do with the paper for which he was working: so closely at times were the interests of the British government and *The Times* identified that Oliphant's successor, Henri Blowitz (1825–1903), promoted to Paris correspondent in 1875, enjoyed a reputation for informing British foreign policy that won him the honorific of *ambassadeur du Times*.

Perhaps the largest cohort of men to emerge from Paris as journalists, however, were those who had gone there to pursue studies designed to prepare them for a different career. William Makepeace Thackeray, Joseph Archer Crowe (1825–96), Augustus Mayhew (1826–75), George Augustus Sala (1828–95), and George du Maurier (1834–96) each sought an artistic apprenticeship with French painters, before lack of talent, poor eyesight, financial need, or finding themselves outclassed by the popular success of a Gavarni or a Daumier variously persuaded them to adapt their art to the demands of the letterpress. John Leech (1817–64) retrained as an artist in Paris after a false start in medicine at London hospital. Returning to London with a portfolio of 'characteristic sketches of Parisian types', such as the *grisette*, the *café garçon*, and the soldier,[13] he made his début in *Punch* with variants on these, depicting foreign loafers in Leicester Square.[14]

Leech's route from medicine to journalism was again not uncommon. According to Thomas Wakley of *The Lancet*, Paris offered Europe's finest medical education, and by 1835 it is reckoned that about 300 British medical students a year could be found in Paris. The city was liberally provided with seven general hospitals and five specialist institutions; attendance at many of the clinics was free for foreigners already enrolled at a home institution, and even private courses of instruction were comparatively cheap.[15]

Martina Lauster has argued that the way in which physiology and zoology, then the leading sciences, could be harnessed to the diagnoses of social conditions helps to explain the phenomenon of the number of medical students turned journalist.[16] A good case can be made for the relationship between the prestigious Parisian disciplines of medicine and natural history and the French journalistic practice of producing taxonomies of Parisian society,[17] but to convert this affinity into a motive for career change may be to over-intellectualize a trend in which young men who had opted without a great deal of thought for one of the few established professions gravitated to a new and more immediately rewarding opening.

The prestige the press seemed to offer in 1830s Paris, and the wealth it seemed to promise under the Second Empire, would have proved alluring: that literary darling of the popular French press Eugène Sue (1804–57) had himself started his career as a naval surgeon before joining the drift to Paris in 1829 to try his hand at painting and writing. Moreover, the insistence of the British medical licensing authorities on a modern foreign language or Greek, in addition to Latin, as an entry requirement designed to restrict the profession to gentlemen, would have lent some of these students the language skills that would have made them useful subeditors in the Anglophone newspapers where many of them started by working freelance in between their studies.[18]

The cast list of medical men turned journalists is in any case impressive. John Chapman (1821–94), the Don Juan of the *Westminster Review*, trained there in 1842, and eventually returned in 1873 to run an office above Galignani's at 22 Rue de Rivoli, where he and his final partner concentrated on medical journalism. It is

[13] It seems unlikely that Henry James knew of Leech's time in Paris when he used his work to form a contrast with what he felt to be the characteristically Anglo-French genius of his friend du Maurier. James wrote of Leech's 'thoroughly English love of sports' and habit of depicting the foreigner as 'an inferior animal', thus ignoring the fact that Leech's comic style had been formed by his Parisian encounters with the work of Daumier and Gavarni, whose lighter touch he came to prefer to the savage caricatures of the Regency. H. James, 'George du Maurier', in *Partial Portraits* (London, Macmillan, 1883), 327–72. First published as 'Du Maurier and Society' in the *Century Magazine*, May 1883.

[14] H. Vizetelly, *Glances Back through Seventy Years: Autobiographical and Other Recollections* (2 vols, London: Kegan Paul, Trench, Trübner, 1893), i, 136.

[15] D. E. Manuel, *Walking the Paris Hospitals: Diary of an Edinburgh Medical Student, 1834–1835* (London: Wellcome Trust, 2004), 15.

[16] M. Lauster, *Sketches of the Nineteenth Century: European Journalism and its Physiologies, 1830–50* (Basingstoke: Palgrave Macmillan, 2007), 115–16.

[17] M. Gill, *Eccentricity and the Cultural Imagination in Nineteenth-Century Paris* (Oxford: Oxford University Press, 2009), 72–5.

[18] M. J. Peterson, *The Medical Profession in Mid-Victorian London* (Berkeley: University of California Press, 1978), 57–8.

possible that George Eliot's portrait, in *Middlemarch*, of Tertius Lydgate, his infatuation with the French actress, Laure, and his interest in the teaching of the Saint-Simonians owed as much to Chapman's reminiscences of his student days in Paris as her more frequently remarked scientific research in back copies of *The Lancet*.

John Delane (1817–79) is reported to have 'attended the hospitals for some terms', and spoke of 'his experience in Paris under the great French physiologist, Magendie', although it is difficult to work out how he managed to fit this and some legal training in between his Oxford undergraduate career and becoming editor of *The Times* at the age of 23.[19] James Macaulay (1817–1902), on completing his medical training in Edinburgh, went to Paris in 1837–8 for a further stint: he was to become editor of *Leisure Hour* and *Sunday at Home*. John O'Leary (1830–1907) had two spells, in 1854 and 1858, as a medical student in Paris before becoming editor of the Fenian *Irish People*; and John O'Shea (1839–1905) was meant to be studying 'at the Pity hospital' (Hôpital de la Pitié-Salpêtrière) when he started his journalistic career.[20]

Albert Smith (1816–60), a surgeon's son, having qualifying at the Middlesex, attended the Hôpital Hôtel-Dieu in 1838. After a brief spell at his father's Chertsey practice, he set up in 1841 on his own account in Percy Street off the Tottenham Court Road, where, according to both Sala and Henry Vizetelly, he continued to combine dentistry with journalism well into the late 1840s.[21] Given his talent for showmanship, which later manifested itself in ballooning stunts and dramatic re-enactments of Alpine ascents, it is possible that he practised expensive cosmetic dentistry for the elderly, which George Reynolds claimed was another Parisian specialty.[22] It is in any case difficult to see Smith and his flamboyant pursuit of his own financial interests as belonging to the trend that Lauster discerns of former medical students seeking to deploy their diagnostic skills in socially committed activities.

The very medical specialisms for which Paris was famed may have served to determine other defections. Anatomy is a case in point. Whereas in Great Britain, until the 1832 Anatomy Act, only the bodies of executed murderers could be used for teaching purposes, in Paris unclaimed cadavers from the hospitals and the morgue were available along with corpses from the guillotine.[23] When he first visited Paris in 1824, Thomas Carlyle had been sufficiently impressed by Baron Cuvier's introductory lecture on comparative anatomy, combined with the free provision of bodies for dissection, that he investigated the possibility of his brother John pursuing his medical training there.[24] However, James Macaulay reported that he and a fellow Edinburgh student had been repulsed by watching the demonstrations of the famous physiologist François Magendie, Chair of Medicine at the

[19] H. Wace, 'John Thadeus Delane', *Cornhill*, Jan. 1909, 95.
[20] J. O'Shea, *Leaves*, 5.
[21] Sala, *Life and Adventures*, i, 196; Vizetelly, *Glances*, i, 314–15.
[22] G. W. M. Reynolds, *Pickwick Abroad: or, The Tour in France* (London: Sherwood, Gilbert, & Piper, 1839), 262.
[23] Vizetelly, *Glances*, ii, 380.
[24] F. Kaplan, *Thomas Carlyle: A Biography* (Cambridge: Cambridge University Press, 1983), 106.

Collège de France. Magendie conducted his experiments on live animals in public. The two Scotsmen left the room 'disgusted less by the cruelty of the professor than by the heartlessness of the spectators', provoking Macaulay to abandon medicine for journalism. Not all Frenchmen were hardened to the spectacle: the poet Alfred de Musset also abandoned medicine because of his distaste for such public dissections. Nevertheless, Parisian medical students continued to retain a reputation for insensitivity: the secret of John O'Shea's defection from medicine may lie in a macabre chapter of his fiction, *Mated from the Morgue: A Tale of the Second Empire* (1889), in which three medical students, fresh from a day in the dissecting room, boast of the body parts they have stolen from a female prostitute who spurned their advances when alive.[25]

9.3 THE IRISH CONTINGENT

When John O'Shea arrived in Paris to study medicine, he found lodgings on the left bank near the Jardin des Plantes, where he joined an Irish colony variously composed of artists, medical students, and writers of one kind and another. O'Shea, like Samuel Beckett and James Joyce after him, was following a long tradition in leaving the 'Fauborg Saint-Patrice called Ireland' for Paris. If anything the Irish were better established there than the English. Irish political exiles had formed one British category exempted from imprisonment when hostilities were declared in the wake of the French Revolution, and in 1803 it had proved possible to recruit an entire legion of Irish soldiers from their numbers, with a view to the invasion of England.[26] In securing a British readership's sympathy for the exilic Irish hero of his 1844 novel, *Tom Burke of 'Ours'*, Charles Lever still found it necessary to insist that the young man made it a condition of his service in Napoleon I's army that, unlike many of his peers, he would never serve against the English, despite their ill-treatment of his own countrymen.[27] By the time Thomas Colley Grattan (1791–1864) arrived in Paris in the early 1820s, he clearly felt confident enough of the contacts and readership necessary to launch his paper, the *Paris Monthly Review of British and Continental Literature* (1822–3).

 The false dawn of pan-European revolution in 1848 brought a fresh wave of Irish to Paris: the Young Irelander movement sent a delegation asking the new republican government for support in their struggle for Irish independence, and the occasional journalist such as Martin MacDermott (1823–1905) stayed on, in his case as a correspondent for *The Nation*. For Irish Catholic families, Paris held the further attraction of providing relatively cheap convent education for their daughters.

 [25] J. O'Shea, *Mated from the Morgue: A Tale of the Second Empire* (London: Spencer Blackett, 1889), 101–3.
 [26] P. Gerbod, 'Voyageurs et résidents britanniques en France en XIXᵉ siècle', *Acta Geographica* 76 (1988), 21.
 [27] *Tom Burke of 'Ours'* (2 vols), in *The Novels of Charles Lever*, ed. by his daughter (36 vols, London: Downey, 1897–99), i, 218–19.

Thackeray's numerous satirical portraits of the Irish have attracted considerable opprobrium as part and parcel of his racial prejudice. His picture in *Pendennis* (1850), for instance, of the Irish as 'the mercenaries of journalism', prepared to write for the Whig or Tory cause as pay dictated, but always as thick as thieves with their fellow countrymen, belongs to the English mythology of 'micks on the make'. The Irish dialect Thackeray delighted in reproducing for comic effect, in private correspondence and published work alike, equally belongs to a long stereotypical tradition. Thackeray's marriage into an Irish family domiciled in Paris may well have intensified his resentment of the scrounging Irish journalist fraternity, each, however impoverished, with his own 'hanger-on' always ready to 'transact the thousand little affairs of an embarrassed Irish gentleman. I never knew an embarrassed Irish gentleman yet', remarks *Pendennis*'s narrator, 'but he had an aide de camp of his own nation, likewise in circumstances of pecuniary discomfort.'

Nevertheless, the observation 'They all stick together those Irish' does seem to have had some basis in the clannishness of the Cork men Thackeray knew in London and Paris.[28] Captain Shandon, *Pendennis*'s gifted Irish journalist, whose twin besetting sins of drink and gambling drag his devoted family into debtor's prison with him, seems to have been an amalgam of two old Paris hands of Thackeray's acquaintance: John ('Jack') Sheehan (1809–82), who came back from Madrid to replace Thackeray on the *Constitutional* in 1837,[29] and an earlier Irish mentor, William Maginn (1794–1842).[30] Maginn, a Protestant schoolmaster from Cork, had befriended fellow Corkman Francis Mahony (1804–66), a disgraced Jesuit who turned his hand to journalism under the pseudonym of 'Father Prout'. The events that caused Mahony's expulsion from the Jesuit order had begun in a night's drinking at the home of the aforesaid Sheehan, who had then been one of the pupils Mahoney was leading on a trip to Maynooth. In the 1850s Mahony settled in Paris, where he had undertaken his Jesuit novitiate some quarter of a century before. He was often to be found hanging about Galignani's reading rooms, and for the last eight years of his life became a Paris correspondent for *The Globe*. William Allingham recalled that he and Thackeray, calling on Mahony in his *entresol* in the Rue des Moulins, had found him 'loosely arrayed, reclining in front of a book and a bottle of Burgundy' and with an indigent 'young Paddy from Cork' to whom he had given temporary lodgings, asleep in a recess.[31] Margaret Oliphant, who met him shortly before he died, recalled his almost 'ascetic' pose as he performed in the *salon* of an 'old lady about whom he circled', and who, she delicately hinted, might have been supporting him.[32]

The plight of Captain Shandon's devoted wife and children reflected Thackeray's private nightmare as he contemplated the lives of the Irish contingent who had been Paris correspondents with him. The careers of Eyre Evans Crowe (1799–1868) and

[28] *The History of Pendennis: His Fortunes and Misfortunes, His Friends and His Greatest Enemy*, ed. J. Sutherland (Oxford: Oxford University Press, 1994), 414, 374.

[29] *Letters of Thackeray*, ed. Ray, i, 321–2n.

[30] The evidence for this amalgam is reviewed in *Pendennis*, ed. Sutherland, 1035–6.

[31] *William Allingham: A Diary*, ed. H. Allingham and D. Radford (London: Macmillan, 1907), 77–8.

[32] *The Autobiography of Margaret Oliphant*, ed. E. Jay (Oxford: Oxford University Press, 1990), 115.

John Frazer Corkran (d. 1884) so nearly mirrored what his own might have been had he remained in Paris to support a growing family by the precarious trade of the correspondent. Eyre Evans Crowe (1799–1868), of Irish extraction and educated in Ireland, left London with his family in the late 1820s to enjoy the cheaper living offered in Boulogne. The need to support his family deflected him from his first ambition of being a historian, and in 1832 he took the role of Paris correspondent to the *Morning Chronicle*. For the next thirteen years he raised his six children in Paris, teaching them himself because he disliked the French educational system, but ensuring that they enjoyed a full range of Parisian extras, from fencing to classes in watercolours and oils. Returning to London in 1844 as the *Chronicle's* leader writer, he launched his second son, Joseph Archer Crowe (1825–96), into journalism, and took him with him in 1846 when he was lured away from the *Chronicle* to the newly launched *Daily News*. When Eyre lost his post at the *Daily News* in 1851, his youngest child was still only 10 years old, and he had little alternative other than to return to Paris. As so often, Thackeray came to the aid of a colleague in distress: he took the oldest son, Eyre Crowe (1824–1910), as his secretary and as drawing-master to his children. A year after the death of Crowe's first wife in 1853, Thackeray also took in their daughter, Amy (b. 1831), into his home as a companion for his two girls, where she stayed until her marriage, nine years later, to a young cousin of Thackeray's. Joseph, he aided by recommending him for the job he himself had been offered of providing letters and sketches of the Crimean War for the *Illustrated London News*.[33]

Given this saga, it is scarcely surprising that when Frazer Corkran turned up destitute in London shortly thereafter, with a wife and five children to support, Thackeray's goodwill was running a little low. Courtesy of his wife's *salon* and his work as correspondent for the *Morning Chronicle* and the *Morning Herald*, Corkran had long been at the heart of press life in Paris. All this foundered fast when the *Morning Herald* dispensed with his services sometime in 1856–7. This was probably not Corkran's fault but brought about by the Baldwin family's need to sell the paper, consequent on a bankruptcy as the result of unwise speculations in the railway boom. Nevertheless, Corkran's difficulty in finding alternative employment in London suggests how dangerous it could be for a 'Paris correspondent' to have no other strings to his bow. By 1861 Thackeray, who had given them money and 'knocked at countless doors to get them work', was tiring of their importunity and complaints.[34]

Despite her own half-Irish extraction, Thackeray's elder daughter, Anne Thackeray Ritchie, seems to have shared something of her father's views about the Irish cohort in Paris. When the young heroine of her novel *Mrs Dymond* is called to Paris, where her widowed mother has remarried, she finds herself in a house very much like the lodgings John O'Shea described in his memoirs. The fictional proprietress's regular visitors, the O'Sheas and the Muldoons, have recently recommended

[33] J. Crowe, *Reminiscences of Thirty-Five Years of My Life* (London: John Murray, 1895), 112.

[34] MS letter of 21 Mar. 1861 to Mrs Crowe, quoted in G. N. Ray, *The Age of Wisdom (1847–63)* (London: Oxford University Press, 1958), 351. The first Mrs Eyre Evans Crowe, whom Thackeray had known in his Paris years, died in 1853. In 1854 Thackeray had given a home to their daughter, Amy.

Michael Marney, an Irish nationalist journalist, and his family to her. The abusive, mendacious Marney, who drinks away whatever money he can lay his hands on and then deserts his long-suffering wife, eventually achieves success as a war correspondent, 'though it was impossible for...experienced newspaper readers to say how much he wrote from his own observation, or what hearsay legends he translated into his own language'.[35]

9.4 THE SECOND GENERATION

Looking at the careers of the children of Paris correspondents, it would appear that ink had entered their bloodstream there. Some continued well into later life to process their early memories of the famous friends their fathers had made in Paris. Henriette Corkran placed a series of articles, variously titled, 'A Child's Recollections ...' and 'A Little Girl's Recollections...' of such famous figures of her Paris childhood as Thackeray and Elizabeth Barrett Browning, in *Temple Bar* before repackaging them in book form as *Celebrities and I* (1902).[36]

Annie Thackeray also adopted Henriette's successful formula, turning the long periods when she and her sister had stayed with their grandparents in the English colony into gossip-filled articles in *Macmillan's Magazine*, and then into a couple of books.[37] The Crowe boys followed suit: Joseph Archer Crowe's *Reminiscences of Thirty-Five Years of My Life* (1895) was swiftly followed by Eyre Crowe's *Thackeray's Haunts and Homes* (1897).

The children of Paris correspondents frequently enjoyed the advantage of a sufficiently good command of French to be able to take over the mantle of Paris correspondent. When Joseph Archer Crowe joined the *Daily News* as a fledgling journalist it was agreed that, despite the new paper's very limited budget, it would be pointless to economize by hiring a Frenchman as a stopgap because a Frenchman's concept of the press and its requirements would be rooted in French conventions. Joseph was therefore sent to Paris for a three-month stint because it was known that he had local knowledge, including the invaluable help of resident journalists. This in turn advanced his career on his return to the London office: 'from casual reporting I turned more and more to the sifting and arranging of news of foreign parts, and my old experience of my father's early occupation, as well as my knowledge of languages, served me in good stead at the office of the *Daily News*.'[38] When Joseph eventually took over the Paris posting, he benefited not only from his father's former connections in the *salons* and the French political world and the press but also from the accumulated knowledge of his predecessor, the notorious Dionysius Lardner (1793–1859), himself an old crony of Crowe senior.

---

[35] *Mrs Dymond, The Works of Miss Thackeray* (10 vols, London: Smith, Elder, 1890), x, 36–7, and 501.
[36] H. Corkran, *Temple Bar*, Oct. 1887, 238–41; Dec. 1888, 539–43; Apr.1889, 580–83; and Dec. 1894, 551–8; *Celebrities and I* (London: Hutchinson, 1902), 114, 192.
[37] See esp. *Records of Tennyson, Ruskin and Browning* (1892); and *Chapters from Some Memoirs* (1894), first published in *Macmillan's Magazine* between July 1890 and Oct. 1894.
[38] Crowe, *Reminiscences*, 55.

A school in Boulogne, run by a Monsieur Bonnefoy, seems to have operated as a veritable forcing-house for second generation Paris correspondents. In 1838 Douglas Jerrold sent his 12-year-old son Blanchard and a younger brother there, where they discovered the future artist and engraver Gustave Doré as a schoolfellow. By 1846 Blanchard was working alongside Joseph Crowe at the *Daily News*, and for his father's own organ, *Douglas Jerrold's Weekly Newspaper*. By his mid-20s, however, he had shifted his centre of operations to Paris, and was to produce books and articles on French culture, a four-volume apologia for Napoleon III (1874–82), letterpress for his former schoolfellow, Doré, and, under the pen name 'Fin-Bec', a short-lived gastronomic periodical, *The Knife and Fork* (1871–2), and a series of books on good eating.

A further scion of a printing family, Frank Vizetelly (1830–1883?), was an alumnus in the 1840s, overlapping with the Jerrold brothers and Doré, and went on to work as Paris correspondent for his brother Henry's weekly, *The Illustrated Times*, until in 1857 he was appointed editor of *Le monde illustré*. At this same school he might have encountered a younger compatriot, William Schwenck Gilbert (1836–1911, sent there by his father, William (1804–90), surgeon, journalist, and novelist, and a regular visitor to the summer colony of journalists' families.[39] Though better known to posterity as a dramatist, W. S. Gilbert's first venture into print was a translation of a French operatic song, and in 1870 the *Observer* appointed him its French correspondent to cover the Franco-Prussian war. Learning from the precariousness of their fathers' careers, these sons each had at least one other string to their bow. W. S. Gilbert was called to the Bar, Joseph Crowe and Blanchard Jerrold had first trained as artists, while Frank Vizetelly was to achieve fame as much as a war artist as war correspondent.

9.5 A QUESTION OF CLASS

As the case of these second generation journalists would suggest, good contacts and good French, rather than a university education, proved key to achieving a Paris posting. Historians of journalism have traditionally stressed a university education as the factor that both distinguished newspaper journalists of the 1840s from their predecessors and continued to exclude women because they had not enjoyed access to this homosocial network. This superior education, in turn, has been credited with setting the interpretive task of foreign correspondents apart from the work of mere reporters,[40] and in that they were presumed to have the local expertise, foreign correspondents may have been subject to less interference than reporters in England; but even those who enjoyed a permanent salary usually needed to top up their income with 'piece-work' sold to other weeklies or dailies.

---

[39] A. W. à Beckett, *The à Becketts of 'Punch': Memories of Father and Sons* (Westminster: Archibald Constable, 1903), 100.

[40] See e.g. A. Aspinall, 'The Social Status of Journalists at the beginning of the Nineteenth Century', *Review of English Studies* 21(1945), 216–32; L. Brown, *Victorian News and Newspapers* (Oxford: Clarendon Press, 1985), 105; B. Onslow, *Women of the Press in Nineteenth-Century Britain* (Basingstoke: Macmillan, 2000), 22.

Yet in the 1830s and 1840s it was more likely to have been a shared public school background than attendance at university that established fellow-feeling among newspaper journalists. Thackeray's Cambridge contemporaries, for instance, were more likely to contribute essays to the periodical press than submit themselves to popular taste in the form of a subeditor slashing their latest contribution, and it was a rather shamefaced Thackeray who in 1836 told his undergraduate friend Edward Fitzgerald, 'I am sorry to say that I like the newspaper work very much, it is a continual excitement, and I fancy I do it very well.'⁴¹ His subsequent desire to represent those early years, jostling with bohemian contemporaries for suitable material or a subeditorial desk, as something of a déclassé youthful episode is captured in the phrase, 'Qu'on est bien à vingt ans', the title of the chapter which describes this Parisian 'down-and-out' phase in the career of the hero of his late novel *The Adventures of Philip*.

Given that some embraced journalism as a brief respite from the more conventional expectations of their class, while for others it was to become a permanent way of life, the social background of the Paris correspondents spanned a wide range. At the one end was a man such as Richard Whiteing (1840–1928), brought up until the age of 8 by his widowed father in one room of a lodging house off the Strand. Sent to a boarding school in Bromley-by-Bow, he was fortunate enough to encounter an inspirational teacher, a refugee from the 1851 coup, who taught him both French and Greek. Displeased by this non-vocational curriculum, his father removed him and eventually apprenticed him to an engraver. During the next seven years Whiteing grew to dislike the trade, but working alongside a German engraver, a refugee from the revolution of 1848, allowed him to acquire the rudiments of a further language. Meanwhile, he used his evenings for self-improvement: courtesy of various initiatives for working men, he attended art classes, and he read voraciously. In 1866 he took his first trip to Paris, as secretary for an Anglo-French working-class exhibition, and back in London he embarked on journalism. The following year he was commissioned by the *Star* to cover the 1867 Paris Exposition, and he soon became Paris correspondent for both the London and the New York branches of *The World*. Paris was to become his base for some twenty years, and according to his own account he only left when it became clear to him that, like so many old Paris hands, he was in danger of going native.⁴²

At the other end of the spectrum was the occasional journalist drawn from the ranks of the minor aristocracy: these attachments usually smacked of opportunism and rarely lasted long. George Smythe (1818–57), eldest son of Viscount Strangford, for instance, joined the newly formed *Morning Post* and reported the 1848 revolution for that paper. His presence in Paris had much to do with London society's disapproval of his latest liaison, and his journalism proved a short-lived retreat from British politics and the periodical press. An upbringing that was not typical of his class probably made him more open to taking on such a role, however briefly. The expatriate existence of a diplomat's son had given him a cosmopolitan outlook, some facility with languages, and an aversion to settling down, while his

---

⁴¹ *Letters of Thackeray*, ed. Ray, i, 322.
⁴² R. Whiteing, *My Harvest* (London: Hodder & Stoughton, 1915).

mother's Roman Catholicism was a further factor in estranging him from the English Establishment.

This combination of a private income and a temperament at odds with the ruling élite of one's own country marked several American journalists in Paris, including the Cambridge-educated Charles Astor Bristed (1820–74), described by the *ODNB* as 'a long-term resident in four different countries' who 'perhaps found it difficult to be completely at home anywhere'. Supported by the Astor money, he moved to Paris in 1851 and, writing under the pseudonym 'Carl Benson', he endeavoured to counter the Puritanism of the Boston Brahmins by defending the work of Baudelaire and George Sand while regaling readers with accounts of Parisian social life.

Even those with rather more tenuous claims to an entrée into aristocratic circles found that they could parlay the gossip of high society into a little ready money. Eustace Murray (1824–81), illegitimate son to a Duke, had transgressed the line between diplomacy and journalism in previous diplomatic postings before carving out a journalistic career in Paris. From 1868 he acted as correspondent for the *Daily News* and the *New York Herald*, while also contributing to the *Pall Mall Gazette*, *Truth*, and the *Illustrated London News*, shamelessly using his social connections to spice his political reporting with more personal information.

Paris also attracted those whose unconventional lifestyles reflected more radical politics. Despite his aristocratic name, Percy Bolingbroke St John (1821–89), who was working as Paris correspondent for *Lloyd's Weekly News* and the *North British Daily Mail* in 1850, was the eldest son of a radical journalist who had started life as plain James John, but had travelled extensively with his eleven children to make foreign news his specialist domain. Percy's first marriage in 1841, to his mother's sister—a prohibited degree of relationship—and a second, apparently bigamous marriage eleven years later may have made Paris a congenial retreat.

George Reynolds married his pregnant bride at the British Embassy in July 1835, as soon as he was 21 and free from the last constraints of his guardian: she gave birth to their first-born the following January. He found the political atmosphere of Paris in the wake of *les Trois Glorieuses* so pleasing to his radical principles that he later claimed to have taken French citizenship and even joined the National Guard while working there between 1830 and 1836. If the names of contemporary European revolutionaries that he gave to his two youngest sons, Ledru Rollin and Kossuth Mazzini, were an insufficient guide to his political leanings, various passages in his Parisian pastiche of Dickens's essentially middle-class comedy *The Pickwick Papers* would have left his readers in little doubt. These include an English translation of the Marseillaise and a satirical speech about aristocrats going scot-free for the type of immorality liable to land the lower classes in prison; by the book's conclusion, Sam Weller feels that the democratic customs of Paris legitimize his wining and dining alongside his master and enjoying an equal voice at a political meeting.[43]

Douglas Jerrold, whose satire at the expense of Establishment figures made Thackeray wonder whether he ought to 'pull any longer in the same boat with such

---

[43] Reynolds, *Pickwick Abroad*, 124–5, 337, 426, 539.

a savage little Robespierre', would, like Reynolds, seem to have acquired these views before going to Paris.[44] Like those of his close friend Charles Dickens, Jerrold's views seem to have been fuelled by a humanitarian-inspired desire for reform rather than sympathy with French egalitarianism. Albert Smith, who continued to flaunt his sympathies in the class war by sporting a French *ouvrier's* smock and exhibiting a model guillotine in his London house, long after his return from France, seems to have done so as much from a desire to parade his view of journalism as a workaday trade, as from principled political convictions.[45] Thackeray's edgy relations with Jerrold and his open dislike of Smith (explored further in Chapter 11) have much to do with his own sense of having betrayed his birthright by entering a world where he was required to keep such socially promiscuous company.

Just how difficult it was to break through the class barrier by means of journalism in Thackeray and Smith's generation is illustrated by a further contemporary who attempted to make his way into Great Britain's governing circles via a spell as a Paris correspondent. Henry Reeve (1813–95), son of an impoverished widow and educated at a day school, made his way by 1832 to Paris, where he worked hard, as a journalist and translator, at cultivating the acquaintance of celebrities such as Hugo, de Vigny, Balzac, and Lizt. When he returned to London in 1838, his knowledge of French politics acquired him the role of leader writer and foreign correspondent for *The Times*, where he was known as 'Il Pomposo', and his report on the French legal system won him the post of clerk of appeals to the Privy Council. Despite managing to make the transition from the newspaper world in 1855 to become editor of the respected periodical the *Edinburgh Review*, he would have been mortified to discover how little his careful husbandry of the contacts he had made abroad counted for when the great and the good came to assess him. Reading Reeve's obituaries, Charles Greville, grandson of the Duke of Portland, confided to a mutual friend that ' "R. would tomber de son haut" if he knew what was being written about him by those whose company he so valued.'

Paris offered the semblance to the British of a more meritocratic society than their own, and in the comparative absence of gentlemens' clubs and their attendant social protocol, the intense sociability of the relatively small British press corps temporarily brought about working camaraderie between men from markedly different social classes. However, few of these trans-class friendships seem to have survived the return to the more hierarchical world of London, and good-humoured boyish rivalry in Paris tended to dissipate when mature journalists ranked themselves and their achievements against one another.

9.6 THE FEMALE CORRESPONDENT

If a male journalist's entitlement to be called a gentleman could be called in question because of his too close proximity to manual labour on the one hand, and the machinery of his industry on the other, it seems at first sight obvious that these

---

[44] *Letters of Thackeray*, ed. Ray, ii, 681.   [45] Vizetelly, *Glances*, i, 315.

associations would entirely compromise a Victorian woman's entitlement to be thought of as a lady. The arguments are rehearsed by Henry James in his picture of Miss Henrietta Stackpole, the American who plies her trade as a journalist in both England and Paris in *The Portrait of a Lady* (1881). In 1875–6, in his early 30s, James himself had worked in Paris as an occasional correspondent for the *New York Tribune*. For the British, Miss Stackpole's nationality serves to underline yet further the unclassifiability of a 'reporter in petticoats'. As Henrietta herself says of Lady Pensil, her ironically named future sister-in-law, 'She think she knows everything; but she doesn't understand a lady-correspondent! It would be so much easier for her if I were only a little better or a little worse.'[46] It is a matter of surprise that Henrietta is unmarked by her trade: in person she is 'scrupulously, fastidiously neat. From top to toe she carried not an inkstain.'[47]

In the course of the novel James indicates the elements of the role of foreign correspondent that seem to call into question its appropriateness for women: the lonely travel from one boarding house or hotel to another, or, alternatively, the gossip provoked by accepting a male escort; the need for the 'vulgar...genius for guessing what the public want'—which, in the case of her American audience, commits her to radical views, and the willingness to be an intrusive interrogator of host, friend, and acquaintance.[48] Although Henrietta is presented as a thoroughly modern American type, in practice her enthusiasm for turning the domestic lives of those she meets into print, and her preference for 'human interest' stories over either politics or the description of scenery, align her very closely with the female reporting from Paris that had been taking place for many years. Frances Trollope's *Paris and the Parisians in 1835* is couched, like Henrietta's reports, in letter form, and insists upon an authority derived from 'finding myself on terms of most pleasant and familiar intercourse with a variety of delightful people, many of them highly distinguished'.[49] Elizabeth Gaskell's articles 'Company Manners' and 'French Life' both capitalized on intimate personal experience, and despite being published anonymously many of those she described would have been easily recognizable to those who knew her.[50]

If women often published their articles in the same periodicals and newspapers as their male counterparts, and like them sometimes collected these in volume form, the typical content of their journalism differed. Female correspondents concentrated on the domestic side of urban life, interiors rather than street scenes, sketches of typical female activities rather than of male leisure pursuits. When women employed the guidebook format this of course involved the description of the major sights, but there

---

[46] H. James, *The Portrait of a Lady*, ed. R. D. Bamberg (New York: W. W. Norton, 1975), 79, 470, 573. By 1908, when James revised this 1881 version for the New York edition, he perhaps felt that 'Lady-correspondents' were no longer so rare as to make his point clear, and revised the phrase to 'a woman of my modern type'.

[47] Ibid. 80, 503. Again revised for the New York edition to read: 'she was as crisp and new and comprehensive as a first issue before the folding. From top to toe she probably had no misprint.'

[48] Ibid. 83–9.

[49] F. Trollope, *Paris and the Parisians in 1835* (2 vols, Paris: Baudry's European Library, 1836), 22.

[50] *The Works of Elizabeth Gaskell*, ed. J. Shattock et al. (10 vols, London: Pickering & Chatto, 2005–6), 295–310, 359–409.

is little of that casual observation of the life of the boulevards, as described by 'that great wanderer about town', Thackeray, or by Dickens from his café vantage point.[51]

When Wilkie Collins found himself confined, by illness, to a one-storey 'Pavilion' abutting the Champs-Élysées, he consciously adopted a feminized role in the article he was writing, describing himself as excluded from the fashionable world outside his window that 'spins and prances by me every afternoon, in all its glory... healthy princes and counts and blood-horses'. In keeping with his domestic imprisonment he focused his sympathetic interest on the exhausting life of the 'portress', or concierge, of his dwelling.[52] This sense of gendered expectation in the contributions from 'a foreign correspondent' is reinforced by the comparison between Dickens's letters and his articles. His private letters, to men and women alike, give detailed descriptions of his domestic arrangements in Paris, of the furniture, of the thorough cleaning he insisted on before he being prepared to take up residence, of the interiors of the mansions where he has dined, but these interior details are not a feature of his press reporting of Paris, which typically deals with the traveller's public encounters or comparisons between French and English systems and mores.

Another distinction that has often been drawn between female and male foreign correspondents is their position as employees, women tending to be paid at piece rate while their male counterparts drew a salary. By the end of the century, however, Emily Crawford, a famous Paris correspondent, claimed, 'The rewards the press affords to clever women who accept its unyielding hard conditions are, in regard to salary, handsome.'[53] The distinction between payment by the piece and a salary also ignores the kind of arrangement arrived at by female travel writers, many of whom made sure of an advance from their publishers before setting out. Frances Trollope, who increasingly turned to fiction, on the grounds that her travelling costs invariably outstripped the money she made on her travel books, obtained £500 from Bentleys before embarking for Paris.[54]

Eliza Lynn Linton has commonly enjoyed the reputation of being England's first salaried female journalist, but during her stint (1851–4) as a correspondent in Paris she no longer drew a fixed salary from the *Morning Chronicle*, working for it freelance while also contributing to the *Leader* and earning £5 an article for contributions to *Household Words*. Her stint as the *Leader's* foreign correspondent began on 6 December 1851 with an article, continued the following week, on 'The Bonaparte Revolution in Paris'. On 20 December her contribution, signed 'L', was

[51] 'A St Philip's Day at Paris', *Britannia* (15 and 22 May 1841), repr. in *The Oxford Thackeray*, ed. G. Saintsbury (17 vols, London: Oxford University Press, 1910), iii, 486; 'Railway Dreaming', *Household Words*, 10 May 1856, 385–8, repr. in *Dickens' Journalism*, ed. M. Slater (4 vols, London: J. M. Dent, 1994–2000), iii, 370–6.

[52] *The Pilgrim Edition of the Letters of Charles Dickens*, ed. G. Storey et al. (12 vols, Oxford: Clarendon Press, 1965–2002), viii, 48n.; [W. Collins,] 'Laid Up in Two Lodgings', *Household Words*, 7 June 1856, 481–7.

[53] E. Crawford, 'Journalism as a Profession for Women', *Contemporary Review* 64 (Sept. 1893), 370.

[54] H. Heineman, *Mrs Trollope: The Triumphant Feminine in the Nineteenth Century* (Athens: Ohio University Press, 1979), 133.

entitled 'The "Masked" Empire in France'. By 27 December this had transmuted into 'Letter from Paris' from a 'Special Correspondent', and by 1 January she was simply described as 'our correspondent'. These initial articles convey a sense of the real danger that English reporters stranded in Paris considered themselves exposed to during this fresh outbreak of violence.

Throughout the following couple of years, Linton's letters offer a running account of the swiftly changing political events in Paris, coloured, as befitted the *Leader*'s radical sympathies, by a deep suspicion of the way in which the harmless working classes were being manipulated by those in authority. The weekly reports adopt a Carlylean method, offering what at first appear to be eyewitness accounts from a spectator capable of being present almost simultaneously in the Chamber of Deputies, at the barricades, or overhearing conversations between various members of government. The earlier articles in particular weave back and forth rather confusingly between direct accounts, letters apparently received from other Parisians, and 'true stories' of police brutality or, alternatively of police resigning rather than fight their fellow workers. Just as Carlyle had created his dramatic retelling of the French Revolution from a variety of other sources, so Linton seems to have relied on the good offices of John Frazer Corkran of the *Morning Herald* to feed her the gossip of his male colleagues and the press cuttings at his disposal.[55] Only once during the exigencies of the events of December 1851 did Linton come close to disclosing her gender when she asked, 'How can (I do not say a susceptible and impressionable being) but any man of common human feeling spin cold well-balanced phrases?'[56]

Meanwhile Linton's articles for the *Morning Chronicle* (1851–4) and *Household Words* overtly addressed subjects, such as 'French Domesticity', conventionally associated with the female correspondent.[57] Nevertheless the French characters in her homely anecdotes stand proxy for national traits, and the warning to English readers against trusting 'in the perpetual sunshine of French love' awakened Dickens's editorial anxieties; he postponed the publication of 'French Love' until Anglo-French relations were no longer hanging in the balance.[58]

The ability to hide behind the anonymity of the byline 'Paris correspondent' may have enabled lesser-known women to undertake the political role Linton filled for the *Leader*. What distinguished Linton from her peers was her decision to make an independent life for herself in Paris. Other British women of her day who became Paris correspondents tended to have come there in a 'dependent' capacity. Louise Costello (1799–1870), Marguerite Power (1815?–1867), Frances Hoey (1830–1908), Kathleen O'Meara (1839–88), and Henriette (n.d.) and Alice Corkran (c.1853–1916)— all of whom incidentally belonged to the Irish diaspora—each fit this category.

Louise Costello moved to Paris with her widowed mother some time after 1815. Developing sufficient skills as a miniaturist and copyist to support her brother Dudley's training at Sandhurst, she also became a published poet and a translator of

---

[55] N. F. Anderson, *Woman against Woman in Victorian England: A Life of Eliza Lynn Linton* (Bloomington: Indiana University Press, 1987), 67; Brown, *Victorian Newspapers*, 77.

[56] *Leader*, 27 Dec. 1851, 1222.   [57] *Household Words*, 24 June 1854, 434–8.

[58] Ibid. 9 June 1855, 442–6; Anderson, *Woman against Woman*, 68.

French poetry. When Dudley (1803–65) returned to Paris in the late 1820s she found him work as a fellow illustrator for the naturalist Baron Cuvier, and over the years moved back and forth between London and Paris with him as he struggled to make his living as a journalist, working briefly in the 1830s for the *Constitutional*, part-owned by Thackeray's stepfather, and in 1846 for the newly-launched *Daily News*. Although she sometimes contributed to the same papers as her brother, her subject matter kept firmly within acceptable female bounds, encompassing travel literature, historical biographies of female subjects, and domestic sketches such as 'My Little French Friend'.[59]

Marguerite Power accompanied her aunt, the notorious Lady Blessington, to Paris in 1849. When her aunt died shortly thereafter, she supported herself by journalism, also taking over her aunt's editorship of the annual *The Keepsake*. In 1853, Thackeray recommended both her and Francis Mahony for the post of Paris correspondent for the *Illustrated London News*, urging that for Power 'the salary would be a perfect god-send of good fortune'. Acquainted with Louis-Napoleon from the days of his London exile, when he would frequent her aunt's soirées, she identified the name of his fiancée a week before the official announcement, though the London press disregarded her information as 'a piece of baseless feminine gossip'.[60]

Frances Hoey was married to a fellow Irish journalist, associated with the Young Ireland Movement. She achieved her scoop as the first English journalist to report on the Commune of 1871, writing it up for the *Spectator* under the pseudonym 'Red Paris'. O'Meara, also known under the pseudonym 'Grace Ramsey', had come from Ireland as a small child with her parents: her mother's Second Empire pension, acquired as a relative of Napoleon's physician, helped to maintain them. For many years O'Meara was Paris correspondent of *The Tablet*.

Henriette Corkran was old enough to recall the company at her mother's *salon* before her father, Frazer, lost his post at the *Morning Herald* some time in 1856–7, when she and her younger sister, Alice, accompanied their parents to Bloomsbury. In her memoirs she recalled that by the time she was 18 her father's financial anxieties were 'a thing of the past'; the family had returned to Paris, and she progressed well enough at her artistic training to earn money as a copyist in the Louvre, and as a society portrait painter, before turning sketch-writer.[61] Alice would appear to have had a similar education, claiming 'sketching from nature' as a favourite hobby, she went on to edit the *Girl's Realm* and the *Bairns' Annual* as well as putting her Parisian upbringing to good use in her short stories.

Family connections and personal recommendations were doubly important to women journalists, as Elizabeth Gaskell explained to George Smith, presumably as he was laying plans for the launch of the *Pall Mall Gazette*; 'I fancy I know your "man", i.e. Miss Courtenay', apparently a well-qualified London-based journalist, 'the daughter of a man of very good family', who would like 'to be put in the way of earning a little quietly and genteelly', and then added,

---

[59] [L. Costello,] 'My Little French Friend', *Household Words*, 8 May 1852, 169–71. Cf. [D. Costello,] 'Blank Babies in Paris', *Household Words*, 17 Dec. 1853, 379–82.

[60] C. Mackay, *Forty Years' Recollections of Life, Literature, and Public Affairs, from 1830 to 1870* (2 vols, London: Chapman & Hall, 1877), ii, 296–7.

[61] Corkran, *Celebrities and I*, 114, 192.

I know her pendant in Paris.—a Mme la Csse de Peyronnet—(ask Lord Houghton about her) if you want such a person \in Paris[.]/She is pretty into the bargain. She is West Indian—brought up & married in Paris to the secretary of Prince Polignac,— who has come to grief because of his politics—she has [?lost] her West Indian property—is witty in either English, French or *Latin*—poor, highly connected—came over to London with her still prettier daughters in the last Exhibition, & was quite fêted by the Houghtons, Palmerstons, Henry Reeve, Nassau Seniors, &c &c—...One of her daughters was engaged to M Prévost Paradol, & she was very intimate with the Guizots—& at the other end of respectability with Alfred de Musset &c &c.—\ She wrote two or three little comedies for the varieties.[62]

De Peyronnet had in fact been a contributor to the *Athenæum* and the *Edinburgh Review* since the early 1850s, and if, as seems likely, Gaskell's letter was written in the wake of London's International Exhibition of 1862, her recommendation was successful, because de Peyronnet wrote for the *Pall Mall Gazette* from its inception in 1865, while simultaneously contributing to the French *Journal de débats*. Hiding behind the mask of genderless anonymity was to serve her particularly well when she started to work for *The Times* as their 'French Correspondent' during the Franco-Prussian war. From 11 July 1870 to 7 February 1871 she submitted columns describing conditions as the siege exerted its grip on Paris, and did not refrain from criticizing Napoleon III's government and expressing admiration for Bismarck—a political stance which would have been highly unpopular with many of her fellow Parisians. The £5 per column this correspondence earned was channelled to her via the bank account of her British son-in-law: married as she was to a well-known scion of the French aristocracy and opponent of the Second Empire, being revealed as in the pay of the British would have exposed the family to yet greater danger.

There were other ways for women to resort to 'undercover' work as a Paris correspondent. Richard Whiteing reported that in the late 1860s the Paris correspondent of the *Star* and his wife worked as a team composing the daily pieces:

> The wife wrote the daily letter from dictation, as to the politics; and, as to the social life, collected the daily gossip of the Imperial *fêtes* from friends who had the entry at the Tuileries. She was a sure guide in regard to the toilettes of the Empress, and the most successful creations of Worth.... She took incredible pains with it, rising sometimes with the sun to catch a reigning beauty in bed, for the details of last night's ball.[63]

The most famous salaried female Paris correspondent of the nineteenth century found her way into journalism in a way that smacked of an earlier period, and then secured her position by working as part of a 'family firm'. Emily Crawford (1831?– 1915) accompanied her widowed mother to Paris in 1863; so interesting were her letters home that a friend suggested she should consider submitting them for publication, which she duly did, both to an American newspaper and to London's *Morning Star*. When, a year later, she married the considerably older George Morland Crawford (1812–85), she was already making £400 per annum. Gradually

[62] *The Letters of Mrs Gaskell*, ed. J. V. Chapple and A. Pollard (Manchester: Manchester University Press, 1966), 440–1. The editors note that the letter has been misdated January 1857.
[63] Whiteing, *My Harvest*, 83.

she and her husband, a late starter in journalism who owed his post of assistant Paris correspondent for the *Daily News* to his friend Thackeray's recommendation, embarked on a job share. His position as the elected press representative in the gallery of the National Assembly, her skills as an interviewer, together with their friendship with many of Europe's leading politicians made them a winning combination. After her husband died, Emily continued as the official correspondent for the *Daily News*, adding the New York *Tribune*, the *Chicago Daily News*, the *Weekly Dispatch*, *Truth*, and the *Calcutta Englishman* to her repertoire, as well as contributing articles to periodicals, including both serious political commentary and literature within her range, and tempering her tone to the paper in question.[64]

These examples suggest that the position of Paris correspondent in the mid-nineteenth century continued for some time to offer a small pocket of journalism where women were not necessarily squeezed out by a growing band of university-educated males. Not only was it possible to combine this role with other money-making genres such as translation, fiction, and travel writing, but the cultural material they collected as journalists nourished their other writing, and the connections they forged with publishers and newspaper editors helped them to place it. For those who wanted to take their journalism into the traditionally male realm of political commentary, a capacity for networking, either through the *salons* or courtesy of a male relation or contact, and an ability to glean information from the foreign press, were essential: Emily Crawford was said to read more than twenty papers a day. The alternative was to offer accounts to women readers that at least appeared to stick safely to proper female concerns. Isabella Beeton's decision in 1860 to report on the Paris fashion shows for the *Englishwoman's Domestic Magazine*, providing illustrations, paper patterns, and prose descriptions, could be seen as extending the traditional territory of the female Paris correspondent into a more public sphere.

Nevertheless, despite Emily Crawford's own highly successful career, and her mention of a handful of other contemporary female journalists, in an article published at the end of the century she still claimed, 'Journalism in Paris is well-nigh closed against women.'[65]

This chapter has indicated the social, cultural, and political heterogeneity of the British press corps in Paris during the period covered by this book. Women journalists have proved not to be as exceptional as previously imagined, although most still had a preference 'to be put in the way of earning a little quietly and genteelly'. It may have been Eliza Lynn Linton's bolder manner of asserting herself as an independent journalist, and living independently of family connections, as much as her ingratiating manner which made her so disliked by her countrywomen in Paris.[66]

---

[64] Ibid. 139.   [65] Crawford, 'Journalism as a Profession for Women', 372.
[66] Anderson, *Woman against Woman*, 67–8; Corkran, *Celebrities and I*, 171–2.

For a number of reasons in the 1830s and 1840s journalism still sat on a relatively low rung of the literary ladder. It was felt to lack creativity and, being largely anonymous, could not make a name for the writer in the way that a book, and particularly a successful novel, was felt to do. By the end of the period, the post of 'the Paris correspondent' for a major newspaper carried greater prestige, and attracted a permanent bureau rather than a café table as a workplace. The next chapter will trace the processes by which this came about, and the changing practices of the foreign correspondent's working life.

10

The working life of the Paris correspondent

This chapter will suggest what it took for a correspondent to succeed in Paris's competitive press environment and in an occupation which was beginning to demand more specialized skills. By concentrating on a specific foreign capital over a limited period of rapid change, this chapter aims at a more nuanced account of the post of foreign correspondent than the comparatively uniform tale emerging from later nineteenth-century memoirs, which address a period when the role had been increasingly absorbed into the editorial structures of a number of British newspapers.

10.1 THE REWARDS OF THE POST

Success as a journalist is often thought to depend upon one or more lucky breaks, upon being in the right place at the right time. The frequency with which young British journalists launched their careers there, suggests that Paris, with its café culture, its supremacy in the arts, and its air of cosmopolitanism, was felt to be this 'right place', offering a round of entertainment, good dining, and social observation that could be enjoyed first-hand and then written up for readers at home. These cultural assets combined with the city's relative proximity to London to make this posting a plum choice. When Palmerston remarked to the incoming Foreign Secretary, Lord Malmesbury, 'You will be struck with a very curious circumstance—namely that no climate agrees with an English diplomatist excepting that of Paris, Florence, or Naples', his observation is likely to have been equally applicable to foreign correspondents.[1]

Young men at the start of their career doubtless found it agreeable to work in a city where, unlike London, the journalist could hold his head high. Furthermore, even the lowest-paid Anglophone journalist, provided he was receiving his pay from Great Britain, felt better off in Paris. Surveying the prospects of writers in mid-century England, France, and Germany, George Henry Lewes claimed that English writers were on the whole better rewarded than their foreign counterparts. Setting aside 'such exceptional cases as Dickens, Eugène Sue, and Thiers', he put the average writer's income in England at £300 per year, and suggested that 'the same men would scarcely be able to keep body and soul together in France or Germany'. The best-known French writers, he averred, were at best paid half the price of their British peers for contributions to the serious quarterlies, while French newspaper

---

[1] Quoted in C. Gladwin, *Paris Embassy* (London: Collins, 1976), 94.

journalists 'are paid well when they are paid five francs [20p]a column; fifteen shillings [75p] a column in England would be considered low terms. Jules Janin, 'the "J. J." of the *Journal des débats*, the first newspaper in France—receives a yearly salary of only 6000 francs [£240] for his weekly twelve columns of criticism.' This he contrasted with the lot of the journalist in England, who would have to 'be very unlucky or very "impracticable," if he do not earn an income varying from a thousand down to two hundred a-year'.[2,3] So the young English journalist, or the family man, finding it difficult to keep his head above water by working for the newspapers in London could at least feel himself better off by crossing the Channel and working as a foreign correspondent. The narrator and fictional hero of Thackeray's *Adventures of Philip* both concur in finding Lewes's sense of comparative rates of pay to have been just as true of the 1830s.

> How do Parisians live at all? is a question which has often set me wondering . . . Paterfamilias, with six hundred a year in London, knows what a straitened life his is, with rent high, and beef at a shilling a pound. Well, in Paris, rent is higher, and meat is dearer. . . . "Sir," Philip used to say . . . "when my income was raised to five thousand francs a year, I give you my word I was considered to be rich by my French acquaintance. . . . I should have been poor in the Rue de la Paix: but I was wealthy in the Luxembourg quarter."[4]

Nevertheless, few journalists of the 1830s and 1840s, even if they were long-established Paris correspondents who had raised their families there, seem to have refused the offer (if it came) of a permanent post as leader writer or subeditor in the London office. This would change as journalism became both more specialized and more professionalized towards the last thirty years of the century.

10.2 THE CHANGING ROLE

Perhaps the clearest trend over the course of the years from 1830 to 1875 is the increasing professionalization of the role of Paris correspondent. As the last chapter revealed, the earlier generation of young men had sometimes fallen into the role almost by chance, counting on their native wit and a reasonable command of the French language to carry them through. A few, such as Thackeray or Wilkie Collins, had polished their French during their respective versions of the Grand Tour, and some in the course of their studies in Paris. Thackeray, who specialized in producing comic Franglais in his fiction, could be harsh on fellow journalists without his own facility in French. Even allowing for the notion that his review was ostensibly penned by 'Fitzboodle at the Travellers' Club', his remarks about

---

[2] [G. H. Lewes,] 'The Condition of Authors in England, Germany, and France', *Fraser's Magazine*, Mar. 1847, 285–95.

[3] Translations of these amounts into their current value will swiftly become outdated: the reader is therefore referred to the following websites: http://www.measuringworth.com; http://projects.exeter.ac.uk/RDavies/arian/current/howmuch.html

[4] *Adventures of Philip, The Oxford Thackeray*, ed. G. Saintsbury (17 vols, London: Oxford University Press, 1910), xvi, 267–8.

James Grant's *Paris and its People* are unpleasantly condescending about 'dear Jim's' ineptitude. Thackeray singles out the spelling mistakes, and the plagiarism from Galignani's *Paris Guide,* to which 'not speaking a word of French' Grant was presumably driven.[5] But then Grant (1802-79), rumoured to have been a baker originally, belonged, like Dickens, to that humbler but ambitious cadre of journalist, the parliamentary reporter, whose efforts to rise in the world often included learning both a foreign language and shorthand.

For gentlemen amateurs, such as Thackeray would like to have been, the trick seems to have been to speak and write French effortlessly but without the suspicious fluency that marked those whose families' impoverished circumstances had resulted in their being brought up abroad. As for shorthand, Thackeray was at pains to emphasize in recounting Philip Firmin's career that he only took it up when, thinking himself 'not clever enough to be a writer of any mark', he elected to become a reporter and subeditor. Nevertheless, Philip's ability to support his family through journalism, together with the satire at the expense of Philip's outrageously snobbish father, who is displeased by his son's descent from putative barrister to a manually skilled 'newspaper reporter', suggests that Thackeray recognized that attitudes had changed since his youth.[6]

The generation of Paris correspondents who followed Thackeray's included many who had been raised or schooled in France; and those who wanted to break into journalism as a profession in the second half of the century, such as Thomas Hardy or Henry Lucy (1843–1924), saw both good French and shorthand as essential to the enterprise. By the end of the century, however, Emily Crawford regarded shorthand as a passé accomplishment: the day of dull verbatim reports was gone, 'and the typewriter is invaluable to those who have few opportunities to correct their proofs'. The advice she gave mothers anxious to launch their daughters on a career in journalism was 'More type-writers and fewer pianos!'.[7]

The gradual democratization of the press that took place between 1830 and 1875, when an increasingly diverse readership wanted different interests met, also had its effect on the range of subject matter that Paris correspondents were required to cover. The doings of polite society in Paris were often considered suitable fare in earlier decades: in 1838 Thackeray wrote of a 'swarry' he had attended as guest of France's Minister of Commerce, 'I could just as well have fancied these places before going but it is as well to have seen—a hall, a crowd of lackies, and antechamber; a great groom of the chambers who shouts out your name, about a hundred gentlemen in black coats, and a dozen ladies—voilà tout, but it will spin into 6 pages or so', and he added, with his mind already on reissuing his articles as a smartly bound collection, that it 'looks well in a book'.[8]

---

[5] [W. M. Thackeray,] 'Grant in Paris. By G. F.S.B.', *Fraser's Magazine,* Dec. 1843, 702–12; repr. in *The Oxford Thackeray,* vi, 366–85.

[6] *Adventures of Philip,* 462, 472.

[7] E. Crawford, 'Journalism as a Profession for Women', *Contemporary Review* 64 (Sept. 1893), 368.

[8] *The Letters and Private Papers of William Makepeace Thackeray,* ed. G. N. Ray (4 vols, Cambridge, Mass.: Harvard University Press, 1945–6).

Official gatherings continued to be reported, but the increasing vogue in British newspapers for campaigning journalism began to be reflected in reports from abroad. Henry Mayhew's reports on the life of the London poor (1851–62) had given middle-class English readers a taste for the frisson of reading about an underworld of poverty and crime. Sala recollected 'blacking up' with an English stockbroker of his acquaintance in early 1852, and heading for Île de la Cité to investigate the criminal haunts described in Eugène Sue's *Mystères de Paris*, though he was duly disappointed to discover only humdrum filth and squalor.[9] Henry Vizetelly's investigative journalism of the late 1860s, however, probably owed more to the French naturalism which would flower in Zola's Rougon-Macquart series, and eventually be translated and published by Vizetelly himself.

10.3 VERSATILITY, THE KEY TO SUCCESS

The versatility desirable in most reporters was a key requirement for the successful foreign correspondent, especially when a newspaper could not afford more than one salaried correspondent to cover a broad spectrum of political and cultural events and issues. When Arthur à Beckett found himself working as a 'roving commissioner' during the siege of Paris, expected simultaneously to provide 'light copy to the *Globe*' and 'heavy work to the *Standard*', he comforted himself: 'It was not altogether a novel experience to have to deal with the same subject from two points of view—comic and sedate. I had done the same sort of thing before as editor of a serious daily and humorous weekly.'[10]

The capacity to range widely, however, had to be balanced against the need to develop a distinctive voice that would be missed by readers at home if the paper dispensed with the journalist's services. This was a particular challenge because throughout most of the middle third of the century the foreign correspondent's contributions continued to appear anonymously. Judy MacKenzie has identified the creation of a public persona as part of the product sold by the successful journalists of the British Empire; and Richard Pearson has similarly traced the way in which the young Thackeray fashioned a series of personas for himself as a self-marketing device, designed to project a recognizable identity to readers, in whichever paper he appeared.[11]

When an old Paris hand like O'Shea looked back on successful contemporaries, what he recalled was the distinctive fields they had carved out for themselves:

[9] *The Life and Adventures of George Augustus Sala written by himself*, 2nd edn (2 vols, London: Cassell, 1895), i, 312.

[10] A. W. à Beckett, *The à Becketts of 'Punch': Memories of Father and Sons* (Westminster: Archibald Constable, 1903), 266.

[11] J. McKenzie, 'Paper Heroes: Special Correspondents and their Narratives of Empire', in B. Garlick and M. Harris (eds), *Victorian Journalism: Exotic and Domestic* (St Lucia: Queensland University Press, 1998), 124–40; R. Pearson, 'Echoes and Narcissisms: Repetitions and Structures of Self across the Periodical Lines. Signature and Persona in the *Paris Literary Gazette* and *Fraser's Magazine*', in *W. M. Thackeray and the Mediated Text: Writing for Periodicals in the Mid-Nineteenth Century* (Aldershot: Ashgate, 2000), 20–47.

authoritative coverage of a particular aspect of Parisian life was apparently what readers appreciated. Felix Whitehurst of the *Daily Telegraph*, for instance, had the trick of making the average British reader feel that 'he was almost the equal of dukes—that is, of foreign dukes' in his knowledge of Parisian society; Hely Bowes of the *Standard* was regarded as the most trustworthy guide to the world of French politics; while Browne of the *Morning Post* had the knack of writing informatively about Paris's contemporary music and art without offending readers.[12]

The restless shape-shifting of Thackeray's early journalism, indicated by the adoption of pseudonyms from 'Michael Angelo Titmarsh', his artistic avatar, to the feeble punning surname of his theatrical alias 'Théophile Wagstaffe', were also indicative of experiments in trying to mark out an area where he was most at home.

One of the most remarkable features of the careers featured in this chapter is the way in which so many of these journalists saw themselves as literary generalists, trying their hand variously in the course of their careers at fiction, play writing, travelogues, biography, and other genres. This ability to move between genres is a characteristic of much mid-nineteenth-century authorship; nevertheless, the requirement to range widely as the sole Paris correspondent of a newspaper must have played its part in shaping the diversity of so many of these journalists' subsequent offerings.

Foreign postings were naturally located in cities of political or mercantile significance to the British, and the political life of Great Britain's nearest neighbour was a matter of great interest, especially during the occasional invasion scare, but it was the arts rather than politics that created the city's special attraction. 'Art is almost the only real priesthood left in France, and by that or by nothing Frenchmen hope to be saved. In its various forms it is regarded as a working substitute for religion,' declaimed one Paris correspondent.[13] Although Whiteing's verdict was expressed somewhat hyperbolically, he backed up his claim by pointing to the state subsidies invested in the Conservatoire and Opéra, the Théâtre Français, and the Odéon, and the pride that families and communities displayed in offspring who succeeded as artists, musicians, or dramatists. Reynolds's *Pickwick Abroad*, briefly recalling its function as a guidebook, despatched the leading characters for an evening at the opera, as an excuse for a lengthy explanation of the funding system:

> For *Robert Le Diable*, Meyerbeeer received from the director of the Opera-house no less than fifteen hundred and eighty pounds sterling for having composed the music; and Scribe, the author of the poem, was paid a similar sum. They both then sold their copyrights to their publishers, and were again largely remunerated; and every time the opera is performed in any theatre in France, they receive ten pound each.[14]

Similarly a French *code dramatique* stabilized the price of play scripts, ensuring that dramatists received their royalties. Established playwrights were even entitled to *les*

[12] J. A. O'Shea, *Leaves from the Life of a Special Correspondent* (2 vols, London: Ward & Downey, 1885), 122–4.

[13] R. Whiteing, *The Life of Paris* (Leipzig: Bernhard Tauchnitz, 1901), 146.

[14] G. W. M. Reynolds, *Pickwick Abroad: or, The Tour in France* (London: Sherwood, Gilbert, & Piper, 1839), 157–9.

primes, the sum of 1,000 francs (£40) per act paid by the theatre manager for permission to read the play. G. H. Lewes, in his commentary on comparative authorial conditions, laboured the advantages of the French system, declaring the theatre in France a goldmine for authors, in which 'one of those light sparkling vaudevilles, which a man may throw off easily in a week' could win infinitely more than a play at one of London's patent theatres. In London, 'aspirants for the laurels of the English legitimate drama are fortunate, indeed, when, with the most triumphant success, they can obtain £300 for a five-act play; whereas a Dumas or a Scribe receives £200 for permitting the manager to read the MS. of a five-act play.'[15] By contrast, Lewes estimated that Douglas Jerrold's sensationally successful *Black-Eyed Susan* (1829) might have earned him about £10, had he not already been a salaried employee contracted to produce regular plays for the theatre where it was first performed. The £60 that Jerrold is in fact reckoned to have earned from it over the years was scarcely comparable to French rates. No wonder then that when Jerrold was forced by his debts to decamp to Paris in 1835, he marvelled, 'It may appear a fiction but dramatists here eat, drink, dress and dwell like gentlemen', and set about writing a play which he hoped to have translated and performed at the Théâtre Français.[16]

In Sala's case the process happened in reverse. He had gone to Paris in December 1851 to report on Napoleon's seizure of power but, finding that his expenses were barely covered, looked about him for other ways of earning his keep. Exploiting the lack of mutual copyright, he sat down at 8.00 p.m. one evening to translate a French play based on Dumas père's novel *Les Frères corses*. According to his own account, by 10.00 a.m. the next morning he had produced *The Corsicans*, which was being performed within the week on the London stage, where it enjoyed a run of 100 performances, for which he and his actor brother were paid a sum, then considered generous, of twenty-five shillings (£1.25) a night.[17]

Dion Boucicault's story of his negotiations with the actor-manager Benjamin Webster, and his own move to Paris in 1842 in search of further material, suggest the comparatively easy source of income that could be made by translations or adaptations by Paris correspondents with adequate French.

> I was a beginner in 1841, and received for my comedy, 'London Assurance,' £300 ... Three years later I offered a new play to a principal London theatre. The manager offered me £100 for it. In reply to my objection he remarked, 'I can go to Paris and select a first-class comedy; having seen it performed, I feel certain of its effect. To get this comedy translated will cost me £25. Why should I give you £300 or £500 for your comedy of the success of which I cannot feel so assured?' The argument was unanswerable and the result inevitable. I sold a work for £100 that took me six months' hard work to compose, and accepted a commission to translate three French plays at £50 apiece. This work afforded me child's play for a fortnight.

Boucicault's well-known anecdote was told as a lament for the fate of the English playwright, 'obliged either to relinquish the stage altogether or to become a French

---

[15] [Lewes,] 'The Condition of Authors', 291.
[16] Quoted in M. Slater, *Douglas Jerrold, 1803–57* (London: Duckworth, 2002), 107.
[17] Sala, *Life and Adventures*, i, 309–10.

copyist',[18] but it also suggests something about mid-nineteenth-century theatre criticism of Paris performances in English newspapers. Although the century witnessed a gradual evolution, from reviews by 'generalist' correspondents with no markedly different expertise from fellow members of the audience to later reviewing by more specialized theatre critics, the development was by no means clear-cut. John Bishop has suggested that theatre critics already seemed well informed about the Parisian theatre by the 1850s, and notes the appearance of a weekly coverage of 'Foreign Theatricals' in the *Spectator* from 1852 and a series of monthly articles in *Blackwood's Magazine* from 1853. However, Frederick Hardman (1814–74), who provided the *Blackwood's* articles, was a jack-of-all trades roving reporter, who had served as a war correspondent and reported from Spain for the magazine in 1853. Conversely, many of the Paris correspondents who were reporting on the quality of the scripts and the acting in the 1830s and 1840s had considerable experience as dramatists, or at the very least translators. Douglas Jerrold and Gilbert à Beckett had demonstrated this ability to move between these two worlds and languages a generation before Sala tried his hand as a translator.

There seems to have been a similar mixture of those with and without practice-based expertise among the Anglophone mid-century music critics working out of Paris. James William Davison (1813–85), the *Times* music critic from 1846 to 1879, who was very much at home in the Parisian musical milieu, had trained at the Royal Academy of Music: he may even have first encountered Berlioz, with whom he was on *tutoyer* terms, in Paris, where Berlioz, having abandoned his medical training, was supporting his musical education through musical journalism.[19] By contrast, the equally influential Henry Chorley, who began his music reviews for the *Athenæum* in 1833 in Paris and continued to supply them until 1868, regretted all his life a utilitarian education that had precluded music. Charles Gruneisen (1806–79), Chorley's successor at the *Athenæum*, had been deflected from his original success as a war correspondent in Spain by being appointed Paris correspondent of the *Morning Post* from 1839 to 1844. He returned from Paris a leading music critic and exponent of contemporary European composition and performance, and was responsible for championing the cause of Meyerbeer, who had first established his reputation in Paris. Similarly, Henry Sutherland Edwards (1828–1906), who had made his way to Paris in early 1852 as part of the posse of British journalists anxious to report on the declaration of the Second Empire, found himself drawn to the company of the musicians and music critics who frequented the Café Leblond in the Passage de l'Opéra.[20] This enthusiasm survived postings in Eastern Europe, a spell as war correspondent during the Franco-Prussian war, and resulted in his publishing *A History of Opera* (2 vols, 1862), *Rossini and his School* (1881), and lives of Rossini (1869) and the opera singer Sims Reeves (1881).

---

[18] Quoted in J. Bishop, '"They Manage Things Better in France": French Plays and English Critics, 1850–55', *Nineteenth-Century Theatre* 22(1) (Summer 1994), 9. An interesting account of the alterations made in the course of adapting French material to the English stage is given in I. Pipinia, 'Casting Identities: French Melodramas on the London Stage', Ph.D, University of Bristol, 2001.

[19] H. S. Edwards, *Personal Recollections* (London: Cassell, 1900), 72.

[20] Ibid. 88.

An interest in art also proved a useful string to the bow of any Paris correspondent in the years prior to the professionalization of the role of art critic, which is usually ascribed to the 1860s.[21] Certainly Thomas Hardy considered art history one of the subjects he should spend his evenings studying in the 1860s in preparation for a journalistic career. Frederick Hardman's eventual appointment in 1874 as a permanent Paris correspondent for *The Times* had originally stemmed from his forwarding to that paper his critique of an 1850 Paris exhibition of art. The capital's national collections, designed to establish the city's claim as the central showcase of European art, promised increasing numbers of British tourists a truncated version of the Grand Tour, and so annual *salons* and special displays, such as the 1855 Exposition in the Palais des Beaux-Arts, were widely reported in the British press. The emergence of British critics who had practical experience as copyists in the Louvre or had trained in the ateliers of French masters brought a new technical vocabulary to the genre and would finally erupt in the famous Ruskin vs Whistler[22] argument of taste vs practical expertise. Henry James was almost certainly wrong, in reviewing P. G. Hamerton's (1834–94) collected newspaper criticism, published as *Contemporary French Painters* (1868), to declare the author a unique English representative of practice-based criticism.[23] Thackeray's early training in Parisian ateliers and hours spent copying in the Louvre, where he was apparently wont to feign ignorance of French to excuse the absence of a student permit, resulted in his publishing no fewer than thirty-eight essays on art.[24] Art criticism also provided a particularly useful route for women to find their way into journalism: Anna Jameson, Lady Eastlake, and Emilia Dilke all honed their expertise as art historians and critics in Paris.

Ultimately, knowledge and skills were less important to a foreign correspondent's success than temperament and adaptability. Where Blanchard Jerrold managed at the end of his long career to be honoured by both the French and the British, his father's skills as a journalist did not transfer across the Channel. When Douglas Jerrold and his wife suddenly had to leave London for Paris in December 1835, he imagined that he would easily be able to turn his hand to journalism. Offering his services as a correspondent of the *New Monthly Magazine*, he wrote to John Forster, 'I think I can send you a few pages of tolerable gossip for the *N.M.* for the present month. As I become more familiar with Parisian matters, and get more into society—which I find opening in many unexpected ways upon me—I have no doubt I can render a monthly commentary more acceptable.'[25]

---

[21] E. Prettejohn, 'Aesthetic Value and the Professionalization of Victorian Art Criticism 1837–78', *Journal of Victorian Culture* 2(1) (1997), 71–94.

[22] Whistler's period as an art student in Paris in 1855 is famously portrayed in du Maurier's *Trilby* (1894), where he figures as Joe Sibley, the idle apprentice.

[23] H. James, 'An English Critic of French Painting', in *The Painter's Eye: Notes and Essays on the Pictorial Arts*, ed. J. L. Sweeney (London: Rupert Hart-Davis, 1956), 33–42.

[24] For a listing of the ateliers where Thackeray studied, an account of his drawings, and his work as an art critic, see J. Fisher (ed.), *Lives of Victorian Literary Figures: William Thackeray* (London: Pickering & Chatto, 2007), 75–85. For the Louvre anecdote, see J. Crowe, *Reminiscences of Thirty-Five Years of My Life* (London: John Murray, 1895), 20.

[25] DJ to JF, 12 Dec. 1835, quoted in Slater, *Douglas Jerrold*, 107.

Since the social introductions into wider society he was relying upon seem to have come from Henry Mayhew (1812–87), and Thackeray, both almost ten years younger than him and themselves scrabbling around for work, it was just as well that Jerrold was able to return to London in January 1836. If anything, this interlude worked to Thackeray's advantage, as he was able to recruit Jerrold as an experienced theatre critic for the *Constitutional* the following year, and to contribute twelve illustrations to Jerrold's essay collection *Men of Character* (1838).

Jerrold's second concerted attempt at reporting from Paris was on Louis-Philippe's overthrow. *Douglas Jerrold's Weekly Newspaper*, launched in July 1846, was badly in need of a fillip by March 1848, so Jerrold set off for Paris. His assistant, George Hodder, recalled being sent out to collect local colour, while his employer's plan was 'to pass the morning in reading the French newspapers, and thus laying in a stock of material, either for his paper or for his weekly contributions to *Punch,* and to devote the remainder of the day to sauntering about the Boulevards, choosing a restaurant to dine at, and visiting a theatre in the evening'.[26] Although Jerrold was capable of reading the local press, he had no talent for eyewitness reporting, no established string of local contacts, and hated working out of a hotel room, preferring domesticity or the to-and-fro of companionable tavern discussion.

The capacity to live out of a suitcase, far from friends and family, combined with the ability to turn one's hand equally to politically trenchant commentary or the intimate tones of gossip, trumped all other considerations. Thackeray's decision to settle in London rather than Paris may well have been influenced by a recognition that his talent, like Jerrold's, was essentially literary rather than political, and that London was more conducive to the club life he enjoyed. The major part played by personality in a foreign correspondent's career can be briefly illustrated by comparing Thackeray's career with that of fellow Trinity man Henry Labouchère (1831–1912). Albeit of different generations, their backgrounds were not dissimilar: both went up to Cambridge from public school with reasonable expectations; both left without a degree and mired in gambling debts. Both later considered themselves of the class and calibre to stand for Parliament. However, where Thackeray was launched on a reduced version of the Grand Tour, Labouchère was dispatched to a family business in South America. Although Thackeray considered foreign correspondent postings further afield—'to Madrid for the Standard with £300 a year' in 1833 and to Constantinople in 1835—he preferred Parisian life to the lure of more remote cultures.[27]

Labouchère, by contrast, made the most of every opportunity that came his way, joining a South American circus troupe and spending six months living in a camp of Objibwe Indians, before spending ten years as a diplomat with postings from Washington to St Petersburg, prior to turning journalist. Despite having recently come into a very substantial family fortune, he was a little daunted when he inadvertently found himself trapped in Paris during the five month siege of the winter

[26] Hodder, *Memories of My Time* (London: Tinsley Brothers, 1870), 118.
[27] *Letters of Thackeray*, ed. Ray, i, 270, 287.

of 1870–71, having mistakenly anticipated, in September, that it would last a month at most. The balconied fourth-floor hotel room in which he had installed himself proved too large to heat in the harsh winter conditions; and his banker had left Paris, so that Labouchère had no money to replace the few clothes he had initially packed. Even this was grist to his mill: he reported himself as looking 'seedy', his shirts threadbare and grubby, pins serving to replace lost buttons as a means of holding his garments together, and his boots holed; but his intimate, witty, and sometimes scathing eyewitness reports secured the fortunes of his paper.[28] Recalling the first time he set eyes on him at a meeting called to discuss how the representatives of the British press planned to get their news out of Paris, O'Shea remarked, 'I wish he had not been in Paris during the siege. He took the wind out of all our sails.'[29]

10.4 THE WAR CORRESPONDENT

War correspondents were slow to appear as a specialist cadre. The correspondents who had reported the convulsions of 1830, 1848, and 1851 had often been resident correspondents in Paris who happened to get caught up in events, or freelance journalists who had rushed across the Channel chasing the story. These men were often warned by the British Embassy to stay off the streets during politically sensitive times: Thackeray claimed he had only managed to offer an eyewitness account of the return of Napoleon I's remains to Paris in December 1840 because he had somehow missed this warning.[30] However, the impact made by their reports of the erection of barricades, street fighting, and the omnipresence of troops in the heart of Paris is produced by the sense of shock such residents experienced in seeing the familiar beats of their peacetime life converted into an impromptu battleground.

W. H. Russell's reporting of the Crimean War for *The Times* is usually seen as the definitive event, setting the pattern for the specialist war correspondent; but the way in which events unfolded in France during 1870–71 meant that here there was still no absolute division between the two types of foreign correspondent. O'Shea recalled how the editor of the *Standard* came to Paris as the talk of war grew more vociferous, instructed Hely Bowes, the paper's long-time Paris correspondent and an expert on French politics, to stay at his post, offered O'Shea, another established correspondent, his choice of sides, and then dispatched his new recruit, G. A. Henty, to report on German manoeuvres. Other papers with long-established Paris correspondents made similarly strategic decisions. The *Daily Telegraph* parcelled out its work between Felix Whitehurst, the Hon. Francis Lawley, and George Sala, although by January 1871 John Merry Le Sage was on hand to achieve the coup of reporting the German army's entry into Paris, hours ahead of rival papers. Sage indeed seems to have adopted the 'Le' as an honorific in acknowledgement of the

[28] [Labouchère, H.,] *Diary of the Besieged Resident in Paris, reprinted from the* Daily News *with Several New Letters and Preface* (London: Hurst & Blackett, 1871), 18, 278.
[29] O'Shea, *Leaves*, ii, 311.
[30] *The Second Funeral of Napoleon*, Oxford Thackeray, iii, 395–449.

enormity of his own achievement. The *Daily News* despatched the team of George and Emily Crawford and their four children to Tours, while Labouchère stayed in Paris, and Forbes followed the troops. The Paris correspondent for the *Star*, prevented from leaving Paris by a recent serious accident, starved to death during the siege, despite his wife feeding him his pet canaries.[31]

Journalists trapped in Paris during the siege felt equally entitled to describe themselves as war correspondents, combining their standard task of reporting domestic details of the way in which the troops ate at the expense of the poor, or grocers profiteered, with commentary on French government policy and rumours from the front. Emily Crawford, who was back in Paris during the Commune, laid equal claim to the title, having experienced 'one of the most furious war storms of modern times':

> Battles, barricades, bombardments were so familiar as to cease to frighten. The noise of cannonading lulled to sleep at night, and the cessation of it kept awake... These dangers and hardships were the best training for subsequent duties. One was deconventionalised and thrown back on first principles. Having gone through such a school, she had no difficulty in taking her life in her hand and walking alone from one end of Paris to the other during the throes of the Commune, to meet her husband coming from Versailles, and be with him should he be arrested as a spy.[32]

Her reward was to be the scoop she achieved by interviewing the leaders of the Commune as they sat in council on 23 March 1871.

The Russell-style war correspondents, selected for reporting from the war zone itself, do seem to have certain shared characteristics. Unsurprisingly, many of them had displayed a long-standing interest in military matters. Archibald Forbes of the *Daily News* had enlisted as a dragoon in 1859 after hearing Russell lecture on his Crimean experiences, and military theory had long been his personal hobby. The *Observer's* correspondent, William Schwenk Gilbert (1836–1911), had hoped as a young man to become an artillery officer, but contented himself with twenty years' voluntary service in the militia. George Alfred Henty (1832–1902) had become a journalist by accident when his father showed his letters home from the Crimea to the editor of the *Morning Advertiser*, which published several as from 'A Military Correspondent'. Army office life back home palled on him; he offered himself to the *Standard* in 1866 as their war correspondent in Italy, and so became a natural choice to report on the Franco-Prussian war for the paper: he was also to extract a boys' adventure tale, *The Young Francs-Tireurs* (1872), from these experiences.

Another noteworthy feature of the wartime press contingent was the way in which 50-something-year-old journalists involved their sons. Henry Mayhew took his son, Athol, to Metz with him and the two together managed to penetrate the front lines; while Henry Vizetelly's 17-year-old, Ernest Alfred, was eventually created a chevalier of the Légion d'honneur for the gallantry he displayed. Whether this is merely further evidence of the way in which journalism had

---

[31] R. Whiteing, *My Harvest* (London: Hodder & Stoughton, 1915), 85.
[32] Crawford, 'Journalism as a Profession for Women', 369–70.

become a family business, or was prompted by the practical need for a subordinate in the field, or showed a wily eye to gaining an early toehold in this new form of reporting, or all of the above, is hard to determine. Both Ernest and Athol certainly had useful language skills; and Henry Vizetelly may have been prompted by the success his youngest brother, Frank, had already achieved as a war correspondent to consider this a suitable career opening for his sons, two of whom achieved fame in this role. Moreover, men of an older generation often did not relish being catapulted into this new role. Sala, suffering the physical penalties of his years as 'prince of Bohemians', was clearly out of his element amid wartime austerities; and Henry Vizetelly's memoirs record how his wartime experiences drove him, in 1874, to leave the role of foreign correspondent to younger and more active men.[33] O'Shea, who, despite being almost twenty years younger than Vizetelly, did not 'have a good war', summed up this new breed of special correspondent as follows:

> The War Correspondent, like the poet, is born, not made. He must have his aptitudes, the two first of which are good temper and good digestion; he must be possessed of tact and activity, be able to ride bare-backed, and write with a fish-bone, be a good linguist and a light sleeper, have a practical knowledge of soldiering and be content, on occasion, to make a meal off the soles of his boots.[34]

10.5 THE WORK–LIFE BALANCE

The world of the Paris correspondent remained predominantly homosocial. For the woman journalist, Emily Crawford claimed, the demanding hours necessitated a freedom and flexibility difficult to combine with domestic duties: a housekeeper was therefore almost a sine qua non; and any children must be despatched to school. Furthermore, the need to remain appropriately dressed and elegantly coiffed during long days of reporting placed an additional strain on women journalists. Crawford recalled an occasion when she had had to resort to 'complicated hair-dressing' twice in one day when invited to report a royal visit that involved a garden party at Versailles, followed by a soirée at the Ministry of Foreign Affairs: the ensuing report had to be composed between 2 and 6 a.m. She noted that Madame Claude Vignon, who doubled as a reporter of the doings of the National Assembly and a professional sculptor, kept a maid with advanced dressmaking skills to ensure that she always 'possessed the gloss of elegance' sufficient to act as an 'Open Sesame' for the places she needed to access for her journalism. Richard Whiteing's appraisal of Madame Claude suggests the terms on which such women practised journalism. Mentioning that she was married to Rouvier, the financial genius of the new government of the Third Republic, he added, 'Her intellectual hold on him was strengthened, with or without need, by her amazing dinners,

---

[33] Whiteing, *My Harvest*, 72; H. Vizetelly, *Glances Back through Seventy Years: Autobiographical and Other Recollections* (2 vols, London: Kegan Paul, Trench, Trübner, 1893), ii, 432.
[34] O'Shea, *Leaves*, ii, 239.

which on Sundays, as a holiday task, she cooked all by herself. It was heroic, for she still had to take due care of her looks.'[35]

Emily Crawford, who was often approached, especially by women, about openings in 'light newspaper work', concluded that there was no such thing. The life was one of unremitting pressure:

> The first requirement...is health and a rich reserve of strength. I don't mean the strength of a railway-porter, but the vitality which enables one to recoup rapidly after an exhausting bout of work. Women of good constitution are more elastic in recovering than men. But elasticity is not enough. There must be staying power. It won't do to suffer from headaches, or to feel easily exhausted. Eager competition between pressmen and presswomen, the more eager competition among newspapers, and the yet greater competition for space among telegrams pouring in from all parts of the globe leave no room in the daily press for the sick and ailing. The same fatalities weigh upon the weekly press. How often have I not written for some weekly paper an article a few days in advance, so as carefully to prune and polish. Before it was sent, and sometimes after, some thunderingly big event burst on the world, and as the public could think of nothing else, I had at once to turn round to hunt this hare.... Night work is usually got through in a state approaching to brain-fever.... Writing or telegraphing from abroad, one does not see one's proofs. When I was more of a novice I used to spend wretched hours between the moment the hurried article was sent off and that of its return in print.[36]

Thackeray who had made this transition from weekly letters for the *National Standard* to the slightly more demanding regime of the daily *Constitutional,* and worked, however briefly, as a subeditor for the twice-daily editions of *Galignani's Messenger,* indicated the changes of pace this demanded in his portrait of Philip Firmin. Philip's initial 'business at Paris was only with a weekly London paper', where 'he could glance over the state of Europe; give the latest news from the salons, imparted to him...for the most part, by some brother hireling scribes; be present at all the theatres by deputy; and smash Louis Philippe or Messieurs Guizot and Thiers in a few easily turned paragraphs'. When Philip's expectations of an inheritance disappeared, he 'gladly sold four hours of his day' to Mr Phipps of the *Daily Intelligencer,* and 'translated page after page of newspapers, French and German; took an occasional turn at the Chamber of Deputies, and gave an account of a sitting of importance'.[37] By the novel's conclusion, however, Philip realises that the irregular hours and lifestyle of the Paris correspondent are incompatible with his new-found family responsibilities, and he returns to London and the office-bound post of subeditor.

Thackeray had in any case been a Paris correspondent of the generation whose working hours were often spent in the cafés, restaurants, theatres, and public spaces of Paris. Café life indeed loomed large in the memoirs of the mid-nineteenth-century fraternity of journalists, even serving as material for their writing. Philip Firmin's breezy account of cheap Parisian eating-places, for instance, was drawn

---

[35] Whiteing, *My Harvest,* 224.　　[36] Crawford, 'Journalism as a Profession for Women', 367.
[37] *Adventures of Philip,* 281, 323.

from Thackeray's earlier 1841 article, 'Memorials of Gormandising [*sic*]', detailing the variety of venue open to the bachelor diner and advising against the dirtiest, cheapest places.[38] In the next generation, Blanchard Jerrold elevated his enthusiasm for a weekly dining-club where, courtesy of the Emperor's chef, the members would sample the menu enjoyed by the head of state himself',[39] into fame as the food critic 'Le Bec'.

In these sociable circles one story fed from and into another, sometimes almost literally. Henry Sutherland Edwards recalled how he had first met the ill-fated Savile Morton of the *Daily News* during the 1851 regime change, filing his copy at the post office of the Rue Lafayette. Morton reopened his letter to include the rumour that Edwards had just heard over lunch, that 100,000 troops were coming from Lille to help put down the impending revolution: as recompense for the information Morton asked Edwards to join him for dinner.[40] It is difficult to estimate to what extent or in what precise ways this sense of belonging to a cadre who knew, in the case of major political events, that they were feasting on the same carrion had an effect on these men's concept of individual authorship and originality. It is certainly the case, as the next chapter will demonstrate, that old Paris hands such as Thackeray and G. W. M. Reynolds were less fazed by the fine distinction between adaptation and plagiarism than some of their London colleagues.[41]

Food and drink continued as an institutionalized part of the journalist's life, even after the advent of the telegraph increased the pressures of the working day. Whiteing recalled of this post-siege 'middle period' of journalism,

> The letters were still written, but they were sent by post, and over above that they were written at the *café* in lieu of an office. The correspondent actually rented a whole table to himself at a place within easy reach of the central post, and his myrmidons came and went, with last items of news to fill up the fat envelope to the bursting point, up to the last minute of the last quarter of an hour.

Only gradually did the provisional and sociable give way to more permanent and formalized arrangements. The *Daily Telegraph* set the fashion by installing their correspondent in an office near the Place de l'Opéra, where the paper's presence was advertised in huge gilt letters hung from the balcony—an altogether better business address, as Whiteing wryly remarked, than '*Café de la Providence*, first table on the left'. The grandees of the press, such as Blowitz of *The Times* or the Crawfords of the *Daily News*, emphasized their dignity and standing by equipping their offices, above which they often lived, with impressively furnished waiting rooms in which to receive visitors.[42]

Living arrangements, 'above the shop', reduced the need for even the single male Paris correspondent to dine out every evening, but does not seem to have eroded

---

[38] Cf. ibid. 266–8; and 'Memorials of Gormandizing. In a Letter to Oliver Yorke Esq. by M.A. Titmarsh', *Fraser's Magazine* 23 (June 1841), 710–25; repr. in *Oxford Thackeray*, iii, 509–36.

[39] Vizetelly, *Glances*, ii, 260.

[40] Edwards, *Personal Recollections*, 28–9.

[41] Cf. R. Macfarlane, *Plagiarism and Originality in Nineteenth-Century Literature* (Oxford: Oxford University Press, 2007), 39.

[42] Whiteing, *My Harvest*, 137–8.

one institution, 'the absinthe hour'. Vizetelly, who devoted a chapter of his memoirs to favourite Parisian watering holes, claimed that it was the 'drink of choice of the latter years of the Empire' when the cafés would be packed with *absintheurs* between 4 and 6 p.m., the English and American journalists foregathering at the Café de la Paix or the Grande Café.[43] It may be that Vizetelly's reinvention of himself as an oenophile led him to remind readers of the health warnings given by the medical profession against this spirit, but he also claimed it as the journalists' favourite tipple because it gave the temporary fillip necessary for the evening's writing, or, as Thackeray's Philip Firmin phrased it, 'It makes the ink run, and imparts a fine eloquence to the style.'[44] The ritual was comfortingly transportable: Sala recalled how quickly he and his fellow English war correspondents had established an absinthe table in their hotel when despatched to Metz at the outbreak of war.[45]

Philip Firmin's rose-coloured memories include how sitting in the 'café opposite the Bourse...Gilligan, of the *Century*, and I used to do our letters...we compared notes and pitched into each other amicably.'[46] Fuelled by absinthe and professional rivalry, the pitching into each other could become less amicable. Vizetelly's memoirs contain tales of journalists passing off invented tales to more naïve colleagues who would telegraph them home only to have the hoax blow up in their face. Wounded pride or imagined insults were sometimes assuaged in print, but towards the end of the Second Empire, Vizetelly claimed, 'quite a duelling epidemic raged among Paris journalists, and scarcely a week went by without the papers chronicling some encounter with swords or pistols, in which prominent contributors to the boulevardian prints were concerned'.[47] Indeed, Robert Browning complained that the Parisian regard for their men of the press was itself to blame for lending a false glamour to fighting which essentially differed little from pub brawling: 'go to-night into half the *estaminets* of Paris, and see whether the quarrels over dice and sour wine present any more pleasing matter of speculation *au fond*.'[48] Flaubert's disaffected picture of mid-century journalism in *L'Éducation sentimentale* seconded Browning's contempt: not only is the ignominious duel in which his protagonist is involved inherently ridiculous, but the part played by the press in such matters is called into question when the editor of a satirical magazine uses his columns for personal vengeance in his report of the affair.

The list of Parisian pressmen involved in such duels includes illustrious names, and Vizetelly claimed that the refusal to fight could ruin a journalist who would find his work no longer acceptable to editors.[49] Browning's remark was made in reference to the 1845 court case prosecuting the duellist who had killed Alexandre Dujarier, part-owner of *La Presse*. Dujarier stood in a long tradition. In 1836 Dujarier's co-editor, Emile de Girardin, had fatally wounded Armand Carrel, editor of *Le National*, in a duel interpreted by Thackeray as the consequence of the

[43] Vizetelly, *Glances*, ii, 253–73.   [44] *Adventures of Philip*, 269.
[45] Sala, *Life and Adventures*, ii, 205.   [46] *Adventures of Philip*, 269.
[47] Vizetelly, *Glances*, ii, 384–6, 132.
[48] Quoted in R. Gridley, *The Brownings and France: A Chronicle with Commentary* (London: Athlone Press, 1982), 45.
[49] Vizetelly, *Glances*, i, 132.

bitter enmity between the Republican and Monarchist press:[50] it was Carrel's third such duel with rival editors. Zola acted as second for Edouard Manet against the art critic Duranty; and Proust was to seek satisfaction from the reviewer of his first book. According to Emily Crawford, the French paper *Le Journal* made it a condition of appointment that a woman journalist, who appeared under the by-line of Séverine, should appoint a male deputy to 'answer for her with sword or pistol' should her words offend.[51]

In a world of inflated egos and exaggerated sense of *amour propre*, where trivial incidents could so easily be exaggerated by rumour and press innuendo into *casus belli*, Thackeray portrayed even staid, elderly family men as swiftly driven to feel that a duel was the appropriate way of avenging rudeness. The duel, averted in this case, prompts the narrator of the *Adventures of Philip* to the more serious reflection:

> The Bois de Boulogne is hard by…with plenty of cool fighting ground. The *octroi* officers [appointed to collect taxes on goods entering the city limits] never stop gentlemen going out at the neighbouring barrier upon duelling business, or prevent the return of the slain victim in the hackney-coach when the dreadful combat is over.[52]

Thackeray had good reason to try to expose the culture of journalists' duels. His friend and Trinity, Cambridge contemporary Savile Morton (1811–52) had died in 1852 at the hands of a fellow Paris correspondent, Harold Elyot Bower (1815–84). When Bower was prosecuted, *Galignani's Messenger* held that this was an 'Interesting Trial Case', precisely because it involved two Paris correspondents for British papers.[53] Morton met his end in a domestic quarrel, as a consequence of a knife wound inflicted by a husband incensed at his delirious wife naming Morton as father of their recently born fifth child; but Morton had fought at least two duels in Paris over women in the previous two years, and after the first, in December 1850, Thackeray had confided to his mother, 'Morton has a genius for scrapes… & the wonder is that he has lasted up to 40 years of age with a whole skin—Why he is always in some feminine mischief.'[54] After the fatal stabbing, Thackeray wrote to Monckton Milnes, another Trinity man, that Morton had 'rushed upon his fate. Haven't I often said to you he would come to a violent death?'[55] Although Morton's philandering makes him an unlikely original for Philip Firmin, the way in which the press fans the flames of a minor fracas in which Philip gets involved at an Embassy ball bears a close relation to the reporting of Morton's death. Philip's fight with his insufferable cousin is narrated in *Galignani's Messenger*, from where the report is posted to America, enabling Philip's father to read the full account in the columns of the *New York Emerald*. Just so was the *Messenger*'s report on 29

[50] First published as 'Parisian Caricatures' in the *London and Westminster Review* 32 (Apr. 1839), 282–305; then republished as 'Caricatures and Lithography', *Paris Sketch Book*, Oxford *Thackeray*, ii, 168–95; 185.

[51] Crawford, 'Journalism as a Profession for Women', 366.

[52] *Adventures of Philip*, 404.

[53] *Galignani's Messenger*, 29 Dec. 1852.

[54] *Letters of Thackeray*, ed. Ray, ii, 726.

[55] *The Letters and Private Papers of William Makepeace Thackeray: A Supplement*, ed. E. F. Harden (2 vols, New York: Garland, 1994), i, 485, 48.

December 1852 concerning Bower's trial repeated verbatim in the *New York Times* for 17 January 1853.

Fatalities were mercifully rarer than these examples would suggest. Vizetelly's claim that 'it far more frequently happened that these duels terminated in a mere scratch or two, with the customary corollary—a reconciliation sealed over a champagne déjeuner' is backed up by Arthur à Beckett's recollection of an occasion in 1867, when as a 22-year-old he had been called out by Whitehurst of the *Daily Telegraph* for an insult in an article he had unwittingly run as editor of the newly launched satirical weekly *Tomahawk* (a paper which itself owed much to Parisian models). The affair was patched up by a man from the British Embassy who took the warring journalists out to dinner.[56] O'Shea's slight tale *Mated from the Morgue: A Tale of the Second Empire* (1889) suggested just how far those involved would go to avoid mortal woundings or legal repercussions. In this case, a nervous Irish second stages the duel in the unlikely setting of the far-flung suburb of Clamart, where he and his principal arrive on bicycles, as if on a holiday jaunt. Once there, he secures suicide notes from both duellists, before filling their pistols with blanks.

———

Journalism offered a precarious enough livelihood and encouraged rivalry: duelling might therefore be seen as an extreme symptom of the highly competitive Parisian press environment, exacerbated in the case of British correspondents by the claustrophobic world in which their comparatively small cohort socialized. In a period when papers were founded, folded, and merged with astounding rapidity, there must have been many journalists who never made the name for themselves which would enable them to escape the perpetual hand-to-mouth existence of the piece-worker. The final chapter in this section explores Thackeray's emergence from this world. The wonder is not that Thackeray took so long to distinguish himself from the herd of his contemporaries, but that he managed to do so at all.

[56] Vizetelly, *Glances*, i, 132.; à Beckett, *The à Becketts of 'Punch'*, 268–9.

11

Thackeray's debt to the print world of Paris

This chapter contends that the time Thackeray spent studying art and practising journalism in Paris profoundly influenced the way in which he saw and represented the world.

11.1 THE NATURE OF THE CLAIM

At the start of his career in the 1830s Thackeray lived intermittently in Paris; after he had transferred his centre of operation to London, he continued to be a regular visitor for the remainder of his life. He wrote French well enough to correspond with educated native speakers—an accomplishment that, as Catherine Gore remarked, was by no means a given among his class of young men.[1] He was well read in both the literature of the *ancien régime* and that of his French contemporaries. One of his earliest articles offered a guide to the latest French novels, explaining that the French appetite for change far outstripped that of her neighbours; and he continued to keep abreast of French fiction:[2] indeed, in later years he was as likely to while away a day reading the latest offering from Dumas *père* as he was to read a novel by an English contemporary.[3] Like other Paris correspondents of his day, Thackeray was not above padding his own columns with chunks of translated quotations from French authors, nor of reworking French tales for an English readership,[4] and at least twice he proposed to publishers that he undertake the relatively menial work of translating French novels.

However, the debts Thackeray owed to the time he had spent in Paris attempting to forge a career went well beyond easily tabulated inventories of his use of

---

[1] C. Gore, *Greville: or, a Season in Paris* (3 vols, London: Henry Colburn, 1841), i, 131.

[2] 29 June 1833, *National Standard*. Thackeray's familiarity with George Sand's fiction is demonstrated in two letters for a New York journal, *The Corsair*, 14 and 21 Sept. 1839; repr. as 'Madame Sand and the New Apocalypse', *Paris Sketch Book*, *Oxford Thackeray*, ed. G. Saintsbury (17 vols, London: Oxford University Press, 1910), ii, 224–50.

[3] 'On a Lazy Idle Boy', *Roundabout Papers*, *Oxford Thackeray*, xvii, 354.

[4] Thackeray acknowledged that 'A Tale of Wonder' (*National Standard*, 2 Oct. 1833, 228–9) 'is translated from a very clever French story'; 'The Bedford Row Conspiracy' (*New Monthly*, Jan.–Apr. 1840), an Anglicized version of Charles de Bernard's 'Le pied d'argile', had been 'stolen from the French': *The Letters and Private Papers of William Makepeace Thackeray*, ed. G. N. Ray (4 vols, Cambridge, Mass.: Harvard University Press, 1945–6), i, 268, 433. A letter to a publisher of 6 Feb. 1844 refers to 'a robbery from the French—a burlesque of a serious romance': derived from Alexandre Dumas's *Othon l'archer*, it was finally published in *George Cruikshank's Table-Book* for 1845 as 'A Legend of the Rhine': *Letters of Thackeray*, ed. Ray, ii, 141, 160.

French phrases, articles on French matters, or accounts of his French fictional char-acters. The following brief indication of the long-term benefits he received from his sojourn in Paris will help in understanding the importance this chapter attaches both to the way in which this pervasive influence has been systematically under-played and to more specific examples of the impression that Parisian life and art left on his work.

Most critics agree that Thackeray hit his stride in the latter half of the 1840s, in the satirical mimicry of the work of fellow British authors in his series 'Punch's Prize Novelists' (1847), and above all in *Vanity Fair*. Both works built upon facets of his experience as a Paris correspondent. Thackeray had increasingly turned to the essentially parasitic skill of the parodic as a means of entertaining distant British readers with reports of French dramas they would probably never see, so that the talent was well honed by the time he came to apply it to British novelists. The confidence to use a wide canvas in *Vanity Fair*—stretching further geographi-cally and socially than the silver-fork novels of either Catherine Gore or Bulwer Lytton—had been primed by long exposure to Parisian cosmopolitanism, topped up by his travels in the Rhineland.

In broader terms still, his Parisian experience affected his attitude to his chosen profession. Having cut his teeth in the dog-eat-dog world of Parisian Anglophone journalism, where much of the work was based upon combing the French press for suitable material for relaying to an English readership, Thackeray took a more relaxed attitude than many of his English contemporaries to the subtle distinctions between literary theft and skilful adaptation of another's work. It would have been difficult to have survived however brief a period slaving for *Galignani's Messenger* without becoming less precious about tampering with another journalist's prose. If, as Robert Macfarlane suggests, the idea of originality, or creation *ex nihilo*, had achieved its high-water mark in England by 1840, Thackeray was already swim-ming strongly against the current when he returned to London.[5] His attitude to the Dumas scandal confirmed his attitude to writing as a craftsman-like business, depending more on ensuring that the right materials and tools are to hand than on the assertion of the isolated nature of individual genius:

> They say that all the works bearing Dumas's name are not written by him. Well? Does not the chief cook have *aides* under him? Did not Rubens's pupils paint on his canvases? Had not Lawrence assistants for his backgrounds? For myself, being also *du metier*, I confess I would often like to have a competent, respectable, and rapid clerk for the business part of my novels; and on his arrival, at eleven o' clock, would say, 'Mr. Jones, if you please, the archbishop must die this morning in about five pages. Turn to article "Dropsy" (or what you will) in Encyclopaedia. Take care there are no medical blunders in his death. Group his daughters, physicians, and chaplains round him. In Wales' *London*, Letter B, third shelf, you will find an account of Lambeth, and some prints of the place. Colour in with local colouring...There is a great deal of carpenter's and joiner's work in novels which surely a smart professional hand might supply.[6]

---

[5] R. Macfarlane, *Plagiarism and Originality in Nineteenth-Century Literature* (Oxford: Oxford University Press, 2007), 39.
[6] 'A Peal of Bells', *Roundabout Papers, Oxford Thackeray*, xvii, 607.

From the late 1830s, Dumas *père* had transferred the collaborative model of literary composition, which he had been accustomed to employ in his theatrical offerings of the 1820 and 1830s, to his hugely successful production of serialized novels for the French press. Had Auguste Maquet, his principal *nègre* or ghost writer, who habitually supplied historical background and early drafts of the novels, not taken Dumas to court over the money owed to him, their arrangement would have provoked little comment in Paris, where such working relationships had become something of an institution.[7]

The impression of the possible status, influence, and morality of literary men that Thackeray had gained in Paris helped to shape his contribution to the mid-century 'dignity of literature' debate in England, which was sparked by the denigratory picture of his own profession that he was alleged to have drawn in *Pendennis*. Paris had shown Thackeray how a journalist might aspire to govern his country, and his later unsuccessful bid to be a member of parliament demonstrated the appeal this idea held for him. The life of his fellow British journalists in Paris of the 1830s, meanwhile, had made him recognize the distance between the desire to see one's name on the title page of a literary work and the humiliating drudgery involved in catering to newspaper editors' whims. Thackeray not only uses journalists as the central consciousness of novels such as *Pendennis* and the *Adventures of Philip*, but displays an interest in the working world they inhabit quite different from the lightly sketched account given by Dickens of David Copperfield's avocation as a writer. The very notion of placing *littérateurs* at the heart of his novels may well have been following the egotistic trend observable in many French writers of Thackeray's period. *Pendennis*, and to an even greater extent the *Adventures of Philip*, demonstrate the lesson that Thackeray had learned in Paris when he found himself having to gauge his English paymasters and rivals in an environment far less socially and ethically homogeneous than Charterhouse or Cambridge. Institutions and Guilds of Art and Literature, designed to elevate the status of authorship in Great Britain, were irrelevant in the Parisian print world, which indulged in some of the lowest practices of his profession: financial skulduggery, slave-wage drudgery, and outright theft of intellectual property. When newspapers, their owners, and their employees could disappear overnight, the only thing left to rely on was personal integrity.[8]

Despite this evidence, twentieth-century Thackeray scholarship, much of which emanated from North America, not only persistently minimized but also denied the significant role Paris had played in Thackeray's evolution as writer and artist. It may be that an older North American practice of dividing Anglophone literary courses into 'British' and 'World' Literature worked in ways that prioritized distinguishing an English tradition, to which Thackeray was then firmly assigned. To understand the nature of the claims this chapter makes, it will be helpful to consider them in the context of previous interpretive models.

[7] See S. Whidden (ed.), *Models of Collaboration in Nineteenth-Century French Literature: Several Authors, One Pen* (Farnham: Ashgate, 2009).

[8] The terms in which the 'dignity of literature' debate was conducted are discussed in C. Pettitt, *Patent Inventions: Intellectual Property and the Victorian Novel* (Oxford: Oxford University Press, 2004), 149–71.

11.2 PREVIOUS INTERPRETIVE MODELS

The fashion for belittling the impact France had on Thackeray seems to have originated with G. N. Ray's 1940 Harvard doctoral dissertation, 'Thackeray and France: Being an Account of the Part Played by Thackeray's Life in France and his Reading of French Literature in the Formation of his Mind and Art'. Submitted to Harvard's Division of Modern Languages, it demonstrated a mastery of French language and literature that few scholars of English literature have since been able to equal. The shaping impulse behind the dissertation becomes clear in claims such as: 'Thackeray's life in France falls naturally into four periods, each marked by a distinctive mode of living correspondent to the position he found himself in in the world that he then occupied.'[9] Convenient though it would be for biographers, few people's lives fall naturally into distinct periods, let alone coherent chapters; but this notion of a Thackeray whose life and writings could be neatly packaged into a series of discrete phases has been remarkably persistent.

Ray's examination of Thackeray's writing was predicated on a very broad-brush conceptual contrast between England and France in which Ray claimed that the Evangelical movement had secured a collusive alliance between the ruling classes and the intelligentsia in early Victorian England, aimed at furthering piety and moral conservatism, whereas in France intellectuals were committed to subverting and destroying the bourgeoisie's hold on the reins of power. Relying on this schema enabled Ray to distance Thackeray from pernicious French influences on two counts: his early exposure to Evangelical mores, and his middle-class preference for dealing in personalities and social mores rather than direct political commentary. Recent scholarship has blurred and complicated this sense of clear-cut boundaries between radically subversive writers and their middle-class counterparts,[10] and this chapter will suggest that Thackeray's spell in Paris had acquainted him more closely with the working practices of radicals such as G. W. M. Reynolds and Albert Smith than he might subsequently have wished to admit. Ray's account of France also took little note of the fact that Thackeray's major spells in Paris fell either side of Louis-Philippe's 1835 crackdown on political satire. Given that Thackeray's early journalism was often highly derivative of the contemporary Parisian press, there was good reason for his own reporting to follow the French trajectory from the early *ad hominem* attacks on political figures—seen in his contributions to the *National Standard* in 1833–4—to the reflections of a more sociophilosophical order apparent in *The Second Funeral of Napoleon* (1841).

Ray concluded that France and its literature had played only a very subordinate role in Thackeray's development: 'His genius was thoroughly English. And he consciously associated himself with one of the greatest native traditions, the line of English humorists extending from Addison to Dickens.'[11] Gradually, as Ray worked

---

[9] G. N. Ray, 'Thackeray and France: Being an Account of the Part Played by Thackeray's Life in France and his Reading of French Literature in the Formation of his Mind and Art', Ph.D, Harvard University, 1940, 47.

[10] e.g. S. Ledger, *Dickens and the Popular Radical Imagination* (Cambridge: Cambridge University Press, 2007).

[11] Ray, 'Thackeray and France', 280.

and reworked his subject's biography, he repudiated the mistaken 'callousness and brutality' of an 'early' Thackeray, tainted by French habits of seeing only the 'harsh and cynical aspects of life',[12] and championed a Thackeray in the 'pattern John Bull' mode, 'almost rivalling Mr Podsnap in his insularity'. Quoting, 'Thank God that, in England, things are not quite managed so', as Thackeray's 'constant refrain', Ray neglected Thackeray's double-edged ironies that frequently rebounded as much on the hypocritical face-saving devices employed by the English as on the open amorality of the French.[13] Nevertheless Ray's mythopoeic biographical studies cast a long shadow.

Christopher Campos's 1965 survey of the French dimension in Victorian literature assigned a chief place to Thackeray, whom he held mainly responsible for the next 100 years of British conceptions of France, while also clinging to Ray's model of Thackeray as John Bull. Ignoring both Isabella Shawe's Irish descent and the Anglo-Indian origins she shared with Thackeray, Campos alleged that 'during his first stay' in Paris Thackeray had 'married the most English girl that he could find', and further opined, 'It is certain, looking back, that Thackeray wrote too much, and was at his worst on the subject of France.'[14]

R. D. Altick's massive study of the early years of *Punch, or the London Charivari* (1997) deepened the faultline Ray had introduced between Thackeray and the Parisian press, by distinguishing *Punch*'s absence of satirical agenda from both the crude raillery of Great Britain's radical press and the political animus of its Parisian namesake, *Le Charivari*. Frank Palmeri's 2004 article 'Cruikshank, Thackeray and the Victorian Eclipse of Satire' completed this tendency by adopting Altick's distinction between the radical satire possible in the England of 1815–25 and the milder comic commentary favoured in the 1840s, and wholly ignoring Thackeray's time in Paris. Instead, he ascribed Thackeray's change from savage caricaturist to the orchestrator of comedic harmony to the changing cultural codes of the English zeitgeist.[15]

It was left to Richard Pearson's *W. M. Thackeray and the Mediated Text* (2000) to throw much-needed fresh light on the significance of Thackeray's Parisian journalism. Pearson sees Thackeray's stint on the *Paris Literary Gazette* as a significant staging point in his developing awareness of the complex relations between author, text, and reader, and suggests that it taught Thackeray to present his subject matter in ways that avoided giving offence to the capital's colony of English expatriates. For Pearson, this explains the occasional embarrassing eruption of patriotism in Thackeray's writing, but he is hard pushed at times to describe—let alone account for—Thackeray's mercurial changes of attitude to either his host country or his own within the space of a single article. Concluding that his exilic writings remain

---

[12] G. N. Ray, *The Buried Life: A Study of the Relation between Thackeray's Fiction and his Personal History* (London: Oxford University Press, 1952), 22.

[13] G. N. Ray, *Thackeray: The Uses of Adversity (1811–1846)* (London: Oxford University Press, 1955), 245.

[14] C. Campos, *The View of France from Arnold to Bloomsbury* (Oxford: Oxford University Press, 1965), 89, 72.

[15] F. Palmeri, 'Cruikshank, Thackeray and the Victorian Eclipse of Satire', *Studies in English Literature* 44 (Autumn 2004), 753–77.

'always complex and ambivalent',[16] Pearson focuses more on Thackeray's obsessive interest in the act of writing itself than on ways in which he might have been influenced by the French press.

It is not merely Thackeray's exilic writings that readers have found discomforting: his attitude to Great Britain frequently betrayed the disenchantment of a man whose Anglo-Indian connections made him identify less readily with England than many of his peers, and may explain why he has never been taken to the nation's heart in the same way as Dickens. Foreign readers, by contrast, found useful ammunition in his critique: Russian critics of Thackeray's own day, for instance, variously held up his unflattering portrait of British materialism and corruption as proof of Great Britain's degeneracy, or used his social and political critique of the snobbery prevalent in England's aristocracy as a covert means of expressing their own anti-monarchical views.[17]

If Thackeray's irony, ambiguities, and changes of stance have made it difficult to discern a consistent set of attitudes or a clear developmental trajectory in his thinking, it may be because the criticism has relied on unhelpful models. The growing complexity that has characterized recent thinking about identity construction and perception may offer more useful insights for considering how an upper-middle-class English writer reacted to his exposure to French culture. Static, monolithic models of national societies have given way to increasingly dynamic models, exposing fluid boundaries, composed as much in terms of class or gender as territorial concepts. Once personal investment in nationality is perceived as a less uniform entity, so it becomes easier to acknowledge the characteristics nations share or their mutual borrowings, and to recognize possible tensions between the individual viewpoint and that of an assumed 'national' outlook. Applying a dynamic model to Thackeray might at the very least help us to think of his contacts with France as a process in which both writer and country were changing, and where personal and professional factors played as great a part as either British foreign policy or national prejudices.

Thackeray's decision in March 1837 to transfer his family and the centre of his literary operations to London, for instance, has frequently been attributed to his dawning realization of the changes to his life that becoming a family man entailed; but to equate this with a repudiation of French culture is to oversimplify. It is true that the disreputable protagonist of *The Memoirs of Barry Lyndon* refers to Paris as 'the only place where a gentleman can live as he likes without being incommoded by his wife', but the thought that London was a convenient distance from his antagonistic Irish mother-in-law, still based in Paris, was just as likely to have influenced Thackeray's choice.[18] In any case, once the decision to pursue a career in journalism had been made, London was a more advantageous base than Paris,

[16] R. Pearson, *W. M. Thackeray and the Mediated Text: Writing for Periodicals in the Mid-Nineteenth Century* (Aldershot: Ashgate, 2000), 52–3.

[17] S. Nuralova, 'W. M. Thackeray and his Cornhill Magazine in Russia: Nineteenth-Century Attitudes', *Victorian Periodicals Review* 35 (Fall 2002), 295–304.

[18] *Memoirs of Barry Lyndon*, Oxford Thackeray, vi, 273.

where the Anglophone press catering for the expatriate community would always experience a limited readership and poor pay.

Furthermore, as early as 1836 Thackeray had recognized one of the problems implicit in opting for a permanent position as a foreign correspondent: 'Perhaps,' he wrote in a despatch of November that year, 'from having resided so long in this country, I have caught the tone of French feeling rather than of English.'[19] The longer the posting, the more remote the journalist risked becoming from both his employers and his core readership. As is so often the case with Thackeray, this moment of apparent self-doubt was somewhat disingenuous, also operating in reverse to advertise the cultural credentials of the *Constitutional*'s Parisian correspondent. The return to London did not in any case make a sudden or definitive break: Thackeray's ability to represent French culture to an English readership depended upon keeping *au courant* with the ever-changing panorama of Parisian life. March 1838 therefore found Thackeray bound for a month in Paris, unaccompanied by either his wife or their first child.

Paris would never hold a monolithic identity for Thackeray because the personal circumstances of his encounters with the city were so varied. His first trip there in the long vacation of 1829 had been undertaken as a truncated version of the Grand Tour, appropriate to the young gentleman of means Thackeray and his family then had good reason to believe him to be. Accompanied by an older friend who was to tutor him in maths, Thackeray hired language tutors in both French and German, took dancing lessons, and viewed French art in the Louvre and at Versailles, all in the approved manner, but also discovered an addictive attraction to gambling on a visit to the elegant café and gambling house of Frascati's.[20]

His second visit, during the Easter vacation of 1830, was a brief, impromptu affair taken shortly before abandoning Cambridge without a degree. A four-month spell of gentlemanly idling in Paris from July to November of 1832 seems to have marked his coming of age and put paid to the further pretence of legal studies at London's Inns of Court. A brief period in the summer of 1833 as Parisian correspondent of the *National Standard* was succeeded by 'a very jolly time' studying painting in the Paris ateliers. Over these nine months gradual disenchantment set in with 'myself, and art, & everything belonging to it', and led instead to the more solitary pastime of 'lying on sofas reading novels, & never touching a pencil'.[21] From September 1834 to March 1837 Thackeray was essentially Paris-based.

Thackeray's contemporary accounts of his periods of residence in Paris in the days of the Citizen King were subsequently overlaid by his revisiting this life in his last completed novel, *The Adventures of Philip On His Way through the World; Shewing Who Robbed Him, Who Helped Him, and Who Passed Him By*. The novel by no means offers a transparent memoir. Complex interpretive cross-currents are created between the forgiving narration of the older writer, Pendennis; the hero's insistence on his own gentlemanly integrity maintained in the face of financial

[19] *The Constitutional*, 14 Nov. 1836, quoted by Pearson, *Thackeray and the Mediated Text*, 56.
[20] *Letters of Thackeray*, ed. Ray, i, 90–102.
[21] *The Letters and Private Papers of William Makepeace Thackeray: A Supplement*, ed. E. F. Harden (2 vols, New York: Garland, 1994), i, 14.

hardship; and the novel's title, which proclaims the hero a victim of circumstance rather than the agent of his own success. Thackeray's recasting of his years spent eagerly chasing fame through journalism may help to explain how two modern scholars have come to characterize this period of his life so differently. While John Sutherland has it that Thackeray 'slaved for most of the 1830s in the anonymous ranks of journalism', Richard Pearson represents him as having the time to look about him, taking a leisurely look at newspaper ownership—in contrast with Dickens, who was busy scuttling around London as a parliamentary reporter.[22] Nor did the re-publication under his own name of many previous journalistic articles in *The Paris Sketch Book* (1840) immediately secure his escape from 'the anonymous ranks of journalism'.

11.3 FINDING A DISTINCTIVE VOICE

Pearson's construction of a writer profiting from Paris's libertarian freedom to try out a series of varying authorial personas needs to be tempered by the notion of a young writer, at a formative period of his life, exposed in quick succession to the sometimes jarring discontinuities of the different lifestyles that Paris sustained. The penchant for playing one set of cultural assumptions off against another that was to become the hallmark of Thackeray's ironic manipulations of character and reader was fed by this challenging period. Writing from or about Paris, Thackeray was simultaneously trying to impress his Cambridge contemporaries (who by and large disapproved of this descent into ephemeral journalism), reassure the staid relatives and acquaintance of the British expatriate colony (where his mother and stepfather lived), and entertain English households with diverse political, moral, and social views.

Sometimes Thackeray's earliest Parisian articles written for the *National Standard* (a short-lived weekly paper of which he was editor) misfired because the tone of his reporting was so unstable as to leave readers mystified. Take, for instance, the report for 6 July 1833, which mainly focused on contemporary Parisian theatre. After the blistering sarcasm meted out to a blasphemously parodic version of Belshazzar's feast, playing at the Ambigu-Comique, it is almost impossible to know whether the concluding observation, 'It would be worth an English actor's while to come to Paris and study the excellent manner of the French comedians', should be taken at face value, despite extratextual knowledge that French and English theatre had developed very distinctive acting styles.

The equivocations and disconcerting moral ambivalences of which Thackeray has repeatedly been accused make an interesting comparison with the work of his direct Paris contemporary G. W. M. Reynolds, purveyor of sensation to the masses. Despite Reynolds's subsequent work as a radical campaigner, Karl Marx accused him of being a bourgeois, cynically pandering to the lowest taste of the working classes to line his own pockets, while a more recent critic, Anne Humpherys, has found it hard 'to

---

[22] *The History of Pendennis: His Fortunes and Misfortunes, His Friends and His Greatest Enemy*, ed. J. Sutherland (Oxford: Oxford University Press, 1994), viii; Pearson, *Thackeray and the Mediated Text*, 1.

separate sincere political expressions from clever careerism' in his work. She attributes Reynolds's success to an inability to resolve contradictions between his social
conformism and political radicalism, amounting to 'a kind of negative capability'
able to sustain multiple audiences.[23] She does not factor Reynold's Parisian experiences into her account, but it is not hard to recognize his kinship with Thackeray in
her diagnosis. Despite his already well-established radicalism, in 1835 Reynolds was
mindful of newly acquired family responsibilities and found himself required as a
literary editor to cater for the more conventional tastes of subscribers to the *Paris
Literary Gazette*: he had the good sense to recognize that Thackeray's gentlemanly
credentials would fit the bill. Thackeray, who later admitted that 'the first money he
ever received in literature...was from G. W. M. Reynolds', contributed eight articles
to the paper between October and December 1835.[24]

Securing a livelihood as a young journalist in the 1830s required a fine balanc-
ing act between jumping on passing journalistic bandwagons and avoiding mere
slavish imitation. Pearson is doubtless right to ascribe Thackeray's multiple journalistic personas of this period to the need to establish his own trademark on otherwise
anonymous articles, though it is also the case that employing different focalizers
allowed Thackeray to reuse the same material.[25] The much-overworked subject of
the Channel crossing and arrival in Paris, for instance, could be told from Titmarsh's
point of view in 'An Invasion of France', and also from the perspective of the valet,
Charles J. Yellowplush, in 'Foring Parts'.[26]

Thackeray also saw his July 1840 publication of a collection of pieces under his own
name as a significant milestone. He told his mother that he hoped *The Paris Sketch
Book* would prove to British publishers, such as 'Chapman & Hall Dickens's publishers', that he was fit for 'something better than that odious magazine-work'.[27] By such
means he hoped to assert the superiority of his ephemera to brief articles such as the
'Sketches of Paris', that Albert Smith had published the year before in the *Mirror of
Literature, Amusement and Instruction*—articles that, Smith proudly admitted in his
first piece, took their cue from the success of Dickens's formula in 'Sketches by Boz'.[28]

Dickens's meteoric success with *The Pickwick Papers* had suddenly made him into
the yardstick against which his generation started to measure their achievements.
In 1836 Thackeray was still based in Paris, but his prompt action in proposing
himself as replacement illustrator when Seymour committed suicide after the second number of Dickens's serial suggests how closely he was following the ups and
downs of London's press world, despite being still mainly based in Paris. Although
he did not secure this assignment, he did not leave his encounter with Pickwick
empty-handed.

[23] A. Humpherys, 'G. W. M. Reynolds: Popular Literature and Popular Politics', *Victorian Periodicals Review* 16 (1983), 79–88.
[24] J. Payn, *Some Literary Recollections* (London: Smith, Elder, 1884), 34.
[25] Pearson, *Thackeray and the Mediated Text*, 40–1.
[26] 'Invasion of France', *Paris Sketch Book, Oxford Thackeray*, ii, 1–13; 'Foring Parts', in *Memoirs of Mr. Charles J. Yellowplush, Oxford Thackeray*, i, 218–30.
[27] *Letters of Thackeray*, ed. Ray, i, 459.
[28] 'Sketches of Paris', by 'Knibs', *Mirror of Literature, Amusement and Instruction*, 12 and 19 Jan., 27 Apr. 1839.

Hard on the heels of the final double number of *The Pickwick Papers* in October 1837 followed Thackeray's creation of Charles Yellowplush in *Fraser's Magazine*, 16 Nov. 1837.

Yellowplush, the Cockney valet who accompanies his master, the blackguardly Honourable Frederick Deuceace, to Paris, owed more than a little to Dickens's worldly-wise Sam Weller. The valet's cockneyfied Franglais might have kept both Thackeray and his readers amused for longer had Thackeray not found himself almost immediately outflanked in December by the first episode of Reynolds's *Pickwick Abroad; or the Tour in France* (1837–8). By transporting the characters to France, Reynolds had effectively given the picaresque format of Dickens's novel a new lease of life. Not only did Reynolds thereby gain a clear advantage over less inventive plagiarisms such as Edward Lloyd's (1815–90) publication *The Penny Pickwick* (1837–9): but, where Thackeray's comic effects largely depended on a single linguistic device, Reynolds had a fuller range of Dickens's palette available to him.[29]

Thackeray in turn also seems to have taken something from Reynolds's version of *Pickwick*. The section of *The Book of Snobs* devoted to English swindlers prowling the French ports and Paris in search of gullible English tourists represents something of a turning away from the straightforward enjoyment of the cynical manoeuvres of Yellowplush and his master, to a tone more akin to Reynolds's sympathy with the exploited, as does chapter 36 of *Vanity Fair*, which deals with the capacity of Rebecca and Rawdon Crawley 'to live well on nothing a year' during their stay in Paris, a city shown at the mercy of a host of marauding English gamblers, debtors, and impostors who are wholly without conscience in their fleecing of French hoteliers, shopkeepers, and servants.[30]

Even if Thackeray was not drawing directly on Reynolds, both owed a clearly traceable debt to an immensely popular French source in the Paris of their day: the legendary Robert Macaire. Thackeray told the tale, in an early sketch, of the way in which this 'type of French roguery' had been fashioned by the actor Frederick Lemaître, who had transformed the villain of a lame 1823 French melodrama into a charming but ruthless swindler, whose many disguises made him a perfect figure for the French cartoonists Daumier and Philipon to use in satirizing the prevailing abuses of the period.[31] Reynolds published the novel *Robert Macaire in England* in 1840: it started with the villain, frequently referred to as 'our hero', committing a robbery in France from which he and his accomplice hope to benefit in England—a pertinent metaphor for Reynolds's own piratical practices.

If Reynolds was seduced by the comic energy of Macaire, Thackeray recognized both 'the rage and rapture' which met the French cartoonists' daring use of this figure to satirize 'no less a personage than the King himself'. It was this bifocal

---

[29] 25 chapters of *Pickwick Abroad* appeared in the *Monthly Magazine* 29 xxix (Dec. 1837)–xxv (June 1838), when it was abruptly withdrawn. Between Jan. 1838 and Aug. 1839 it was published in 20 monthly parts by Sherwood, Gilbert & Piper, achieving a weekly sale of 12,000. It was then reissued in 79 penny parts by Willoughby & Co. sometime in 1840: L. James, *Fiction for the Working Man 1830–1850: A Study of Literature Produced for the Working Classes in Early Victorian Urban England* (London: Oxford University Press, 1963), 53–4.

[30] 'English Snobs on the Continent', *The Book of Snobs*, *Oxford Thackeray*, ix, 385–8.

[31] 'Caricatures and Lithography', in *Paris Sketch Book*, *Oxford Thackeray*, i, 168–95.

vision, capable of arousing contradictory responses in the reader, that became the central structural plank of *Vanity Fair*, and made of Becky a consummate actress capable of knowingly exploiting her society's follies and vices. In *Vanity Fair* Thackeray also discovered a way of using his narrator to capitalize upon those sudden switches of perspective that had sometimes proved so disconcerting in his journalism. In the novel, he could pit a range of authorial personas and their varying social and moral perspectives against one another, and these deliberately staged discontinuities became a lynchpin of Thackeray's ironic manipulation of character and reader alike.

In the early 1840s, however, Thackeray's financial needs still occasionally drove him to contemplate using French material in ways that would scarcely have distinguished his voice from those of other old Paris hands. His letters to publishers in the early 1840s, when he was commuting between his London base and Paris, continued to teem with ideas for English spin-offs from French ventures. In a letter of 19 January 1843 to Chapman & Hall Thackeray rattled off the following list of such proposals: 'humorous-pathetic verse' to accompany the enclosed set of French illustrations to fairy tales; an article on 'The Paris Almanacks'; and a further one on 'Eugene Sues last novel Les Mysteres de Paris…with some such title as "Thieve's Literature in France [*sic*]'. [32,33]

Thackeray's diary entry for 6 January 1844 records him as engaged in translating Eugène Sue's immensely popular serial *Les mystères de Paris*, originally published in *Le journal des débats* during 1842–3.[34] The failure of Giraldon, the French publisher, to pay him promptly has usually been cited as the reason for Thackeray not completing this project. While this would certainly have been a contributory factor, the fact that six other translations became available in Great Britain in the course of 1844 would have acted as a further disincentive. The *coup de grâce* seems likely to have been the news that Reynolds was once again promising to outflank him and threaten damage by association, by publishing a year-long serial in penny numbers, beginning in October 1844, entitled *The Mysteries of London*. Although the title suggested that it was an adaptation of Sue's novel for English audiences, Reynolds's populist radical, aristocrat-bashing fiction was very different in tone from the French original, which had promoted social cohesion and pleaded for the sympathetic understanding of the sufferings of the poor in ways reminiscent of the agenda launched in England by Gaskell, Disraeli, and Kingsley later that decade.

Thackeray's subsequent canonical status, combined with Reynolds's increased identification with working-class movements and mass literature, has made it

[32] *Letters of Thackeray*, ed. Ray ii, 92. 'Thieves' Literature of France' appeared in *Foreign Quarterly Review* (31 Apr. 1843), 231–49; repr. in *Oxford Thackeray*, v, 459–80.

[33] The proposed verse was almost certainly designed to accompany illustrations by 'Cham' (Charles Amédée de Noé, 1818–79) for Charles Philipon's 1842 edn of Perrault's popular *Histoires ou contes du temps passé*, 1697. Thackeray apparently knew de Noé, a noted raconteur of Parisian gossip, well enough to host a breakfast and dinner for him during his 1848 visit to London: H. Vizetelly, *Glances Back through Seventy Years: Autobiographical and Other Recollections* (2 vols, London: Kegan Paul, Trench, Trübner, 1893), i, 286; *Letters of Thackeray*, ed. Ray, ii, 389–90.

[34] For Thackeray's references to Sue, see B. Chevasco, *Mysterymania: The Reception of Eugène Sue in Britain 1838–1860* (Oxford: Peter Lang, 2003), 140–56.

difficult to recognize what a thorn in the flesh Reynolds's extraordinarily rapid adaptations of other mens' ideas must have been for Thackeray. By 1848, when Thackeray was asked to give a speech to an assembly of literary men, his own recent success and Reynolds's very public move into radical politics as a member of the Chartist executive afforded Thackeray the opportunity to cast himself as a novelist and member of the literary set, rather than a mere journalist, and to distance himself simultaneously from Reynolds's populism and from his association with French revolutionary politics.

> But arriving at my own country, I beseech you to remember that there was a time, a little time ago, on the '10th of April last,' when a great novelist—a great member of my own profession—was standing upon Kennington Common in the van of liberty, prepared to assume any responsibility, to take upon himself any direction of government, to decorate himself with the tricolour sash, or the Robespierre waistcoat; and but for the timely, and I may say 'special' interposition of many who are here present, you might have been commanded by a president of a literary republic, instead of by our present sovereign...I don't believe that the country as yet requires so much of our literary men.[35]

11.4 LEARNING FROM THE FRENCH PRESS

Thackeray relied more on combing Parisian newsprint than on *vox populi* material or the press cohort for his journalism. In 1836 he wrote to his mother from Paris that it was 'the very reading of the papers' that preoccupied him: '[I]t is not what I send, but what I shall not send, that takes time;—I am very glad I have not been about for rumours, I am sure they only mislead.'[36] He rightly judged his own creative procedures to be notably slower than those of many other English journalists in the Paris corps.

Thackeray indeed took longer than many of his contemporaries in selecting, processing, and adapting new French print models for his own use. For instance, when he agreed to contribute three sketches to Douglas Jerrold's *Heads of the People; or, Portraits of the English* (1838–40), a serial publication sketching contemporary types, eventually published in two-volume form, Thackeray showed no signs of recognizing its relation to French typological literature. Martine Lauster argues that this was because between 1830 and 1850 such 'intermedial genre-painting and exercises in early sociology' formed a pan-European development, and cites Jerrold's collection as evidence that London was sometimes ahead of Paris in the development of its print culture. Despite the fact that the work of Jerrold and Meadows predated and, in translation, influenced the massive eight-volume *Les*

---

[35] Quoted in T. Taylor, *Thackeray the Humourist and the Man of Letters* (London: John Camden Hotten, 1864), 208–9. R. A. Colby reads this as a straight endorsement of Reynolds 'both as a man and an author' in *Thackeray's Canvass of Humanity* (Columbus: Ohio State University Press, 1979), 272, n. 65.
[36] *Letters of Thackeray*, ed. Ray, i, 321.

Français peints par eux-mêmes (1840–42)[37] and the German *Wien und die Wiener* version, serialized from 1841, two contributors who (like Thackeray) were old Paris hands clearly understood the project in relation to French typological literature of the period. Douglas Jerrold, in his sketch of a pawnbroker, interpreted his brief in a way that resonated with the analytical mode of the French *physiologies*, while Catherine Gore's portrait of the English débutante began by differentiating it from the characteristics the French would understand by this term. Although Thackeray's contributions, under his own name and in the persona of Michael Angelo Titmarsh, also featured generic types, they offered no allusions or comparisons to French equivalents, and he seems to have thought of this as a thoroughly English enterprise.[38] Nor did he contribute to the accompanying illustrations, which were all produced by Joseph Kenny Meadows (*c*.1790–1874).

By early 1841 Thackeray hoped to make his living by books, rather than journalism, before returning to his 'old painting mania'; but the bills he was facing for his wife's treatment in France meant a return to working as a Paris correspondent, so that the up-to-date textual material contained in the 422 instalments of *Les Français peints par eux-mêmes* was likely to have attracted him.[39] The claim made in the work's preface that the work should be viewed, not as ephemeral journalism, but as a treasure-house of information for future generations would have satisfied Thackeray's pretensions as a historian, while contributions by the likes of Balzac acted as a guarantee of the contributors' literary standing. However, the quality of the French publication's artwork seems to have proved an equal attraction. On his return to Paris, Thackeray told a correspondent that by March 1841 he had 'made seventeen engravings—that is 1 of the reasons I wish to continue here for a while to learn the mechanical parts of that profitable pleasant art'.[40] In the lists of contributors to the volumes of the 1841 Curmer edition of *Les Français peints par eux-mêmes*, equal typological prominence was given to illustrators and engravers.

Nor could Thackeray have failed to notice that some of the same artists who had contributed to *Les Français peints par eux-mêmes* were also benefitting from another publishing fashion, at its height between 1840 and 1842: the *physiologie*. The skills demanded were eminently transferable, since the initial run of *Les Français peints par eux-mêmes* and the *physiologies* shared urban life as their subject matter; the chief difference was that the latters' anatomies of urban types, occupations, and institutions adopted a comic tone, often parodying the remorseless sociological interest of the former, heavier-weight publication. By the peak of the *physiologies*' popularity it has been reckoned that about 120 of these pocket-sized booklets,

---

[37] By late 1838 *The Heads of the People* was already being serialized in Paris in translation under the title *Les Anglais peints par eux-mêmes*. Similarly, *Les Français peints par eux-mêmes* reached English readers in book form between 1840 and 1841 as *Pictures of the French: A Series of Literary and Graphic Delineations of the French Character*. M. Lauster, *Sketches of the Nineteenth Century: European Journalism and its Physiologies, 1830–50* (Basingstoke: Palgrave Macmillan, 2007), 42–3, 54, 76 n. 50, 276 n. 51.

[38] 'Captain Rook and Mr Pigeon', by William Thacker[a]y; 'The Fashionable Authoress' by William Thackeray; and 'The Artists' by Michael Angelo Titmarsh, in *Heads of the People, or, Portraits of the English* (2 vols, London: Robert Tyas, 1840–41), i, 305–20; ii, 73–84, 161–76.

[39] *Letters of Thackeray*, ed. Ray, ii, 9–10.

[40] *Letters of Thackeray: Supplement*, ed. Harden, i, 98.

each of 120 pages or so, and enjoying an average print run of 3,500, were achieving street sales of some 500,000, selling at one franc a piece to a population of about 1 million.[41] If at their finest these productions proudly displayed the names of the author, illustrator, and engraver, they were also related to the world of journalism. The *Collection des Physiologies* from the Maison Aubert came out of the same stable as the illustrated satirical daily paper *Le Charivari* (1832–1937), a less politically contentious successor to *La Caricature* (1830–35). These papers were both started by the bookseller Gabriel Aubert (1789–1847), in concert with his brother-in-law, the caricaturist, journalist, and sometime editor of both papers Charles Philipon (1800–1861), while Louis Huart (1813–65), who wrote some twenty-five of these *physiologies*, also did a spell as editor of *Le Charivari*. Gavarni (1804–66) and Honoré Daumier (1808–79), who had established reputations as painters, were two of the best-known illustrators of the *physiologies*, and were also regularly employed by these newspapers.

The values of the bourgeoisie under the reign of Louis-Philippe, the Citizen King interrogated by these Parisian caricaturists, readily translated into satire of middle-class English pretensions. Although both Altick and Lauster have been determined to establish an English genealogy for *Punch*, albeit through different antecedents,[42] it is hard to ignore the allusion to a Parisian forebear in the subtitle and the copied use of enterwined figures in the heading of *Punch, or the London Charivari*, when it was launched on 17 July 1841. It is indeed remarkable that the early *Punch* circle included Gilbert à Beckett, Douglas Jerrold, John Leech, the Mayhew brothers, Augustus and Henry, and Albert Smith, who had all studied, lived, or worked in Paris during the previous decade. À Beckett, and Henry Mayhew already behind them had *Figaro in London* (December 1831–9), another attempt at a cross-Channel satirical transplant, and throughout the 1840s many of this group of men continued to manifest a strong interest in the taxonomy of metropolitan life that they had found so abundantly displayed in the Parisian press.

In late 1842 Albert Smith claimed that he needed to drop the word 'physiology' from the title of his new series on 'The Medical Student' in *Punch*: he had 'borrowed it from France', but was dismayed by the 'crowd of imitators' this genre was attracting, particularly in the despised *New Monthly*.[43] Nevertheless, he proceeded to employ a translation of *physiologie* in the title of his best-seller, *The Natural History of the Gent* (1847), and edited the collection *Gavarni in London: Sketches of Life and Character* (1849). Douglas Jerrold's satirical fiction *A Man Made of Money* (1848) was modelled on Balzac's *Peau de chagrin*, the first of the gallery of types collected in his *Comédie humaine*. The Mayhew brothers produced a slew of comic novels in the vein of the comic urban anatomy before Henry took the sketch in a fresh direction in the engaged campaigning of *London Labour and the London Poor*.

---

[41] A. Zevin, 'Panoramic Literature in 19th Century Paris: Robert Macaire as a Type of the Everyday': <http://dl.lib.brown.edu/paris/Zevin.html>; Lauster, *Sketches*, 289.
[42] R. D. Altick, *Punch: the Lively Youth of a British Institution, 1841–1851* (Columbus: Ohio State University Press, 1997), 496–9; Lauster, *Sketches*, 39–40.
[43] *Punch* 3 (1842), 198.

Press historians have sometimes expressed surprise at the gap of six or seven years between the zenith of the *physiologies'* popularity in Paris and their appearance as a separately published genre in London; but in its early years *Punch* seems to have provided the convenient outlet for this interest shared by a group of men who were energetically involved in trying to make an individual mark and a regular income however they could. Douglas Jerrold launched two monthly papers, the *Illuminated Magazine* (1843–4) and *Douglas Jerrold's Shilling Magazine* (1845–8), followed by *Douglas Jerrold's Weekly Newspaper* (1846-8), in this period. From 1841 Gilbert à Beckett combined his continuing activities as a journalist and playwright with a legal career, and the Mayhew brothers, together and severally, were continually involving themselves in new ventures.

In mid-1842, when Thackeray joined this circle of men he had known in Paris, he also needed to take work wherever he could get it. Nevertheless, he told his mother that he wanted the connection kept secret, because although this new weekly offered 'good pay', and 'great opportunity for unrestrained laughing sneering kicking and gambadoing', it was 'a very low paper'.[44] *Punch's* editors and writers were unlikely to be subject to the frequent prosecution and periods of imprisonment suffered by Philipon and his colleagues, but, in England the association of satire with radical working-class journalism, or with the 'scandal and ribaldry organs' of the cheap Sunday press, denounced by Thackeray as worse than anything seen in the French press at its most licentious, lingered on.[45] Meanwhile Thackeray's former Paris colleague, Reynolds, a man with whose name, Dickens would claim towards the end of this decade, 'no lady's, and no gentleman's, should be associated', was providing new fuel for this particular fire.[46] Although Thackeray continued to work for 'the worthy Mr Punch, whose pay is more than double of that I get anywhere else',[47] a letter of February 1844 to Bradbury & Evans suggests the image he would prefer to have been developing.

> I have got a good public now, I should be glad to bring out a good stout book full of tales—reprints from Fraser—literary articles &c. with illustrations by myself…Or will you bring me to London and put me at the head of a slashing, brilliant, gentlemanlike, sixpeny, aristocratic, literary paper?—containing each week *good* reviews of a book or two, not notices: good novels in series: good theatrical articles &c.—a paper that should not look for a large but a gentlemanlike circulation: and have a decided air of white-kid gloves.[48]

Thackeray's lively sense of the discrepancy between the company he was keeping on *Punch* and the world of his aspirations eventually found its finest self-mockery in the picture of Captain Shandon penning the prospectus for the *Pall Mall Gazette*, 'written by gentlemen for gentlemen', from a debtors' prison.[49]

[44] *Letters of Thackeray*, ed. Ray, ii, 54.
[45] 'Caricatures and Lithography in Paris', *Paris Sketch Book, Oxford Thackeray*, ii, 173.
[46] *The Pilgrim Edition of the Letters of Charles Dickens*, ed. G. Storey et al. (12 vols, Oxford: Clarendon Press, 1965–2002), v, 603.
[47] *Letters of Thackeray*, ed. Ray, ii, 135.
[48] *Letters of Thackeray: Supplement*, ed. Harden, i, 144.
[49] *Pendennis*, ed. Sutherland, 410.

The *physiologies* held particular risks for those aiming at 'Gentlemanlike circula-tion' in the less egalitarian world of the English press. As Balzac's novels, and the *physiologies* alike suggested, the dissection of the urban scene offered an almost infinitely extendable panorama,[50] embracing the aristocracy at one end but also shading off into murkier underworlds of deprivation and vice at the other. The promiscuous blurring of boundaries afforded by urban streets, where a *grisette* might rub shoulders with a staid member of the bourgeoisie, was simultaneously fascinating and potentially contaminating, as Thackeray discovered when in 1841–2 he took on the mantle of 'a great wanderer about town' for a series of sketches in the weekly magazine *Britannia*, describing Parisians amusing themselves *en fête*.[51] In effect, while retaining his trade mark signature of Michael Angelo Titmarsh, he was taking on the role described that same year in Louis Huart's *Physiologie du flaneur* [*sic*], where amongst the categories of those who took their enjoyment in the free spectacles offered by the Parisian boulevards he included the *badaud étranger* (the idle onlooker as tourist). The opening paragraphs of the first article, 'A St Philip's Day at Paris', demonstrate Thackeray's deliberate attempts to inhabit the happy, non-judgemental sociability of the *flâneur*.[52]

> But let us take things as we find them: let us, contented with effects, not be too squeamish and curious about the causes. Here is the sun shining, the heavens fault-lessly blue, the leaves bright, the fountains playing, and five hundred thousand people happy. What can one want more?[53]

Such a pose held an attraction for Thackeray, who had every reason to distance his authorial persona from the husband and father plagued by the worry and expense of his wife's medical treatment and the breakdown of family life. The device was not entirely successful: the insouciant gaze dissolved by the end of the third article into an envious glimpse of the intimate happiness still possible for other families no matter how poor. Moreover, if boulevards *en fête* offered to protect him from domestic melancholy, they also rapidly exposed him to carnivalesque disorder, excess, and lawlessness: the first article proceeds by way of displaced beggars, gambling

---

[50] For the notable interest, post-1830, in observing and interpreting the social order of Paris, see section 5.1.2. Walter Benjamin and his disciples diagnose the *philologies* as simultaneously displacing sharper political protest and offering the illusion that the urban world was knowable and thus con-trollable. Miranda Gill has extended this notion of the genre's duality to an interpretation of its social function as both 'reassuring and orienting city dwellers' whilst also being capable of registering the novel and the ephemeral in city culture: *Eccentricity and the Cultural Imagination in Nineteenth-Century Paris* (Oxford: Oxford University Pres, 2009), 73. Critics such as Margaret Rose (*Flaneurs and Idlers* (Bielefeld: Aisthesis), 2007, 4) and Martina Lauster (*Sketches*, 3) have argued that this view fails to do adequate justice to the irony and knowing capacity for self-criticism that characterized the genre.

[51] 'A St Philip's Day in Paris' and 'Shrove Tuesday in Paris', *Loose Sketches*, *Oxford Thackeray*, iii, 461–507.

[52] Rose, *Flaneurs and Idlers*, Lauster, *Sketches*, and M. Gluck, 'The Flâneur and the Aesthetic: Appropriation of Urban Culture in Mid-Nineteenth-Century Paris', *Theory, Culture and Society* 20 (Oct. 2003), 53–80, all emphasize the error of conflating the happy 'sociable presence' of the inquir-ing city stroller with the later Baudelairean *flâneur*—by turn one of the crowd, an observer, and an artist—or with Walter Benjamin's more complicated interpretation of the Baudelairean figure.

[53] 'A St Philip's Day in Paris', *Oxford Thackeray*, iii, 485.

booths, and vendors of stolen goods on the Champs-Élysées, before the evening ends in drunken revelry and a missed train back from Saint-Cloud.

A further article, 'Shrove Tuesday in Paris', contains the famous recollection of an encounter at a masked ball, ten years previously, with Madame or Mademoiselle Pauline, a *grisette* (an independent working-class girl with bohemian morals), known to him formerly as 'a governess in a very sober, worthy family in England, where she brought up the daughters, and had been selected especially because she was *a Protestant*'.[54] The circumstantial detail in which this episode is recounted has caused it to be treated by Thackeray's biographers as straightforward autobiograph-ical confession. Ray claims that it was a 'censored version' of a personal encounter, while Harden's chronological record of Thackeray's life simply records as fact that in April 1830 'at a masquerade ball he is approached by a woman whom he had known as a governess for a respectable family in England, but who has become a Parisian grisette'.[55] Their 'evidence' for the assumption that Thackeray was up to no good on this trip would seem to rest on Thackeray's much later admission that he was guilty of having told his 'benighted parents' nothing about his sudden deci-sion to visit his friend Edward Fitzgerald in Paris, and that he had subsequently lied to his tutor about his whereabouts during the Easter vacation.[56] However, the nature of the detail Thackeray provides, plus the likelihood of this article coming to his mother's attention, makes it more likely that the portrait, like many another of Thackeray's, stemmed from contemporary literary sources which were then woven into the personal history of Thackeray's fictional persona, Titmarsh.

The figure of the governess, whose unverifiable continental references are an alibi for a disreputable past, is a stock device of mid-century fiction, designed to strike terror into the hearts of respectable middle-class readers lest their own fami-lies should unwittingly be harbouring such an employee. Both Frances Trollope's *The Robertses on their Travels* (1846) and Anne Brontë's *The Tenant of Wildfell Hall* (1848) feature a lover imported by the master of the house in the guise of a gov-erness, though the return in disguise of the heroine of Ellen Wood's *East Lynne* (1861) is probably the most famous example of this stereotype.

A dalliance with a *grisette* or with her close sister, the *lorette* (kept woman), at a carnival ball seems similarly to have been almost obligatory in accounts of Paris *en fête* by the 'many hundred English writers' Thackeray's Titmarsh admits have already described such a scene.[57] Reynolds's *Pickwick Abroad* described these masked balls as much frequented by foreigners because they were open to anyone who could afford the price of a ticket.[58] Albert Smith praised the dancing at such feast days precisely because it afforded an Englishman the opportunity of speaking

---

[54] 'Shrove Tuesday in Paris', 501.
[55] Ray, *Uses of Adversity*, i, 125; E. F. Harden, *A William Makepeace Thackeray Chronology* (Basingstoke: Palgrave Macmillan, 2003), 18.
[56] 'Desseins', in *Roundabout Papers, Oxford Thackeray*, xvii, 617; *The Letters of Edward Fitzgerald*, ed. A. M. Terhune and A. B. Terhune (4 vols, Princeton, NJ: Princeton University Press, 1980), i, 82.
[57] 'Shrove Tuesday in Paris', 499.
[58] G. W. M. Reynolds, *Pickwick Abroad: or, The Tour in France* (London: Sherwood, Gilbert, & Piper, 1839), 398–400.

to 'a pretty grisette'.[59] In 1831, the year after Thackeray's encounter allegedly occurred, Edward Planta's travel guide, subtitled *The Stranger's Guide to the French Metropolis*, suggests that such encounters at masked and fancy dress balls have already become a species of urban myth: 'The utmost order and decorum prevail, although it is said that many a young man has cause to lament the seducing acquaintance which he has formed at this ball.'[60] Evidence that these accounts created their own expectations can be found in a letter written almost twenty years later to Wilkie Collins from Charles Dickens in his apartment on the Champs-Élysées: 'Tomorrow week, a fête is coming off at the Jardin d'Hiver, next door but one here, which I must certainly go to, and which I should think can hardly fail to attract all the Lorettes in Paris.'[61]

An entire subset of the *physiologies* was devoted to taxonomies of the *grisette* and the *lorette*. It is difficult to determine exact publication dates, but each of the following appeared in either 1841 or early 1842. Aubert issued three works, each illustrated by Gavarni: *Physiologie du débardeur* and *Physiologie de la lorette* by Maurice Alhoy and *Physiologie de la grisette* by Louis Huart, and Jules Janin contributed 'La Grisette' to *Les Français peints par eux-mêmes*. They provide details of masquerade balls where women and men alike adopted the disguise of the *débardeur* (a docker unloading the rafts carrying timber down the Seine).[62] An illusion of specialized scientific analysis appropriate to the *physiologie* is maintained by a system of cross-referencing, so that when Huart alludes to a *débardeur* he refers readers to Alhoy's work.[63]

The distinctive features of Madame Pauline, Thackeray's ex-governess figure—her love of dancing, her readiness to pawn her gown to hire the dirty costume of a *débardeur*, her scraping a living as a needlewoman, and her temperamental preference for this happy-go-lucky way of life over the stricter habits that might have won her a bourgeois marriage, are all drawn from Huart's and Janin's catalogue of characteristics. Thackeray's description shared with Alhoy's account of the *débardeur* not only the Shrove Tuesday promenade of masqued actors following an oxen, and Alhoy's allusions to rustic versions of the Carnival, but also his emphasis on the annual rhythms of Carnival which end abruptly on Ash Wednesday, when the woman is driven to the pawn shop again, this time to barter the dirty trousers and oilskin hat of her *débardeur* disguise.

Typically the *physiologistes* sought to impart a sense of familiarity with the objects of their gaze, dramatizing the typology by giving names to the girl and her lovers, or presenting a case history. Alhoy and Huart both invent dialogues for their characters, and Janin presents the story of Jenny, the flower seller turned artist's model.

[59] *Mirror of Literature, Amusement and Instruction* 33 (19 Jan., 27 Apr. 1839).

[60] E. Planta, *A New Picture of Paris or, the Stranger's Guide to the French Metropolis* (London: Samuel Leigh and Baldwin & Cradock, 1831), 425.

[61] 19 Jan. 1856; *Letters of Charles Dickens*, ed. Storey et al., viii, 30.

[62] The *débardeur's* distinctive red sash, retained long after egalitarianism had erased many class-based clothing distinctions, rendered him a symbolic figure of working-class heroism, as evidenced in an 1839 comic melodrama, *Le débardeur, ou Le gros-caillou et Alger* by Paul de Kock and Valory, in which the eponymous hero's occupation has no relevance to the plot, other than indicating his staunchly honourable values.

[63] L. Huart, *Physiologie de la grisette* (Paris: Aubert, 1841), 87n.

Thackeray's portrait similarly ranges back and forth between the personal anecdote and a sense of the generic, taking us from glimpses of Madame Pauline's current accommodation in a seventh-floor apartment on Rue Neuve Saint-Augustin to the type: 'There are a hundred thousand Paulines in Paris, cheerful in poverty, careless and prodigal in good fortune, but dreadfully lax in some points of morals in which our own females are praiseworthily severe.'

However, Thackeray's device for personalizing the *grisette*'s history by incorporating her within the biographical backhistory of his persona, Titmarsh, presented a problem. The anecdotal flourish provided by Titmarsh's recollection of having met with her in England in her previous incarnation as a French governess may have been designed to offered a pleasurable frisson of the 'there but for the grace of God go I' variety to middle-class British readers, but for those unaware of this tale's literary antecedents, it was to implicate Thackeray rather too closely in the events of his alter ego's life. In sacrificing the protection of detached scientific interest ostensibly lent by the *physiologie* or 'natural history' in favour of verisimilitude, Thackeray was then confronted by the question of what a British readership would stomach. The contrast between the moral codes of France where 'a French gentleman thinks no more of proclaiming that he has a mistress than that he has a tailor' and the British preference for leaving such matters unmentioned was one to which Thackeray frequently returned.[64] He therefore sought to exempt the married Titmarsh from the harsh assumptions of English moralists by proceeding to justify his seeking out Madame Pauline in her attic apartment, claiming that he required her shirt-making skills. As he concluded his description of her, Thackeray fell back on the *physiologie* format of the urban typology to explain his departure from English norms and values, merging Pauline back into her genus as a 'type... quite unknown in England; it tells a whole social history, and speaks of manners and morals widely different from those which obtain in our own country.'[65] Thackeray's sense that British prudery would draw the line at an English gentleman, such as Titmarsh, openly proclaiming the kind of detailed, non-judgemental knowledge of a *grisette*'s lifestyle to be found in the amoral French *physiologies* drove him to provide the very fictional flourishes which ironically have led to a series of biographers viewing the 'Shrove Tuesday' article as an ill-concealed admission of a just such a youthful liaison in Thackeray's past.

11.5 ADAPTING FRENCH GENRES FOR THE ENGLISH MARKET

Like others of the *Punch* set who had worked in Paris, it was not until the later 1840s that Thackeray sought to adapt the *physiologie* recipe to English settings in works independent of the magazine's pages. His 1847 Christmas publication, *Mrs Perkins's Ball*, itemizing the guests at a London middle-class suburban evening-party, could

[64] 'On Some French Fashionable Novels', *Paris Sketch Book*, *Oxford Thackeray*, ii, 109.
[65] 'Shrove Tuesday in Paris', 502.

be seen as an adaptation of the Parisian *physiologie*. Certainly Albert Smith, who claimed to have been first on the scene with the *physiologie* in *Punch* in 1841, recognized it as such, complaining to 'Father Prout' that 'he, Albert Smith, had "done it all before" in various sketches of evening parties'.[66] Smith and Thackeray's mutual aversion, the subject of much literary gossip by contemporaries and biographers, has a particular relevance to following the way in which Thackeray sought to profit from his Paris years while simultaneously distancing himself from the taint of having kept 'low' company and absorbed vulgar literary habits there.

The origin of this hostility has been attributed to Thackeray assuming Smith's place at the *Punch* table, when Smith was banished in 1843, either for showing proofs to rival journalists or for being detected in an unacknowledged plagiarism from a French piece.[67] Henry Vizetelly, who did not hesitate to accuse the later Thackeray of becoming a 'tuft-hunter', could nevertheless understand why a man 'who had an abhorrence of things vulgar, found Smith's mauvais goût more than he could stand'. Smith's 'unpleasant falsetto voice', and his habit of declaring his own work superior to Shakespeare's, may have been unattractive,[68] but far more significant was the way in which this apothecary's son, with his flaunted French sympathies, threatened Thackeray's sense of journalism as compatible with gentlemanliness. It was probably not by chance that Thackeray's journalist hero, Pendennis, is frequently required to engage in salutary looks in the mirror provided by a vulgar, ill-educated apothecary's son from his home town who eventually marries the *grisette* with whom Pendennis has enjoyed a brief flirtation. Looked at as an attempt to translate the *grisette* to an English setting it was not successful: though he strove to make Fanny part *naïf* and part minx, his reluctance to offend readers by allowing the hero anything beyond an ill-advised flirtation with her led him into an unsympathetic debate between the moral prudishness of the hero's bourgeois mother and the laissez-faire attitude of the hero's worldly-wise uncle.[69]

In 1840s London, Smith continued to behave as though he were still living the bohemian life of the Parisian medical student, championing the vulgar romances of Paul de Koch,[70] or 'caper[ing] to some masked ball in the guise of a Gavarni *débardeur*...or a booted and bewigged French postilion, dancing energetically till daylight with some fourth rate actress of whom he had become temporarily enamoured'.[71] Worst of all, Smith made all too clear his view of journalism as a trade rather than a gentlemanly pursuit. In the days when anonymity was in vogue, he refused to publish anything without his own name under it, and, in chatting with other journalists, thought nothing of taking out his notebook and asking whether a fellow writer wanted this or that item. If he did, it was all the

---

[66] H. S. Edwards, *Personal Recollections* (London: Cassell, 1900), 39.

[67] Ray, *Uses of Adversity*, i, 349. Arthur à Beckett found the latter rumour unlikely: 'I remember as a boy that every dramatic author went to Paris for inspiration, and never thought of making the slightest reference to the colleague on the other side of the Channel': *The à Becketts of 'Punch': Memories of Father and Sons* (Westminster: Archibald Constable, 1903), 256–7.

[68] Vizetelly, *Glances*, i, 317–19.   [69] *Pendennis*, ed. Sutherland, 687–91.

[70] Paul de Kock was treated as 'a literary pariah' by serious French critics like Janin: H. S. Edwards, *Personal Recollections* (London: Cassell, 1900), 75.

[71] Vizetelly, *Glances*, i, 315.

same as he would see it the following week under Smith's name in the *Illustrated London News*.[72] His open contempt for the *noblesse oblige* Thackeray held dear was displayed by having a 'lithographic circular' printed, when he began to make money as a lecturer, 'embodying the trite remark that "—loan often loses both itself and friend"'.[73]

It must have been galling for Thackeray to know that he was drawing from the same well as Smith, and later in life Thackeray reputedly admitted to hating his own series of character typologies, begun in *Punch* in February 1846 under the title *The Book of Snobs. By One of Themselves*.[74] The prefatory note, stating that '*Snobs are to be studied like other objects of the Natural Sciences*', made apparent their debt to the physiological vogue of social analysis. The second part of Thackeray's title had the double advantage of alluding to the more heavyweight *Les Français peints par eux-mêmes* and of associating the author with the royal and aristocratic circles with which his series of typologies began, rather than with the parvenu Spangle Lacquer family and other cockneyfied denizens of Smith's 'Natural Histories'.[75] A final proof that, despite the best efforts of a succession of Thackeray scholars to search elsewhere for antecedents to *The Book of Snobs*, contemporaries recognized its French provenance is Henry Vizetelly's evidence. On behalf of David Bogue, a publisher renowned for importing French lithographs, Vizetelly, the house's printer and engraver, approached Thackeray—'a single chapter of whose "Snob papers" contained more wit than any half-dozen of Albert Smith's'—with the proposition that he write as many 'physiologies' as he chose' for a prospective series, 'at the price of one hundred guineas each'.

> This being double the amount Thackeray was then receiving for a monthly part of 'Vanity Fair' (including the etching of a couple of plates),[76] he frankly admitted that the offer was a tempting one, but he eventually declined it, by reason of his strong disinclination to ally himself with anything that Albert Smith was connected with.

Personal antipathy aside, Thackeray seems to have judged rightly that Smith's close association with the genre had reduced its literary standing. In Vizetelly's opinion, the comparatively poor sales of *Gavarni in London* (1849), a collection of twenty-two urban sketches edited by Smith, who also contributed a third of the contents, could partly be explained by Gavarni's illustrations being 'too much of a French character', but was mainly because other famous names, known for their facility in the genre, followed Thackeray's lead and 'drew back... from the strong objections they had to writing for any publication edited by Albert Smith'.[77]

Bogue's proposal offered Thackeray easy money for reworking a familiar genre, but lending his name once again to a collective enterprise could not advance his

---

[72] Edwards, *Personal Recollections*, 188.

[73] Vizetelly, *Glances*, i, 322.   [74] Ray, *Uses of Adversity*, i, 380.

[75] A. Smith, *The Natural History of Stuck-Up People* (London: Ward & Lock, 1847).

[76] Thackeray was in fact paid £60 a part for each serialized portion: N. Pickwoad, 'Commentary on Illustrations', in P. L. Shillingsburg (ed.), *Vanity Fair: A Novel without a Hero* (New York: Garland, 1989), 641. He also probably stood to make more money from the publication of the completed novel in volume form than the collected *physiologies* could guarantee.

[77] Vizetelly, *Glances*, i, 317, 339.

career, in ways that the early episodes of *Vanity Fair* appeared to be doing. By January 1848, Thackeray felt confident enough to tell his mother, 'I am become a sort of great man in my way—all but at the top of the tree: indeed there if the truth were known and having a great fight up there with Dickens.'[78]

Far from pursuing very different routes from fellow Paris correspondents, arriving at the formula for *Vanity Fair* had involved Thackeray in picking his way very carefully between alternative models for indigenizing French material. Reviewing Catherine Gore's two-volume *Sketches of English Character* (1846) for the *Morning Chronicle*,[79] while he was writing the early episodes of *Vanity Fair*, he noted that her portraits of Cabinet ministers, diplomatic attachés, the hapless English tourist abroad, and their servants provided 'a good guide book' to Pall Mall and its ways, but lamented the book's characteristically French lack of moral feeling: 'If it be as here represented, the world is the most hollow, heartless, vulgar, brazen world, and those are luckiest who are out of it.' The counterpointing of the detached amorality of the French, with the sentimental idealization of domestic life practised by the English, formed both theme and structural foundation for *Vanity Fair*, when he first offered it to Bradbury & Evans under the title, *The Novel without a Hero: Pen and Pencil Sketches of English Society*.

In *Vanity Fair* Thackeray tackled the problem of accommodating French literary typology within an English context head on. Becky Sharp, the product of a dissolute English drawing-master's marriage to a French soubrette, and so endowed with the ability to deploy her French expertise to advance herself in English society, is a shockingly knowing, or 'sharp', example of hybridity. Thackeray's habit of using Becky for self-reflexive commentary on his own artistic practices extends to this aspect of her life.[80] A sufficiently good actress to mimic the code of behaviour of whatever company she finds herself in, she discomforts the reader by half-inhabiting and half-challenging each national stereotype. Thus the grateful charity pupil turned governess, of English mythology, nurses Napoleonic sympathies, and although her career may follow the pathways mapped out in the French *physiologies* for the good-humoured little *grisette*, Rebecca is emphatically pronounced not 'in the least kind or placable'.[81]

Becky's childhood function as precocious muse to her father's Bohemian set is a perverted version of the role of atelier playmate and model enjoyed in her leisure time by Huart's *grisette*. Despite scheming to rise to heights undreamed of by her Parisian counterpart, Rebecca's instinct for carnivalesque pleasure remains that of a Parisian working girl. Like Madame Pauline, of whom Thackeray had written, 'A grisette she was, and a grisette she would be; and left dreary Londres...for her quarters, habits, and companions, and that dear old gutter in the Rue du Bac of which

[78] *Letters of Thackeray*, ed. Ray, ii, 333.

[79] 'Mrs Gore's *Sketches of English Character*', *Morning Chronicle*, 4 May 1846; repr. in *William Makepeace Thackeray's Contributions to the* Morning Chronicle, ed. G. N. Ray (Urbana: University of Illinois Press, 1955), 139–42.

[80] A. Byerly, *Realism, Representation, and the Arts in Nineteenth-Century Literature* (Cambridge: Cambridge University Press 1997), 56–85.

[81] *Vanity Fair: A Novel without a Hero*, ed. J. Sutherland (Oxford: Oxford University Press, 1991), 14–15.

Madame de Staël has spoken so fondly', Becky, at the very height of her success in London society, inwardly yearns for a gaudier, carefree life: 'oh, how much gayer it would be to wear spangles and trousers, and dance before a booth at a fair.'[82] Titmarsh's speculation that, had Madame Pauline, the *grisette* he encountered at the Shrove Tuesday masked ball, continued as a French governess in an English family she might well have been able to marry either the son of the family or a widowed employer, surely informs the incident in *Vanity Fair* where Becky's marriage to Rawdon involves her in a moment of genuine regret at having missed the chance of becoming his stepmother.[83] After the Steyne debacle, Becky tries out each of the endings to a *grisette*'s career detailed in Huart's *Physiologie de la grisette*. After the age of 30 there were no *grisettes*, Huart declared: some became *lorettes*; others made bourgeois marriages to merchants whom they tyrannized; and those who achieved neither of these outcomes became pious.[84] Becky's days of Continental wandering, squired by dubious rogues, her domination of the Indian nabob Joss Sedley, followed by her final apotheosis as devout churchgoer, precisely follow Huart's recipe.

Thackeray's illustrations also showed their debt to the Parisian urban sketch industry. By the time that it had become clear to Thackeray that he was unlikely to make his name or fortune as a watercolourist, the talent for caricature that he had enjoyed since childhood was gaining French illustrators, such as Cham, Daumier, and Gavarni, commissions and fame aplenty. The writers who supplied the text for French *physiologies* openly admitted that they served in a secondary capacity to their illustrators.[85] Seen against this background, Thackeray's oft-quoted remark that, had Dickens accepted his services to replace Seymour as illustrator for *Pickwick Papers*, he would never have taken up writing as his profession, takes on a less self-abasing tone; indeed, he may well have been more taken aback by Dickens's refusal of his services than his later retelling of the incident suggested.[86] Having come across from Paris expressly to arrange for the publication in both cities of his series of captioned lithograph caricatures of neoclassical balletic poses, *Flore et Zéphyr* (1836), he might reasonably have assumed that the art and writing would at least enjoy equal status in such a partnership.

Thackeray was every bit as much a 'snapper-up' of other men's 'unconsidered trifles' in his art as in his writing. His first published illustration (Fig. 7), a caricature of Louis-Philippe in the *National Standard* of 4 May 1833, depicting a stout gentleman, equipped with an umbrella rather than a sword, accompanied by verses, simply echoed the criticisms of Louis-Philippe's despotic greed being levelled at him by a host of French caricaturists.[87,88] Thackeray's lengthy 1839

---

[82] 'Shrove Tuesday in Paris', 502; *Vanity Fair*, ed. Sutherland, 636.

[83] Ibid. 185.   [84] Huart, *Physiologie de la grisette*, 109–14.

[85] e.g. M. Alhoy, *Physiologie du débardeur* (Paris: Aubert, 1842), 10.

[86] L. Melville, *The Life of William Makepeace Thackeray* (2 vols, London: Hutchinson, 1899), ii, 182–3.

[87] E. C. Childs, 'The Body Impolitic: Press Censorship and the Caricaturist Honoré Daumier', in D. de la Motte and J. M. Przylblyski (eds), *Making the News: Modernity and the Mass Press in Nineteenth-Century France* (Amherst: University of Massachusetts Press, 1999), 43–81.

[88] Philipon's famous caricature in *Le Charivari* of 17 Jan. 1832 ensured that 'caricatures of him were visible on house walls or in comic prints. His face, in the shape of a pear, was on every available

LOUIS PHILIPPE.

[*See page* 17.

Fig. 7. 'Louis Philippe', illustration by W. M. Thackeray, *National Standard*, 4 May 1833.

essay 'Parisian Caricatures' amply demonstrated the impression the artwork of the Parisian press had made on him. There he listed the major lithographers practising in Paris, describing the '*loisirs* of these men of genius' as infinitely superior to English 'finikin performances of laboured mediocrity'. It was here too that he spoke of 'pondering over' the Philipon and Daumier 'Macaire Picture

spot that could be reached with a piece of coal': J. Crowe, *Reminiscences of Thirty-Five Years of My Life* (London: John Murray, 1895), 11. Later that year Sébastien-Benoît Peytel (a name well known to Thackeray: see 'The Case of Peytel; in a letter to Edward Briefless, Esquire, of Pump Court Temple', *Paris Sketch Book, Oxford Thackeray*, ii, 251–79) published *Physiologie de la poire*, which counted on readers making the necessary connection to discern the message of his political satire depicting the erstwhile regal duc d'Orléans posturing, in his role as Citizen King, as representative of the urban bourgeoisie.

Gallery' for 'some hours'.[89] In view of this, it seems surprising how keen critics have been to place his illustrations as well as his writing in a definitively English satirical tradition, working back through Cruikshank and Gilray to Hogarth. Thackeray indeed alluded to these British artists in a lengthy tribute to Cruikshank's work in the *Westminster Review* of 1840,[90] but the essay, acknowledging his school-boy debt to the artist, also judges him to have reached his peak in 1825. In his 1839 article Thackeray had already declared Daumier the superior caricaturist and nothing he later wrote or said would appear to have undermined this position.[91] *Vanity Fair*'s 'motifs of clown, puppet show, and children's pantomime', as Robert Colby reminds us, were part of the recurrent iconography of recent *Punch* editions, but that again returns us to a shared European inheritance in the pages of the Parisian press and the older traditions of the *commedia dell'arte*.[92]

The hybridity or transnational cross-fertilization at work in Thackeray's illustrations for the novel are clearly displayed in the title page for the first edition of *Vanity Fair* in book format (Fig. 8), with its picture of a melancholy fool, gazing at his own reflection in a cracked mirror and lounging 'before the curtain' on an impromptu travelling stage, which in turn frames a provincial English scene with a twin-towered church at its heart. The following comment from Thackeray's *Westminster Review* essay on Cruikshank suggests what he had learned, or appropriated, from his youthful admiration for the English artist:

> The little glimpse of the church seen through the open door of the room is very beautiful and poetical: it is in such small hints that an artist especially excels; they are the morals which he loves to append to his stories, and are always appropriate and welcome.

In Thackeray's illustration, however, the nature of Cruikshank's moral reference is complicated by being intertwined with French symbolic devices. The central figure, often described as a harlequin but wearing a cockscomb, indicative of foolish vanity, above his skull-cap, is markedly different from the jester, with his wide ruff and ass's ears, portrayed on the wrapper of the monthly numbers (Fig. 9). The figure on the new title page has more in common with the pierrot, the pathetically deluded lover brought to prominence by the popular performances of the mime artist Jean Gaspard Deburau (1796–1846), at the Théâtre des Funambules in Paris, subsequently immortalized in the film *Les enfants du paradis* (1945).[93] The jester, raised on his tub, apparently preaching to the crowd, has given way to the silent

[89] 'Caricatures and Lithography', *Paris Sketch Book*, *Oxford Thackeray*, ii, 193.

[90] *Westminster Review* 34 (June1840), 1–60; repr. in *Oxford Thackeray*, ii, 407–92.

[91] Cf. 'Cruikshank's Gallery', *The Times*, 15 May 1863; repr. in *Oxford Thackeray*, ii, 719–23. F. Locker-Lampson, *My Confidences: An Autobiographical Sketch Addressed to my Descendants*, ed. A. Birrell (London: Smith, Elder, 1896), 299.

[92] R. Colby, 'Historical Introduction', in P. L. Shillingsburg (ed.), *Vanity Fair*, ed. Shillingsburg, 629; Lauster, *Sketches*, 54–7, 164.

[93] Thackeray expressed his preference for watching Deburau over attending classical French tragedy in 'French Dramas and Melodramas', and accompanied the essay by a sketch entitled 'The Gallery at Deburau's Theatre Sketched from Nature': *Paris Sketch Book*, *Oxford Thackeray*, ii, 291, 303.

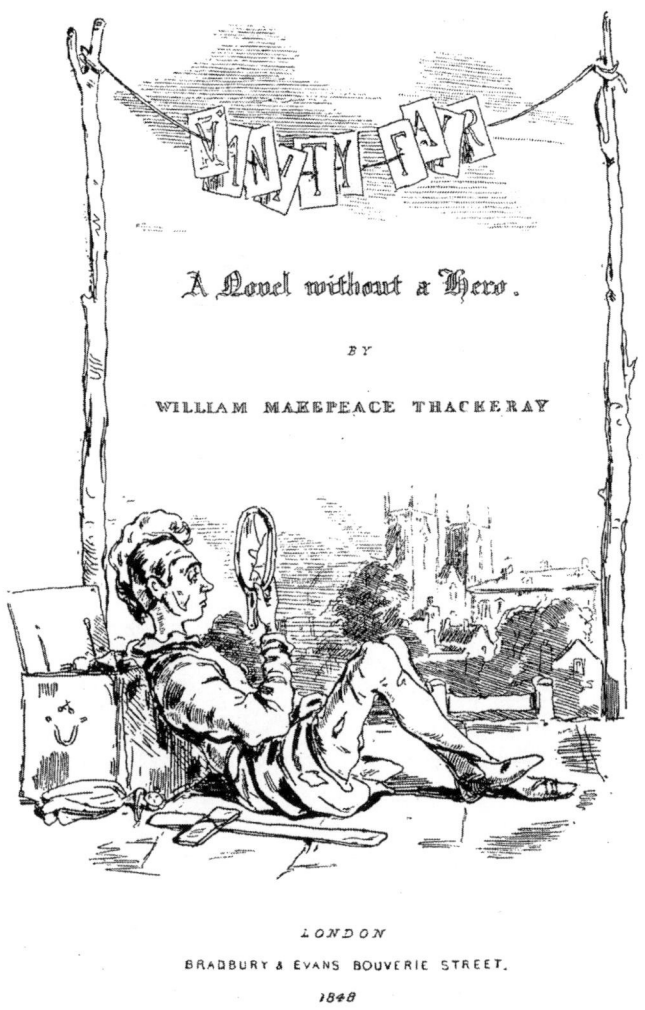

[*Facsimile of title-page to the first edition.*]

Fig. 8. Title page design by Thackeray for the first edition of *Vanity Fair* in book format.

self-communing of the pierrot, who ignores both the consolations of the discarded cross to his left and the sturdy values of a national church rooted in parochial custom suggested by the scene glimpsed beyond the stage. The behaviour of the novel's Revd Bute Crawley and his wife suggest that the pierrot is right to avert his gaze, but this does not fully exhaust the implications of Thackeray's juxtaposition of visual codes here, playing off a world of faith and stability against the impermanence of theatrical illusion, and calling upon the well-known French maxim: 'The

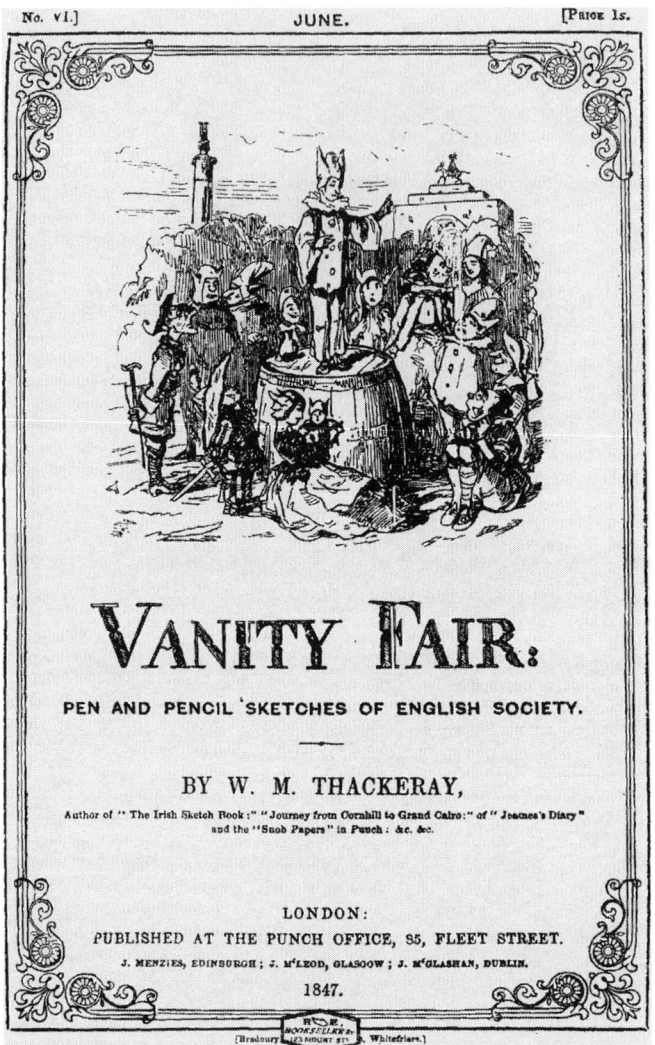

Fig. 9. Thackeray's wrapper design for *Vanity Fair* as first published in monthly parts.

world is full of fools, and he who would not see it should live alone and smash his mirror'[94] to make his final cynical pronouncement.

As issued in serial form, the novel had concluded with the pictorial conceit of the characters as doll-size puppets being returned to their box (Fig. 10), and it is this same box that forms the uncomfortable support for the prostrate form of the crumpled pierrot resting from his labours in the new title page illustration.

---

[94] Adapted from an axiom in *Discours satiriques* (1686) by Claude Le Petit.

Fig. 10. Illustration by Thackeray following the last paragraph of *Vanity Fair* in both serial and volume format.

The concept of his characters as puppets was allegedly suggested to Thackeray by a friend as the novel was nearing completion in June 1848,[95] but his chosen way of representing this idea once again strongly recalls a French source. The end-piece of the first volume of *Les Français peints par eux-mêmes* had depicted the collector of this panorama of social and moral types as a Gulliver-size figure popping the Lilliputian figures back into their wicker basket (Fig. 11)—an image that may well have prompted Thackeray to think further about the missing figure of the writer and illustrator and so to devote the new prologue to the first edition of the novel to his own role as 'Manager of the performance'.

Thackeray's closing image of children packing their small puppets away scarcely seems to belong to the world of *Vanity Fair*, but this, together with the novel's abrupt concluding paragraph, smack of his exhaustion at having to provide fourteen illustrations for this last episode, in a month when he had also undertaken a further ten, unrelated illustrations for *Punch*. Under this strain Thackeray seems to have borrowed fairly extensively. The final plate, showing Rebecca, Lady Crawley tending her 'booth in Vanity Fair' (Fig. 12), bears a marked resemblance to the composition of Archibald Henning's illustration for a similar scene in Albert Smith's *The Natural History of Stuck-Up People* (1847) (Fig. 13). Vizetelly

---

[95] E. Crowe, *Thackeray's Haunts and Homes* (London: Smith, Elder, 1897), 55–6.

Fig. 11. The final illustration in the first volume of *Les Français peints par eux-mêmes* (1841).

claimed that Henning was considered a 'vulgar' artist, but Thackeray was none too fussy where he took his initial inspiration.[96] Although the scene must have been a Victorian commonplace, the similar positioning of the figures suggests that he may also have developed the earlier plate of Becky entangling Joss (Fig. 14) from the same source (Fig. 15)—a theft which would have left him time to extemporize the witty framing device he provided for the scene.

The strongest influence on Thackeray's illustrations for *Vanity Fair*, however, was that of the Frenchman Gavarni (the nom de plume of Sulpice Guillaume Chevalier, 1804–66), and was to be seen in the novel's characteristic feature of starting each chapter with an illustrated capital letter. Illustrated capital letters were in themselves nothing new—indeed, alphabet books of majuscule characters flooded the Victorian market—but Gavarni had made them into something of a personal trademark, claiming that he typically launched himself on new projects by covering a woodblock with initial letters and fantastic designs.[97] Where fellow illustrators for *Les Français peints par eux-mêmes* would insert an illustration

[96] Vizetelly, *Glances*, i, 316.
[97] H. Tucker, 'Literal Illustration in Victorian Print', in R. Maxwell (ed.), *The Victorian Illustrated Book* (Charlottesville: University of Virginia Press, 2002), 163–208; Edwards, *Personal Recollections*, 94.

VIRTUE REWARDED: A BOOTH IN VANITY FAIR

Fig. 12. 'Virtue Rewarded: A Booth in Vanity Fair', final plate by Thackeray in *Vanity Fair*.

to the side of the letter, Gavarni's device of forcing the reader to disentangle the two in order to discern the letter focused the reader's attention on his drawing. Encountering Meissonier's opening capital for 'Le Viveur' (Fig. 16), the eye drifts swiftly through the group of men to find the 'L' that completes the opening word, 'La'. Gavarni's design for the initial capital of the essay 'La Grande Dame de 1830' (Fig. 17) is intended to strike the eye as a contrast between the grandeur of the assembly shown in the headpiece illustration and the simplicity of the shield emblazoned with two crossed pens and a pen-wipe, surrounded by humble items such as a smoking tallow candle and loaves of bread. This enacts the point

Fig. 13. Illustration of a charity fair, by Archibald Henning, in Albert Smith's *The Natural History of Stuck-Up People* (1847).

being made in the article that the *grande dame* of mid-nineteenth-century France is a very different matter from her aristocratic forebear. The nineteenth-century woman has risen, often from humble origins, on the back of her husband's political career. Her grandeur is a matter of surface polish, and, in place of the largesse distributed by her pre-Revolutionary predecessor to the needy, once a year she plays the stall-keeper, for which her bourgeois instincts suit her, forcing her

MR. JOSEPH ENTANGLED

Fig. 14. 'Mr. Joseph Entangled', plate by Thackeray in *Vanity Fair*.

guests to purchase items such as pen-wipes manufactured by her daughter and herself.[98] It also seems likely that the motif with which this capital is illustrated

---

[98] The constant performance required of the woman who must both embody high fashion and act with calculated simplicity is predicated upon the sense that money and social approbation, unlike the privilege of birth, can disappear at any time. These elements of the stereotypical 'femme à la mode', together with a 'masculine' heartless ambition (analysed in Gill, *Eccentricity*, 85) can also be detected

Fig. 15. Illustration by Archibald Henning of a young man holding a skein of silk for a lady, in Albert Smith's *The Natural History of Stuck-Up People* (1847).

gave Thackeray the idea for his version of the Thackeray coat of arms, where he surmounted the shield with a crossed pen and brush, and at the base placed his characteristic signature of a pair of round spectacles (Fig. 18).[99]

Gavarni did not invariably illustrate his capitals in this way, but something of the distinctive style he achieved can be seen by comparing his illustration for Chapter 14 of Louis Huart's *Physiologie de la grisette* (Fig. 19), with Meissonier's perfunctory effort (Fig. 16), which simply places the relevant capital alongside, rather than integrating it.

In Gavarni's illustration, by contrast, the tipsy angle of the opening capital 'T', the wine bottle, the suggestion of a table set for meal but covered with hastily discarded attire, the shadows behind the 'Cabinets' sign, all tell their own story in response to the question the chapter addresses: 'Is a grisette more faith-

feeding into Becky Sharp's capacity to transform herself from darling of the *salons* to charity stallholder.

[99] My dating for this heraldic device is based on Lewis Melville giving 1843 as the date for Thackeray's first known usage of the spectacles device: *Life of Thackeray*, ii, 189.

Fig. 16. J.-L. E. Meissonier's illustrated initial capital for 'Le Viveur' in the first volume of *Les Français peints par eux-mêmes* (1841).

Fig. 17. Gavarni's illustrated initial capital appears below Gagniet's headpiece for 'La Grande Dame de 1830' in the first volume of *Les Français peints par eux-mêmes* (1841).

ful than other women?' Fig. 20, by comparison, shows a capital illustration from Huart's *Physiologie du flaneur* [*sic*], variously illustrated by Alophe, Daumier, and Maurisset, where the initial 'D' is quite simply superimposed on the picture. Thackeray's fellow English illustrators seem generally to have followed the dominant mode of planting the illustration next to the relevant capital, as Henning does in Fig. 21.

In keeping with the hybrid practices he employed in the prose text of *Vanity Fair*, Thackeray both employed the standard English approach and tried his hand at Gavarni-like capital letters. My confidence in asserting Gavarni's influence was considerably increased by discovering Henriette Corkran's recollection of

Fig. 18. Thackeray's design for his personal 'coat of arms', reproduced on the cover of L. Melville, *The Life of William Makepeace Thackeray* (2 vols, London: Hutchinson, 1899).

Thackeray's admiration for ' "G." . . . a clever draughtsman', and his striving for Gavarni's effects. Not only did she know Thackeray as a child but, having herself studied in a Parisian atelier, she had a trained eye in such matters.[100] It has to be admitted that for all Thackeray's 'striving', his majuscules are rarely either as conceptually sophisticated or as well-executed as his French counterpart's, but in studying two fairly typical designs for the letter 'S', the reader's eye is invited to linger and decipher meaning. The first (Fig. 22) echoes Chapter 9's title, 'Family Portraits', in presenting a sketch of Sir Pitt Crawley, seated in the upper portion of the 'S' but always poised to slip to the lower regions in search of the pitcher: an apt representation of his membership of the landed gentry and his preference for below-stairs company and entertainment. The second 'S' illustration (Fig. 23) at first seems strikingly at odds with Chapter's 24's title, 'In which Mr. Osborne takes down the Family Bible'. Nevertheless, the diminutive figure resonates both with the mock-heroic opening sentence in which Captain Dobbin prepares 'to perform the rest and most difficult part of the task which he had undertaken', wrestling with the mighty dragon of Mr Osborne's wrath, and, more seriously, with Dobbin's reminder to Mr Osborne of 'the great and certain risk that hangs

---

[100]　H. Corkran, *Celebrities and I* (London: Hutchinson, 1902), 107.

Fig. 19. Gavarni's illustrated initial capital for chapter 14 of L. Huart, *Physiologie de la grisette* (1841) (by courtesy of the Getty Research Institute, Los Angeles (1558–274)).

Fig. 20. An illustrated capital from Louis Huart, *Physiologie du flaneur* [*sic*] (1841), variously illustrated by Alophe, Daumier, and Maurisset, (by courtesy of the Getty Research Institute, Los Angeles (2911–378)).

Fig. 21. Archibald Henning's illustration inserted beside the initial capital for chapter 3 of Albert Smith's *The Natural History of Stuck-Up People* (1847).

over every one of us' as the army awaits its imminent orders to embark for the Continent.[101]

Such examples, though not as well known as those depicting Becky and her machinations, suggest how Thackeray had profited from those hours in Paris spent 'pondering over' French cartoonists' work. *Vanity Fair* speaks to the profound impression the typographical devices of the French press had made on Thackeray when he was learning his skills as both writer and illustrator. It is one of the ironies of literary history that Galignani's, the firm that had once employed Thackeray in Paris, ran *Vanity Fair* as their pirated serial in the *London and Paris Observer: Journal of English and Foreign Literature, Science, and the Fine arts* during 1847–8, unaccompanied by any illustrations.

---

[101] *Vanity Fair*, ed. Sutherland, 278.

Fig. 22. Thackeray's illustrated initial capital 'S' for chapter 9 of *Vanity Fair*.

Fig. 23. Thackeray's illustrated initial capital 'S' for chapter 24 of *Vanity Fair*.

In demonstrating the debts Thackeray's mature fiction owed to the Parisian print culture he had come to know in the early stages of his career, this chapter forms a bridge between the world of the Paris correspondent considered in the last four chapters and the final section of this book, which turns to British fictional representations of mid-nineteenth-century Paris.

PART III

THE FICTIONAL FORMATTING OF PARIS

The first two sections of this book have tended to use literary material with comparatively little attention to differentiating between the genres in which it was found. The final section of this book addresses the aesthetics of British fictional representations of Paris more directly. Fiction will be broadly conceived in this section to include articles written under a fictive persona, but will exclude drama, which would require expertise in nineteenth-century theatrical conventions on both sides of the Channel.

If, as Part II demonstrated, the techniques and practice of journalism experienced extensive change over the middle decades of the nineteenth century, so did the sections of the publishing world devoted to the production of fiction. As a junior branch of literature, never subject to the constraint of rules derived from classical antiquity, fiction was particularly marked by the fluidity between genres characteristic of the print culture of the 1830s and 1840s. Authors who wrote for a living learned to move back and forth between the production of occasional articles, both informative and satirical, travel writing, or guidebooks, incorporating many of these genres, which literary histories have often tended to treat as discrete, within their fiction. Chapter 12 briefly indicates the relevance of the swift democratization of the literary marketplace for the fictional representation of Paris, while Chapters 13 and 14 categorize the fictional subgenres and stereotypical formulas characteristically employed by mid-nineteenth-century British writers.

12

The democratization of British fiction

The period covered by this book saw the rapid expansion of the literary market-place, increasingly diverse modes for publishing fiction, and the growth of a broader and more diverse readership. This chapter briefly considers the ways in which these factors influenced the fictional representation of Paris.

12.1 THE SIGNIFICANCE OF DEMOCRATIZATION

Although the mid-nineteenth century has traditionally been considered one of the richest periods in the evolution of British fiction, publishers with a keen eye to the market also exerted a contrary pressure in favour of mining previous success rather than encouraging innovation. The story of the young Mary Elizabeth Braddon being offered £10 by a printer in Beverley for a tale combining 'the humour of Dickens with the dramatic quality of G. W. M. Reynolds' offers a telling example of this tendency.[1] The propensity such advice encouraged to splice successful for-mulas into new hybrid forms meant a constant leakage between subgenres, inci-dentally making it almost inevitable that the taxonomy attempted in the next chapter will occasionally include a work under more than one category.

Thackeray identified a further force at work encouraging writers to settle for a limited range of basic plotlines, stock scenes, and stereotypical characters when attempting representations of Paris. In an imaginary conversation with Mr Punch, his commissioning editor, Thackeray tries to sell him further accounts of foreign travels and is roundly put down: 'Have you lived so long in this our country as not to know that Britons do not care a fig for foreign affairs? . . . In print as in art,' Mr Punch reminds him, 'The British public like to see representations of what they have seen before!'[2] As so often, Thackeray's irony here is double-edged, directed as much at the imagined reader as the publisher. Part of *Punch*'s appeal as a comic threepenny weekly directed at the middle classes was that it could afford to exchange knowing winks with readers who enjoyed seeing the faults of their own class exposed.

As magazines had multiplied so they had became more fiercely competitive and anxious to please a particular section of the market. G.W. M. Reynolds's choice of

[1] M. Sadleir, *Things Past* (London: Constable, 1944), 72.
[2] 'Sketches and Travels in London; Introductory', *Punch*, 20 Nov. 1847; repr. in *Miscellaneous Contributions to 'Punch'*, *Oxford Thackeray*, ed. G. Saintsbury (17 vols, London: Oxford University Press, 1910), viii, 180–1.

the *Monthly Magazine* as the vehicle for *Pickwick Abroad* was, for instance, an astute choice in that it had been in the *Monthly Magazine* that Dickens had placed much of his early work before the phenomenal success of *Pickwick Papers* as a stand-alone part publication. Reynolds could therefore reasonably anticipate an audience already acclimatized to this fictional brand and receptive to 'more of the same'. *Pickwick Abroad* did indeed improve the magazine's circulation, though Reynolds failed to predict that the shameless plagiarism and piracies to which Paris had accustomed him would lead to the abrupt termination of both the serial and his contract by the magazine's proprietors.

The chequered history of Reynolds's novel, which progressed to publication in separate monthly parts after it was curtailed as a magazine serial, and subsequently appeared both in penny parts and between hard covers, all within the space of two years, is a reminder of the very different classes of purchaser who might access a popular work of fiction. Meanwhile, the middle decades of the nineteenth century also witnessed educational changes which had a bearing on the audience whom an author anxious to maximize his sales could anticipate, and this in turn influenced the use of the French language within fiction depicting Paris.

12.2 THE USE OF THE FRENCH LANGUAGE IN FICTION REPRESENTING PARIS

Bilingual dictionaries, updating earlier eighteenth-century volumes or marking out fresh territory, multiplied rapidly during this period; but the appearance of those only offering Franco-English translation, together with guidebooks listing useful French phrases, suggests there were probably increasing numbers of readers who had not received French as part of their education.[3] Indeed, when the first French–English pocket dictionary, measuring 4×2 inches and containing 340, 000 words was published in Paris in 1873, Mark Twain dubbed it the 'church of the gratis lesson'. Perhaps it was the work's democratizing force that the Communards recognized when they granted a permit for the manuscript to be removed to a place of safety after it had narrowly escaped destruction during the siege of Paris when the next-door house was shelled.[4]

In the early part of the nineteenth century, modern languages, normally taught by a governess or tutor, had formed one of the requisites of an accomplished gentleman or gentlewoman, and it was expected that a young man of Thackeray's class would hire a language tutor on his first trip to Paris.[5] Knowledge of French therefore became increasingly desirable to the aspirational middle classes: the Brontë

---

[3] C. Marello, 'Bilingual Dictionaries of the Nineteenth and Twentieth Centuries', in A. Cowie (ed.), *The Oxford History of English Lexicography* (2 vols, Oxford: Clarendon Press, 2009), ii, 86–104, 89.

[4] J. E. Bellows, *John Bellows, 1831–1931: A Biographical Sketch and Tribute* (n.p., 1931), 11.

[5] Cf. J. Austen, *Pride and Prejudice*, ed. P. Rogers (Cambridge: Cambridge University Press, 2006), 43. *The Letters and Private Papers of William Makepeace Thackeray*, ed. G. N. Ray (4 vols, Cambridge, Mass.: Harvard University Press, 1945–6), i, 95.

sisters were, for instance, convinced that good French would be necessary to the success of their projected private Yorkshire boarding school. Meanwhile, a stream of French exiles seeking to earn a living ensured that French featured on the curriculum of England's burgeoning number of private schools: modern languages, for example, featured strongly in the private education provided during the 1840s for Samuel Beeton by his publican father, and for Samuel's future wife, Isabella, by her stepfather, a printer and clerk of the Epsom racecourse.[6]

By the closing decades of the century knowledge of French would seem to have ceased to act as a clear social marker. In 1886 the *Pall Mall Gazette,* under the crusading editorship of W. T. Stead, was to deplore the 'cheerful optimism' that 'the people of England are not likely to be corrupted by literature published in a language they do not understand', since 'the schoolmaster is abroad and every clerk and shopboy knows enough French to pick out the obscenity in a pornographic pamphlet'.[7] The rapidity with which these shifts took place led to an interestingly varied range of decisions as to the advisability of using French within Anglophone fiction. The choice seems to have been variously determined by the social background of the author, the target readership, the type of publication, and the publisher.

When the hero of Bulwer Lytton's silver-fork novel *Pelham: or, Adventures of a Gentleman* (1828) reaches Paris, like Thackeray, he is swift to hire a language tutor, and the first edition of the novel is sprinkled with untranslated French quotations and phrases, along with the Latin tags a man of his class would have acquired during his schooling. However, as part of her son's educational programme, the hero's cynical aristocratic mother advises:

> You will also be careful, in returning to England, to make very little use of French phrases; no vulgarity is more unpleasing. I could not help being exceedingly amused by a book written the other day, which professes to give an accurate description of good society. Not knowing what to make us say in English, the author has made us talk nothing but French. I have often wondered what common people think of us, since in their novels they always affect to pourtray us so different from themselves. I am very much afraid we are in all things exactly like them, except in being more simple and unaffected...This is the chief reason why our manners are better than low persons: ours are more natural, because they imitate no one else; theirs are affected, because they think to imitate ours; and whatever is evidently borrowed becomes vulgar.[8]

In 'good society' the ability to read French literature and write grammatically correct French, rather than fluency, was what counted. Bulwer Lytton claimed that it was a mark of the English aristocracy that few spoke French either accurately or elegantly; he himself favoured the *salons* of the Faubourg Saint-Germain partly because his French hosts often spoke immaculate English whereas he 'expressed

[6] K. Hughes, *The Short Life and Long Times of Mrs Beeton* (London: Harper Perennial, 2005), 65–6, 70, 85–6.

[7] [W.T. Stead,] 'Occasional Notes', *Pall Mall Gazette,* 5 Nov. 1886.

[8] [E. G. E. L. Bulwer-Lytton,] *Pelham: or, the Adventures of a Gentleman* (3 vols, London: Henry Colburn, 1828), 104, 232–3.

[himself] awkwardly', preferring to reply to his French interlocutors in English.[9] Even in *The Parisians*, a novel of the 1870s, he felt the need to explain the ease with which his English hero communicates in French society by attributing it to a former spell at the British Embassy.[10]

Nevertheless, Bulwer Lytton's preface to the 1849 edition of *Pelham* made it clear that he was all too aware that his novel of twenty years back was appearing in an altogether changed climate: 'The popular changes in the Constitution have brought the several classes more intimately into connection with each other', and while, 'We have not talked of equality, like our neighbours the French', cheap books now existed 'not written down to the supposed level of uninformed and humble readers, but such books as refine the gentleman and instruct the scholar'.[11] In keeping with this recognition, the text of the 1849 edition included a footnote announcing that the frequent quotations in Latin and French would be translated 'for the convenience of the general reader', except when they involved untranslatable puns or where the context made the meaning clear. Quite what the new class of readers whom the 1849 edition of *Pelham* was intended to embrace made of Bulwer Lytton's satire on the bankrupt ethics of a Regency aristocratic milieu it is hard to guess, since he claimed, in his 1840 preface to the novel, that its initial critics had often failed to perceive his ironies.[12]

Catherine Gore, a successor in the silver-fork school of fiction, was altogether less certain as to whether her novels were designed to satirize or offer painstaking lessons in the manners and argot current in the best society. Anxious to demonstrate her own cosmopolitan credentials, Gore has a character involved in the diplomatic world of *The Ambassador's Wife* inform the reader, 'The aristocracies of all the countries in Europe are of one and the same nation.... People of rank and fortune eat, drink, dress, dance, and talk French, all over the world.'[13] In *Greville, or a Season in Paris*, the reader is told that it is sheer idleness that prevents Fred Massingberd, her specimen of an idle English traveller with vulgar tastes, from learning sufficient French to pen an apology for being unable to attend a dinner given by French hosts. Diligent readers are offered revision lessons to update their conversational knowledge: while '*un lion*', as used by the French, is different from the London meaning of 'lion', so '*un lion*', they are informed, is now fossilized slang and as much out of date as '*muscadin, -incroyable, -merveilleux*'.[14] Gore's cultural capital is further on display in the untranslated French quotations appearing at the heads of chapters, and in a series of intertextual allusions to French literature.

A fellow silver-fork novelist, Lady Charlotte Bury, displays a greater unease both about her target audience's facility in French, and indeed their attitude to the

---

[9] E. R. Bulwer Lytton, *The Life and Literary Remains of Edward Bulwer, Lord Lytton* (2 vols, London: Kegan Paul, Trench, 1883), i, 366; L. Mitchell, *Bulwer Lytton: The Rise and Fall of a Victorian Man of Letters* (London: Hambledon Continuum, 2003), 151.

[10] Lord [E. G. E. L. Bulwer-]Lytton, *The Parisians* (2 vols, London: George Routledge, 1875), i, 56.

[11] E. G. E. L. Bulwer-Lytton, *Pelham, or, the Adventures of a Gentleman* (London: Chapman & Hall, 1849), pp. xv, 11.

[12] E. G. E. L. Bulwer-Lytton, 'Preface to the Edition of 1840'; repr. in *Pelham* (1849), pp. x–xii.

[13] C. Gore, *The Ambassador's Wife* (3 vols, London: Richard Bentley, 1842), ii, 44.

[14] C. Gore, *Greville: or, a Season in Paris* (3 vols, London: Henry Colburn, 1841), i, 131; ii, 157; iii, 93.

French themselves. Anxious to emphasize the impeccable upbringing and inno-cence of the English heroine of *Family Records* (1841), she reveals that, having learned her French solely 'from books', this new wife finds conversational French with her husband's former Parisian friends difficult. In the effort to convey the awful 'Frenchness' of the husband's former mistress, the Comtesse de Rambouillet, Bury peppers the Comtesse's talk with untranslated French phrases; but when a letter from the mistress is important for the plot, she reminds her readers that the recipients of this letter 'read the following words in French', though the text is actually given in English.[15]

By the second half of the century fiction clearly directed at women, such as Henrietta Jenkin's novel *Once and Again* (1856), whose story is concerned with the disastrous effects of a bad relation between an indigent middle-class English mother and daughter, did not baulk at including an entire letter in French. The accompanying narrative commentary, it is true, would have made its gist clear, but the author's desire to offer a little language tuition en route to upwardly mobile readers still emerges in conversations such as the following between a French mother and son:

> 'If you don't marry her, he will. Trust a woman's penetration: our cousin is in love with Mdlle. Louisa.'
> The French expression was more forcible. 'Nôtre cher cousin est féru. Acceptes, tu hériteras à cause d'elle.'[16]

Thackeray, unsurprisingly, given his acute consciousness of the class gap between his own sense of his gentlemanly background and the varying expectations of the publishing outlets he used, was very varied in his usage. He was well aware of the gentlemanly convention that poor written French was the mark of an inferior education: excursions into French in his own letters to friends would sometimes include a pre-emptory apology for unintentional faux pas. It was perhaps Thackeray's uneasy sense that his behaviour was not quite going to be that of an English gentleman that caused him to employ French when he decided to declare himself to his friend Brookfield's wife.[17] On the other hand, Thackeray was undoubtedly irked by the boorish ignorance on occasion displayed by his com-patriots, and frequently portrayed the average Englishman abroad as a 'brutal ignorant, peevish bully', wholly incompetent at communicating in French, and bolstered in his sense of superiority by 'never speak[ing] to any native above the rank of a waiter or shopman'.[18] Yet fluency in spoken French was equally suspect. It is Becky Sharp's too perfect French that pronounces her part-French parentage, distinguishes her from the other pupils at the Miss Pinkertons' academy for young

---

[15] Lady C. Bury, *Family Records; or, The Two Sisters* (3 vols, London: Saunders & Otley, 1841), ii, 248; iii, 22.

[16] [H. Jenkin,] *Once and Again: A Novel* (3 vols, London: Smith, Elder, 1865), ii, 228–31.

[17] *The Letters and Private Papers of William Makepeace Thackeray: A Supplement*, ed. E. F. Harden (2 vols, New York: Garland, 1994), i, 244–6.

[18] 'Continental Snobbery Continued', in *The Book of Snobs, Oxford Thackeray*, ix, 383; *The Adventures of Philip, Oxford Thackeray*, xvi, 298.

ladies, and enables her to earn her living as a governess.[19] Thackeray's fictional alter ego, Philip Firmin, despite having (like his creator) lived in the Latin quarter, worked as an Anglophone journalist, and 'had occasion to speak a little French', found 'it never came very trippingly from his stout English tongue. "You don't suppose I would like to be taken for a Frenchman he would say with much gravity." '[20]

Writing an article in 1839 for the six-shilling quarterly the *London and Westminster Review*, Thackeray was on safe ground in assuming an audience sufficiently interested in Parisian mores to be capable of understanding continuous passages in untranslated French.[21] The more heavyweight periodicals of the day often carried a regular section reviewing foreign literature. His mid-1840s articles for *Punch* were more cautious, demanding only a minimal level of familiarity with French words and phrases: his articles on 'Continental Snobs', for instance, drop French expressions for things and roles into the text, either where they had no one-word English equivalent (e.g. *estaminets* and *cabarets*) or where the meaning is fairly transparent (e.g. 'a brazen-looking, tawdry French *femme-de-chambre* (none but a female pen can do justice to that wonderful tawdry toilette of the lady's maid *en voyage*).'[22] As early as 1838 he had recognized that endowing his Cockney servant, Yellowplush, with Franglais would simultaneously indicate the lad's aspirations and differentiate him from G. W. M. Reynolds's Samivel Weller, whose exploits in Paris had only just finished their serialization.

If his story of joining the National Guard is to be believed, Reynolds's colloquial French was almost certainly better than Thackeray's, and as narrator he remarks the generational differences between an old Frenchwoman's scarcely intelligible *patois*, her soldier son's more accessible use of language, and her grandchild's good command of grammar.[23] However, given the readership at which he aimed, Reynolds was wary about the prospect of alienating monoglot readers. Where he employs French to provide a little local colour in *Pickwick Abroad* (1837–8) he also tactfully includes a translation, as in the following example.

> "*Silence, Messieurs!*" exclaimed one of the town-serjeants fiercely, while the other twirled his moustachios and looked very much like a savage bear in the Garden of Plants in Paris.
>
> "*Appellez l'interprete!*" cried the Commissary of Police; and in five minutes the interpreter made his appearance.

Such comedy as Reynolds derives from linguistic misunderstanding is skilfully manipulated so that its arrows are deflected away from the reader. An episode set in a restaurant simultaneously ridicules Francis Coghlan's *A Guide to France, or,*

---

[19] W. M. Thackeray, *Vanity Fair: A Novel without a Hero*, ed. J. Sutherland (Oxford: Oxford University Press, 1991), 14, 356.

[20] *Adventures of Philip*, 448.

[21] 'Parisian Caricatures', *London and Westminster Review*, Apr. 1839, 282–305; republished as 'Caricatures and Lithography', in *Paris Sketch Book*, *Oxford Thackeray*, ii, 185.

[22] 'Some Continental Snobs', in *The Book of Snobs*, *Oxford Thackeray*, ix, 376–80.

[23] G. W. M. Reynolds, *Alfred de Rosann: or, the Adventures of a French Gentleman* (London: J. W. Southgate, 1839), 78.

Travellers their own Commissioners for failing to provide phonetic equivalents for the useful dining-out phrases it included, and manages to teach the correct pronunciation in the course of the scene: phonetics were to form the first item in the instruction manual, *The French Self-Instructor* (1846), that Reynolds himself published. In *Pickwick Abroad* only characters such as Weller Senior, to whom even his son Samivel condescends, are mocked for their invincible deafness of ear, and a typical episode in which he confuses 'cocher' with 'cochon' is there as an excuse for more of the plentiful fisticuffs on which the novel thrived.²⁴

Dickens was enormously keen to master French himself and to ensure his children received a good grounding.²⁵ 'MON AMI, he wrote to John Forster, 'je trouve que j'aime tant la République, qu'il me faut renoncer ma langue et écrire seulment le langage de la République de France—langage des Dieux et des Anges [My friend, I find myself liking the Republic so much that I must renounce my own language and only write in the language of the Republic—the language of gods and angels].²⁶ His decision not to employ French in his fiction therefore seems very deliberately tailored to his desire for a wide audience. The narrative commentary in *A Tale of Two Cities* reminds readers that the exiled Darnay, though he might have achieved a university post by the mid-nineteenth century, would previously have depended for a living in England on being paid by young men with sufficient 'leisure and interest' to hire his services as a French tutor.²⁷ In both *A Tale of Two Cities,* and the Marseilles prison scene that opens *Little Dorrit,* Dickens adopted the device of producing pedantically literal English translations of dialogue supposedly uttered in French, and it can presumably only have been the fear that the phrase 'Quartier Latin' smacked of privileged knowledge that led to its substitution by 'the Student-Quarter of Paris' in the second edition of *A Tale of Two Cities.*²⁸

In Dickens's fiction, learning French is often associated with crude ambition. Carker, the villain of Dickens's *Dombey and Son* (1847), has worked to become a proficient linguist, speaking French 'like an Angel—or a Frenchman' only so that he can penetrate all the secrets of his employer's merchant-shipping firm.²⁹ By contrast, Sydney Carton, the languid hero of *A Tale of Two Cities*, reminds Stryver, the pointedly named barrister for whom he devils, 'Even when we were fellow-students in the Student-Quarter in Paris, picking up French, and French law, and other French crumbs that we didn't get much good of, you were always somewhere, and I was always—nowhere.'³⁰

However, Sala's novel *Quite Alone,* serialized in *All the Year Round* only four years after Dickens's *A Tale of Two Cities,* was almost belligerent in its use of untranslated

²⁴ G. W. M. Reynolds, *Pickwick Abroad: or, The Tour in France* (London: Sherwood, Gilbert, & Piper, 1839), 35, 280–1, 537–8.
²⁵ *The Pilgrim Edition of the Letters of Charles Dickens*, ed. G. Storey et al. (12 vols, Oxford: Clarendon Press, 1965–2002), iv, 669.
²⁶ *Letters of Charles Dickens*, ed. Storey et al., v, 256.
²⁷ C. Dickens, *A Tale of Two Cities*, ed. A. Sanders (Oxford: Oxford University Press, 2008), 124.
²⁸ Ibid. 381, n. 86.
²⁹ C. Dickens, *Dombey and Son*, ed. A. Horsman (Oxford: Clarendon Press, 1974), 292, 721.
³⁰ Dickens, *A Tale of Two Cities*, ed. Sanders, 85–6.

French, and the French slang in the denunciatory rants of the characters who people its trans-Channel demi-monde and milieux of tawdry artistes makes no pretence at educating readers. Sala undoubtedly enjoyed showing off his familiarity with a Paris well outside the experience of the average British tourist, and was knowing enough to rely upon the capacity of bad language to titillate readers into their own acts of translation.

———

The examples given above suggest that the decision of whether, how much, and how to use French in fiction relied quite heavily upon the writer's judgement of the expectations or linguistic ability of his or her target audience. This capacity to assess the education and cultural interests of one's likely readership became all the more important as fictional subgenres proliferated, and the next chapter will turn to the choice of fictional format or mould faced by British novelists intent on representing Paris.

13

Fictional subgenres

Drawing on both French and English nineteenth-century fictional models, this chapter offers a taxonomic guide to the most frequently used subgenres for representing Paris.

13.1 A NARROW FICTIONAL PALETTE

> Can we, while discussing English fiction, quite ignore fiction written in other languages? particularly French and Russian? We could ignore it, for our writers have never been much influenced by the Continentals.[1]

The swift expansion of British cities during the nineteenth century was accompanied by a growing literary interest in the distinctive nature of urban experience. The radical shift in population from the countryside to the cities, and the consequent alterations that took place in hierarchical structures, familial relationships, and neighbourly intimacies, provoked debates and emotions that eventually touched every genre. The theme proved so pervasive in fiction that when it came to considering Paris, British novelists tended to adapt models that already lay to hand to the business of variously representing, critiquing, or satirizing the French capital. Yet, because Parisian urban development was very different from the British—less piecemeal, more *dirigiste*, and productive of very different types of urban accommodation and lifestyle—by no means all of the swiftly burgeoning subgenres of nineteenth-century English urban fiction proved appropriate to the Parisian experience. This comparatively restricted palette contributes to the sense English Parisian fiction so often induces of being in a world of narrow, and thus frequently exaggerated, variations on a few set themes.

The counterpointing of closely observed family life with larger economic, social, and religious rhythms which formed so marked a feature of English fiction in the mid-nineteenth century proved beyond the capacity of most British novelists to translate into a Parisian context. Since *intra muros* Paris did not confront visitors with the size and scale of the factory-based industries that had mushroomed in England's northern cities, British writers were more likely to meet servants, artisans, and shopkeepers than to inquire into the living conditions of the immigrant labour involved in Paris's flourishing recycling and construction industries. It

---

[1] E. M. Forster, *Aspects of the Novel* (Harmondsworth: Penguin, 1971), 14–15.

was therefore difficult, if not impossible, to set up the contrasts between crowded streets or poor working conditions and the welcoming serenity of the ideal familial hearth that formed part of the underlying critique of urban alienation in English fiction. In imagining a salvific alternative to the chaos and terror of revolutionary Paris for a French family in *A Tale of Two Cities*, Dickens was driven to the recourse of a secluded house in London's Soho.

Nor could the likes of Gaskell or Dickens summon up the kind of emotional or intellectual investment in the life of this foreign city that drove the reforming animus in their novels of British urban life. Gaskell observed both Protestant and Catholic Parisian charity in action but, acknowledging herself out of her depth in any real grasp of French labouring conditions, referred her readers to French sociopolitical authorities.[2] Dickens confined himself to comparing individual national organizational features, such as the disposition of French and English abattoirs.[3] Bowled over as they often were by the dramatic signs of the French state's powers to bring about rapid, visible change in Paris, appeals to the transformative powers of the individual may have seemed almost beside the point.

Vizetelly's journalistic forays of 1868 into the shanty dwellings of the dispossessed and the ghettos of immigrant workers had little chance of provoking a Zolaesque turn in British fiction, partly because the events of the Commune swiftly intervened to refocus English attitudes to such areas as breeding grounds for anarchy and discontent.[4] As the third chapter of this book suggested, British fictional portraits of the Commune, whatever their political hue, came from middle-class pens that found it difficult to see the Parisian Communards as people with individual life histories and family connections. Anne Thackeray Ritchie had briefly been in the midst of the fighting, but readers of *Mrs Dymond* are distracted from a comparably tense fictional moment by the back-story of Papa Caron, whose profit-sharing schemes as a benevolent employer can only be explained by referring readers to real life Frenchman Edmé Jean Leclaire (1801–72). Meanwhile Caron's former workmen are reduced to a 'mad crowd' led by a drunken brute.[5]

When the avenging angel of Braddon's *Under the Red Flag* determines to track down 'the Ajax of the gutter', whom she believes has been responsible for her husband's death at the barricades, she discovers that he was formerly a currier. Whereas in an English industrial novel of the 1840s this melodramatic plot might have provided the platform on which to build an investigation of working-class conditions, in Braddon's novel mention of the 232 curriers' workshops in Paris, found by the heroine in a trade directory, tells the reader precious little about the

---

[2] E. C. Gaskell, 'French Life', in *The Works of Elizabeth Gaskell*, ed. J. Shattock et al. (10 vols, London: Pickering & Chatto, 2005–6), 392–4.

[3] C. Dickens, 'A Monument of French Folly', in *The Uncommercial Traveller and Reprinted Pieces* (London: Oxford University Press, 1958), 589–600.

[4] [H. Vizetelly,] 'Night Rambles in Paris', *Pall Mall Gazette*, 3, 5, 6, 9, 13 June 1868. The notion of the 'dangerous classes' formed by the link between poverty and crime had been given currency by H.-A. Frégier's *Des classes dangereuses dans la population des grandes villes et des moyens de les rendre meilleures* (Paris: J.-B. Baillière, 1840).

[5] *Mrs Dymond; Works of Miss Thackeray* (10 vols, London: Smith, Elder, 1890), x, 466, 504–5.

conditions operating in tanning factories, and serves merely to delay the discovery of a working-class villain apparently animated by motiveless malice.[6]

The handful of novels that attempted to offer a sympathetic portrayal of the disadvantaged in Paris suggest how heavily their authors had to rely on literary sources, often lending their works the quality of moral fable at odds with the very plea they were mounting for understanding the real sufferings of the poor. Ouida's *Tricotrin* (1869), for instance, describes the heroic exploits and good deeds of a vagabond philosopher, whose portrait appears to have been derived from the anti-dogmatic, human visionary of Ernest Renan's immensely popular *La Vie de Jésus* (1863). Tricotrin performs his individual works of redemption in a curious world, loosely historically located in the July Monarchy, but depicted in a series of stylized, sensational tableaux designed to be emblematic of working-class affliction. Most of these episodes, involving the turpitude of police spies, convicts escaped from the galleys in Toulon, the unemployed dying *in extremis*, or Tricotrin attempting to stem the conflict at the barricades between the crowd and the approaching troops, smack of Victor Hugo's *Les Misérables* (1862), topped up with information from Vizetelly on the Parisian lime quarries that harboured bands of thieves and down-and-outs.

Having grown up in Paris, Alice Corkran knew enough to give a real location 'at the fag end of the city…in the rue Mouffetard', to 'Père Perrault's Legacy' (1887), a tale purporting to describe the mindset of Paris's community of rag-and-bone men, yet her title's allusion to Charles Perrault's *Histoires ou Contes du temps passé* (1697) means that the initial quasi-realistic delineation of a community characterized by illiteracy, immorality, filth, avarice, and revolutionary tendencies swiftly dissolves into the romance world of folktale.[7]

As some of the examples above have demonstrated, British novelists were frequently stumped in finding convenient home-grown equivalents through which to convey a sense of life in this foreign city, and driven either to referring readers to non-fictional sources or to using fable and romance to erode the need for documentary specificity. However, when it came to exploring national difference, rather than straightforwardly engaging with the life of Paris, there was a French literary model to hand: Germaine de Staël's *Corinne, ou l'Italie* (1807).

13.2 PARIS *À LA* CORINNE

The first reading of 'Corinne' is an epoch a woman never forgets.[8]

Although women writers were likely to find peculiarly pertinent the plight of Madame de Staël's heroine Corinne, doomed by her artistic genius to be denied marriage to the man she loves, writers of both sexes discovered in her novel *Corinne*,

[6] M. E. Braddon, *Under the Red Flag* (Leipzig: Tauchnitz, 1884), 217, 219–20.

[7] A. Corkran, 'Père Perrault's Legacy', in *The Young Philistine and Other Stories* (London: Burns & Oates, 1887), 89–126.

[8] G. Jewsbury, *The Half-Sisters* (1848), ed. J. Wilkes (Oxford: Oxford University Press, 1994), 60.

ou l'Italie a format suited to the exploration of national differences.[9] *Corinne's* nineteenth-century influence was by no means confined to Great Britain, but its plot, which pitted the cautious northern temperament and familial loyalties of a Scots aristocrat against the independent spirit of a southern European woman of genius, offered a template which could be easily adapted to contrasting Anglo-Saxon and Gallic attitudes. Bulwer Lytton aside, few of de Staël's British successors attempted to compete with her use of the novel as a vehicle for sophisticated discussion of contemporary European politics; and perhaps only Elizabeth Barrett Browning, by endowing the heroine of *Aurora Leigh* with similarly hybrid national origins, came close to recognizing the complexity of the choices between the mores of 'father-land' and 'motherland' facing de Staël's self-exiled heroine.

Few heroes or heroines of British fiction, transported to Paris, experience an inner crisis of identity comparable to de Staël's heroic prototype Lord Nevil, who is caught between the seductive allure of the exotic other, embodied in Corinne, and filial duty to the conventions and dictates of his homeland. De Staël refused to provide final narrative blame or approval for Lord Nevil's eventual decision, clearly wishing to provoke further debate: 'Was he consoled by society's approval? Was he content with the common lot after what he had lost? I do not know, and, on that matter, I want neither to blame nor to absolve him.'[10] Nevertheless, embodying this choice in two women, Corinne and her half-sister, linked the erotics of romantic desire to patriotism. Whereas de Staël, a Frenchwoman, might have been thought impartial in having her British male protagonist eventually opt for the purity and order of British domestic life over Italian grand passion, subsequent British uses of this device, of which there were many, frequently carried unpleasant undertones of guarding the purity of the race against dilution or contamination by foreign bodies.

The many examples of British fiction bearing the trace of de Staël's influence rarely tolerated her degree of ambivalence and were on the whole inclined to condemn cultural exogamy. In the few cases where an English hero intends marrying a woman of foreign extraction, as in Elizabeth Barrett Browning's *Aurora Leigh* or Amelia Edwards's *In The Days of My Youth* (1874), he usually has to burn his bridges and abandon England to achieve marital bliss. Barrett Browning's Aurora is finally united to Romney on Italian soil, and the visionary new Jerusalem to which they aspire lacks any geographical specificity. In Amelia Edwards's novel the impossibility of a true marriage of minds occurring through either the hero or his wife adopting the other's country is firmly underlined. The hero sells up his childhood home in the symbolically named English village of Saxenholme, and the possibility of the Frenchwoman he has met in Paris regaining possession of her

---

[9] See U. Jung, 'The Reception of Germaine de Staël and George Sand among Female Novelists in Nineteenth-Century Spain'; G. Stedman, 'Passion and Talent, Fulfilment or Death? Germaine de Staël's Novel *Corinne* Crosses the Channel', in H. Brown and G. Dow (eds), *European Connections: Readers, Writer, Salonnières* (Oxford: Peter Lang, 2011), 179–216. Gilbert Osmond's mother, with her 'pretensions to "culture"', liked to be known as 'the American Corinne': H. James, *The Portrait of a Lady*, ed. R. D. Bamberg (New York: W. W. Norton, 1975), 240.

[10] Mme de Staël, *Corinne, or Italy*, trans. S. Raphael, intro. J. Isbell (Oxford: World's Classics, 2008), 404.

family's château, lost in the course of the French Revolution, is left unresolved: in the hero's view the couple's best chance of happiness lies in the neutral space of Italy.

In *Corinne* the question of national characteristics is closely bound up with gendered cultural expectations. Previous to the novel's main events Corinne has repudiated British provincial life, where 'One would have seemed a troublemaker, a woman of doubtful virtue, if one had indulged in speaking or putting oneself forward in any way', as a bitter denial of 'natures called to a destiny unique to them'.[11] As the novel opens, this consummate poet, writer, tragedian, dancer, and artist is being granted the accolade, previously granted to Petrarch and Tasso, of being crowned in the Capitol at Rome. The national prejudice of England, we are told, is wholly opposed to women, however talented, becoming a figure for public remark, whereas for the Italians, artistic genius, wherever it is found, is a matter for public celebration.

Corinne's example unleashed a string of Victorian English heroines whose artistic aspirations felt cramped by the prospect of a conventional English marriage; and often these women's ambitions were marked as un-English by their being of partly foreign extraction. Lady Blessington felt that readers of her novel *The Victims of Society* (1837) would have no trouble either in understanding what it meant to produce 'a tirade a la De Stael', replete with literary allusions, nor to recognize its use as part of the seductive repertoire of a French-educated English temptress.

Bulwer Lytton had keen personal reasons for responding to this theme in *Corinne*: he had married a woman who had been raised with a strong commitment to women's rights, and in the wake of their rancorous separation she used both fiction and journalism to denounce her husband's behaviour. For a nineteenth-century readership the plot parallels between Bulwer Lytton's novel *The Parisians* and de Staël's *Corinne*, scarcely necessary and at times detrimental to the concerns of his wider political novel, could not have been more clearly indicated. Bulwer's Corinne, simply known as 'Isaura', has had a cosmopolitan upbringing closely resembling Corinne's: Isaura is the daughter of an Italian, and stepdaughter to an unsympathetic Frenchwoman who on the death of Isaura's father marries an Englishman. Transported to Second Empire Paris, Bulwer's version of Corinne contemplates a choice between the careers of singer and actress before becoming a successful novelist, yet where de Staël's Corinne's cornucopia of talent receives ample public testimony, it is as if the vocations in which Isaura shines scarcely matter other than as a source of romantic friction.

Like her predecessor, Isaura falls in love with an Englishman, devoid of Lord Nevil's various peccadilloes but constitutionally unable to marry a woman 'whose life could not be narrowed to the Home she adorned and blessed'.[12] Unlike Corinne, however, Isaura is given a female confidante, a Madame Eulalie de Grantmesnil, with whom she discusses the shaping of her career in the novel's opening epistolary

---

[11] Ibid. 249–50.
[12] Lord [E. G. E. L. Bulwer-]Lytton, *The Parisians* (2 vols, London: George Routledge, 1875), ii, 136.

exchange. This confidante, who never makes an on-stage appearance, is superfluous to the plot and is gradually phased out, but provided Bulwer with the opportunity to subvert the teaching of George Sand, on whom she is recognizably based. Whatever personal ambivalence later critics have detected, Sand's fiction and behaviour had made her into a feminist icon for nineteenth-century readers, so the chance of introducing her into his novel only to make her revoke her life's teaching proved irresistible to Bulwer Lytton.[13]

Madame de Grantmesnil advises Isaura that she would be content to see her 'safe in the woman's best sphere—a contented home, safe from calumny, safe from gossip' and, reflecting on her own failed relationships, adds that she would have been only too happy to have sacrificed all her fame for such a lot.[14] Isaura finds little difficulty in renouncing the notion of performing in public, but is still made to undergo indignity and disillusion when, as a successful novelist, she becomes easy prey for calculating suitors: she eventually opts for the privacy of domestic bliss with her English husband, living quietly by the Bay of Sorrento.

The long shadow of *Corinne*'s influence can even be seen in du Maurier's *Trilby* (1894), although by then it had been cross-fertilized with Dumas's popular mid-nineteenth-century success *La Dame aux Camélias* (1848). The *grisette* heroine of du Maurier's novel, who has been raised in Paris, is a hybrid, born to Irish-Scottish parents, though even this is left uncertain given that she was born ten months after her father died. The Englishman she loves sufficiently to be persuaded to renounce him before embarking on her remarkable singing career resembles Lord Nevil in that he 'adored piety in woman, though he was not pious by any means', and wished to Anglicize her, having 'a longing that Trilby could be turned into a young lady—say the vicar's daughter in a little Devonshire village—his sister's friend and co-teacher at the Sunday school, a simple, pure, and pious maiden of gentle birth'.[15]

Paris in the nineteenth century, as represented in the English fictional repertoire, assumed Rome's place as the site of dangerous artistic opportunity for women. In the aptly titled *A Woman's Trials* (1867), Kathleen O'Meara, alias 'Grace Ramsay', depicted an upper-class English girl temporarily thrown on her own capacity to earn a living in Paris. Unable to find pupils for watercolour lessons, she is insulted by the one offer she receives of acting as either saleswoman or model for a male artist. At a low ebb, she is groomed by an aristocratic French artist and statesman who starts his campaign by lending her a selection of French works, including de Staël's *Corinne*, which implicitly encourage the view that the emancipated female artist is entitled to form equally unconventional sexual relationships. Disaster is averted by the timely intervention of her English baronet father, who rescues her from penury and irremediable loss of reputation.

The gendered code embedded in such Parisian tales for the English market persisted, often in the face of the evidence provided by real life. O'Meara, for instance,

---

[13] S. van Dijk, 'Sociability and Mentoring by Correspondence: George Sand and Contemporary Female Writers', in Brown and Dow, *Readers, Writers, Salonnières*, 119–44.

[14] Lytton, *The Parisians*, i, 214.

[15] G. du Maurier, *Trilby*, intro. E. Showalter, ed. D. Denisoff (Oxford: Oxford University Press, 1995), 34.

earned her own living as a journalist in Paris. An even stranger example of bending Parisian realities to British sensibilities is to be found in Alice Corkran's tale for adolescent girls: *Margery Merton's Girlhood* (1888). The Corkran girls, Alice and Henriette, had witnessed their father's loss of his post as Paris correspondent, and the family's consequent period of poverty in London would have brought sharply home to them the need for a woman to be able to earn her own living. By the age of 18 Henriette was back in Paris, studying in the atelier of Mme Frederika (Emily) O'Connell (née Miethe), a German-Belgian painter and engraver (1823–85).[16] From there she progressed to the study of nude models in a male artist's atelier, while earning her living as a copyist in the Louvre. Both sisters, even if they did not rise to Corinne's heights of acclaim, aspired to careers in the arts—Henriette as a society portrait painter and Alice as a magazine editor and author—and neither appears to have married.

Alice's fictional heroine Margery Merton, an Anglo-Indian orphan who is raised in Paris by an English spinster aunt, possesses both artistic talent and ambition. Her aunt plans a wealthy marriage for her niece's future security, but Margery's ambitions are reflected in her personal calendar of saints: 'Mrs Browning; George Eliot, Mrs Somerville, Rosa Bonheur, Mrs Butler, and Sister Rosalie', the last-mentioned fictional character being an artist-turned-nun who runs a teaching studio where Margery studies.[17] When her aunt dies penniless, Margery's hopes lie in winning a coveted scholarship for further artistic training: her telling choice for the exhibition painting being Joan of Arc listening to her voices.

Nevertheless, Margery's ambitions are carefully hedged about by various types of warning scene. On a sketching expedition to the Fontainebleau forest, undertaken because it had inspired Rousseau and Corot, she encounters one of its 'ghosts' in the form of a mad woman, reputed once to have been an artist's model, and has to be rescued from this frightening episode by a stalwart young Englishman. A fellow art student accepts the 'deathly' prospect of becoming a nun as her only alternative to winning the scholarship which could lead to an independent career. As Margery's chances of winning the scholarship appear to diminish, in a moment of depression, reminiscent of Charlotte Bronte's heroine in *Villette*, she visits the Roman Catholic church of Saint-Roch in the heart of the English quarter, where the stalwart Englishman reappears, and in the course of their conversation Margery reaffirms her Protestantism. His intervention helps to counteract the accusations that have surrounded her winning exhibition picture, so that in gaining the coveted prize her talent and ambition are confirmed. However, the ending on a note of budding romance equally allowed readers of a conventional turn of mind see Margery's coveted prize as marriage rather than the life of the artist, and to associate her artistic ambitions with the immaturity of 'girlhood'. Oscar Wilde's dismissive summary of the story's issues in his review in *Woman's World* as 'Miss Corkran's little story, in which the creation of a picture forms the dominant *motif* suggests that a tale for adolescent English girls was never likely to provide the appropriate mould for righting Corinne's wrongs.[18]

[16] H. Corkran, *Celebrities and I* (London: Hutchinson, 1902), 114, 192.
[17] A. Corkran, *Margery Merton's Girlhood* (London: Blackie & Sons, 1888), 131.
[18] O. Wilde (ed.), *The Woman's World* (London: Cassell, 1888), 135.

The questions of nationality, gender, and genius broached in *Corinne, or Italy* were what best survived for late nineteenth-century readers; but when it was originally published in 1807, it held the additional attraction of acting as an up-to-date cultural travel guide. Set in the very recent past (1794–1803), the novel deploys the arts, archaeology, and literature of Italy to evoke the phases of the lovers' relationship, and in the process introduces the reader to Italy's leading tourist sites. British imitations, such as Anna Jameson's *A Lady's Diary* (1826), were swift to capitalize on the success of this formula, and before long many a British nineteenth-century novelist was happy to send his or her characters on an abbreviated Grand Tour, with commentary, to eke out the middle part of the story.[19]

13.3 THE NOVEL AS GUIDEBOOK

> I m--m--mean to exhaust P--P--Paris. I'm going to write a b--b--book about it, when I get home.[20]

It was not necessary, of course, for British writers to look to Mme de Staël for devices to move the story on by means of attention to changing scenes and customs. Dickens had only to look to the picaresque form as popularized by Fielding or Scott to find a way of reinvigorating *Martin Chuzzlewit* (1843–4) by despatching its hero to America. Nor is it likely that G. W. M. Reynolds had *Corinne* in mind when writing *Pickwick Abroad, or the Tour in France*—de Staël was not one of the authors featured in his work *The Modern Literature of France* (1839). Nevertheless, alive to the possibilities created by a contemporary print world in which publishers and authors restlessly shifted genre between *feuilletons, physiologies*, guidebooks, and novels, Reynolds determined to move beyond simple plagiarism in this book.

When compared with Dickens's *Pickwick Papers*, or their common ancestor, Pierce Egan's *Life in London, or The Day and Night Scenes of Jerry Hawthorn, Esq. and his elegant friend Corinthian Tom in their Rambles and Sprees through the Metropolis* (1821), Reynolds's novel swiftly emerges as more interested in describing specific sites. Egan's Regency bucks are introduced to fashionable drinking, gaming, sporting London, but the emphasis is on the generic atmosphere of these places, rather than their individual architecture. When Dickens's Pickwickians visit Ipswich, the town is little differentiated from the fictional Muggleton, scene of an earlier adventure, and it is not until his characters move to Bath in the latter half of the novel that Dickens begins to deploy the specifics of place to any real effect. When Reynolds's Pickwickians arrive in Paris in chapter 6, however, their first day's sightseeing, or 'lionising', initially has on its itinerary the Chamber of Deputies, the Luxembourg Palace, Saint-Sulpice, the Panthéon, the Garden of Plants [*sic*], Notre Dame, and the Morgue. Anxious not to 'fatigue' the reader, and probably equally wary of exhausting his material too fast, the narrator confines himself to a

---

[19] Jameson's novel was retitled *Diary of an Ennuyée* in subsequent editions.
[20] A. B. Edwards, *In the Days of My Youth* (3 vols, London: Hurst & Blackett, 1873), i, 90.

brief description of the form and function of the Chamber of Deputies, and a discussion between Pickwick and the *valet-de-place* about the unfortunate damage done to the sculptures of earlier national heroes during the French Revolution.[21]

By the time of the first book edition of *Pickwick Abroad*, Reynolds had decided to interpolate 'two exquisite wood-cuts representing some of the public buildings or scenes of Paris and its environs' along with the two steel engravings which had featured in the original serialization. Calculated as a value-added device to induce readers to invest again in the book version, these woodcuts, Reynolds realized, would 'form no inconsiderable feature in a book, which, by their aid, and on account of the information it contains, may almost be termed a manual for English travellers in France'.[22] Perhaps equally significantly, like the panorama or diorama, this experiment would have brought a Paris they had never visited imaginatively closer for some of Reynolds's audience, and consequently opened them to the experience of reading further fiction set in a city whose major sites and monuments they knew at least pictorially.

Reynolds also found a way to adapt to his own purposes Dickens's device of the interpolated tale in *Pickwick Papers*. His solution to the problem of subordinating his own, largely original, tales to the primary purpose of introducing English readers to French culture was twofold. First, he introduced a Parisian policeman who tells tales that serve as a warning to Reynolds's innocents abroad of the vice lying just under the surface of the tourist haunts of Paris. His second method was to tie the interpolated stories into a building or site which Pickwick and his companions intend to visit.

His partiality for the country which had been his home for nearly ten years led Reynolds to conclude his preface with the pious hope that his work would serve 'to clear away from the minds of my untravelled fellow-countrymen, a few of those prejudices, in reference to the French, which are still so tenaciously adhered to, and place the character of our great and gallant neighbours—and, thank God! present and sure allies—in a new and better light than they have ever yet been viewed in'.[23]

If healing Anglo-Gallic relations had indeed been Reynolds's primary aim, he had set himself something of a challenge in adopting the Pickwickians as his vehicle. Ultimately the conversational and recreational interests of this hedonistic, very English crew were at odds with the possibility of penetrating French mores. Reynolds's guide swiftly becomes the fun-loving British tourist's guide to Paris. Eating and drinking figure large, and Reynolds's enthusiasm for the French songs and ballads to be heard in the *estaminets* is reflected in his own translations, with which the text is liberally sprinkled. Claiming that a man would require 'perhaps a year, perhaps two—perhaps more—to make himself perfectly acquainted with the French and their characteristics', Reynolds repeatedly denounces travel writers who feel entitled, after the briefest of stays, to produce two-volume guides. One such, rejoicing in the soubriquet of Wegsworth Muffley—perhaps a jibe at John Murray, whose

---

[21] G. W. M. Reynolds, *Pickwick Abroad: or, The Tour in France* (London: Sherwood, Gilbert, & Piper, 1839), 62–3.
[22] Ibid. v–vi.   [23] Ibid. vii.

first *Handbook for Travellers on the Continent* had appeared in 1836—is lampooned for having passed only three days in Paris compiling spiteful impressions of Parisian behaviour, in order to 'flatter the vanity of the English'. A further side-swipe at Frances Trollope's *Paris and the Parisians* (1837) asserted that a certain 'Mrs Baggage, who was in the habit of visiting large cities, partaking of the hospitality of the inhabitants, and then abusing them' had brought out a two-volume guide, which a local tobacconist had recently bought in bulk 'at twopence a volume, for waste-paper'.[24]

Reynolds may have started his venture as an act of easy plagiarism, but in the course of this long-running compilation, he learned how to present factual hand-book material in an entertaining fashion, and discovered the intrinsic advantages of the polyphonic and dialogic novel form for an author with split national and class loyalties. As a wily servant Sam Weller, for instance, not only experiences dif-ferent layers of Parisian life but offers the occasional comment to Pickwick on the different assumptions governing French class relations, thus prompting the reader to consider how far Pickwick is justified in clinging to his insular view of master–servant relations.

Reynolds's format could scarcely be held responsible for the numbers of fictional guidebooks that followed, though its success would have offered encouragement.[25] Thackeray (whose sense at this stage in his career of Reynolds as a competitor was discussed in Chapter 11) saw his own two-volume publication *The Paris Sketch Book* (1840) as a step on the ladder of literature rather than journalism; yet the book's mixture of literary and artistic reviews, fictional tales, and illustrations might be seen as having been in part legitimated by the gallimaufry that consti-tuted Reynolds's *Pickwick Abroad*. A series of allusions in *The Paris Sketch Book* in any case show Thackeray to have been keenly alive to the competition: the first essay refers the reader to Bulwer Lytton's *Pelham* for the description of a particular Parisian hotel, while an article on French novels contains a slighting reference to 'such authors as Lady Morgan and Mrs. Trollope, [who] having frequented a cer-tain number of tea-parties in the French capital, begin to prattle about French manners and men'.[26]

The move back and forth between the informative and the fictional was not always easy to manage. Frances Trollope had first recognized the lucrative potential in making travel writing work double-time when she used a transatlantic trip to fuel the publication in 1832 of both *The Domestic Manners of the Americans* and *The Refugee in America*. The trick in moving from the one genre to the other lay in knowing how to transform or pare down factual knowledge into material pertinent to plot or character development. The virtue of her epistolary work *Paris and the Parisians in 1835* (1836) lay in its spirited sense of the worth of her own experi-ences, but her satirical novel, *The Robertses on their Travels* (1846), got off on the wrong foot from chapter 1, where she announced, 'Those who have travelled

---

[24] Ibid. 316, 506.   [25] For details, see Ch. 11, n. 31.
[26] Thackeray, 'On Some French Fashionable Novels', in *The Paris Sketch Book*, *The Oxford Thackeray*, ed. G. Saintsbury (17 vols, London: Oxford University Press, 1910), ii, 97.

much, and still more, perhaps, those who have *resided* for a time in any of the continental capitals of Europe, must, I think, have observed how very much more conspicuous those English travellers, who are not of the most polished class of society, make themselves, than do those who are.' Unsure whether readers less well versed than herself in Parisian habits would understand the nature of the mistakes the Robertses made, Trollope felt the need to rectify their errors at every stage. Thus, when Mrs Roberts protests at the fare she is charged by the cab driver who has taken her accommodation-hunting, the local magistrate to whom she refers the dispute explains that she needs in future to hire 'a coach "*a l'heure*," as, without this precaution, every stoppage may be legally reckoned a separate fare'.[27] This trait of offloading on the reader snippets of hard-won personal experience recurred in many another Parisian-based novel: Henrietta Jenkin, for instance, thought nothing of breaking the dramatic thread of her novel *Once and Again* with advice to the unwary on French rental practices, or information on the ways in which French inheritance laws differed from those in England.[28]

Neither the choice of a largely passive figure as the focalizer nor a historical setting nor the determination to show off a command of Parisian haunts beyond the normal tourist range were necessarily inimical to a gripping novel. Sala's *Quite Alone* manages to impart suspense to his hapless young heroine's day-long exploration of Paris's seedier side, as a voyage of discovery driven by fear and ignorance of the dangers to which she is exposed. The resemblance between his heroine and Henry James's central intelligence in *What Maisie Knew* (1897) extends well beyond the parallel of their both being victims whose fate is driven by the mutual animosity of demi-monde parents. In both cases Sala and James's travel-writing practice, as self-conscious investigators of foreign places and customs, had led them to grasp the distinction between seeing and knowing, and to recognize that novel readers required more than accurate descriptions.[29]

From Sala's sprawling novel, readers finally received little more than a series of lively episodes, but in *The Ambassadors* (1903) James was to bring his knowledge of the Parisian streets and their history into play to underpin the social, psychological, and emotional lives of his characters, from Lambert Strether's initial strolls reacquainting himself with a city visited in his youth to the changes of address of the American playboy, Chad. 'The complexion of the stone, a cold, fair grey, warmed and polished a little by life' of the Haussmannian buildings in the Boulevard Malesherbes tells us much about Chad, whose acquisition of worldly sophistication is marked by his removal to a third-floor apartment there from his student digs in the Latin quarter. His freedom to move back and forth over the Seine measures the distance between him and his aristocratic mistress, Mme de Vionnet, the *salonnière* to whom he owes the Parisian polish he has acquired. Her first-floor apartment in the Rue de Bellechasse, at the heart of the aristocratic Faubourg

---

[27] F. Trollope, *The Robertses on their Travels* (3 vols, London: Henry Colburn, 1846), i, 4, 61–2.
[28] [H. Jenkin,] *Once and Again: A Novel* (3 vols, London: Smith, Elder, 1865), i, 94–7; ii, 235–41.
[29] J. Rignall, *Realist Fiction and the Strolling Spectator* (London: Routledge, 1992) provides much interesting commentary on adult observer-narrators.

Saint-Germain, speaks, by contrast, of old ties and loyalties. Where Chad finds himself at home in a world of boulevard commerce, and free to pick and choose, the mode of 'chastened ease' amid the inherited antique furniture amidst which his mistress lives conveys that she is condemned to live 'passive under the spell of transmission', trapped by an unhappy and indissoluble marriage to a member of the *ancien régime*.[30]

Few English novelists possessed James's capacity for Parisian psychogeography. George Eliot, who might have managed this had she been able to avoid the penchant for 'instructive antiquarianism' that bedevilled *Romola*, was so slow in overcoming her dislike of Paris that it was not until 1865 she agreed to accompany Lewes on a prolonged visit.[31] For the most part, English novelists who wrote about Paris relied on drawing broad distinctions between the urban attractions and vicissitudes of central Paris and the more relaxed charms of rusticity to be found in Saint-Cloud or Versailles. Male protagonists' expeditions to these venues were occasionally used as a brief escape from the emotional problems they were facing in the feverish environment of the city, but more often as an opportunity to disport themselves in casual dalliances with lower-class French women who would not have proved acceptable companions within the Parisian social hierarchies where English gentlemen hoped to be accepted.

13.4 THE SILVER-FORK NOVEL

From the mid-1820s British fiction had afforded a popular subgenre exclusively devoted to the behaviour of the British upper classes, and it seemed safe to assume that glimpses into a privileged world of Parisian glamour could only enhance the voyeuristic attractions of the silver-fork school of fiction for English readers.[32] In Bulwer Lytton's best-selling example of the genre, *Pelham* (1828), the narrator prefaces his account of his sojourn in Paris by announcing his credentials as guide:

> Young, well born, tolerably good-looking, and never utterly destitute of money, nor grudging whatever enjoyment it could procure, I entered Paris with the ability and the resolution to make the best of those *beaux jours* which so rapidly glide from our possession.[33]

As a young dandy Pelham spends his social life in predominantly Anglo-French circles, and on the right bank, where he attends fashionable salons, indulges in two duels—soon to become an obligatory ingredient of this subgenre—samples the best restaurants, and contemptuously inspects the lower-class English and Frenchmen

---

[30] H. James, *The Ambassadors* (1909) (2 vols, New York: A. M. Kelley, 1971), i, 96–7, 245.

[31] *Saturday Review*, 25 July 1863, 124–5; repr. in D. Carroll (ed.), *George Eliot: The Critical Heritage* (London: Routledge & Kegan Paul, 1971), 208.

[32] Franco Moretti notes that the specific nature of the silver-fork novel's appeal limited its readership abroad to determined Anglophiles: *Atlas of the European Novel 1800–1900* (London: Verso, 1998), 177–80.

[33] Lord [E. G. E. L. Bulwer-]Lytton, *Pelham: or, Adventures of a Gentleman* (London: George Routledge, 1873), 33.

to be found in the cafés of the Palais Royal and nearby private gaming establishments. As a casual guarantee of his aristocratic pedigree, Pelham casts a swift eye over the ancient splendours of the Faubourg Saint-Germain, announcing, 'if ever I go to Paris again I shall reside there', and, the night before his stay ends, briefly attends an intimate party where he swaps courtly pleasantries with Charles X and his family.[34] Bulwer Lytton's decision to place the bulk of the action in the shallow social round enjoyed by the upper-class inhabitants of the English quarter meant that his satire at the expense of his conceited young hero was largely undimmed by any serious desire to educate less well-travelled readers. *Pelham* may mock the shallow lives of the fashionable aristocracy, but the Paris it presents is nevertheless a world of binaries, dividing between an exclusive circle of entitlement, marked by birth and breeding, and those beyond its pale.

Catherine Gore's *Greville, or a Season in Paris* (1841) announces its intention of trading on brand recognition from the first by using a quotation from *Pelham* as epigraph: 'O! English people, English people! why can you not stay and perish of apoplexy and Yorkshire pudding at home?'[35] However, by detaching this snippet of dialogue from its original context, where it had served as the peroration to a particularly odious outpouring of Pelham's gastronomic snobbery, Gore obscures its original parodic thrust and uses it to suggest that she is appealing to the kind of 'discerning' readers anxious to mark themselves out from their more insular compatriots.[36] *Greville* is therefore structured around the contrast between the Paris open to a boorish young son of the English squirearchy and the aristocratic Hugo Greville who penetrates the society of the *ancien régime* in the Faubourg St Germain; yet the desire to demonstrate an insider knowledge of the shifting Parisian power structures unsettles the simpler contrasts demanded by satire. By the third volume, Greville's aristocratic cachet has been compromised by uncertainty as to the legitimacy of his claim to an earldom, and in Paris this translates to his moving away from the elegant understatement of the old aristocratic families and towards the wealth and political power centred on the Citizen King's court at the Tuileries, together with the more ostentatious splendour and attainments of the Chaussée d'Antin. Gore is anxious to persuade her readers that dining at embassies or with French ministers, and visiting lesser-known cultural attractions such as the Hôtel des Archives, still opens worthwhile doors to Greville. Nevertheless, she still hankers after the illusion of viewing life from an aristocratic perspective: dinner at the French Ministry of the Interior disappoints because this regime is of too recent a date to have laid down good cellars.[37] Her novel of the following year, *The Ambassador's Wife*, set back in the Restoration monarchy of Charles X, left her on more sure-footed territory by focusing on the closed world of embassy intrigue.

As ostentatious display gained further ground over the more understated gatherings of the old French aristocracy, and power seeped from the left to the right bank, so the minutiae of class distinctions between newly acquired wealth and old

---

[34] Ibid. 33, 87, 115–17.   [35] Cf. ibid. 41.
[36] Perhaps it was a similar inclination to please the cognoscenti that led her to name the novel's hero after Henry William Greville (1801–72), one of her husband's colleagues at the Embassy.
[37] C. Gore, *Greville: or, a Season in Paris* (3 vols, London: Henry Colburn, 1841), iii, 269–70.

breeding, upon which the silver-fork novel depended, became obsolete. Despite the promise conveyed by its title, and its setting in the early 1830s, Frances Trollope's *Hargrave; or, the Adventures of a Man of Fashion* (1843) belongs to a world in which the clear aristocratic/bourgeois divide has disappeared. Her protagonist is only ever an impostor in the Faubourg Saint-Germain: his wealth derives from his father's career as a London banker, and his foothold on French aristocratic life depends on a second marriage to the widow of a French vicomte. His ostentatious entertainment of society's finest is driven by the vainglorious dream of securing a princely suitor for his younger daughter's hand, and is financed by a secret life of reckless gambling, supported by robbery with violence. As the novel advances Trollope herself is seduced by the bourgeois banker's aspirations. When Hargrave hires the most famous opera singers in town to perform as a trio at a champagne supper thrown to encourage the Prince's attentions, she names real singers—Grisi, Lablache, and Tamburini—and eulogizes their performance as if it added lustre to her own.[38,39] Although Hargrave is disappointed in his social ambition of becoming father-in-law to a member of Louis-Philippe's family, and turns into a romantic outcast in the German mountains before his final incarceration in a Trappist order, Trollope is left free to realize Hargrave's vulgar daydreams by eventually bringing about the unlikely marriage of Hargrave's daughter to a prince of the house of Orléans. By the time she published *Fashionable Life; or, Paris and London* (1856), the silver-fork novel had run its course, and in *The Robertses on their Travels* (1846) Trollope opted for the simpler course of sneering at the English middle classes' attempts to enter Parisian society.

It was the insecurity these women's novels revealed, perched uneasily somewhere between a fascination with profligate excess and a fundamental respect for more bourgeois values, that Thackeray pilloried so mercilessly in *Vanity Fair*. Unlike Pelham with his secure title and fortune, the arriviste Becky Sharp can never be wholly at ease. At the height of her conquest of Parisian society, she experiences an inner distrust of its triviality: she tires of the 'idle social life...she could not live upon knickknacks, laced handkerchiefs, and kid gloves. She felt the frivolity of pleasure, and longed for more substantial benefits.'[40]

13.5 CRIME FICTION

Although *Vanity Fair* is ostensibly set back in the Regency period, Becky and her card-sharping husband belong to the mid-nineteenth-century world where the

---

[38] F. Trollope, *Hargrave; or, the Adventures of a Man of Fashion* (3 vols, London: Henry Colburn, 1843), i, 184.

[39] It seems probable that Trollope is boasting of her own attendance at the first performance of Bellini's *I Puritani* at the Théâtre-Italien in Paris on 24 Jan. 1835, in which this trio of soprano, bass, and baritone, along with the tenor Rubini, won lasting fame as the 'Puritani Quartet'. As part of a European tour that same year they gave a private command performance at Kensington Palace to Crown Princess Victoria on her 16th birthday.

[40] W. M. Thackeray, *Vanity Fair: A Novel without a Hero*, ed. J. Sutherland (Oxford: Oxford University Press, 1991), 457–8.

social anxiety of betraying a lack of blue blood had been overtaken by the fear of being taken in by the socially fraudulent. Increased geographical and social mobility meant that it was no longer easy to judge a man by his local antecedents, and so (it was feared) allowed those on the move to reinvent themselves as they pleased. 'Roguery', as Thackeray noted, might be 'of no country nor clime'; but if it was difficult to be sure of identifying confidence tricksters in London, it stood to reason that it would be harder for first-time British visitors to identify the social origins of those they met in Paris.[41]

The disruption to the social hierarchy of the *ancien régime* effected by the French Revolution made it all too easy, it was felt, for a French confidence trickster to claim to be a deposed aristocrat reduced to impoverished circumstances. The prostitute Anastasie who targets Reynolds's Pickwickians, for example, boasts of a mother who is a marchioness and a brother who is a count.[42] The English, in any case, often claimed they found it difficult to grasp the various orders of French nobility and cast frequent aspersions on those suspected to have ennobled themselves by the interpolation of 'de' before their surname. Charles X's decision to restore reduced privileges to the aristocracy seems to have brought this anxiety to a peak, and, if fiction set during Louis-Philippe's reign was to be believed, the cafés of the Palais-Royal were awash with self-styled comtes and vicomtes. The cosmopolitan nature of city life doubled the risk of being taken in by crooks posing as titled exiles from some other European country. Perhaps the most implausible use of such shape-shifting for non-comedic purposes occurs in Henrietta Jenkin's *Once and Again*, where a certain M. le Vicomte Granson uses a fellow chess-player in the Café de la Régence in the Palais-Royal to effect an introduction to an affluent English widow. He explains the curious Scots inflection to his French accent by his birth in Edinburgh when his father accompanied the Comte d'Artois into exile. Many years after the self-styled vicomte has defrauded the widow and her daughter of their inheritance, he reappears in rural France as a colporteur, claiming British citizenship. Finally, imprisoned for a murder committed in trying to cover his traces, it emerges that he had been an officer in the British army who, when he was cashiered in Spain, had stolen the papers of the real Vicomte Granson, an émigré killed on the battlefield.

These fears of Paris as the favoured resort of British crooks had a certain basis in reality, in that, after Boulogne, it was the most convenient destination for those in flight from the English law and debtors' prison. From 1832 two years' imprisonment sufficed in France to expunge debts of less than £20, and ten years was the maximum a foreigner could serve no matter how great the debt, whereas in England until the late 1860s there could be no exit from debtors' prison until an agreement had been reached with the creditors.[43] As travel conditions became easier, those in

---

[41] 'Parisian Caricatures', *London and Westminster Review*, Apr. 1839, 282–305; repr. as 'Caricatures and Lithography', *Paris Sketch Book*, 184.

[42] Reynolds, *Pickwick Abroad*, 75.

[43] Reynolds, who twice went bankrupt, first in Paris in 1836 and later in London, devoted an early episode of *Pickwick Abroad* to explaining why France's more lenient bankruptcy laws proved attractive to Englishmen.

trouble with the law could slip back and forth between capital cities, changing name and persona as it suited, and often (in fiction at least) offering political exile rather than financial ruin as their motive for a moonlight flight. The sheer frequency with which these elements feature in the back-histories of mid-nineteenth-century fictional villains suggests that they had become a part of British urban myth.

Just as the techniques employed by thieves and scoundrels differed little on either side of the Channel, so fictional rogues' galleries proved adaptable. The vogue for Newgate novels, or melodramatic tales of criminality, which flourished in England in the 1830s and 1840s had clear French counterparts, of which the best known was Eugène Sue's serialized melodrama *Les Mystères de Londres* (1842–3), which not only achieved almost instant translation into English but swiftly inspired G. W. M. Reynolds's syndicated spin-off, *The Mysteries of London* (1845–55). The Newgate novel enjoyed traceable native antecedents in the plays of Gay or the fiction of Defoe or Smollett, but Thackeray, who inherited the role of scourge of the genre in *Fraser's Magazine*, was quick to point out the analogies with French literary traditions. He identified the story of Cartouche, an eighteenth-century robber, legendary in France for his daring exploits and courageous death, as an early progenitor of a genre which he repeatedly denounced for its tendency to glamorize the criminal. 'As Newgate and the highways are so much the fashion with us in England, we may be allowed to look abroad for histories of a similar tendency,' he wrote, before turning the tale on its head to represent Cartouche's life as a series of cruel and dishonourable episodes.[44]

A further common source for both French and English fiction was the equally legendary real-life French criminal, turned 'cop', turned private eye, Vidocq (1775–1857). In the aftermath of the publication of the first volume of his self-aggrandizing *Memoirs* (1828), this charismatic giant of a man, master of disguise and escapee par excellence, provided inspiration for both Balzac and Victor Hugo. He also sparked interest in an English public, witnessing the evolution of its own police force, but troubled by its implications for the intrusion of the supervisory powers of the state into the intimacy of domestic life.[45] Not the least of Vidocq's more sinister abilities had been his capacity to survive changes of political regime, perhaps by acting as a double spy or perhaps because of the incriminating evidence he had gathered in his secret records. So famous were his exploits that he attracted large crowds in the summer of 1845 when he acted as raconteur at a London exhibition of disguises and assorted items connected with his versatile career.

Reynolds, who had lived in Paris during the troubling period when Vidocq's activities had seemed to morph between working for the police bureau and on his own account, was much fascinated by Vidocq and could be said to have led the field in

[44] 'The French Plutarch', *Fraser's Magazine*, Oct. 1839, 447–59; repr. as 'Cartouche' in *Paris Sketch Book*, 78.

[45] See F. Trollope, *Hargrave*, ii, 97–8; E. S. Dixon, 'The Right of French Women', *Household Words*, 22 May 1852, 218–21. For a further development of this argument see C. Dever, ' "An Occult and Immoral Tyranny": The Novel, the Police, and the Agent Provocateur', in M. Cohen and C. Dever (eds), *The Literary Channel: The Inter-National Development of the Novel* (Princeton, NJ: Princeton University Press, 2002), 225–50.

the English fiction of transnational criminality. Reynolds's own early history had after all included cheating at gambling and fraud.[46] Early in *Pickwick Abroad*, the susceptible Tupman, who accompanies Pickwick to Paris, is attracted by a girl who conveniently drops her handkerchief in front of him in the gardens of the Palais-Royal. She smartly invites Tupman to meet her mother, the aptly named, Marchioness de Volage (a surname meaning inconstancy), living, since deprived of her fortune by the July Revolution, in a sixth-floor apartment. Attending a soirée held there, Tupman is promptly fleeced at a card game and his expensive watch disappears. Eventually Vidocq, 'an ex-galley-slave and ex-President of the Board of Public Safety', himself restores the watch, for a fee, to Tupman, along with a lecture in which he explains the pedigree of the prostitute, Anastasie, who had first attracted Tupman's attentions. The convoluted tale of her downward trajectory from treading the boards to becoming so notorious that her only prey are now foreigners too ashamed to prosecute her, is prefaced by Vidocq's admission, 'She has as many names...as I have had in my time—and those are not a few.' When next encountered, many chapters later, Anastasie is posing as Countess Loveminski, cousin to a Polish Count Boloski: the Count in due course turns out to be the latest alias of William Sugden, a London publican's son, who after a career of petty crime in England had crossed the Channel and assumed the more genteel name of Adolphus Crashem.[47]

It has been customary to denigrate Reynolds's early work as so much methodical plagiarism, but focusing on the imitative element of Dickens's amiable Pickwickians misses the creative pleasure Reynolds derived from describing his crooks' shameless capacity for self-reinvention—a characteristic mirrored in the author's own versatile appropriations of other writer's ideas and forms. In his second novel, *Alfred de Rosann or, the Adventures of a French Gentleman* (1839), Alfred is merely the honourable cipher whose misadventures allow the reader insights into the murky world of the French criminal fraternity. Betrayed by his French business partner, who promptly absconds to London, Alfred finds himself part of a convict chain-gang making its way slowly down to the 'galleys', or purpose-built prisons, at Brest. Although ostensibly sickened by the coarseness and immorality of his companions, Alfred, like the reader, soon succumbs to listening to the convicts' 'anecdotes of blood, of lust, of incest, and of terror'.[48] In point of fact, these convicts' tales more often recount tales of theft and trickery, almost certainly prompted by the publication the previous year of Vidocq's *Les Voleurs*. However, where Vidocq's manual of criminal techniques and argot had been intended to demystify and thus disempower swindlers, Reynolds' stories act as an introduction to the intoxicating pleasures of imposture and deceit.

The episode in the Brest prison, which includes a guillotining, followed by a prison riot in which the prisoner-turned-executioner is dismembered by fellow

[46] R. McWilliam, 'The French Connection: G. W. M. Reynolds and the Outlaw Robert Macaire', in A. Humpherys and L. James (eds), *G. W. M. Reynolds: Nineteenth-Century Fiction, Politics, and the Press* (Aldershot: Ashgate, 2008), 33–49.

[47] Reynolds, *Pickwick Abroad*, 77, 134–5, 332.

[48] G. W. M. Reynolds, *Alfred de Rosann: or, the Adventures of a French Gentleman* (London: J. W. Southgate, 1839), 57.

convicts, for a time threatens to derail Reynolds's farcical tale of underworld decep-
tion. However, Alfred and his two companions escape under cover of the riot; once
back on the road, the trio proceed to take on such a series of aliases that the narrator is driven to admit that it will be necessary to revert to the names under which
they were first introduced lest the reader should become confused.[49] When a further twist of the long-forgotten romantic plot leads Alfred to London, he soon
encounters both the former French partner whose double-crossing first put him
in prison and a French prison cellmate, now masquerading as the exiled Count
d'Elsigny. Deciding that a swindler's career is easier in Paris than in London, the
cellmate returns to France, where he eventually dies a hero's death on the barricades during the July Revolution. Despite the fact that this villain has not scrupled
to trick the poor and has hired thugs to achieve his ends, ultimately Reynolds finds
himself in thrall to the sheer effrontery, charm, and swagger such men exude.

An 1839 article by Thackeray makes it easy to guess where Reynolds next turned
his attention. If Cartouche could be seen as the Dick Turpin of French literature,
Thackeray found the figure of Robert Macaire (see section 11.3) in his 'dandified
rags' an altogether more disturbing contemporary example of the villain as potential
hero, attractive in his comic energy. When taken up by the political caricaturists
Philipon and Daumier, Macaire and his clumsy stooge, Bertrand, had been repeatedly reconfigured as hypocritical rogues whose 'lies, crimes and absurdities' could be
identified as playing their role in politics, law, medicine, commerce, and the press.[50]
It was but a short step therefore for Reynolds to make that popular French villain
the equivocal hero of *Robert Macaire in England* (1840). The later addition of the
subtitle *The French Bandit in England* (1849) simply served to underline the creep-
ing menace of French brigandry to which honest English citizens stood exposed.[51]

The novels of sensation which flourished in the 1860s revisited the Parisian
fraternity of gamblers, cheats, and tricksters, but the world they presented now
contained cold-blooded villains rather than lovable rogues and chancers. The plot
and ambience of Mary Elizabeth Braddon's first novel, *Three Times Dead; or, the
Secret of the Heath* (1854), repackaged a few years later under the more lurid title
The Trail of the Serpent,[52] is in some ways a throwback to the world of social
extremes that met in her mentor Bulwer Lytton's Newgate novel, *Paul Clifford*
(1830), but Braddon's murdering scoundrel has none of Clifford's potential as a
romantic hero. Nor is the Paris he heads for to reinvent himself Reynolds's city of
petty crime, where deceivers and their victims alike belong to a broadly middle-class
spectrum. Instead it is an exotic world of melodrama, where titles and money ride
roughshod over the normal moral conventions.

Sala's novels of the 1860s confirm this shift in tone. *Quite Alone* proposes the
minor aristocracy as the milieu where villainy is most to be feared. Sir Francis

---

[49] Ibid. 51.   [50] 'Caricatures and Lithography', *Paris Sketch Book*, 168–95.

[51] For a plot synopsis see McWilliam, 'The French Connection', 33–49.

[52] For James Fitzjames Stephen, this evocative title became the hallmark of the genre: 'It is impossible to mistake what is now-a-days called sensation literature when you see it. Whether it takes the
shape of minute detail or ghastly calmness, or conscious inconsciousness, the trail of the serpent is over
it all': 'Sentimentalism', *Cornhill Magazine*, July 1864, 72.

Blunt, at the outset of the novel already a dandy bearing a duelling scar, knows his way around the demi-monde society of both London and Paris, though club gossip speculates as to how he keeps himself afloat. Utterly heartless, he beats and deserts his wife and uses their child as a pawn in his revenge. Once known for the 'brilliant depravity' with which he fleeced rich scions of the peerage, fifteen years later he is pictured as a dissolute, decrepit old man, dependent on his winnings for the price of a bed in the cheapest Paris lodging-place, and now at the mercy of a generation of titled reprobates even less honourable than himself.[53] The fifteen years between the novel's 1836 opening and its ending is of course necessary for the heroine to reach maturity, but the precise time-span chosen is significant in that by the end of the novel the Second Empire is about to dawn. Yet, just as *Vanity Fair* operates in two chronological periods, the Regency past of its historical events and the later 1840s of its narrative perspective, so *Quite Alone* uses Louis-Philippe's reign for its narrative time-scheme while often reminding the reader of the brasher, harsher days in which the novel is being read.

Similarly, in *The Seven Sons of Mammon* (1862), Sala went back to Vidocq as inspiration for the lynchpin of his inordinately complicated plot, while very deliberately setting the events of the novel between December 1849 and early 1851, that 'perturbed period of transition and suspense' between Republic and Empire.[54] Sala's Vidocq figure appears, under a host of different names, as the *éminence grise* of a Parisian courtesan, the partner of an English speculator, the power behind his own embezzling franchise in London, and a travelling salesman in Parisian corsetry, before turning up at the Epsom races as a French officer of the law, working in concert with the English police, to spirit the courtesan back to Paris on charges of forgery and theft. This joint Anglo-French operation allows for a discussion in which the English police note the lavish state funding available for informers in France, and the secrecy in which the French can operate as opposed to the authorizations the English require. Back in Paris, the Vidocq figure resumes the role of legal officer and manages, while obviously enjoying the proceeds of the courtesan's blackmailing activities, to have her murder charge dropped. His secret influence has also enabled him to exert absolute control over the fate of an unfortunate Englishman, first exiled to a punitive Belgian monastery, then to the role of a loathed French prison warder, all because he spurned the courtesan's love.

Sala's fascination with and anxiety about the inherent corruption of a system which permits such extraordinary freelance activity under the auspices of the legal system is made clear in the choice of this figure's chief nomenclature as Simon Le Franc. A retrospective narrative, which frequently pauses to defend the plausibility of its sensational plot, is thus able to suggest that rumours of increasingly despotic powers, exercised through a secret police, that had once seemed so far-fetched form the daily order of Napoleon's III's Empire.

On the one hand, the marked divide between pre- and post-Haussmannian Paris might be said to have facilitated a minor resurgence in the historical, or retrospective,

[53] G. A. Sala, *Quite Alone* (3 vols, London: Chapman & Hall, 1864), i, 225.
[54] G. A. Sala, *The Seven Sons of Mammon* (London: Tinsley Brothers, 1862), i, 88.

novel as a suitable genre for considering Paris. On the other, the frequency with which novels written during the Second Empire looked back to the times of the Citizen King indicates a politics of representation at work, celebrating an era when the state's attempts at interfering in the lives of its private citizens had ultimately proved less successful.

13.6 THE HISTORICAL NOVEL

In 1846 Thackeray was to be heard lamenting that, in the relative dearth of the historical novel in England, English readers had to rely on translations of the copious historical fiction flowing from the pens of Dumas *père*, Soulié, Sue, and Féval.[55] Since the death of Sir Walter Scott, the acknowledged doyen of the genre, British novelists who had turned to history had either (like Ainsworth) concentrated on the English heritage or, in the case of a slew of novels inspired by the religious ferment of the 1840s, chosen periods of history, however remote, where current controversies could be aptly replayed. Meanwhile the originality of Carlyle's *French Revolution* presented a formidable obstacle to English novelists anxious to try their hands at that episode in French history.

The coming of Napoleon III to the French throne was to change all of this. Suddenly, the immediate past of Louis-Philippe's reign seemed another era, somehow instantly more historic than comparable decades in Great Britain. In the pithy summary of a recent historian, 'Paris experienced a dramatic shift from the introverted, private and personalized urbanism of the July Monarchy to an extroverted, public and collectivized style of urbanism under the Second Empire.'[56] The glittering surfaces and dazzling displays of Second Empire boulevards proved unsympathetic to the quiet interiors of domestic fiction; and when novelists strove to suggest the way in which small fish could be caught up in the interplay of larger political forces, they often reverted to the topography of Louis-Philippe's Paris, before the days when the class distinction between the various arrondissements had become so marked.

Those novelists who had been born too late to recall much of pre-Haussmannian days laboured at a disadvantage when they came to recreate an environment which many of their readers did remember. Amelia Edwards's *In The Days of My Youth* (1873) suffered from her penchant for research: two years' background work were said to go into her novels. This novel, set towards the close of Louis-Philippe's reign, faced the double challenge of recreating the topography of pre-Haussmannian Paris and viewing it through the eyes of a male English medical student. Using him as her focalizer enabled Edwards to penetrate a *grisette's* room, student drinking clubs, and a salon whose hostess did not welcome other women—but at the price of laborious historical reconstruction. The narrator's recollection of setting foot in

---

[55] W. M. Thackeray, 'Proposals for a Continuation of Ivanhoe', *Fraser's Magazine*, Aug. 1846, 237–45; Sept. 1846, 359–67; repr. in *Oxford Thackeray*, x, 463–95.

[56] D. Harvey, *Consciousness and the Urban Experience* (Oxford: Blackwell, 1985), 204.

the student quarter for the first time, for instance, begins with the ominous words: 'The dear old Quartier Latin of my time—the Quartier Latin of Balzac, of Béranger, of Henry Murger...exists no longer.'[57]

Ouida, whose *Tricotrin* (1869) ends with the close of the July Monarchy, was only born in 1839. Her reliance on a variety of literary sources, including the typologies of urban life popular in the early 1840s and Vidocq's *Memoirs*, as a base for her saintly hero's adventures mean that her scenes set in garrets, thieves' dens, theatres of the 'boule du Crime', or the 1848 barricades appear as topographically unconnected *tableaux*, leaving it unclear how anyone but a hero with semi-magical powers could travel from one site to the next. The lack of material historical grounding in this novel becomes all the more marked if compared with Victor Hugo's *Les Misérables* (1862). Despite relying similarly heavily on Vidocq's tales, and writing much of the novel in self-imposed exile, Hugo had the inestimable advantage of having known Paris in the period 1815–32 in which his novel was set, and of having lived through the subsequent transformations in which the plight of the poorest was increasingly distanced from the city's heart.

By the time that Braddon wrote her historical reconstruction of the Commune, *Under the Red Flag* (1883), the homes of the poor were (as she correctly observed) in small neighbourhoods where such social life as there was tended to be centred on the local crèmerie, and so, since she did not allow herself the epic breadth and multiple characters' crossings and recrossings of Paris which occur in Bulwer Lytton's panoramic contemporary account of the end of the Second Empire in *The Parisians* (1872), she had to resort to the unlikely agency of one man, a disenchanted, impoverished aristocrat, to connect the parochialism of such life with the larger political movements of the day. Only Anne Thackeray Ritchie, familiar over the years with the changes Paris had experienced, managed in *Mrs Dymond* (1885) to convey something of the disconnect between the various enclaves, the quiet domesticity, and the street violence.

Although the violent disruptions marking successive regime changes attempted to sweep away the past as if it had never been, the demolition and excavation work involved in creating these successive 'new' Parises also inevitably disclosed ancient secrets. The practice of erasure, of everything from political leaders to buildings and street names, evoked in the British consciousness a fear of the loss of memory's moral function, and reinforced a commensurately strong commitment to tracing origins and lines of descent. These two features permeate *A Tale of Two Cities* (1860), which remains to this day the most famous British historical novel about Paris.[58] Ostensibly devoted to the first Revolution and its antecedents, which by 1859 were beyond the living memory of all but the novel's oldest readers, its events fall outside the chronological purview of this book, but *A Tale of Two Cities* was nevertheless an intervention in a contemporary debate. Did the promise of a 'beautiful city and a brilliant people rising from this abyss', envisaged by a character who

---

[57] Edwards, *In the Days of My Youth*, ii, 98.
[58] Nevertheless, it was scarcely a tactful choice of gift for Margaret Thatcher to offer to President Mitterrand during the commemoration of the second centenary of the French Revolution in 1989.

is about to die unjustly, in any way justify 'the long ranks of the new oppressors'?[59]
The immediate relevance of this question to Napoleon III's grand imperial project
of transforming the city, cost what it might to its poorest inhabitants, was further
spelt out by Dickens in his 1862 article 'Some Recollections of Immortality':

> The subject of my meditations was the question whether it is positively in the essence
> and nature of things, as a certain school of Britons would seem to think it, that a
> Capital must be ensnared and enslaved before it can be made beautiful: when I lifted
> up my eyes and found that my feet, straying like my mind, had brought me to
> Notre-Dame.
>
> That is to say, Notre-Dame was before me, but there was a large open space between
> us. A very little while gone, I had left that space covered with buildings densely
> crowded; and now it was cleared for some new wonder in the way of public Street,
> Place, Garden, Fountain, or all four.[60]

Commenting on the 1839 anniversary celebrations of the July Revolution, com-
memorated in 'the Place Louis Quinze, otherwise called the Place Louis Seize, or
else the Place de la Révolution, or else the Place de la Concorde (who can say
why?)', Thackeray had suggested that 'instead of having Carlyle to write a History
of the French Revolution, I often think it should be handed over to Dickens or
Theodore Hook'. For British observers accustomed to take the longer view, Paris's
annual commemorations of recent regime changes were inherently ludicrous yet
inevitably provoked reflection, both on previous occasions when revolutionary
mobs had hurled 'royalty, loyalty, and a thousand years of Kings, head-over-heels
out of yonder Tuileries windows' and on the likelihood of forthcoming repetitions
of this cycle.[61]

It is this same sense of cyclical inevitability, punctuated by brutal acts of destruction and betrayal, on which the complex time sequence of *A Tale of Two Cities* is
built. The book's opening metaphors of the silent growth of trees already marked
by the Woodman, Fate, who works with 'muffled tread', become audible in the
narrative's 'echoing footsteps' and the rumble of the death-carts in the final chapter, only to serve as harbinger of future repetition:

> Crush humanity out of shape *once more*, under *similar* hammers, and it will twist itself
> into the *same* tormented forms. Sow the *same* seed of rapacious license and oppression
> *over again*, and it will surely yield the *same* fruit according to its kind. [my italics][62]

By the novel's conclusion, the notion of history as safely confining or irrevocably
sealing off the past as settled fact has been destabilized. Miss Pross may experience
a 'fixed and unchangeable' stillness' caused by the gunshot which deafens her, but
readers, like the rest of Paris's inhabitants, are only too conscious of the noise of
approaching tumbrils. The novel makes little attempt to recreate a frozen time past
by presenting major historical figures or detailed Parisian topography. Instead, if the

[59] C. Dickens, *A Tale of Two Cities*, ed. A. Sanders (Oxford: Oxford University Press, 2008), 360.
[60] C. Dickens, 'Some Recollections of Immortality', in *The Uncommercial Traveller*, 188; first published in *All the Year Round*, 16 May 1863, 276–80.
[61] 'The Fêtes of July', *Paris Sketch Book*, 34, 36. Cf. Sala, *Quite Alone*, iii, 5–9.
[62] Dickens, *A Tale of Two Cities*, ed. Sanders, 356.

past was to be 'recalled to life' so as to interest readers in history's processes, Dickens needed to bear in mind formats and devices that resonated with contemporary readers. *A Tale of Two Cities* therefore calls upon the resources of the contemporary novel of sensation, in constituents such as the unmasking of hidden papers and family secrets, rape and murder, and in its interest in such matters as the relation between mind and body, and instances of trauma and monomania.

If these aspects played upon contemporary anxieties, the novel also made knowing allusion to familiar formats and conventions for representing Paris. The central notion of having the action oscillate between Paris and London had long been standard in the silver-fork novel, from which the description of the Marquis's salon in 'Monseigneur in Town' and the notion of juxtaposing life on the aristocratic country estate with the town establishment also derive. For the most part, however, the novel operates in the bourgeois and working-class circles favoured by Reynolds. The first volume of Reynolds's *The Mysteries of London*, for instance, had featured a London banker linked with Paris by his business dealings; trials at the Old Bailey, accompanied by adverse commentary on the lawyers who conduct them; and a trio of 'resurrectionists' who composed a central plank of his tale. Dickens's grave-robber, the 'resurrectionist' Jerry Cruncher and his two accomplices surely tipped a knowing nod to Reynolds's 'Body-Snatchers'. Like Jerry, Reynolds's gang leader, Anthony Tidkins, crosses the Channel, and is supplied with a family life in which he regularly indulges in domestic violence. The opening scene of *A Tale of Two Cities*, in which the mailcoach making its way to a Channel crossing seems likely to be interrupted by a highwayman, plays a similar role in moving characters back and forth from Paris to London in Reynolds's earlier novel *Alfred de Rosann; or, the Adventures of a French Gentleman* (1838), and the double-dealing turncoat, confidence trickster, and spy, Solomon Pross, who operates under the alias of Barsad in Paris, could easily have come, courtesy of Vidocq, from Reynolds's extensive rogues' gallery.

My point is not to accuse Dickens of plagiarism—he swiftly endows his borrowings from a common pool with highly individualized tics—but to confirm the fairly tight range of stereotypical situations and characters from which mid-Victorian novelists constructed their pictures of city life, and more specifically Parisian life, which they mostly knew less well than London. In a matter of a decade Madame Defarge and her band of maenad *citoyennes*, pitiless in their destructive vengeance, would re-enter the mythology of Parisian revolution and inform the fictional pictures of the *pétroleuses*. The final chapter of the book addresses the underlying structures, repetitive tropes, and stock characters employed by British fiction in voicing attitudes to Paris.

14

Stereotype and prejudice

We most of us transact our moral and spiritual affairs in our own country.[1]

What does travel ultimately produce if it is not, by a sort of reversal, 'an exploration of the deserted places of my memory,' the return to nearby exoticism by way of a detour through distant places, and the discovery' of relics and legends?...What this walking exile produces is precisely the body of legends that is currently lacking in one's own vicinity; it is a fiction, which moreover has the double characteristic, of being the effect of displacements and condensations.[2]

The final chapter of this book examines some of the deep-seated, and sometimes contradictory, convictions and prejudices about Paris and the Parisians that surfaced in mid-nineteenth-century British fiction, and the way in which these both influenced fictional structures, and led to the regular reappearance of stereotypical characters and situations.

The vogue for domestic realism that flourished at home in the mid-nineteenth-century English novel was beyond the reach of the majority of British writers when they came to depict Parisian life. Staying in the house of the acculturated Madame Mohl, Elizabeth Gaskell explained: 'Here in a French family, I get glimpses of life for which I am not prepared by any previous reading of French romances, or even by former visits to Paris, when I remained in a hotel frequented by English, and close to the street which seems to belong almost exclusively to them.'[3] Consequently, despite two long articles informing British readers about contemporary French living, Gaskell's fiction remained relatively untouched by this direct experience of Parisian domestic and social life.[4] Instead the French and their doings continued to be absorbed into her tales in forms beloved of Gothic fiction, as women abandoned or imprisoned, or dispossessed French aristocrats reduced to humble servitude in England. Even though parts of her final novel, *Wives and Daughters*, were written in Madame Mohl's home, the sole French references—to a squire's eldest son who has made a *mésalliance* with a French maid, a scientific article whose worth is vouched for by being published in France, and an English girl's character rendered cold and

[1] H. James, 'Paris Revisited', in *Parisian Sketches* (London: Rupert Hart-Davis, 1958), 5.

[2] M. de Certeau, *The Practice of Everyday Life*, trans. S. Rendell (Berkeley: University of California Press, 1988), 107.

[3] 'French Life', in *The Works of Elizabeth Gaskell*, ed. J. Shattock et al. (10 vols, London: Pickering & Chatto, 2005–6), i, 392.

[4] 'Company Manners' and 'French Life', in *Works of Elizabeth Gaskell*, ed. Shattock et. al., i, 295–310, 359–409.

preferring to feature the observations in her journalism

shallow by a French education—could all have been retrieved from the British store of French stereotypes.

If the rhythms of bourgeois Parisian domesticity proved untranslatable into English fiction, the aristocracy and the working classes (as the previous chapter's sections on the silver-fork novel and crime fiction suggested) were allotted to categories of novel where psychologically realistic characterization counted for little. Domestic servants, shop assistants, and *grisettes*, meanwhile, tended to be depicted solely in their moments of interaction with those they served. Often reduced to a nameless pair of hands in British domestic fiction, the domestic servants who appear in English pictures of Parisian life were usually subject to extreme stereotyping as either family treasures, prepared to contribute their life's savings to their now impoverished pre-Revolutionary masters, or, surly underlings, inclined to theft and ready to turn on their current masters at the slightest hint of either revolutionary activity or bribery.[5] Such faults as mendacity and disloyalty were represented as part and parcel of a police state, and thus characteristic national failings. Fanny Trollope indeed employed one from each of the first and third categories in *Hargrave; or, the Adventures of a Man of Fashion* (1843).[6] Only Anne Thackeray Ritchie, who had spent childhood years domiciled in Paris, produced a brief sketch of the kind of loyal family retainer, capable of offering tart advice, that Gaskell was capable of doing so well in novels such as *Ruth* or *North and South*.[7]

Moreover, whether they were enthusiastic Francophiles, confirmed xenophobes, or, more rarely, anxious to present a balanced appraisal, British novelists worked within or against a tradition created by a growing body of earlier imaginings of the city. Those who felt rejected by British society, or who actively opposed dominant British cultural mores, were supremely conscious of needing to redress previous bias but, in seeking to complicate the picture, often drew as much attention to the standard simplifications as to their own endeavours to produce a more nuanced understanding. Take for instance the frequent claim that, by comparison with the English cultivation of hearth and home, the French were notably deficient in domestic affection. Both Eliza Lynn Linton and Gaskell wrote articles which set out to scotch this libel, but their very anxiety to offer documentary evidence based on 'insider' knowledge led them to emphasize national differences in ways which threatened their original project.[8]

14.1 COMPARATIVE STRUCTURES

[Y]ou assert that you travel to be amused; but instead of finding interest, or amusement, in what you behold, you discover only faults. Every thing is compared with you and your country,—that country whence your *ennui* drove

---

[5] e.g. G. A. Sala, *Quite Alone* (3 vols, London: Chapman & Hall, 1864), ii, 163–5; [E. Linton,] 'Marie's Fever', *Household Words*, 30 July 1853, 523.

[6] F. Trollope, *Hargrave; or, the Adventures of a Man of Fashion* (3 vols, London: Henry Colburn, 1843), i, 17–19; ii, 97–8.

[7] *The Story of Elizabeth*; *The Works of Miss Thackeray* (10 vols, London: Smith, Elder, 1890), vi, 87–91.

[8] Gaskell, 'French Life'; [E. Linton,] 'French Domesticity', *Household Words*, 24 June 1854, 434–8.

you, and which, while in it, you decry, but the moment you desert it, you exalt. We, however, always find our *belle France* the best of countries, and, consequently, rarely leave it.[9]

The paradigms of fiction are essentially the same whatever the medium. Words or images, it makes no difference at the structural level.[10]

The pressure to address past British imaginings of Paris dictated deeper structural choices, and at first sight the structure of the epistolary novel, with its opportunities for presenting differing points of view, would have seemed an obvious choice for swapping impressions between the two capital cities, but in practice this device was rarely used. Lady Blessington's *The Victims of Society* was probably the only relevant novel conducted wholly in epistolary mode, but here the correspondence between two women, the one born in France and the other raised there, is so obviously skewed to illustrate the demoralizing effects of French cynicism that no fruitful comparative stance emerges. The problem may have been that since its eighteenth-century heyday the epistolary form had begun to seem outdated, and had in any case been overtaken by the 'letters home' reports of English correspondents abroad. These journalistic pieces depended for their success on the writer's capacity to produce authoritative impressions, and so tended to discourage the notion of alternative points of view.

The fact that the majority of British novels about Paris could have carried 'A Tale of Two Cities' as their subtitle does not mean that the two cities would necessarily gain equal page space, nor that balanced comparisons would be made, nor that any great effort would be made to devise a plot linking the characters' comings and goings between two capitals. In all these respects, indeed, Dickens could lay claim to considerable originality. He had devised a tightly plotted novel in which larger political forces could be made to appear to be playing as great a part as individual histories in driving the travel between London and Paris. It of course forms part of Dickens's Carlylean message that the fates of the two nations are too deeply imbricated ever to be separated. Tellson's bank is 'quite a French House, as well as an English one', and that belligerent patriot Miss Pross easily acquires culinary skills 'half English, and half French' from Soho's long-established Gallic community.[11] Further significant comparative gestures are made. Late eighteenth-century Great Britain is not free from the lawlessness and violence that afflicts Revolutionary France: travellers on the London–Dover road fear highwaymen, and spies are as plentiful in London as in Paris. Yet, at base, London, and British values form Dickens's moral yardstick. His Parisians are types—their working classes are less individually realized than their London counterparts, and the wicked marquis is a caricature of aristocratic indifference.

The standard binary model had been given currency by the part played by Lord Nevil within de Staël's *Corinne*. In such plots a young, unmarried British protagonist is sent to Paris to acquire social polish before responding to a parental

---

[9] Countess of Blessington, *The Victims of Society* (3 vols, London: Saunders & Otley, 1837), ii, 5–6.
[10] D. Lodge, *Changing Places* (Harmondsworth: Penguin, 1978), 251.
[11] C. Dickens, *A Tale of Two Cities*, ed. A. Sanders (Oxford: Oxford University Press, 2008), 21, 95.

call to return home to assume adult responsibilities. Since the duties at home frequently include embarking on marriage to a partner of impeccable English heritage, Paris is implicitly equated with the last irresponsible throes of adolescence. Bulwer's Pelham, responding to just such a maternal summons, leaves Paris without a backward glance: 'crack went the whips—off went the steeds, and so terminated my adventures at dear Paris'.[12] Multi-volume novels of manners regularly despatched their protagonist to Paris for one volume, to enjoy an agreeable flirtation with a foreign culture, without the stay having any crucial influence on subsequent events or behaviour: a little exposure to temptation has merely bolstered those sterling British qualities that have proved impregnable to foreign assault. In his parody of the silver-fork novels of Bulwer Lytton and Gore, Thackeray perfectly captured this sense that Paris could only temporarily 'pervert' or 'turn aside' an English aristocrat:

> Bitter, bitter tears did Emily de Pentonville weep, when, on Alured's return from the Continent, she beheld the awful change that dissipation had wrought in her beautiful, her blue-eyed, her perverted, her still beloved boy![13]

Fiction reflected the likelihood that whatever financial woes beset him, an educated young gentleman enjoyed greater agency than his sister. It is a heroine's socioeconomic inability to break free from the morally endangering atmosphere of Paris that distinguishes her predicament from that of a series of heroes who, though they may become temporarily ensnared by French women of dubious morality, emerge to embark on adult life, emotionally unscarred and with their reputations and morals relatively unscathed.

Exploring Britain's fears of the invasive power of Paris through female susceptibility formed the reverse side of the coin to the male imperviousness which represented Britain's confidence in its powers to remain true to itself. When a novel examining the moral and psychological forces that shape character took its heroine to Paris, it was as an intensifier of the rites of passage through which the adolescent British girl must pass if she were to emerge into marriageable adulthood. Whether the girl in question is cast adrift by parental ambition, a guardian's indifference, or the need to earn her own living, these tales concur in indicating the potentially fatal consequences of exposing an adolescent female, hitherto brought up according to English values, to French mores. If moral contamination could be caught merely through reading the representation of French immorality in its contemporary fiction, as often suggested in Victorian literature and art, the danger constituted by being sent to inhale its essence on a daily basis must be worse. The extreme vulnerability of these overly emotional, adolescent girls at a formative point in their lives formed the common impetus behind such fictions: as the author of *The Schoolgirl in France* (1840) expressed it in her preface:

> It has fallen to her lot, to witness many of the evils attendant on that too-common practice of sending young persons to the continent, at that very period of life when

---

[12] Lord [E. G. E. L. Bulwer-]Lytton, *Pelham: or, the Adventures of a Gentleman* (London: George Routledge, 1873), 123.

[13] 'Lords and Liveries', in *Miscellaneous Contributions to 'Punch'*, *The Oxford Thackeray*, ed. G. Saintsbury (17 vols, London: Oxford University Press, 1910), viii, 115.

the mind is most unguarded, the feelings most susceptible, and the principles most uncertain.

Each of the following coming-of-age novels displays several similar structural features: Rachel McCrindell's *The Schoolgirl in France* (1840); Sarah Fitton's *How I Became a Governess* (1861); Anne Thackeray Ritchie's *The Story of Elizabeth* (1860); Henrietta Jenkin's *Once and Again* (1865); 'Grace Ramsay's' *A Woman's Trials*; and Alice Corkran's *Margery Merton's Girlhood*. Many of these novels inspect the salutary consequences for an English girl who encounters the kind of young man who might well have formed the hero of a novel of manners:[14] French or English, he has come to Paris with pleasure and dalliance in mind. All of these novels depict a crisis in which, before the heroine can regain the healthy normality and respectable marriage promised on English shores, she, or a comparator female figure who exists merely to offer a timely warning, will have to endure a life-threatening illness brought on by the moral dangers to which France has exposed them. It is indeed a mark of the exceptionality of Charlotte Brontë's *Villette* (1853)—a novel which, though set in Belgium, in so many other respects enjoys the structures of these other tales—that at the end of the story she leaves her heroine, Lucy Snowe, abroad, her marital fate suspended.

The structural tension in these stories is fuelled by a series of interlocking prejudices. The tedium the visiting English girl experiences in the stifling monotony and constant surveillance practised at her French school, or in the hours of preparation for the polished performance expected in the *salons*, is contrasted with the seductive allure and heightened sensation offered by Parisian public life—in the hectic amusement of festival crowds, the charged atmosphere of a theatre audience, or the aesthetic and confessional consolations offered by Roman Catholic churches. The libertine, duplicitous, and intensely competitive fashionable society for which Parisian women were being prepared was measurable, to British eyes at least, by an education system which relied on constant supervision, rivalry, and spying to safeguard its girls' virtue until marriage was safely accomplished.[15] Above all, the heartless superficiality of a nation which valued social polish over individual integrity, and conformity to external forms over a good conscience, is repeatedly linked to and embedded in the two nations' differing religious traditions.

14.2 RELIGIOUS PREJUDICE

A dreadful suspicion had lately forced itself on her mind;—she could not avoid admitting, however unwillingly, that Caroline's conduct evinced a

---

[14] For a detailed analysis of Anne Thackeray Ritchie's fictional critique of the insouciant young Englishman abroad in Paris as portrayed in her father's largely autobiographical novel *The Adventures of Philip*, see E. Jay, '"In Her Father's Steps She Trod": Anne Thackeray Ritchie Imagining Paris', *Yearbook of English Studies* 36(2) (2006), 197–211.

[15] C. de Bellaigue, *Educating Women: Schooling and Identity in Britain and France 1800–1867* (Oxford: Oxford University Press, 2007) offers detailed discussion of the different national traditions and the concepts that informed them.

growing partiality for everything French, and a leaning to the doctrines and observances of Popery.[16]

The fact is, there is no religion in Paris... there is no satirizing religious cant in France; for its contrary, true religion, has disappeared altogether; and having no substance can cast no shadow. If a satirist would lash the religious hypocrites in *England* now—the High-Church hypocrites, the Low-Church hypocrites, the promiscuous Dissenting hypocrites, the No-Popery hypocrites—he would have ample subject enough. In France, the religious hypocrites went out with the Bourbons.[17]

As these two comments indicate, the British were capable of simultaneously embracing at least two contradictory prejudices about the state of religion in France, each of which was intimately related to their sense of the threats offered to their own distinctiveness as a nation. On the one hand, memories of the French Revolution's outright attack upon religion, and the sacrilegious excesses it had witnessed, confirmed British views that the French were an essentially irreligious nation, posing a subversive menace to a kingdom where a constitutionally embedded religion formed a bulwark against sedition and anarchy. On the other hand, France's traditional adherence to Roman Catholicism as its majority religion was perceived as offering a neighbouring haven to those—be they Irish Catholics, seceding Tractarians, or Anglo-Catholics—who were continually seeking to subvert Protestant Britain from within.

Although Protestantism, and more particularly Anglicanism, was the British default position, it did not speak with one voice. Dissenting attitudes were inclined to be complicated by a deep-rooted suspicion of religion of any kind when it worked hand in glove with government. Thus Robert Browning distrusted both the Protestant politician Guizot, who had shown so little enthusiasm for helping to oust Papal power in Italy, and Montalembert, the ultramontane lay leader of France's Roman Catholics, who had nevertheless supported Napoleon III's rise to power for as long as he thought he could gain his support for church-controlled education. Their hypocrisy, Browning suggested in his poem 'Respectability', was part and parcel of Parisian public life where social civilities counted for more than conviction.[18] Meanwhile the socialist Dissenter, Matilda Betham-Edwards, nursed a more pervasive conspiracy theory that Roman Catholic interests had kept Napoleon III in power and even fostered the immorality of the Second Empire.[19]

The very different constitutional relations pertaining between politics and religion, and indeed between various forms of Christianity, in the two countries made impartial comparison difficult. Nevertheless, British writers were often acutely

---

[16] R. McCrindell, *The Schoolgirl in France* (London: R. B. Seeley & W. Burnside, 1840), 213.

[17] 'Caricatures and Lithography in France', in *Paris Sketch Book, Oxford Thackeray*, ii, 189.

[18] *Letters of the Brownings to George Barrett*, ed. P. Landis and R. E. Freeman (Urbana: University of Illinois Press, 1958), 168; *Learned Lady: Letters from Robert Browning to Mrs Thomas Fitzgerald 1876–1889*, ed. E. C. McAleer (Cambridge, Mass: Harvard University Press, 1966), 92.

[19] M. Betham-Edwards, *Brother Gabriel* (3 vols, London: Hurst & Blackett, 1878), iii, 236.

conscious that their English readers would expect some reflection on how the religious life of Paris related to ecclesiastical affairs on the home front. Only six months after roundly asserting that religion scarcely existed in Paris, Thackeray published an article on George Sand's novels, in which his brief review of Paris's changing fashions of religiosity is used as a peg on which to hang an address to his British readers upon the blasphemous oversimplifications contained in Martha Sherwood's Evangelical tracts, German theological scholarship, and the latest gossip concerning the leading members of Britain's Catholic Apostolic Church, otherwise known as the Irvingites.

This desire to make religious commentary relevant to British readers could have an oddly distorting effect. The end of the second volume of Frances Trollope's *Hargrave; or, the Adventures of a Man of Fashion* (1843) suddenly lurches into discussion of the religious affiliations of the two half-sisters at the centre of the story. Until this point the fact that one has followed her dead mother into the Roman Catholic Church, while the other has reverted to her mother's Protestant faith, had been scarcely mentioned. 1843, however, saw the rumours about Newman's retreat to Littlemore growing, and Frances Trollope took this opportunity to nail her colours to the mast. A learned Catholic priest is introduced whose allegiance has been tested by reading conflicting opinions before opting to bend to Rome's authority. This priest's capacity to be bamboozled by anyone who claims to have papal interests at heart is made the occasion for advertising the practical counselling and preaching of M. Coquerel, a real Protestant pastor with a considerable Parisian following.[20]

French Protestantism, however, did not automatically win approval. Most commentators would have agreed with Henrietta Jenkin's heroine, who feels sorry for a French *pasteur* to whom she has taken a liking, for 'It's quite different, isn't it mamma, from being an English clergyman?'[21] The Calvinist severity and gloom of the services and classes presided over by Pasteur Monod at the fashionable Parisian Chapelle Taitbout, where Prime Minister Guizot worshipped, seemed overwhelmingly oppressive to adolescent girls like Thackeray's daughters and the Corkran girls.[22] In adulthood, Annie Thackeray Ritchie recalled how this rendered the Roman Catholic services glimpsed from her grandparents' country house outside Paris seem attractively fête-like by comparison.[23] With the memory of her unhappy sojourn in the English Protestant enclave still fresh in her mind, she wrote *The Story of Elizabeth,* in which the sudden shock of immersion in the austere joylessness of a French *pasteur*'s family is offered as quite sufficient explanation for the heroine's clandestine outings to a theatre with her cousin's fiancé.

Since in cosmopolitan Paris most varieties of Protestantism boasted a place of worship, British visitors, unless they were cradle Catholics, treated Roman Catholicism as a tourist activity, visiting its churches, or securing a seat for a course

[20] F. Trollope, *Hargrave; or, the Adventures of a Man of Fashion* (3 vols, London: Henry Colburn, 1843), ii, 221–40.

[21] [H. Jenkin,] *Once and Again: A Novel* (3 vols, London: Smith, Elder, 1865), ii, 41.

[22] H. Corkran, *Celebrities and I* (London: Hutchinson, 1902), 66–8.

[23] A. T. Ritchie, *Chapters from Some Memoirs* (London: Macmillan, 1894), 151–4.

of sermons by a particularly noted preacher.[24] Bulwer Lytton, whose purpose was largely to remark the political split between the revolutionary lower classes and the fading power of the *ancien régime*, arranged a scene in the Madeleine explicitly to comment on the state of religion in the city at the end of the Second Empire. Two bourgeois Frenchmen drop in and observe a devout congregation composed primarily of aristocrats, accompanied by a sprinkling of the older working classes, and large numbers of Breton soldiers. 'Religion', the narrator remarked, 'still existed in Paris, and largely exist it does, though little seen on the surface of society, little to be estimated by the articles of journals and the reports of foreigners.'[25]

The point was well made: what struck British observers more forcibly, because unavoidable, was the Parisian failure to observe the Sabbath as a commerce-free day. For Dickens the bustling trade in the open shops provided a further example of the exploitation of the working classes which had fuelled his campaign against sabbatarian legislation at home: 'so much toil and sweat on what one would like to see, apart from religious observances, a sensible holiday, is painful.'[26] For the average middle-class Briton, however, the flagrant consumerism evident on the Parisian streets of a Sunday epitomized the essential foreignness of this neighbouring capital. These reactions imputed to the young hero of a novel, fresh from his village of Saxenholme, express his Protestant inheritance by means of Biblical prose rhythms and by respect for the Word, and for a tradition rooted in the continuity of the English countryside.

> Where there had been the silence of early morning there was now the confusion of a great city. Where there had been closed shutters and deserted thoroughfares, there was the bustle of life, gayety, business, and pleasure. The shops blazed with jewels and merchandise; the stonemasons were at work on the new buildings; the lemonade venders, with their gay reservoirs upon their backs, were plying a noisy trade...the merchant was in his counting-house, the stock-broker at the Bourse, and the lounger, whose name is Legion, was sitting in the open air outside his favorite café, drinking chocolate, and yawning over the *Charivari*.
>
> I thought I must be dreaming. I scarcely believed the evidence of my own eyes. Was this Sunday? Was it possible that in our own little church at home,—in our own little church, where we could hear the birds twittering outside in every interval of the quiet service—the old familiar faces, row beyond row, were even now upturned in reverent attention to the words of the preacher?[27]

The British habit of viewing Roman Catholicism as at best a spectator activity reinforced the habit of commenting mainly on the external features which differentiated it from the reformed churches of most Protestant persuasions: the Roman religion's highly decorated churches, the smell of incense, the queues for the confessional, or the gluttony of its priests. Margaret Oliphant's recollections of attending

[24] e.g. F. Trollope, *Paris and the Parisians in 1835* (2 vols, Paris: Baudry's European Library, 1836), i, 52, 85; *The Autobiography of Margaret Oliphant*, ed. E. Jay (Oxford: Oxford University Press, 1990), 113.

[25] Lord [E. G. E. L. Bulwer-]Lytton, *The Parisians* (2 vols, London: George Routledge, 1875), ii, 262.

[26] *The Pilgrim Edition of the Letters of Charles Dickens*, ed. G. Storey et al. (12 vols, Oxford: Clarendon Press, 1965–2002), iv, 663.

[27] A. B. Edwards, *In the Days of My Youth* (3 vols, London: Hurst & Blackett, 1873), i, 129–31.

Lenten and Easter services in Notre Dame are deliberately composed as a painting or operatic spectacle:

> The nave was packed closely with men, a dark mass, their immoveable faces whitening the whole surface of that great area under the not abundant lights, and the spare figure of the monk in the pulpit, his face whiter still, like ivory. It was very dark in the side chapels, and we did not hear very well, but the sight was very impressive, and specially so I think the Thursday of Holy Week, when this immense crowd of men sang the Stabat Mater in unison,—the most wonderful volume of sound ... a perfectly new and extraordinary effect ...
>
> On the Easter morning we went very early to Notre Dame to see the communion of these men, which was also a very touching sight ... I ... smiled a little ... at the air of conscious solemnity with which most of the men came up to the altar, very devout, but yet with a certain sense of forming part of a very great and ennobling spectacle.[28]

This focus on the materiality of the experience served to intensify the prejudice that, whereas Protestantism encouraged introspection and individual spiritual accountability, Catholicism was largely a matter of conforming to certain rites, and so accounted for French superficiality. Only nunneries and monasteries were exempt from this wholesale condemnation. When not invoked as Gothic places of imprisonment, or suitable depositories for women who had in some way besmirched their genteel reputation, nunneries were generally recognized as performing charitable, educational, or nursing functions which to an extent compensated for their heretical beliefs.[29] The defence of the monasteries and their inhabitants usually took the form of a reaction to the violent anti-clericalism of French radicalism rather than a positive endorsement of the education or values they offered.[30]

The only fiction which claimed to portray a more intimate picture of Roman Catholic mores were the tales of Parisian boarding schools for girls, which were often couched as playing a serious part in a national debate. The departing advice 'never to forget in a foreign land that I was an Englishwoman and a member of the Church of England', given by a family friend to the heroine of Sarah Fitton's *How I Became a Governess* (1860), captures the solemnity with which even less polemical authors approached their task.[31,32]

Rachel McCrindell's tale *The Schoolgirl in France* (1840), however, was explicitly designed to dissuade English parents from the fashionable habit of sending daughters to French finishing school;[33] and if her principal aim proved unsuccessful,

---

[28] *Autobiography of Margaret Oliphant*, ed. Jay, 113.

[29] The former type is exemplified in C. Gore, *The Ambassador's Wife* (3 vols, London: Richard Bentley, 1842), iii, 310–21, and the latter in [Jenkin,] *Once and Again*, iii, 281; [Linton,] 'Marie's Fever', 522; 'Ouida' [M. L. de la Ramée], *Tricotrin; the Story of a Waif and Stray* (3 vols, London: Chapman & Hall, 1869), i, 86.

[30] M. Betham-Edwards, *Brother Gabriel*, (3 vols, London: Hurst & Blackett, 1878), iii, 242–7; M. E. Braddon, *Under the Red Flag* (Leipzig: Tauchnitz, 1884), 76–87.

[31] Fitton was a long-standing member of the English resident community in Paris: her other works for children on botany and music suggest that she was more interested in educational than religious issues.

[32] [S. Fitton,] *How I Became a Governess* (London: Griffith & Farran, 1861), 26.

[33] By 1847–8, English girls formed the majority of foreign pupils, composing 9% of the 1,382 girls in the 34 boarding schools in the 1st arrondissement of Paris: de Bellaigue, *Educating Women*, 200.

McCrindell was determined to provide these girls with the doctrinal wherewithal to withstand the Catholic foe, in the event of conversion attempts. British readers may have taken for granted the bias of a book with this title, especially when it was published out of the Seeley evangelical stable; but America, accustomed to such lurid titles as *The Awful Disclosures of Maria Monk; or, The Hidden Secrets of a Nun's Life in a Convent Exposed* (1836), required more obvious signposting, so in New York McCrindell's work acquired the subtitle '*The Snares of Popery: A Warning to Protestants Against Education in Catholic Seminaries*' (1845), while in Philadelphia the tale was baldly retitled as *The Protestant Girl in a French Nunnery* (1846).

Much of the debate conducted in these school stories was centred on the extent to which Roman Catholic establishments actively sought to convert English pupils. Even McCrindell agreed that French schools customarily made arrangements for English pupils to attend Protestant places of worship, but in a convent school, the desire to join the Catholic pupils in witnessing the celebration of a feast day or a first communion could sow the first seed of disquiet, just as the 'spiritual desolation' apparent in laicized French schools could awaken a fervour for the intense atmosphere of the convent. As an Irish Catholic raised in Paris, Kathleen O'Meara stoutly maintained that it was not in the financial interests of Catholic schools to seek to proselytize; in any case, 'beyond a few words interchanged along the passages with the regular pensionnaires, or a chance word to servants, the [English] parlour-boarders would pass an entire day without speaking French.'[34] The second and third volumes of her novel *A Woman's Trials* (1867) tell how a Protestant girl's conversion forces the principal of her Catholic school to expel her in order to preserve the school's reputation. Her Protestant father's act, of disowning his convert Catholic daughter, allows the tale to throw back onto Protestant consciences the need to deal with the solitary state that leads beleaguered young Englishwomen to seek consolation in Roman Catholicism. Repeatedly such novels replay the drama of the isolated Lucy Snowe meeting with 'all that was tender, and comforting, and gentle,' from the priestly confessor in a local Roman Catholic church in Charlotte Bronte's *Villette*.[35] In Margaret Oliphant's experience, troubled Englishwomen abroad often had recourse to the prayerful silence of such churches, not because they were drawn to Rome, but because they had been alienated by the gossipy cliquishness of Protestant churches catering for English expatriates.[36]

In the wake of the anti-clericalism manifested during the Commune, there was less emphasis upon what Frances Trollope had proclaimed 'that most precious of all Roman Catholic triumphs, the conversion of a wealthy infidel'.[37] It may be that the secular foundation of the Third Republic allayed fears, but later novelists tended to mitigate the mistaken revolutionary zeal of their young heroes by having them attempt to rescue their former monastic teachers from the violent clutches

---

[34] [K. O'Meara,] *A Woman's Trials*, by 'Grace Ramsay' (3 vols, London: Hurst & Blackett, 1867), i, 152.

[35] C. Bronte, *Villette*, ed. H. Rosengarten and M. Smith (Oxford: Clarendon Press, 1984), 228.

[36] M. O. W. Oliphant, 'Madame Saint-Ange', *Good Cheer*, Dec. 1867, 33–44.

[37] F. Trollope, *Fashionable Life; or, Paris and London* (3 vols, London: Hurst & Blackett, 1856), ii, 19–20.

of the mob,[38] or to dwell on the inherent defects of the French educational system,[39] rather than on French Roman Catholicism's insidious attempts to undermine Protestantism through concentrating on its weakest link: susceptible young girls.

The total absence in British writers' convent novels of any hint that French priests betrayed the kind of sexual interest in their flock alleged in Maria Monk's 'awful disclosures' may have been because this aspersion had been reserved for attacking Jesuits and Anglo-Catholics doing the Pope's work in England, or it may have been that Paris's reputation for secular sins of the flesh sufficed.

14.3 THE WICKEDNESS OF PARIS

> Paris?' I hear you exclaim: 'Unhappy soul! what has taken *thee* to Paris? . . . where vanity and Sensuality have set up their chosen shrine, and every one that falls not down to worship them is as an alien and an interloper!'[40]

> He was not a good man,—he had not led a good life. Pretty women had called him 'Enfant!' in the dim mysterious shades of lamplit conservatories, upon the curtain-shrouded thresholds of moonlit balconies. Arch soubrettes in little Parisian theatres, bewitching Marthons and Margots and Jeannettons, with brooms in their hands and diamonds in their ears, had smiled at him, and acted at him, and sung at him, as he lounged in the dusky recesses of a cavernous box.[41]

Matthew Arnold's bizarre ethnographic construction of 'the sensuousness of the Latinised Frenchman' who typified Paris probably did not seem so wide of the mark to his contemporaries as it does to us.[42] Deploying his theory as an explanation of France's defeat in the Franco-Prussian war, he contrived to suggest an intimate relation between Paris's two besetting sins of sexual hedonism and revolutionary politics:

> Paris is the city of *l'homme sensual moyen*. This has an attraction for all of us. We all have in us this *homme sensual*, the man of the 'wishes of the flesh and of the current thoughts . . . France takes the wishes of the flesh and of the current thoughts' for man's *rights*; and human happiness, and the perfection of society, she places in everybody's being enabled to gratify these wishes, to get these rights, as equally as possible and as much as possible.[43]

Regendered as female, these twin evils emerged in pictorial and literary representations of the unfettered passion, both personal and political, fuelling the activities

---

[38] e.g. Betham-Edwards, *Brother Gabriel* (1878); Braddon, *Under the Red Flag* (1883).

[39] e.g. A. Corkran, *Margery Merton's Girlhood* (London: Blackie & Sons, 1888); 'The English Teacher at the Convent', in *The Young Philistine and Other Stories* (London: Burns & Oates, 1887), 1–30.

[40] *The Collected Letters of Thomas and Jane Welsh Carlyle*, ed. C. R. Sanders, K. J. Fielding, et al. (40 vols, Durham, NC: Duke University Press, 1970–2012), iii, 178.

[41] M. E. Braddon, *The Doctor's Wife*, ed. L. Pykett (Oxford: Oxford University Press, 2008), 201.

[42] 'On the Study of Celtic Literature' (1866), in *The Complete Prose Works of Matthew Arnold*, ed. R. H. Super (11 vols, Ann Arbor: University of Michigan Press, 1960–77), iii, 346.

[43] M. Arnold, *Literature and Dogma* (1873), in *Works*, ed. Super, vi, 390–1.

of the *pétroleuses*. Delacroix's famous painting of the 1830s barricades, 'Liberty leading the People', showing the bare-footed, bare-breasted figure of Liberty bestriding corpses underfoot, was later adopted as a symbol of republican France, and may have played its part in literary depictions of revolutionary maenads whose behaviour was the antithesis of everything the English middle classes valued in their women. 'Ouida's' description of a woman of the barricades, as a prostitute leading her countrymen into evil, 'her bosom bare, and her arms akimbo, and her garments all in rags', is typical. The similarity of these depictions to those of madwomen underlines the irrationality of the ill-educated, working-class female revolutionary, invariably driven by misplaced love or revenge.[44]

British novelists showed less interest in the working-class male revolutionary. More to their taste was the eccentric figure of the French aristocrat turned revolutionary. This character's antipathy to the politics of central government is usually emphasized by siting his ancestral lands in far-flung Brittany. Scant attention is paid to the specific nature of the character's political ideas. His desire that France should be freed 'slowly' from mismanagement and oppression scarcely qualify Dickens's Charles Darnay as a revolutionary, but his generalized diagnosis of the ills from which France was suffering would have sufficed for the credo of most of his more politically committed fictional equivalents: 'it is a crumbling tower of waste, mismanagement, extortion, debt, mortgage, oppression, hunger, nakedness and suffering.'[45] British novels offer nothing to match the more nuanced choice between the politics of his father and grandfather that the young hero of the barricades, Marius Pontmercy, must make in Victor Hugo's *Les Misérables* (1862).

Ideologically driven betrayals of class loyalty appear to have been so unimaginable to most British novelists that the typical revolutionary aristocrat's estrangement from his class origins is usually precipitated by some personal wrong experienced at the hands of his family or social set.[46] Always slightly embarrassed by the folly and excesses of his working-class fellow-travellers, he either dies trying to restrain them or is ultimately redeemed from his youthful enthusiasm by marriage to a good middle-class woman.

This focus on the private romance simultaneously works to suggest that public evils are chronic, capable only of minor mitigation at the personal level, and severs the political alliance, most disliked by the British middle classes, between the aristocrat and the masses. Even Bulwer Lytton's Vicomte de Mauléon, whose role as agent provocateur is initially motivated by cynical self-interest, is manipulated in the novel's coda to serve the message that revolution based upon 'principles that demand the demolition of all upon which the civilisation of Europe has its basis— worship, property, and marriage—in order to reconstruct a new civilisation adapted to a new humanity' is doomed to failure. Too old by now for marriage himself, the Vicomte secures respectable marriages for others for whom he feels responsible,

---

[44] e.g. Madame Defarge in Dickens, *A Tale of Two Cities*, or Suzon Michel in Braddon, *Under the Red Flag*.

[45] Dickens, *A Tale of Two Cities*, ed. Sanders, 119.

[46] e.g. the hero of 'Ouida's' *Tricotrin*, or the Vicomte de Mauléon in Bulwer Lytton's *The Parisians*.

and, finding he cannot impose discipline on the Communards, joins 'the party of Order' at Versailles, only to be stabbed on the ramparts on the last day of *la Semaine Sanglante* by 'a Red Republican and Socialist', whose initial forays into revolutionary activity he had encouraged. The last word on post-Communard Paris is allotted to a bourgeois dandy, who offers a ringing endorsement of the stereotypes of Parisians beloved to the British:

> Certain moralising journals tell us that, sobered by misfortunes, the Parisians are going to turn over a new leaf, become studious and reflective, despise pleasure and luxury, and live like German professors. Don't believe a word of it. My conviction is that, whatever may be said as to our frivolity, extravagance, &c., under the Empire, we shall be just the same under any form of government.[47]

The French bourgeois, though free from revolutionary wickedness, were held to be equally immoral in contracting marriages of cold dynastic calculation, made tolerable only by the complaisant eyes with which spouses subsequently regarded each other's flirtations and infidelities—subject only to the proviso that these did not threaten the wider family or cause unnecessary scandal. The occasional female practitioner of domestic fiction, such as Elizabeth Gaskell or Margaret Oliphant, would attempt to get readers to see the pros and cons of arranged marriages, such as the plentiful post-marital support available from two families, in whose interest it was to see the marriage flourish; but such comparisons rarely ventured beyond the confines of an article or short story because they demanded too much sympathetic engagement with an alien culture and disposition.[48] For the most part the mutually indifferent partners in French marriages served to paint the backdrop of an immoral society at which the English could only purse their lips, or thank God they had been born into a superior civilization where romantic attachment formed the desirable precondition for marriage. English fiction agreed in asserting that it was only the respectable married women of Paris's English Quarter who shunned *salons* hosted or frequented by Frenchwomen known to be involved in an extramarital liaison. This peculiarly English behaviour is variously interpreted by fictional Parisians as a failure in cosmopolitan savoir-faire, rank hypocrisy, or, more simply, a striking and inexplicable example of cultural difference. As Frances Trollope remarked:

> [The] remarkable difference between the two countries [is] that the theme which is first brought under discussion with us, when scandal is the business of the hour, is the last alluded to; whereas it is never alluded to at all by our neighbours. No, nobody talked about Madame de Soissonac's lovers, but a great many people talked about her extravagance, her horses, her carriages, her dresses, and above all, of the absurd, and every-way-detestable vanity of which she and her husband had been guilty in prefixing *de* before their name. But not for this were the *salons* of Madame de Soissonac the less brilliantly filled.[49]

---

[47] Bulwer Lytton, *The Parisians*, ii, 376, 383.
[48] 'French Life', 369–70; M. O. W. Oliphant, 'The Count's Daughters', *Good Cheer*, Dec. 1874, 1–31.
[49] F. Trollope, *The Robertses on their Travels* (3 vols, London: Henry Colburn, 1846), i, 77.

Older, unmarried French women added to the repertoire of English fiction's comic spinsters by being prepared to welcome an invitation to an affair as avidly as a proposal of marriage.[50]

Whether mid-nineteenth-century Paris, either in the private lives of its wealthier classes or the seamier life of the street, was in truth more libidinous than mid-nineteenth-century London is probably impossible to answer. By 1830 street prostitution had been banned in both capitals. The 'politico-statistical' enthusiasm of an underemployed French bureaucracy, to which William Acton attributed Parent-Duchâtelet's influential study of Paris's native prostitutes and their cohorts of sisters from the provinces, lent a surface impression of scientific evidence for a more pervasive working-class sex industry than the impressionistic accounts provided for English cities by Bracebridge Hemyng or William Acton.[51] English fiction and art certainly reflected a belief that Paris offered a likely destination for the ruined English woman. Elizabeth Barrett Browning's *Aurora Leigh* (1857) famously depicted Marian Erle, a travellers' child, as drugged and transported to a French brothel, and a year later, Augustus Egg displayed his narrative triptych of a middle-class fallen woman's history, 'Past and Present', finally picturing her under the Adelphi arches giving onto the Thames, with a poster behind her, advertising 'Pleasure Excursions to Paris'. A letter from the Parisian *salonnière* Mary Mohl confirmed that these fictional histories of English girls had some basis in reality.

> I am much interested in a sort of establishment here, only just beginning, called a Home for English Young Women. It is a horrible fact that there are people who catch handsome young English girls in London and send them over here for vice, because the lower class is so much handsomer there and more delicate in complexion and shape. Others...come to get places as governesses, nursemaids, etc., and get snapped up; then if they want to get out of these vices, they can't.[52]

The louche night-time expeditions conducted by Egg and Dickens in Paris give some credence to Catherine Gore's claim that 'the moment an Englishman feels the pragmaticality of his native land too much for his spirits, off he goes, to relieve himself abroad; and, like a high pressure boiler, of which the safety-valve has been obstructed, the explosion is terrible.'[53]

What seems to have shocked Victorians more than the tales, common to both countries, of poor women fallen on hard times was the high social visibility of mistresses and wealthy courtesans in Paris. Thackeray referred to the 'rich store

---

[50] e.g. the heroine's governess in C. Gore, *The Diary of a Désennuyée* (2 vols, London: Henry Colburn, 1836); and the villain's sister-in-law in F. Trollope's *Hargrave*.

[51] A. J.-B. Parent-Duchâtelet, *De la prostitution dans la ville de Paris: considérée sous le rapport de l'hygiène publique, de la morale et de l'administration* (2 vols, 1836; Paris: Baillière, 1857); B. Hemyng, 'Prostitution in London', in Henry Mayhew, *London Labour and the London Poor: A Selected Edition*, ed. R. Douglas-Fairhurst (1861–2: Oxford: Oxford University Press, 2010), 332–40; W. Acton, *Prostitution, considered in its moral, social, and sanitary aspects, in London and other large cities* (London: J. Churchill, 1857), 2. See also M. Mason, *The Making of Victorian Sexuality* (Oxford: Oxford University Press, 1994), 80–90, for the difficulty of forming a clear view from such estimates.

[52] M. Lesser, *Clarkey: A Portrait in Letters of Mary Clarke Mohl (1793–1883)* (Oxford: Oxford University Press, 1984), 129–30.

[53] C. Gore, *Sketches of English Character* (2 vols, London: Richard Bentley, 1846), 5.

of calm internal *debauch*' which allowed French gentlemen of the July Monarchy to admit to possessing a mistress as readily as mentioning their tailor—an openness which he contrasted with 'the decency of secrecy' observed on such matters in England.[54] The journalist Vizetelly wondered how Victoria and Albert would cope during their 1855 visit with the court of Napoleon III, where the Emperor's affairs, and those of his niece, Princess Mathilde, and his cousin, Prince Napoleon, were common knowledge.[55] Gradually the simpler style of *salon* hosted by wives in the marital home was giving way to the rise of a male club culture where it became the practice to welcome and celebrate the charms of actresses and courtesans. The club gossip about the spectacular horsewomanship of a mysterious newcomer to Rotten Row with which Sala's *Quite Alone* begins had its real life equivalent in Thomas Hardy's recollection of the chat among the 'architect's pupils and other young men' with whom he socialized when he first went to London in the early 1860s: it was of 'Coral Pearl, "Skittles", Agnes Willoughby, Adah Menken, and others... of whom they professed to know many romantic and *risqué* details, but really knew nothing at all'.[56]

The cult of Catherine Walters (alias 'Skittles'), almost as renowned for her skill as a horsewoman as for her abilities as a high-flying courtesan, not only acted as the inspiration for Sala's novel but produced a long narrative poem by Wilfrid Scawen Blunt. Having been captivated by her in the early 1860s, when her star was in the ascendant at Napoleon's summer residence, he spent the next thirty years polishing a self-pitying sonnet sequence about the circumstances of his seduction. In his rewriting of this episode, the already sexually experienced Blunt became the ingénu and Catherine is reinvented as a young French actress: 'Boy as I was, she had not lived a nun.'[57]

The fashionable éclat such humbly born young English women won for themselves by entering the demi-monde world was an insult to Protestant principle, and the clear contrast their lives offered to the English womanly ideal of virginal purity, designed to flower into wifely and maternal solicitude, became an accepted shorthand for indicating the inherent depravity of the French female character. While a French education was sufficient to explain the callous flirtatiousness of English girls like Charlotte Brontë's Ginevra Fanshawe, or Gaskell's Cynthia Kirkpatrick, being born French set a female character at an almost irrecuperable moral disadvantage. Even though Adèle Varens is removed 'from the slime and mud of Paris, and transplanted... to grow up clean in the wholesome soil of an English country garden', it takes many years of Jane Eyre's tutelage and two English boarding schools to correct 'in a great measure her French defects'. Thus, by the end of Charlotte Brontë's novel, the specific circumstances of Adèle's birth as the 'illegitimate offspring of a French opera-girl' who preferred her own amatory

---

[54] Thackeray, 'On Some French Fashionable Novels', in *Paris Sketch Book*, ii, 108–9.

[55] H. Vizetelly, *Glances Back through Seventy years: Autobiographical and Other Recollections* (2 vols, London: Kegan Paul, Trench, Trübner, 1893), i, 401–2.

[56] M. Millgate (ed.), *The Life and Work of Thomas Hardy* (London: Macmillan, 1984), 43.

[57] 'Esther: A Young Man's Tragedy', sonnet 17 in *The Poetry of Wilfrid Blunt*, ed. W. E. Henley and G. Wyndham (London: William Heinemann, 1898), 71.

pleasures to the bonds of maternity have become absorbed into an overriding national disposition.[58]

Self-seeking ambition and the love of adulation so frequently filled the place of 'normal' maternal feeling in French-born characters—consider half-French Becky Sharp's antipathy to her son—that it became increasingly difficult to convey the additional wickedness necessarily involved in being an actress. If women who appeared on the London stage, flaunting their bodies in public and immersed in a hothouse world of lavish adulation, at best enjoyed a dubious fictional reputation, those who succeeded in Paris's famed melodramas, in which illicit affairs of the heart played so prominent a role, were automatically assumed to be meretricious. Moreover, since such shows and their stars were so popular in Paris, these women must embody a peculiarly French womanly ideal: superficially sophisticated, promiscuous, and essentially heartless.

Sala, for instance, seemed unable to understand that ambition alone might drive a beautiful girl from languishing unadmired in a provincial auberge to securing a position as a salaried actress at the Porte Saint-Martin theatre. Instead his actress, Valerie, exhibits symptoms of insanity, and her wild mood swings and drunken rages justify her child being taken from her. The deep-seated misogyny of 'Ouida's' *Tricotrin*, apparent in narrative comments such as 'The devil is never so brutal as when he comes into a woman's form', produces a novel in which every beautiful Frenchwoman is a further instance of the sex's corruptibility. The story of the orphaned baby, Viva, found abandoned in the French countryside, and raised a child of nature only to hanker for the bright lights of Paris, is interwoven with the tale of the mother who abandoned her, the famous French actress and courtesan Coriolis, 'wicked, because things all sense and no soul must be so'. When Coriolis's sailor husband, who has spent twenty years in pursuit of the wife who abandoned him, finds her on a Parisian stage, he repudiates her as a devil who has assumed his wife's form, before vomiting blood and expiring on stage. Viva, who has narrowly escaped the life inevitable for success on the Parisian stage—honest, pure women who turn actresses are 'hissed off the boards'—instead opts for the alternative Parisian form of prostitution involved in marrying without love for riches and power.[59]

At first sight George Eliot's picture in *Middlemarch* of Lydgate, distracted from his medical studies in Paris by an *amour fou* for the actress Madame Laure, famed for her performances in the melodramas at the Porte Saint-Martin theatre, appears to be nothing more than a *réchauffé* of the same literary cliché. Madame Laure's revelation that she intentionally stabbed her actor husband on stage one night, out of boredom with his uxoriousness, may confirm Eliot's revulsion against this female profession; but Lydgate's subsequent entrapment by that perfect English rose Rosamond Vincy, who 'flourished wonderfully on a murdered man's brains',[60] suggests that Eliot at least did not perceive the self-centred female concern with the material as peculiarly French. Concerned to show how resistant provincial English

---

[58] C. Brontë, *Jane Eyre*, ed. J. Jack and M. Smith (Oxford: Clarendon Press, 1969), 178, 576.
[59] 'Ouida', *Tricotrin*, ii, 26, 12, 90.
[60] G. Eliot, *Middlemarch*, ed. D. Carroll (Oxford: Clarendon Press, 1986), 821.

society of the mid-nineteenth century had been to the alien and the exotic, George Eliot drew upon and complicated the stereotypes of the 'continental novel' for both her junior romantic leads. Lydgate nurses aristocratic pretensions, but lacks both the financial freedom and moral insouciance of the silver-fork hero, while Will Ladislaw originates in that other archetype of the Parisian novel, 'the bohemian'.

14.4 THE BOHEMIAN

La Bohème, the ideal, free, pleasurable life of Paris, is a kind of paradise of Ishmael.[61]

Matthew Arnold's bracketing of the permissive life of the Latin Quarter with the life of a biblical nomadic exile was striking enough to be quoted a couple of years later in 'Ouida's' novel *Tricotrin*.[62] His paradox not only incorporates something of the ambivalence with which British writers regarded this community of impoverished artists, writers, and students but also suggests how bohemia had swiftly become more metaphor than actuality in English minds. Appropriately, the process by which this had happened provides *Middlemarch*'s final and clearest demonstration of the complex ways in which contemporary French literary culture proved important to successive generations of nineteenth-century Anglophone writers.

George Eliot's Will Ladislaw finds his bohemian enclave in Rome rather than Paris, but its treatment in *Middlemarch* neatly illustrates the conflicted attitudes apparent in Arnold's formulation. From the view of Casaubon, the clerical relative funding his travel, Will's desire 'to go abroad again, without any special object, save the vague purpose of what he calls culture', constitutes irresponsible self-indulgence. As if to confirm this point of view, the narrator tells us of Will's experiments with alcohol and opium, but we subsequently learn that it was this exposure to cosmopolitan student culture that allowed him to detect the insular parochialism of his clerical relative's scholarship. Nevertheless, Will repudiates the bohemian life for the better path of earning his own living in the English provinces. In a scene redolent of Thackeray's use of the erotics of the Louvre, the German artist Naumann draws Will's attention to the picture Casaubon's wife presents as she stands close to the reclining 'marble voluptuousness' of Ariadne, and then suggests they pursue her. Disgusted by the notion that 'English ladies' should ever endure the contamination of serving as studio models, Will instantly repudiates the homosocial camaraderie and sexual licence for which bohemian coteries were famed.[63]

---

[61] Arnold, *Literature and Dogma*, in *Works*, ed. Super, vi, 391.
[62] 'Ouida', *Tricotrin*, ii, 458.
[63] For Thackeray and the erotics of the Louvre, see section 5.1.3. Eliot, *Middlemarch*, ed. Carroll, 79, 82, 184–6.

While Eliot's scene set in Rome is part of her broader discussion of a sculptural trope which reduced women to spectacular objects,[64] the reaching back to Thackeray—whether conscious or not (she had read *The Newcomes*, with its scene in the Louvre, in 1855)—for a British response to bohemian mores was apposite. Until the appearance of George du Maurier's *Trilby* (1894), Thackeray's series of vignettes, written over a number of years, formed the major part of the Anglophone discourse of bohemia. However, Thackeray's pictures too were constructed from literature rather than life, owing more to the changing depictions of the bohemian figure in French literature between the days of the July Monarchy and the Second Empire than to his own brief experience of the Latin Quarter.[65] His 1840 description of 'the Paris student, whose exploits among the *grisettes* are so celebrated, and whose fierce republicanism keeps gendarmes for ever on the alert' was, he openly admitted, taken from a satirical account in Charles de Bernard's novel *Les Ailes d'Icare* (1840).[66] This emphasized the deliberately eccentric appearance and anti-bourgeois attitudes struck by the 'dandy...of the Pays Latin', while also predicting that 'age, sense and a little government pay' would soon bring these youths back into the bourgeois fold.

However, by Thackeray's next venture into this territory, the French literary picture of the Latin Quarter had changed, thanks to Henry Murger's stories, begun in March 1845 in the Parisian magazine *Le Corsaire*, and eventually turned into the novel *Scènes de la vie de bohème* (1851). Dismissive of precisely such gentlemen amateurs as Thackeray, who could readily rejoin the bourgeois world, Murger's portrait of bohemia revealed a life of poverty, male camaraderie, and free love. It is clear that by the last instalment of *Vanity Fair*, in July 1848, Thackeray had encountered Murger's tales, and his new, figurative use of the word 'Bohemian'. Now firmly ensconced himself in the ranks of the bourgeois, Thackeray saw seediness as the substratum of Murger's sentimental celebration of the artistic life. Ignoring Murger's claim that the bohemian lifestyle was unique to Paris, Thackeray applied the adjective 'Bohemian' to Becky's life as an outcast from polite society, glossing his meaning thus: 'her taste for disrespectability grew more and more remarkable. She became a perfect Bohemian ere long, herding with people whom it would make your hair stand on end to meet.'[67]

If Murger's work had helped to make the moral laxity of bohemia more explicit than it had been in Charles de Bernard's fiction, it had also undermined that earlier notion of the bohemian life as carefree. 'In a word,' wrote a journalist who had also clearly read his Murger, in *Household Words* for 1851, 'the Parisian Bohemians of to-day are a tribe of unfortunate artists of all kinds—poets, painters, musicians and dramatists—who haunt obscure cafés in all parts of Paris, but more especially in

---

[64] See G. Marshall, *Actresses on the Victorian Stage* (Cambridge: Cambridge University Press, 1998), 79–92.

[65] See M. Gill, *Eccentricity and the Cultural Imagination in Nineteenth-Century Paris* (Oxford: Oxford University Press, 2009), 170–5.

[66] 'On Some French Fashionable Novels', 102–5.

[67] W. M. Thackeray, *Vanity Fair: A Novel without a Hero*, ed. J. Sutherland (Oxford: Oxford University Press, 1991), 822.

the Quartier Latin.' Only the author who subsequently achieved success enjoyed the privilege of 'look[ing] back upon his Bohemian days as perhaps the most happy, and certainly not the least useful portion of his experience'.[68]

Certainly in the early 1860s, when Thackeray came to revisit the Latin Quarter of Louis-Philippe's day in *The Adventures of Philip*, his account was penned from a harsher and more complicated critical perspective. His quasi-autobiographical hero may have chosen his lodgings in the Luxembourg quarter to save money, but soon elevates the life of cheap drink, tobacco, song, and shabby dress into a conviction of his own literary and moral integrity. Happy to boast that these virtues differentiate him from the bourgeois prejudices of his more successful compatriots, he continues to accept hospitality from a wealthy relative on the right bank. Thackeray's own elevation to the ranks of successful novelists, combined with repeatedly being called upon to bail out colleagues who had not made the transition, no doubt also rendered him sympathetic to the turn Second Empire French literary circles was taking in ranking authors with a name on the title-page above the journalist's 'humiliating dependence on editors'.[69]

It was the wholesale capitulation of artistic idealism to wealth and power, which Bulwer Lytton believed had occurred during the Second Empire, that his portrait of the young poet Rameau illustrates in his novel *The Parisians*. The choice of name was not accidental: this was an updating of the discussions aired in Diderot's *Le Neveu de Rameau* (1763), of such matters as what it means to be a successful artist, how an artist makes a living, and women's contribution to this process. Bulwer Lytton's Rameau deserts the *lorette* who has been a feature of his Bohemian life, but is equally prepared to prostitute the artistic talents of the wealthier, more talented Isaura, and then willing to break their engagement when bribed to marry the *lorette* who has all the while remained devoted to him. His poetic ambition fades into the desire to star in the *salons*, and his earlier radical allegiance to hack journalism is sold to the highest bidder. Throughout, his vanity prevents him from seeing the extent to which he has become a pawn in the schemes of more powerful men. Finally, however, Bulwer Lytton's own sharp distrust of the Parisian fêting of such *hommes de lettres* undermines his own project. In revealing Rameau to be the spoilt son of doting shopkeeping parents with impeccably bourgeois values, Bulwer Lytton produced a selfish poseur rather than a Bohemian artist overcome by the forces of materialism.

The delicate balance between artistic idealism, romantic feeling, and the socially unconventional to be found in Murger's portrait of bohemia was essentially a mid-century French literary construct finally incomprehensible to the Anglo-Saxon system of values. Even du Maurier, partly raised in a French environment and inclined in *Trilby* (1894) to satirize English prudery, found himself creating a fantasy bohemia: the supposed good-hearted camaraderie of the 1850s is overlaid in the course of the novel by the harsher, more commercially exploitative spirit of later generations. Perhaps of all the Anglophone writers who attempted to depict

---

[68] [S. Blanchard,] 'The True Bohemians of Paris', *Household Words*, 15 Nov. 1851, 190–2.
[69] See Gill, *Eccentricity*, 174.

the never-never land of Parisian bohemia, only Henry James truly discerned the extent to which it had always been a literary artefact.

Developing this perception in *The Ambassadors* (1909), James used 'Melancholy Murger' and his fictional cast to indicate the nostalgia for a dream never to be fulfilled. Lambert Strether, the American for whom Paris and French literature have long been emblematic of a life desired rather than achieved, has over the years treasured his copy of 'Melancholy Murger', which he had taken back to America in the 1860s, for its 'old imaginations of the Latin Quarter'. Idle Chad Newsome, the product of a younger generation, has meanwhile cynically exploited an older America's belief in the existence of the life of the artist lived out among the 'young painters, sculptors, architects [and] medical students' of the Latin Quarter, even hinting in his letters home that he has found a vocation and enrolled in an atelier. Instead, Chad has pursued a series of unromantic liaisons with modern-day examples of Murger's *lorettes* and *grisettes*, 'vulgarised by the larger evolution of the type'. No longer pictured as relationships with free-spirited girls willingly giving themselves to their student lovers, Chad's liaisons have been conducted with 'one ferociously "interested" little person after another'.[70] Nor does Chad's decision to abandon the Latin Quarter represent the entry into the responsibilities of bourgeois adult life which it had for Murger's maturing students: rather it merely marks another stage in his exploration of Parisian hedonism. Chad's exploitation of the bohemian fantasy has in effect shown it up for what it always was; a literary conceit allowing a young man's wish-fulfilment dream of a life without responsibility to gain a spurious artistic gloss.

14.5 EPILOGUE

The representation of the bohemian, discussed in the final part of this last chapter, encapsulates many of the lessons of this book's investigation into British writers' engagement with Paris. First, it shows how heavily dependent they often were for their descriptions of Parisian life on their reading of French literature. Despite the much-bruited moral dangers of French novels, there were apparently few educated Victorian writers who felt their own moral compass would be seriously affected by reading them. Second, this episode re-emphasizes how, in considering the ways in which transnational cultural influence works, it is important to consider literature non-canonically: the canon sifts out and elevates the exceptional, whereas writers wanting to take the temperature of majority attitudes and passing fashions in a foreign city turned to popular, and often ephemeral, contemporary literature. Third, it shows that although tropes born of a particular moment could swiftly become ossified stereotypes, equally, in the hands of consummate artists, they could be reconsidered and refashioned.

Above all I hope that this book has proved how significant Paris was for British literary culture in the mid-nineteenth century. If it has achieved nothing else it will

---

[70] H. James, The *Ambassadors* (2 vols, 1909; New York: A. M. Kelley, 1971), i, 86–94.

have provided another buttress against the tendency, faced with the long years of Victoria's reign, to collapse distinctive decades, or concepts such as the urban, into homogenized wholes. In its engagement with the alien environment of Parisian society, mores, and literature, mid-nineteenth-century Victorian writing reveals its fracturing along lines dictated by political, aesthetic, class, and gender preoccupations, and demonstrates the ways in which, even during the most expansionist stage of the nation's imperialist self-confidence, many of its writers continued to seek out, borrow, and steal from French culture.

Works cited

PRIMARY SOURCES

à Beckett, A. W., *The à Becketts of 'Punch': Memories of Father and Sons* (Westminster: Archibald Constable, 1903).

Acton, W., *Prostitution, considered in its moral, social, and sanitary aspects, in London and other large cities* (London: J. Churchill, 1857).

Addison, H. R., *Forty-Eight Hours in Paris Amidst the Ruins* (London: C. H. Clarke, 1871).

Alhoy, M., *Physiologie de la lorette* (Paris: Aubert, 1841).

Alhoy, M., *Physiologie du débardeur* (Paris: Aubert, 1842).

Allingham, W., *William Allingham: A Diary*, ed. H. Allingham and D. Radford (London: Macmillan, 1907).

Anon., 'Street Names in Paris', *Pall Mall Gazette*, 8 Dec. 1868, p. 9.

Arnold, M., *The Complete Prose Works of Matthew Arnold*, ed. R. H. Super (11 vols, Ann Arbor: University of Michigan Press, 1960–77).

Arnold, M., *The Poems of Matthew Arnold*, ed. K. Allott (London: Longmans, 1965).

Arnold, M., *The Letters of Matthew Arnold*, ed. C. Y. Lang. (6 vols, Charlottesville: University Press of Virginia, 1996–2001).

Austen, J., *Pride and Prejudice*, ed. P. Rogers (Cambridge: Cambridge University Press, 2006).

Bagehot, W., *Bagehot: The English Constitution*, ed. P. Smith (Cambridge: Cambridge University Press, 2001).

Balzac, H. de, *Le Père Goriot*, trans. A. J. Krailsheimer (Oxford: Oxford University Press, 2009).

Balzac, H. de, *A Harlot High and Low [Splendeurs et misères des courtisanes]*, trans. R. Heppenstall (Harmondsworth: Penguin, 1970).

Bennett, A., *The Old Wives' Tale*, ed. M. Harris (Oxford: Oxford University Press, 1995).

Betham-Edwards, M., *Brother Gabriel* (3 vols, London: Hurst & Blackett, 1878).

[Blanchard, S.,] 'The True Bohemians of Paris', *Household Words*, 15 Nov. 1851, 190–2.

Blessington, Countess of [Marguerite Gardiner], *The Victims of Society* (3 vols, London: Saunders & Otley, 1837).

Blessington, Countess of, *The Idler in France* (2 vols, London: Henry Colburn, 1841).

Blunt, W., *The Poetry of Wilfrid Blunt*, ed. W. E. Henley and G. Wyndham (London: William Heinemann, 1898).

Braddon, M. E., *Three Times Dead; or, the Secret of the Heath* (London: W. M. Clark, 1854); repr. as *The Trail of the Serpent* (London: W. M. Clark, 1861).

Braddon, M. E., *The Doctor's Wife*, ed. L. Pykett (1864; repr. Oxford: Oxford University Press, 2008).

Braddon, M. E., *Under the Red Flag* (Leipzig: Tauchnitz, 1884).

Braddon, M. E., *Under the Red Flag, and Other Tales* (London: John & Robert Maxwell, 1886).

Brontë, A., *The Tenant of Wildfell Hall*, ed. H. Rosengarten (Oxford: Clarendon Press, 1992).

Brontë, C., *Jane Eyre*, ed. J. Jack and M. Smith (Oxford: Clarendon Press, 1969).

Brontë, C., *Villette*, ed. H. Rosengarten and M. Smith (Oxford: Clarendon Press, 1984).

Brontë, C., *The Letters of Charlotte Brontë, with a Selection of Letters by Family and Friends*, ed. M. Smith (3 vols, Oxford: Clarendon Press, 1995–2004).

Browning, E. B., *Elizabeth Barrett Browning: Letters to her Sister, 1846–1859*, ed. L. Huxley (London: John Murray, 1929).

Browning, E. B., *Elizabeth Barrett Browning's Letters to Mrs. David Ogilvy, 1849–1861*, ed. P. N. Heydon and P. Kelley (New York: Browning Institute, 1973).

Browning, E. B., *The Letters of Elizabeth Barrett Browning*, ed. F. G. Kenyon, 2nd edn (2 vols, London: Smith, Elder, 1897).

Browning, E. B., *The Works of Elizabeth Barrett Browning*, ed. S. Donaldson (5 vols, London: Pickering & Chatto, 2010).

Browning, E. B., and Browning, R.: *Letters of the Brownings to George Barrett*, ed. P. Landis and R. E. Freeman (Urbana: University of Illinois Press, 1958).

Browning, R., *Dearest Isa: Robert Browning's Letters to Isabella Blagden*, ed. E. C. McAleer (Edinburgh: Thomas Nelson, 1951).

Browning, R., *Learned Lady: Letters from Robert Browning to Mrs Thomas Fitzgerald 1876–1889*, ed. E. C. McAleer (Cambridge, Mass.: Harvard University Press, 1966).

Browning, R., *Robert Browning: The Poems*, ed. J. Pettigrew and T. J. Collins (2 vols, Harmondsworth: Penguin, 1981).

Buchanan, R., *Napoleon Fallen: A Lyrical Drama* (London: Strahan, 1871).

[Bulwer-Lytton, E. G. E. L.,] *Pelham: or, the Adventures of a Gentleman* (3 vols, London: Henry Colburn, 1828).

Bulwer-Lytton, E. G. E. L., *Pelham: or, the Adventures of a Gentleman* (London: Chapman & Hall, 1849).

Bulwer-Lytton, E. G. E. L., *Pelham: or, the Adventures of a Gentleman* (London: George Routledge, 1873).

Bulwer-Lytton, E. G. E. L., *Paul Clifford* (London: George Routledge & Sons, 1874).

Lytton, [E. G. E. L. Bulwer-], Lord, *The Parisians* (2 vols, London: George Routledge, 1875).

Bulwer-Lytton, E. R., *The Life, Letters, and Literary Remains of Edward Bulwer, Lord Lytton* (2 vols, London: Kegan Paul, Trench, 1883).

Bury, Lady Charlotte, *Family Records; or, The Two Sisters* (3 vols, London: Saunders & Otley, 1841).

Carlyle, T., 'Excursion (Futile Enough) to Paris; Autumn 1851: thrown on paper, pen galloping, from Saturday to Tuesday October 4–7, 1851', in *Last Words of Thomas Carlyle* (London: Longmans, Green, 1892).

Carlyle, T., *Rescued Essays of Thomas Carlyle*, ed. P. Newberry (London: Leadenhall Press, 1892).

Carlyle, T., *The Works of Thomas Carlyle*, ed. H. D. Traill (30 vols, London: Chapman & Hall, 1896–1901).

Carlyle, T., *The French Revolution*, intro. H. Belloc (2 vols, London: J. M. Dent & Sons, 1906).

Carlyle, T., *The Collected Letters of Thomas and Jane Welsh Carlyle*, ed. C. R. Sanders, K. J. Fielding, et al. (40 vols, Durham, NC: Duke University Press, 1970–2012).

[Chorley, H.,] *Athenæum* (25 July 1840), '*The Paris Sketch-Book. By Mr. Titmarsh*', 589.

Clough, A. H., *The Correspondence of Arthur Hugh Clough*, ed. F. L. Mulhauser (2 vols, Oxford: Clarendon Press, 1957).

Coghlan, F., *A Guide to France, or, Travellers their own Commissioners* (London: J. Onwhyn, 1828).

[Collins, W.,] 'Laid Up in Two Lodgings', *Household Words* (7 June 1856), 481–7.

Collins, W., *The Woman in White*, ed. H. Sucksmith (London: Oxford University Press, 1975).

Collins, W., *The Letters of Wilkie Collins*, ed. W. Baker and W. Clarke (2 vols, London: Macmillan, 1999).

Collins, W., *The Public Face of Wilkie Collins: The Collected Letters*, ed. W. Baker, A. Gasson, G. Law, and P. Lewis (4 vols, London: Pickering & Chatto, 2005).

Corkran, A., *The Young Philistine and Other Stories* (London: Burns & Oates, 1887).

Corkran, A., *Margery Merton's Girlhood* (London: Blackie & Sons, 1888).

Corkran, H., *Celebrities and I* (London: Hutchinson, 1902).

[Costello, D.,] 'Blank Babies in Paris', *Household Words*, 17 Dec. 1853, 379–82.

[Costello, L.,] ' My Little French Friend', *Household Words*, 8 May 1852, 169–71.

Crawford, E., 'Journalism as a Profession for Women', *Contemporary Review* 64 (Sept. 1893), 362–72.

Crowe, E., *Thackeray's Haunts and Homes* (London: Smith, Elder, 1897).

Crowe, J., *Reminiscences of Thirty-Five Years of My Life* (London: John Murray, 1895).

de Kock, P., and Valory, *Le débardeur, ou Le gros-caillou et Alger* (Paris: Barba, 1839).

de Staël, Mme G., *Corinne, or Italy*, trans. S. Raphael, intro. J. Isbell (Oxford: Oxford University Press, 2008).

Dickens, C., *Little Dorrit* (London: Oxford University Press, 1953).

Dickens, C., *Christmas Stories* (London: Oxford University Press, 1956).

Dickens, C., *The Uncommercial Traveller and Reprinted Pieces* (London: Oxford University Press, 1958).

Dickens, C., *The Pilgrim Edition of the Letters of Charles Dickens*, ed. G. Storey et al. (12 vols, Oxford: Clarendon Press, 1965–2002).

Dickens, C., *Dombey and Son*, ed. A. Horsman (Oxford: Clarendon Press, 1974).

Dickens, C., *Charles Dickens: The Public Readings*, ed. P. Collins (Oxford: Clarendon Press, 1975).

Dickens, C., *Dickens' Journalism*, ed. M. Slater (4 vols, London: J. M. Dent, 1994–2000).

Dickens, C., *Our Mutual Friend*, ed. A. Poole (London: Penguin, 1997).

Dickens, C., *Dickens on France*, ed. J. Edmondson (Oxford: Signal Books, 2006).

Dickens, C., *A Tale of Two Cities*, ed. A. Sanders (Oxford: Oxford University Press, 2008).

Diderot, D., *Le neveu de Rameau* (1762; Paris: Gallimard, 1972).

Dixon, E. S., 'The Right of French Women', *Household Words*, 22 May 1852, 218–21.

du Maurier, G., *Trilby*, intro. E. Showalter, ed. D. Denisoff (Oxford: Oxford University Press, 1995).

Edwards, A. B., *In the Days of My Youth* (3 vols, London: Hurst & Blackett, 1873).

Edwards, H. S., *Personal Recollections* (London: Cassell, 1900).

Egan, P., *Life in London, or The Day and Night Scenes of Jerry Hawthorn, Esq. and his elegant friend Corinthian Tom in their Rambles and Sprees through the Metropolis* (1821).

Eliot, G., *The George Eliot Letters*, ed. G. S. Haight (9 vols, New Haven, Conn.: Yale University Press, 1954–6, 1978).

Eliot, G., 'Woman in France: Madame de Sablé', in *Essays of George Eliot*, ed. T. Pinney (London: Routledge & Kegan Paul, 1968).

Eliot, G., *Middlemarch*, ed. D. Carroll (Oxford: Clarendon Press, 1986).

'English Amusements', *Paris Satirist*, 14 Apr. 1836, p. 3.

Fisher, J. (ed.), *Lives of Victorian Literary Figures by their Contemporaries: William Thackeray* (London: Pickering & Chatto, 2007).

[Fitton, S.,] *How I Became a Governess* (London: Griffith & Farran, 1861).

Fitzgerald, E., *The Letters of Edward Fitzgerald*, ed. A. M. Terhune and A. B. Terhune (4 vols, Princeton, NJ: Princeton University Press, 1980).

Flaubert, G., *A Sentimental Education* [*L'Éducation sentimentale*], trans. D. Parmée (Oxford: Oxford University Press, 2008).

Forester, T. (ed.), *Paris and its Environs: An Illustrated Handbook* (London: Henry G. Bohn, 1859).

Frégier, H.-A., *Des classes dangereuses dans la population des grandes villes et des moyens de les rendre meilleures* (Paris: J.-B. Baillière, 1840).

Gaskell, E. C., *The Letters of Mrs Gaskell*, ed. J. V. Chapple and A. Pollard (Manchester: Manchester University Press, 1966).

Gaskell, E. C., *Further Letters of Mrs Gaskell*, ed. J. Chapple and A. Shelston (Manchester: Manchester University Press, 2003).

Gaskell, E. C., *The Works of Elizabeth Gaskell*, ed. J. Shattock et al. (10 vols, London: Pickering & Chatto, 2005–6).

Gore, C., *The Diary of a Désennuyée* (2 vols, London: Henry Colburn, 1836).

Gore, C., *Greville: or, a Season in Paris* (3 vols, London: Henry Colburn, 1841).

Gore, C., *The Ambassador's Wife* (3 vols, London: Richard Bentley, 1842).

Gore, C., *Paris in 1841* (London: Longman, Brown, Green, & Longmans, 1842).

Gore, C., *Sketches of English Character* (2 vols, London: Richard Bentley, 1846).

Hand-book for Travellers on the Continent, A (London: John Murray; Paris: A & W. Galignani; Leipzig: Longman, 1844).

Heads of the People: or, Portraits of the English, Drawn by Kenny Meadows, with Original Essays by Distinguished Writers, ed. D. Jerrold (2 vols, London: Robert Tyas, 1840–41).

Hemyn, B., 'Prostitution in London', in Henry Mayhew, *London Labour and the London Poor: A Selected Edition*, ed. R. Douglas-Fairhurst (Oxford: Oxford University Press Press, 2010).

Hodder, G., *Memories of My Time* (London: Tinsley Brothers, 1870).

Hofland, B., *Emily's Reward, or the Holiday Trip to Paris* (London: Grant & Griffith, 1844).

Huart, L., *Physiologie de la grisette* (Paris: Aubert, 1841).

Huart, L., *Physiologie du flaneur* (Paris: Aubert, 1841).

Hugo, V., *Le dernier jour d'un condamné* (Paris: Barba, 1829).

Hugo, V., *Les Misérables*, trans. C. Donougher (London: Penguin, 2012).

James, H., 'George du Maurier', in *Partial Portraits* (London: Macmillan, 1883), 327–72.

James, H., *A Small Boy and Others* (London: Macmillan, 1913).

James, H., 'An English Critic of French Painting', in *The Painter's Eye: Notes and Essays on the Pictorial Arts*, ed. J. L. Sweeney (London: Rupert Hart-Davis, 1956), 33–42.

James, H., 'Paris Revisited', in *Parisian Sketches* (London: Rupert Hart-Davis, 1958), 5.

James, H., *The Ambassadors* (2 vols, 1909; New York: A. M. Kelley, 1971).

James, H., *The Portrait of a Lady*, ed. R. D. Bamberg (New York: W. W. Norton, 1975).

James, H., *The Complete Notebooks of Henry James*, ed. L. Edel and L. H. Powers (New York: Oxford University Press, 1987).

James, H., *What Maisie Knew*, ed. A. Poole (Oxford: Oxford University Press, 1998).

Jameson, A. B., *The Diary of an Ennuyée* (Paris: Baudry's European Library, 1836).

Jameson, A. B., *A Commonplace Book of Thoughts, Memories and Fancies* (London: Longman, Brown, Green & Longmans, 1854).

[Jenkin, H.,] *Once and Again: A Novel* (3 vols, London: Smith, Elder, 1865).

Jerrold, B., 'Departed this Life in Paris', in *Imperial Paris; including new scenes for old visitors* (London: Bradbury & Evans, 1855), 43–62.

Jerrold, B., 'Paris upon Wheels', in *Imperial Paris; including new scenes for old visitors* (London: Bradbury & Evans, 1855).

Jerrold, B., *Paris for the English* (London: Bradbury, Evans, 1867).

Jerrold, B., *The Cockaynes in Paris, or 'Gone Abroad' with sketches by Gustave Doré and other illustrations of the English Abroad from a French point of view* (London: John Camden Hotten, 1871).

Jewsbury, G., *The Half-Sisters*, ed. J. Wilkes (Oxford: Oxford University Press, 1994).

Kavanagh, J., *Bessie* (3 vols, London: Hurst & Blackett, 1872).

[Labouchère, H.,] *Diary of the Besieged Resident in Paris, reprinted from the* Daily News *with Several New Letters and Preface* (London: Hurst & Blackett, 1871).

Les Français peints par eux-mêmes: encyclopédie morale du dix-neuvième siècle (8 vols, Paris: L. Curmer, 1840–42).

Lever, C., *The Novels of Charles Lever*, edited by his daughter (36 vols, London: Downey, 1897–99).

[Lewes, G. H.,] 'The Condition of Authors in England, Germany, and France', *Fraser's Magazine*, Mar. 1847, 285–95.

[Linton, E.,] 'Marie's Fever', *Household Words*, 30 July 1853, 518–26.

[Linton, E.,] 'French Domesticity', *Household Words*, 24 June 1854, 434–8.

Linton, E., *The True History of Joshua Davidson, Christian and Communist* (London: Strahan, 1872).

Littré, E., *Dictionnaire de la langue française*, vol. 3 (Paris: Pauvert, 1863).

Locker-Lampson, F., *My Confidences: An Autobiographical Sketch Addressed to my Descendants*, ed. A. Birrell (London: Smith, Elder, 1896).

Mackay, C., *Forty Years' Recollections of Life, Literature, and Public Affairs, from 1830 to 1870* (2 vols, London: Chapman & Hall, 1877).

Mayer, G. T., *Women of Letters* (2 vols, London: Richard Bentley, 1894).

McCrindell, R., *The Schoolgirl in France* (London: R. B. Seeley & W. Burnside, 1840).

Melville, L., *The Life of William Makepeace Thackeray* (2 vols, London: Hutchinson, 1899).

Mill, J. S., *Collected Works of John Stuart Mill*, ed. J. M. Robson and J. Stillinger (33 vols, Toronto: University of Toronto Press, 1963–91).

Mill, J. S., *The Earlier Letters of John Stuart Mill, 1812–1848*, ed. F. E. Minneka, intro. F. A. Hayek (2 vols, London: Routledge & Kegan Paul, 1996).

Millgate, M. (ed.), *The Life and Work of Thomas Hardy* (London: Macmillan, 1982).

Morgan, Lady S., *France* (London: Henry Colburn, 1817).

Morgan, Lady S., *France in 1829–30*, 2nd edn (2 vols, London: Saunders & Otley, 1831).

Noel, R., *The Red Flag and Other Poems* (London: Strahan, 1872).

[O'Meara, K.,] *A Woman's Trials*, by 'Grace Ramsay' (3 vols, London: Hurst & Blackett, 1867).

O'Meara, K., *Madame Mohl: Her Salon and her Friends: A Study of Social Life in Paris* (London: Richard Bentley, 1885).

O'Shea, J. A., *Leaves from the Life of a Special Correspondent* (2 vols, London: Ward & Downey, 1885).

O'Shea, J. A., *Mated from the Morgue: A Tale of the Second Empire* (London: Spencer Blackett, 1889).

Oliphant, M. O. W., 'Madame Saint-Ange', *Good Cheer*, Dec. 1867, 33–44.

Oliphant, M. O. W., 'The Count's Daughters', *Good Cheer*, Dec. 1874, 1–31.

Oliphant, M. O. W., *A Memoir of the Life of John Tulloch* (Edinburgh: William Blackwood & Sons, 1888).

Oliphant, M. O. W., *Memoir of the Life of Laurence Oliphant and of Alice Oliphant, his wife*, 6th edn (2 vols, Edinburgh: William Blackwood & Sons, 1891).

Oliphant, M. O. W., *The Autobiography and Letters of Mrs. M. O. W. Oliphant*, ed. Mrs H. Coghill, intro. Q. D. Leavis (Leicester: Leicester University Press, 1974).

Oliphant, M. O. W., *The Autobiography of Margaret Oliphant*, ed. E. Jay (Oxford: Oxford University Press, 1990).

Oliphant, M. O. W., *Miss Marjoribanks*, ed. E. Jay (London: Penguin, 1998).

Opie, A., 'A Morning at Paris in 1829', in *The Aurora Borealis, a Literary Annual*, ed. The Society of Friends (Newcastle upon Tyne, 1833), 234–40.

'Ouida' [M. L. de la Ramée], *Tricotrin: The Story of a Waif and Stray* (3 vols, London: Chapman & Hall, 1869).

Parent-Duchâtelet, A. J.-B., *De la prostitution dans la ville de Paris: considérée sous le rapport de l'hygiène publique, de la morale et de l'administration* (2 vols, 1836; Paris: Baillière, 1857).

Payn, J., *Some Literary Recollections* (London: Smith, Elder, 1884).

Peytel, S.-B., *La physiologie de la poire* (Paris: Librairies de la Place de la Bourse, 1832).

Phipps, C. H., *A Year of Revolution from a Journal kept in Paris in 1848 by the Marquess of Normanby* (London: Longman, Green, Longmans, & Roberts, 1857).

Planta, E., *A New Picture of Paris or, the Stranger's Guide to the French Metropolis* (London: Samuel Leigh and Baldwin & Cradock, 1831).

Poe, E. A., *The Murders in the Rue Morgue* (1841; London: Phoenix, 1996).

Renan, E., *Vie de Jésus* (1863).

Reynolds, G. W. M., *Alfred de Rosann: or, the Adventures of a French Gentleman* (London: J. W. Southgate, 1839).

Reynolds, G. W. M., *The Modern Literature of France* (2 vols, London: George Henderson, 1839).

Reynolds, G. W. M., *Pickwick Abroad: or, The Tour in France* (London: Sherwood, Gilbert, & Piper, 1839).

Reynolds, G. W. M., *Last Day of a Condemned Man, translated without abridgement from the French of Victor Hugo*, trans. G. W. M. Reynolds (London: George Henderson, 1840).

Reynolds, G. W. M., *Robert Macaire in England* (3 vols, London: Thomas Tegg, 1840); repr. as *Robert Macaire in England; or, The French Bandit in England* (London: John Dicks [n.d.]).

Reynolds, G. W. M., *The French Self-Instructor* (London: G. Vickers, 1846).

Reynolds, G. W. M., *The Mysteries of London*, ed. T. Thomas (1844–; repr. Keele: Keele University Press, 1996).

Ritchie, A. T., *Records of Tennyson, Ruskin and Browning* (London: Macmillan, 1892).

Ritchie, A. T., *Chapters from Some Memoirs* (London: Macmillan, 1894).

Ritchie, A. T., *Letters of Anne Thackeray Ritchie*, ed. H. Ritchie (London: John Murray, 1924).

Ritchie, A. T., *Anne Thackeray Ritchie: Journals and Letters. Biographical Commentary and Notes by Lilian Shankman*, ed. A. B. Bloom and J. Maynard (Columbus: Ohio State University Press, 1994).

Ritchie, A. T., *The Works of Miss Thackeray* (10 vols, London: Smith, Elder, 1890).

Rossetti, D. G., *The Poetical Works of Dante Gabriel Rossetti*, ed. W. M. Rossetti, (London: Ellis & Elvey, 1898).

Rossetti, D. G., *The Correspondence of Dante Gabriel Rossetti*, ed. W. E. Fredeman et al. (8 vols, Cambridge: D. S. Brewer, 2002–9).

Rossetti, W. M., *The Diary of W. M. Rossetti 1870–1873*, ed. O. Bornand (Oxford: Clarendon Press, 1977).

Rossetti, W. M., *Democratic Sonnets* (2 vols, London: Alston Rivers, 1907).

Ruskin, J., *The Works of John Ruskin*, ed. E. T. Cook and A. Wedderburn (39 vols, London: George Allen; New York: Longmans, Green, 1903–12).

[Sala, G. A.,] 'Liberty, Equality, Fraternity, and Musketry', *Household Words*, 27 Dec. 1851, 313–17.

Sala, G. A., *The Seven Sons of Mammon* (London: Tinsley Brothers, 1862).

Sala, G. A., *Quite Alone* (3 vols, London: Chapman & Hall, 1864).

Sala, G. A., 'The Cant of Modern Criticism', *Belgravia: A London Magazine*, 4 (Nov. 1867), 45–55.

Sala, G. A., *Paris Herself Again in 1878–9* (2 vols, London: Remington, 1879).

Sala, G. A., *The Life and Adventures of George Augustus Sala written by himself*, 2nd edn (2 vols, London: Cassell, 1895).

Senior, N., *Journals kept in France and Italy from 1848 to 1852, with a Sketch of the Revolution of 1848 by the late Nassau William Senior*, ed. M. C. M. Simpson (2 vols, 1871; repr. New York: Da Capo Press, 1973).

Sherwood, M. M., *Père La Chaise* (Wellington, Salop: F. Houlston & Son, 1823).

Simpson, J. P., *Pictures from Revolutionary Paris: sketched during the first phase of the Revolution of 1848* (2 vols, Edinburgh: William Blackwood & Sons, 1849).

Simpson, M. C. M., 'Some Personal Recollections of Madame Mohl', *Macmillan's Magazine* (Sept. 1883), 424–36.

Simpson, M. C. M., *Letters and Recollections of Julius and Mary Mohl* (London: Kegan, Paul, Trench & Co, 1887).

Simpson, M. C. M., *Many Memories of Many People* (London: Edward Arnold, 1898).

Smith, A., 'Sketches of Paris', by 'Knibs', *Mirror of Literature, Amusement and Instruction*, 12 and 19 Jan., 27 Apr. 1839.

Smith, A., *The Natural History of the Gent* (London: David Bogue, 1847).

Smith, A., *The Natural History of Stuck-Up People* (London: Ward & Lock, 1847).

Smith, A. (ed.), *Gavarni in London: Sketches of Life and Character, with illustrative essays by popular writers* (London: David Bogue, 1849).

[Stead, W. T.,] 'Occasional Notes', *Pall Mall Gazette* (5 Nov. 1886).

[Stephen, J. F.,] 'Sentimentalism', *Cornhill Magazine* (10 July 1864), 65–75.

Swinburne, A. C., *The Poems of Algernon Charles Swinburne* (6 vols, London: Chatto & Windus, 1904).

Swinburne, A. C., *The Swinburne Letters*, ed. C. Y. Lang (6 vols, New Haven, Conn.: Yale University Press, 1959–62).

Taylor, T., *Thackeray the Humourist and the Man of Letters* (London: John Camden Hotten, 1864).

Tennyson, A., *The Poems of Tennyson*, ed. C. Ricks (3 vols, Harlow: Longman, 1987).

Thackeray, W. M., *The Works of William Makepeace Thackeray with biographical introductions by his daughter, Anne Ritchie* (13 vols, London: Smith, Elder, 1899).

Thackeray, W. M., *Stray Papers by William Thackeray, being Stories, Reviews, Verses, and Sketches (1821–1847)*, ed. L. Melville (London: Hutchinson, 1901).

Thackeray, W. M., *The Oxford Thackeray*, ed. G. Saintsbury (17 vols, London: Oxford University Press, 1910).

Thackeray, W. M., *The Letters and Private Papers of William Makepeace Thackeray*, ed. G. N. Ray (4 vols, Cambridge, Mass.: Harvard University Press, 1945–6).

Thackeray, W. M., *William Makepeace Thackeray's Contributions to the* Morning Chronicle, ed. G. N. Ray (Urbana: University of Illinois Press, 1955).

Thackeray, W. M., *Vanity Fair: A Novel without a Hero*, ed. P. L. Shillingsburg (New York: Garland, 1989).

Thackeray, W. M., *Vanity Fair: A Novel without a Hero*, ed. J. Sutherland (Oxford: Oxford University Press, 1991).

Thackeray, W. M., *The History of Pendennis: His Fortunes and Misfortunes, His Friends and His Greatest Enemy*, ed. J. Sutherland (Oxford: Oxford University Press, 1994).

Thackeray, W. M., *The Letters and Private Papers of William Makepeace Thackeray: A Supplement*, ed. E. F. Harden (2 vols, New York: Garland, 1994).

Thackeray, W. M., *Vanity Fair: An Authoritative Text*, ed. P. Shillingsburg (New York: W. W. Norton, 1994).

Trollope, A., 'The National Gallery', *St James's Magazine* (Sept. 1861), 163–76.

Trollope, A., *Travelling Sketches*, ed. A. Briggs (New York: Arno Press, 1981).

Trollope, F., *Paris and the Parisians in 1835* (2 vols, Paris: Baudry's European Library, 1836).

Trollope, F., *Hargrave; or, the Adventures of a Man of Fashion* (3 vols, London: Henry Colburn, 1843).

Trollope, F., *The Robertses on their Travels* (3 vols, London: Henry Colburn, 1846).

Trollope, F., *The Old World and the New* (3 vols, London: Henry Colburn, 1849).

Trollope, F., *Fashionable Life; or, Paris and London* (3 vols: London: Hurst & Blackett, 1856).

Trollope, T. A., *What I Remember*, ed. H. van Thal (London: William Kimber, 1973).

Turnbull, D., *The French Revolution of 1830; the events which produced it, and the scenes by which it was accompanied* (London: Henry Colburn & Richard Bentley, 1830).

Queen Victoria: Leaves from a Journal: A Record of the Visit of the Emperor and Empress of the French to the Queen, and of the Visit of the Queen and H.R.H the Prince Consort to the Emperor of the French, 1855, intro. R. Mortimer (London: André Deutsch, 1961).

Vidocq, E. F., *Memoirs of Vidocq, principal agent of the French police until 1827 and now proprietor of the paper manufactory at St. Mandé* (4 vols, London: Whittaker, Treacher, & Arnot, 1829).

Vidocq, E. F., *Les voleurs: physiologies de leurs moeurs et de leur langage. Ouvrage qui dévoile les ruses de tous les fripons, et destiné à devenir le Vade Mecum de tous les honnêtes gens* (2 vols, Paris: chez l'auteur, 1838).

[Vizetelly, H.,] 'Night Rambles in Paris', *Pall Mall Gazette*, 3, 5, 6, 9, 13 June 1868.

Vizetelly, H. (ed.), *Paris in Peril* (2 vols, London: Tinsley Brothers, 1882).

Vizetelly, H., *Glances Back through Seventy Years: Autobiographical and Other Recollections* (2 vols, London: Kegan Paul, Trench, Trübner, 1893).

Wace, H., 'John Thadeus Delane', *Cornhill*, Jan. 1909, 93–100.

Ward, Mrs H. [M. A.], *A Writer's Recollections 1856–1900* (London: William Collins, 1918).

Ward, Mrs H., *Robert Elsmere*, ed. C. de Ryals (Lincoln: University of Nebraska Press, 1967).

Whiteing, R., *The Life of Paris* (Leipzig: Bernhard Tauchnitz, 1901).

Whiteing, R., *My Harvest* (London: Hodder & Stoughton, 1915).

Wilde, O. (ed.), *The Woman's World* (London: Cassell, 1888).

Williams, H. M., *Sketches of the state of manners and opinions in the French Republic, towards the Close of the Eighteenth Century: in a Series of Letters* (London: G. G. and J. Robinson, 1801).

Williams, H. M., *A Narrative of the Events which have taken place in France, with an account of the Present State of Society and Public Opinion*, 2nd edn (London: John Murray, 1816).

Williams, H. M., *Letters on the Events which have passed in France since the Restoration in 1815* (London: Baldwin, Cradock & Joy, 1819).

Williams, H. M., *Letters from France*, intro J. M. Todd (2 vols, Delmar, NY: Scholars' Facsimiles and Reprints, 1975).

Williams, H. M., *Letters Written in France in the Summer of 1790, to a Friend in England, Containing Various Anecdotes Relative to the French Revolution* (Oxford: Woodstock Books, 1989).

[Wills, W. H.,] 'Paris Improved', *Household Words*, 17 Nov. 1855, 361–5.

Wollstonecraft, M., *An Historical and Moral View of the Origin and Progress of the French Revolution; and the effect it has produced in Europe*, intro. J. M. Todd (Delmar, NY: Scholars' Facsimiles and Reprints, 1975).

Wood, E., *East Lynne*, ed. E. Jay (Oxford: Oxford University Press, 2005).

Wordsworth, W., *William Wordsworth*, ed. S. Gill (Oxford: Oxford University Press, 1984).

Zola, É., *The Belly of Paris* [*Le Ventre de Paris*], trans. B. Nelson (New York: Oxford University Press, 2005).

NINETEENTH-CENTURY JOURNALS AND NEWSPAPERS

All the Year Round

Athenæum

Bentley's Miscellany

Blackwood's Edinburgh Magazine

Britannia

La Caricature

Le Charivari

Constitutional and Public Ledger

Daily News

Daily Telegraph

Douglas Jerrold's Shilling Magazine

Douglas Jerrold's Weekly Newspaper

Dugdale's Messenger

Edinburgh Review

Englishwoman's Domestic Magazine

Evening Star

Figaro in London

Fraser's Magazine

Galignani's Messenger, or the Spirit of English Journals

Le Gaulois

Globe

Le Globe

Harper's New Monthly Magazine

Household Words

Illuminated Magazine

Illustrated London News

Le Journal

Le Journal des débats

The Lancet

Leader

Leisure Hour

Lloyd's Weekly News

London and Paris Courier

London and Paris Observer: Journal of English and Foreign Literature, Science, and the Fine Arts

London Examiner

London Express and Advertiser

Macmillan's Magazine

Le Monde Illustré

Monitor

Monthly Magazine

Morning Advertiser

Morning Chronicle

Morning Herald

Morning Post
Morning Star (check is this the same as the Star ch9., p.316
Le National
National Review
National Standard
New Monthly Magazine,
New York Herald
North British Daily Mail
Observer
Pall Mall Gazette,
Paris Advertiser and Journal of English and Foreign Literature
Paris and London Chronicle
Paris et Londres: revue de la littérature des beaux-arts
Paris Herald
Paris Literary Gazette
Paris Monthly Review of British and Continental Literature
Paris Satirist
Paris Sun
Paris Sun-Beam
La Presse
Punch
Railway Chronicle
Revue des deux mondes
Spectator
Standard
Star
Tablet
Temple Bar
The Times
Tomahawk
Truth
World

SECONDARY SOURCES

Allen, J. S., *In the Public Eye: A History of Reading in Modern France, 1800–1940* (Princeton, NJ: Princeton University Press, 1991).

Alter, R., *Imagined Cities* (New Haven, Conn.: Yale University Press, 2005).

Altick, R. D., *The English Common Reader* (Chicago: Chicago University Press, 1957).

Altick, R. D., *Punch: The Lively Youth of a British Institution, 1841–1851* (Columbus: Ohio State University Press, 1997).

Anderson, B. R. O'G., *Imagined Communities: Reflections on the Origin and Spread of Nationalism*, 2nd edn (London: Verso, 2006).

Anderson, N. F., *Woman against Woman in Victorian England: A Life of Eliza Lynn Linton* (Bloomington: Indiana University Press,1987).

Ashton, R., *142 Strand: A Radical Address in Victorian London* (London: Chatto & Windus, 2006).

Aspinall, A., 'The Social Status of Journalists at the Beginning of the Nineteenth Century', *Review of English Studies* 21 (1945), 216–32.

Bainbridge, S., *Napoleon and English Romanticism* (Cambridge: Cambridge University Press, 1995).

Barber, G., 'Galignani's and the Publication of English Books in France from 1800 to 1852', *The Library*, ser. 5, 16(4) (Dec. 1961), 267–86.

Barnes, J. J., 'Galignani and the Publication of English Books in France: A Postcript', *The Library*, 5th ser. (Dec. 1970), 294–313.

Bellows, J. E., *John Bellows, 1831–1931: A Biographical Sketch and Tribute* (n.p., 1931).

Benjamin, W., *Charles Baudelaire: A Lyric Poet in the Era of High Capitalism*, trans. H. Zohn (London: NLB, 1973).

Bibliography of British Diplomats, A (London: Foreign and Commonwealth Office, 1999).

Bishop, J., '"They Manage Things Better in France": French Plays and English Critics 1850–55', *Nineteenth-Century Theatre* 22(1) (Summer 1994), 5–29.

Brake, L., and Demoo, M. (eds), *Dictionary of Nineteenth-Century Journalism in Great Britain and Ireland* (London: British Library, 2009).

Brooks, B., and Gergits, J. M. (eds), *British Travel Writers, 1837–1875: Dictionary of Literary Biography*, vol. 166 (Detroit: Gale Research, 1996), 353–61.

Brown, H., and Dow, G. (eds), *European Connections: Readers, Writer, Salonnières* (Oxford: Peter Lang, 2011).

Brown, L., 'The Treatment of the News in Mid-Victorian Newspapers', *Transactions of the Royal Historical Society*, 5th ser., 27 (1977), 23–39.

Brown, L., *Victorian News and Newspapers* (Oxford: Clarendon Press, 1985).

Burton, R. D. E., *Blood in the City: Violence and Revelation in Paris, 1789–1945* (Ithaca, NY: Cornell University Press, 2001).

Buzard, J., *The Beaten Track: European Tourism, Literature, and the Ways to 'Culture' 1800–1900* (Oxford: Clarendon Press, 1993).

Byerly, A., *Realism, Representation, and the Arts in Nineteenth-Century Literature* (Cambridge: Cambridge University Press, 1997).

Campos, C., *The View of France from Arnold to Bloomsbury* (Oxford: Oxford University Press, 1965).

Carnell, J., *The Literary Lives of Mary Elizabeth Braddon: A Study of her Life and Work* (Hastings: Sensation Press, 2000).

Carroll, D. (ed.), *George Eliot: The Critical Heritage* (London: Routledge & Kegan Paul, 1971).

Charle, C., Vincent, J., and Winter, J. (eds), *Anglo-French Attitudes: Comparisons and Transfers between English and French Intellectuals since the Eighteenth Century* (Manchester: Manchester University Press, 2007).

Chevasco B. P., *Mysterymania: The Reception of Eugène Sue in Britain 1838–1860* (Oxford: Peter Lang, 2003).

Childs, E. C., 'The Body Impolitic: Press Censorship and the Caricaturist Honoré Daumier', in *Making the News: Modernity and the Mass Press in Nineteenth-Century France*, ed. D. de la Motte and J. M. Przylblyski (Amherst, Mass: University of Massachusetts Press, 1999), 43–81.

Clark, R. 'Threading the Maze: Nineteenth-Century Guides for British Travellers to Paris', in *Parisian Fields*, ed. M. Sheringham (London: Reaktion, 1996), 8–29.

Clarke, N., *Ambitious Heights: Writing, Friendship, Love—the Jewsbury Sisters, Felicia Hemans, and Jane Welsh Carlyle* (London: Routledge, 1990).

Clubbe, J. (ed.), *Carlyle and his Contemporaries: Essays in Honor of Charles Richard Sanders* (Durham, NC: Duke University Press, 1977).

Colbert, B., 'Bibliography of British Travel Writing, 1780-1840', *Cardiff Corvey Articles*, 13 (Winter 2004): <http://www.cardiff.ac.uk/ecap/journals/corvey/cc13_n01.html>

Colby, R. A., *Thackeray's Canvass of Humanity: An Author and His Public* (Columbus: Ohio State University Press, 1979).

Colley, L., *Britons: Forging the Nation 1707–1837* (New Haven, Conn.: Yale University Press, 1992).

Conboy, M., *Journalism: A Critical History* (London: Sage, 2004).

Cooper-Richet, D., and Borgeaud, E., *Galignani*, trans. I. Watson (Paris: Galignani, 1999).

Cromwell, J. L., *Dorothea Lieven: A Russian Princess in London and Paris, 1785–1857* (London: McFarland, 2006).

Crossley, C., and Small, I. (eds), *Studies in Anglo-French Cultural Relations* (Basingstoke: Macmillan, 1988).

Dales, R. C., *The Intellectual Life of Western Europe in the Middle Ages* (Leiden: E. J. Brill, 1992).

Dames, N., 'Britain and Europe', in *The Cambridge History of Victorian Literature*, ed. K. Flint (Cambridge: Cambridge University Press, 2012), 622–40.

Dawson, G., 'Stranger than Fiction: Spiritualism, Intertextuality, and William Makepeace Thackeray's Editorship of the *Cornhill Magazine*, 1860-62', *Journal of Victorian Culture* 7(2) (2002), 220–38.

de Bellaigue, C., *Educating Women: Schooling and Identity in Britain and France 1800–1867* (Oxford: Oxford University Press, 2007).

de Certeau, M., *The Practice of Everyday Life*, trans. S. Rendall (Berkeley: University of California Press, 1988).

DeVane, W. C., *A Browning Handbook* (New York: Appleton-Century-Crofts, 1955).

Dever, C., '"An Occult and Immoral Tyranny": The Novel, the Police, and the Agent Provocateur', in *The Literary Channel: The Inter-National Development of the Novel*, ed. M. Cohen and C. Dever (Princeton, NJ: Princeton University Press, 2002), 225–50.

Dunn, W. H., *James Anthony Froude: A Biography* (2 vols, Oxford: Clarendon Press, 1961).

Farrell, M. P., *Collaborative Circles: Friendship Dynamics and Creative Work* (Chicago: University of Chicago Press, 2001).

Ferguson, P. P., 'The Flâneur On and Off the Streets of Paris', in *The Flâneur*, ed. K. Tester (London and New York: Routledge, 1994).

Ferguson, P. P., *Paris as Revolution: Writing the Nineteenth-Century City* (Berkeley: University of California Press, 1994).

Flint, K., *The Victorians and the Visual Imagination* (Cambridge: Cambridge University Press, 2000).

Forster, E. M., *Aspects of the Novel* (Harmondsworth: Penguin, 1971).

Gaillard, M., *Paris sous le Second Empire au temps de Charles Baudelaire* (Étrépilly: Presses du Village, 2002).

Gerbod, P., 'Voyageurs et résidents britanniques en France en XIXe siècle', *Acta Geographica* 76 (1988), 19–36.

Gill, M., *Eccentricity and the Cultural Imagination in Nineteenth-Century Paris* (Oxford: Oxford University Press, 2009).

Girard, L., *La Deuxième République et le Second Empire* (Paris: Association pour la publication d'une histoire de Paris, 1981).

Gladwin, C., *The Paris Embassy* (London: Collins, 1976).

Glinoer, A., 'Collaboration and Solidarity: The Collective Strategies of the Romantic Cenacle', in *Models of Collaboration in Nineteenth-Century French Literature: Several Authors, One Pen*, ed. S. Whidden (Farnham: Ashgate, 2009), 37–54.

Gluck, M., 'The Flâneur and the Aesthetic: Appropriation of Urban Culture in Mid-Nineteenth-Century Paris', *Theory, Culture and Society* 20 (Oct. 2003), 53–80.

Gregory, D., *Geographical Imaginations* (Oxford: Blackwell, 1994).

Gridley, R., *The Brownings and France: A Chronicle with Commentary* (London: Athlone Press, 1982).

Griffin, S. M., *Anti-Catholicism and Nineteenth-Century Fiction* (Cambridge: Cambridge University Press, 2004.

Hall, S., 'Cultural Identity and the Diaspora', in *Identity, Community, Culture, Difference*, ed. J. Rutherford (London: Lawrence & Wishart, 1990).

Hamburger, L., and Hamburger, J., *Contemplating Adultery: The Secret Life of a Victorian Woman* (London: Pan, 1994).

Harden, E. F., *A Checklist of Contributions by William Makepeace Thackeray to Newspapers, Periodicals, Books, and Serial Part Issues, 1828–1864* (Victoria, Canada: University of Victoria, 1996).

Harden, E. F., *A William Makepeace Thackeray Chronology* (Basingstoke: Palgrave Macmillan, 2003).

Harter, J. *World Railways of the Nineteenth-Century: A Pictorial History in Victorian Engravings* (Baltimore, Md.: Johns Hopkins University Press, 2005).

Harvey, D., *Consciousness and the Urban Experience* (Oxford: Blackwell, 1985).

Hayek, F. A., *John Stuart Mill and Harriet Taylor: Their Correspondence and Subsequent Marriage* (London: Routledge & Kegan Paul, 1951).

Haynes, C., *Lost Illusions: The Politics of Publishing in Nineteenth-Century France* (Cambridge, Mass.: Harvard University Press, 2010).

Heineman, H., *Mrs Trollope: The Triumphant Feminine in the Nineteenth Century* (Athens: Ohio University Press, 1979).

Hemmings, F. W. J., *The Theatre Industry in Nineteenth-Century France* (Cambridge: Cambridge University Press, 1998).

Henderson, P., *Tennyson: Poet and Prophet* (London: Routledge & Kegan Paul, 1978).

Heyrendt, C., ' "A Rain of Balderdash": Thomas Carlyle and Victorian Attitudes toward the Franco-Prussian War', *Carlyle Studies Annual* 22 (Spring 2006), 243–54.

Hickman, K., *Daughters of Britannia: The Lives and Times of Diplomatic Wives* (London: Flamingo, 2000).

Hill, A. G., 'Wordsworth, Louis-Philippe, and "England in 1840"', *Modern Language Review*, July 2002, 529–38.

Hollington, M., 'Dickens, Sala, and the London Arcades', *Dickens Quarterly* 28(4) (Dec. 2011), 273–84.

Hoppen, K. T., *The Mid-Victorian Generation: 1846–1886* (Oxford: Clarendon Press, 1998).

Howe, S. K., *Geraldine Jewsbury, Her Life and Errors* (London: Allen & Unwin, 1935).

Hughes, K., *The Short Life and Long Times of Mrs Beeton* (London: Harper Perennial, 2005).

Humpherys, A., 'G. W. M. Reynolds: Popular Literature and Popular Politics', *Victorian Periodicals Review* 16 (1983), 79–88.

Hussey, A., *Paris: The Secret History* (London: Penguin, 2007).

James, L., *Fiction for the Working Man 1830–1850: A Study of Literature Produced for the Working Classes in Early Victorian Urban England* (London: Oxford University Press, 1963).

Janowitz, A. F., 'The Pilgrims of Hope: William Morris and the Dialectic of Romanticism', in *Cultural Politics at the Fin de Siècle*, ed. S. Ledger and S. McCracken (Cambridge: Cambridge University Press, 1995), 160–83.

Jay, E., ' "In Her Father's Steps She Trod": Anne Thackeray Ritchie Imagining Paris', *Yearbook of English Studies* 36(2) (2006), 197–211.

Jay, E., 'British Women Writers and the Mid-Nineteenth-Century Parisian Salon', in *European Connections: Readers, Writer, Salonnières*, ed. H. Brown and G. Dow (Oxford: Peter Lang, 2011), 145–62.

Jones, C., *Paris: Biography of a City* (London: Penguin, 2006).

Jones, C., McDonagh, J., and Mee, J. (eds), *Charles Dickens, A Tale of Two Cities and the French Revolution* (Basingstoke: Palgrave Macmillan, 2009).

Kale, S., *French Salons: High Society and Political Sociability from the Old Regime to the Revolution of 1848* (Baltimore: Johns Hopkins University Press, 2004).

Kaplan, F., *Thomas Carlyle: A Biography* (Cambridge: Cambridge University Press, 1983).

Kessler, M., 'Dusting the Surface, or the Bourgeois, the Veil, and Haussmann's Paris', in *The Invisible Flâneuses? Gender, Public Space, and Visual Culture in Nineteenth-Century Paris*, ed. A. D'Souza and T. McDonough (Manchester: Manchester University Press, 2006), 49–64.

Kucich, J., and Bourne Taylor, J., *Oxford History of the Novel in English: The Nineteenth-Century Novel* (Oxford: Oxford University Press, 2012).

Lauster, M., *Sketches of the Nineteenth Century: European Journalism and its Physiologies, 1830–50* (Basingstoke: Palgrave Macmillan, 2007).

Leask, N., 'Salons, Alps and Cordilleras: Helen Maria Williams, Alexander von Humboldt, and the Discourse of Romantic Travel', in *Women, Writing and the Public Sphere, 1700–1800*, ed. E. Eger, C. Grant, C. ó Gallchoir, and P. Warburton (Cambridge: Cambridge University Press, 2001), 217–35.

Ledger, S., *Dickens and the Popular Radical Imagination* (Cambridge: Cambridge University Press, 2007).

Lesser, M., *Clarkey: A Portrait in Letters of Mary Clarke Mohl (1793–1883)* (Oxford: Oxford University Press, 1984).

Lodge, D., *Changing Places* (Harmondsworth: Penguin, 1978).

Lyons, M., *Reading Culture and Writing Practices in Nineteenth-Century France* (Toronto: University of Toronto Press, 2008).

MacCallum, C., 'Visconti et l'ambassade de Grande-Bretagne', in *Rue du Faubourg St Honoré*, ed. B. De Andia and D. Fernandes (Paris: Délégation à l'action artistique de la ville de Paris, 1994).

Macfarlane, R., *Plagiarism and Originality in Nineteenth-Century Literature* (Oxford: Oxford University Press, 2007).

Mansel, P., *Paris Between Empires, 1814–52: Monarchy and Revolution* (London: Phoenix, 2001).

Manuel, D. E., *Walking the Paris Hospitals: Diary of an Edinburgh Medical Student, 1834–1835* (London: Wellcome Trust, 2004).

Marcus, S., *Apartment Stories: City and Home in Nineteenth-Century Paris and London* (Berkeley: University of California Press, 1999).

Marello, C., 'Bilingual Dictionaries of the Nineteenth and Twentieth Centuries', in *The Oxford History of English Lexicography*, ed. A. P. Cowie (2 vols, Oxford: Clarendon Press, 2009).

Marsh, J., *Christina Rossetti: A Literary Biography* (London: Pimlico, 1995).

Marshall, G., *Actresses on the Victorian Stage* (Cambridge: Cambridge University Press, 1998).

Mason, M., *The Making of Victorian Sexuality* (Oxford: Oxford University Press, 1994).

Maxwell, C., 'Swinburne and Thackeray's *The Newcomes*', *Victorian Poetry*, Winter 2009, 733–46.

McDonough, T., 'City of Strangers', in *The Invisible Flâneuse? Gender, Public Space, and Visual Culture in Nineteenth-Century Paris*, ed. A. D'Souza and T. McDonough (Manchester: Manchester University Press, 2006), 148–63.

McKenzie, J., 'Paper Heroes: Special Correspondents and their Narratives of Empire', in *Victorian Journalism: Exotic and Domestic*, ed. B. Garlick and M. Harris (St. Lucia: Queensland University Press, 1998).

McWilliam, R., 'The French Connection: G. W. M. Reynolds and the Outlaw Robert Macaire', in *G. W. M. Reynolds: Nineteenth-Century Fiction, Politics, and the Press*, ed. A. Humpherys and L. James (Aldershot: Ashgate, 2008).

Meisel, M., *Realizations* (Princeton, NJ: Princeton University Press, 1983).

Millgate, M., *Thomas Hardy: A Biography* (Oxford: Oxford University Press, 1982).

Millgate, M. (ed.), *The Life and Work of Thomas Hardy* (London: Macmillan, 1984).

Milner, J., *The Studios of Paris: The Capital of Art in the Late Nineteenth Century* (New Haven, Conn.: Yale University Press).

Mitchell, L., *Bulwer Lytton: The Rise and Fall of a Victorian Man of Letters* (London: Hambledon Continuum, 2003).

Moers, E., 'Mme de Stael and the Woman of Genius', *American Scholar* 44(2) (Spring 1975), 225–41.

Moretti, F., *Atlas of the European Novel 1800–1900* (London: Verso, 1998).

Morgan, M., *National Identities and Travel in Victorian Britain* (Basingstoke: Palgrave, 2001).

Mullen, R., and J. Munson, J., *'The Smell of the Continent': The British Discover Europe* (Basingstoke: Macmillan, 2009).

Nairn, T., *The Break-Up of Britain: Crisis and Neo-nationalism* (Altona, Vic.: Common Ground, 2003).

Nuralova, S., 'W. M. Thackeray and his *Cornhill Magazine* in Russia: Nineteenth-Century Attitudes', *Victorian Periodicals Review* 35 (Fall 2002), 295–304.

Onslow, B., *Women of the Press in Nineteenth-Century Britain* (Basingstoke: Macmillan, 2000).

Oxford Dictionary of National Biography, The (Oxford: Oxford University Press, 2004).

Paglia, C. A., 'Oscar Wilde and the English Epicene', *Raritan* 4(3) (Winter 1985), 85–109.

Palmeri, F., 'Cruikshank, Thackeray and the Victorian Eclipse of Satire', *Studies in English Literature* 44 (Autumn 2004), 753–77.

Parent-Lardeur, F., *Lire à Paris au temps de Balzac: les cabinets de lecture à Paris (1815–1830)* (Paris: EHESS, 1982).

Patmore, D., *The Life and Times of Coventry Patmore* (London: Constable, 1949).

Pearson, R., *W. M. Thackeray and the Mediated Text: Writing for Periodicals in the Mid-Nineteenth Century* (Aldershot: Ashgate, 2000).

Peterson, M. J., *The Medical Profession in Mid-Victorian London* (Berkeley: University of California Press, 1978).

Pettitt, C., *Patent Inventions: Intellectual Property and the Victorian Novel* (Oxford: Oxford University Press, 2004).

Pope-Hennessy, U., *Charles Dickens, 1812–1870* (London: Reprint Society, 1947).

Popkin, J. D., 'Press and "Counter- Discourse" in the Early July Monarchy', in *Making the News: Modernity and the Mass Press in Nineteenth-Century France*, ed. D. de la Motte and J. M. Przylblyski (Amherst: University of Massachusetts Press, 1999), 15–42.

Prendergast, C., *Paris and the Nineteenth Century* (Oxford: Blackwell, 1992).

Prettejohn, E., 'Aesthetic Value and the Professionalization of Victorian Art Criticism 1837–78', *Journal of Victorian Culture* 2(1) (1997), 71–94.

Rainsford, D., *Literature, Identity and the English Channel: Narrow Seas Expanded* (Basingstoke: Palgrave, 2002).

Ray, G. N., *The Buried Life: A Study of the Relation between Thackeray's Fiction and his Personal History* (London: Oxford University Press, 1952).

Ray, G. N., *Thackeray: The Uses of Adversity (1811–1846)* (London: Oxford University Press, 1955).

Ray, G. N., *The Age of Wisdom (1847–63)* (London: Oxford University Press, 1958).

Read, D., *The Power of News: the History of Reuters* (Oxford: Oxford University Press, 1992).

Reynolds, S., *Paris–Edinburgh: Cultural Connections in the* Belle Époque (Aldershot: Ashgate, 2007).

Rignall, J., *Realist Fiction and the Strolling Spectator* (London: Routledge, 1992).

Rignall, J. (ed.), *George Eliot and Europe* (Aldershot: Scolar, 1996).

Rignall, J., *George Eliot, European Novelist* (Aldershot: Ashgate, 2011).

Robb, G., *The Discovery of France* (London: Picador, 2007).

Rose, M., *Flaneurs and Idlers* (Bielefeld: Aisthesis, 2007).

Rubery, M., *The Novelty of Newspapers: Victorian Fiction after the Invention of the News* (New York: Oxford University Press, 2009).

Sadleir, M., *Things Past* (London: Constable, 1944).

Seville, C., *The Internationalisation of Copyright Law: Books, Buccaneers, and the Black Flag in the Nineteenth Century* (Cambridge: Cambridge University Press, 2006).

Simmons, C. A., *Eyes Across the Channel: French Revolutions, Party History, and British Writing 1830–82* (Amsterdam: Harwood, 2000).

Slater, M., *Douglas Jerrold, 1803–57* (London: Duckworth, 2002).

Sorensen, D., '"Je suis la Révolution française": Carlyle, Napoleon, and the Napoleonic Mythus', *Carlyle Studies Annual* 22 (Spring 2006), 283–302.

Stern, M. B., 'The English Press in Paris and its Successors, 1793–1852', *Papers of the Bibliographical Society of America* 74 (1980), 307–59.

Surtees, V., *The Ludovisi Goddess: The Life of Lady Ashburton* (Salisbury: Michael Russell, 1984).

Thomas, G. M., 'Women in Public: The Display of Femininity in the Parks of Paris', in *The Invisible Flâneuses? Gender, Public Space, and Visual Culture in Nineteenth-Century Paris*, ed. A. D'Souza and T. McDonough (Manchester: Manchester University Press, 2006), 32–48.

Thorold, P., *The British in France: Visitors and Residents since the Revolution* (London: Continuum, 2008).

Tombs, R., *The Paris Commune, 1871* (London: Longman, 1999).

Tombs, R. P., and Tombs, I., *That Sweet Enemy: The British and the French from the Sun King to the Present* (London: Heinemann, 2006).

Tucker, H., 'Literal Illustration in Victorian Print', in *The Victorian Illustrated Book*, ed. R. Maxwell (Charlottesville: University of Virginia Press, 2002).

Whidden, S., ' On Collaboration', in *Models of Collaboration in Nineteenth-Century French Literature: Several Authors, One Pen*, ed. S. Whidden (Farnham: Ashgate, 2009), 1–18.

White, J., *London in the Nineteenth Century* (London: Jonathan Cape, 2007).

Withey, L., *Grand Tours and Cook's Tours: A History of Leisure Travel 1750–1915* (London: Aurum Press, 1998).

Wolkenstein, J., 'Henry James in France', in *A Companion to Henry James*, ed. G. W. Zacharias (Oxford: Wiley-Blackwell, 2008), 416–33.

Woodworth, E., 'Elizabeth Barrett Browning, Coventry Patmore, and Alfred Tennyson on Napoleon III: The Hero-Poet and Carlylean Heroics', *Victorian Poetry* (Winter 2006), 543–60.

Vigier, P., *Paris pendant la Monarchie de Juillet* (Paris: Association pour la publication d'une histoire de Paris, 1991).

Weisz, G., 'The Politics of Medical Professionalization in France 1845–1848', *Journal of Social History* 12(1) (Autumn 1978), 3–30.

Yon, J.-C., *Le théâtre français à l'étranger: histoire d'une suprématie culturelle* (Versailles: Université de Versailles Saint-Quentin-en-Yvelines, 2008).

Yon, J.-C., *Les spectacles sous le Second Empire* (Paris: Armand Colin, 2010).

Zeldin, T., *France, 1848–1945: Intellect and Pride* (Oxford: Oxford University Press, 1980).

Zevin, A., 'Panoramic Literature in 19th Century Paris: Robert Macaire as a Type of the Everyday': <http://dl.lib.brown.edu/paris/Zevin.html>.

UNPUBLISHED

Letters of Robert and Elizabeth Barrett Browning; and the Victorian Collection, held in the Armstrong Browning Library, Baylor University, Texas.

L'Hopital, S. A., 'Joseph Milsand: esthéticien–théologien', thèse présentée à la Faculté de Lettres de Dijon pour le doctorat d'université, 1955.

Linder, K. A., 'Travel and Cosmopolitanism in the Anglo-French Relationship, c. 1840-1880', Ph.D dissertation, University of Cambridge, 2010.

Pipina, I., 'Casting Identities: French Melodramas on the London Stage', Ph.D dissertation, University of Bristol, 2001.

Ray, G. N., 'Thackeray and France: Being an Account of the Part Played by Thackeray's Life in France and his Reading of French Literature in the Formation of his Mind and Art', Ph.D dissertation, Harvard University, 1940.

Index

Note: Figures are indicated by an italic *f* following the page number.

Printed and bound by CPI Group (UK) Ltd, Croydon, CR0 4YY